T0398855

A New Etruscan Archaeology

A New Etruscan Archaeology

Twenty-First Century Techniques and Methods

Edited by

Maurizio Forte

OXFORD
UNIVERSITY PRESS

OXFORD
UNIVERSITY PRESS

Oxford University Press is a department of the University of Oxford.
It furthers the University's objective of excellence in research, scholarship,
and education by publishing worldwide. Oxford is a registered trade mark of
Oxford University Press in the UK and in certain other countries.

Published in the United States of America by Oxford University Press
198 Madison Avenue, New York, NY 10016, United States of America.

© Oxford University Press 2025

All rights reserved. No part of this publication may be reproduced, stored in a retrieval system,
transmitted, used for text and data mining, or used for training artificial intelligence, in any form or
by any means, without the prior permission in writing of Oxford University Press, or as expressly
permitted by law, by license or under terms agreed with the appropriate reprographics rights
organization. Inquiries concerning reproduction outside the scope of the above should be sent
to the Rights Department, Oxford University Press, at the address above.

You must not circulate this work in any other form
and you must impose this same condition on any acquirer.

Library of Congress Cataloging-in-Publication Data
Names: Forte, Maurizio editor
Title: A new Etruscan archaeology : twenty-first century techniques and
methods / edited by Maurizio Forte.
Description: New York, NY : Oxford University Press, [2025] |
Includes bibliographical references and index
Identifiers: LCCN 2025002434 | ISBN 9780197582022 hardback
| ISBN 9780197582046 epub
Subjects: LCSH: Etruscans—Study and teaching | Etruria--Antiquities |
Archaeology—Methodology
Classification: LCC DG223 .N477 2025 | DDC 937/.5—dc23/eng/20250519
LC record available at https://lccn.loc.gov/2025002434

DOI: 10.1093/9780197582053.001.0001

Printed by Marquis Book Printing, Canada

MIX
Paper | Supporting
responsible forestry
FSC® C103567

The manufacturer's authorised representative in the EU for product safety is Oxford
University Press España S.A. of El Parque Empresarial San Fernando de Henares, Avenida
de Castilla, 2 – 28830 Madrid (www.oup.es/en or product.safety@oup.com). OUP España
S.A. also acts as importer into Spain of products made by the manufacturer.

To my parents, Umberto and Maria Luisa, dedicated to their seventy years spent together.

Contents

Contributors

Pierfrancesco Alaimo Di Loro is Assistant Professor of Statistics,Libera Universita Maria Santissima Assunta, Rome, Italy.

Fabio Babiloni is Professor of Physiology at the Faculty of Medicine of the University of Rome "Sapienza", Sapienza University of Rome, Rome, Italy.

Fabiana Battistin is Postdoctoral Fellow in Classical Archaeology, University of Tuscia, Viterbo, Italy.

Stefano Campana is Professor of Landscape Archaeology, University of Siena, Siena, Italy.

Teresa Carta is Restorer, Fondazione Vulci, Montalto di Castro, VT, Italy.

Adele Cecchini is a Restorer, Associazione Amici delle Tombe Dipinte di Tarquinia, Italy.

Vincenza Ferrara is Contract Professor of Special Pedagogy, Nursing Degree, Sapienza University of Rome, Rome, Italy.

Assunta Florenzano is Professor of Systematic Botany, Laboratory of Palynology and Palaeobotany, Department of Life Sciences, University of Modena and Reggio Emilia, Modena, Italy.

Maurizio Forte is Professor of Classical Studies, Art, Art History and Visual Studies, Department of Classical Studies, Duke University, Durham, NC, USA.

Antonio Giglio is President of Consorzio Kavaklik Restauro, Rome, Italy.

Andrea Giorgi is Biosignals Data Analyst, BrainSigns, Rome, Italy.

Margarita Gleba is Associate Professor, Department of Cultural Heritage, University of Padua, Padua, Italy.

Felipe Infante de Castro is Chief Technical Officer of FollowFox.AI, Chapel Hill, NC, USA.

Marco Iosa is Professor of Psychometry, Department of Psychology, University of Rome Sapienza and Head of the SmArt Lab, IRCCS Fondazione Santa Lucia, Rome, Italy.

Antonio LoPiano is Digital Humanities Program Specialist Boston College, Boston, Massachusetts, USA.

Daniele Federico Maras is Director of the National Archaeology Museum of Firenze, Florence, Italy.

Katherine McCusker is Geospatial Analyst, Durham, NC, USA.

Stefano Menicocci is Neuromarketing Reseacher, BrainSigns, Rome, Italy.

Anna Maria Mercuri is Professor of Systematic Botany, Department of Life Sciences, University of Modena and Reggio Emilia, Modena, Italy.

Marco Mingione is Researcher, Department of Political Sciences, Roma Tre University, Rome, Italy.

Alessandro Nocentini is Contract Professor of Design, University of Florence, Florence, Italy.

Jacqueline K. Ortoleva is Leverhulme Early Career Fellow (forthcoming, May/2025), University of Oxford, Oxford, UK.

Meryl Shriver-Rice is Assistant Professor, Rutgers University, New Brunswick, NJ, USA.

Simon Stoddart is Professor of Prehistory, Department of Archaeology, University of Cambridge, Cambridge, UK.

Michael L. Thomas is Richard R. Brettell Distinguished University Chair

Director—Edith O'Donnell Institute of Art History Associate Provost, University of Texas at Dallas, Dallas, TX, USA.

Angela Trentacoste is PJ Smith Senior Fellow in Archaeology, The British School at Rome, Italy.

P. Gregory Warden is Director of the Custard Institute, Meadows Museum, and Professor of Art History Emeritus, Southern Methodist University, Dallas, TX, USA.

Introduction: Beyond Time and Space

Digital Frontiers, Cognitive Perspectives, and AI in Etruscan Archaeology

Maurizio Forte

The study of Etruscan archaeology, or in a broad sense, Etruscology, is crucial for understanding the pre-Roman and Roman world and, more generally, the entire Mediterranean culture. It is interesting to notice that this topic is (particularly in US) incorporated within the broader field of Roman archaeology as a kind of complementary part of Roman archaeology. There are also still several stereotypes in the representation of Etruscan society, for example, the emphasis on the preponderant influence of Greek culture and the overwhelming use of Greek or Latin terminology in the description of objects, rituals, funerary practices or cities descriptions. This kind of misrepresentation of the Etruscan world marginalized this category of study to a range of "minor topics" or subtopics.

As editor of this volume, by contrast, I believe that Etruscan and pre-Roman archaeology is essential for understanding the complexity of the ancient world at the core of the Mediterranean basin in the first millennium BCE and the interactions among different populations and societies.

In 2018, I collaborated on the archaeological exhibition "Ancient Mediterranean Cultures in Contact," held at the Field Museum of Chicago. This exhibit highlighted how the Etruscans interacted with Egyptians, Romans, and Greeks in the Mediterranean basin. These interactions led to commerce and exchange of goods, but they also encouraged the sharing of ideas across continents and seas, which sparked innovation in language, literature, art, and religion. Those cultural and commercial exchanges continued during the Roman period, but the Etruscan were first actors in this scenario.

Substantial publications such as *The Etruscan World* (J. Macintosh Turfa, 2013) and *Etruscology* (A. Naso, 2015) showed a growing international interest for the discipline at the academic level and beyond. However, these volumes reflect the state of the art of the discipline according to a schematic-thematic repetitive structure: society, religion, architecture, history, and the problem of the origins, among others. What is missing is a focus on new multidisciplinary research methods and technologies of investigation. What's new? How can we teach and approach new methods in Etruscology in the third millennium? Do new technologies promote a better understanding of Etruscan society, and are they relevant to this kind of study?

Most of these methods are not taught at the university level because they involve specialization, skills, and very expensive devices whose cost is beyond the reach of individual labs or institutions. Moreover, it is difficult to integrate advanced methods of investigation into the academic curriculum, and the result is often a sort of marginalization of several technological applications and methods.

This volume had a longstanding conceptual development due to the rapid growth of new methods and technologies, the negative effects of the post-COVID period, and the difficulties of rearranging the contents in light of the progress being made in new research field projects and data analyses. I take full responsibility for this delay, despite the wonderful work done by my colleagues as contributors to the volume.

This volume presents a representative overview of technologies and methods that, in the past decade, have shifted Etruscan archaeology beyond its original borders and substantially contributed to its advancement. In particular, the volume explores case studies and applications in the fields of digital technologies (virtual reality, three-dimensional modeling), spatial analyses and remote sensing, applications of artificial intelligence (AI), textiles analyses, conservation technologies, neuroarchaeology, paleoenvironmental studies, and material culture.

The field of Etruscan archaeology has undergone substantial development over time, wherein the integration of novel methodologies and technology has played a pivotal part in the progression of our comprehension pertaining to this ancient society. The field of Etruscan archaeology has experienced significant advancements since its inception in the eighteenth century, and this continues to the present day. These advancements encompass a diverse array of new methodologies that have played a crucial role in the excavation, examination, and comprehension of the material artifacts left behind by the Etruscan civilization. The development of Etruscology has gone hand in hand with that of archaeology and anthropology, at least in recent years.

The early period of "Etruscan" archaeology, spanning the eighteenth and nineteenth centuries, was characterized by a profound sense of curiosity about and intrigue surrounding the ancient Etruscan civilization. The initial wave of explorers and antiquarians initiated the process of unearthing Etruscan tombs, art, and inscriptions, thus generating a surge of curiosity aimed at comprehending the enigmatic nature (at that time) of this ancient culture. Nevertheless, the initial endeavors in this field were deficient in systematic procedures and mainly relied on the practices of looting and random digs. For example, during the Grand Tour, many Americans and other travelers to Italy became fascinated by the "mysterious" Etruscan culture and language and try to collect artifacts as souvenirs.

The advent of scientific archaeology in the twentieth century witnessed a notable transition toward methodologies grounded in scientific principles within the field of Etruscan archaeology. Giuseppe Fiorelli,[1] an esteemed archaeologist, implemented stratigraphic excavation methodologies with the objective of enhancing the

[1] Fiorelli, G. (1875), *Descrizione di Pompei*, Tipografia Italiana; G. Fiorelli (1860–1864), *Pompeianarum Antiquitatum Historia*, Napoli: Tipografia Poliglotta.

precision of reconstructing the chronological succession of archaeological sites. During this era, there was also notable progress in the typological examinations of artifacts, which played a crucial role in the categorization and chronological assessment of Etruscan material culture.

The mid-twentieth century witnessed notable progress in the realm of documentation, characterized by the use of various techniques such as photography, precise drawings, and complete field notes. This enabled archaeologists to effectively document the contextual information of objects in their original locations prior to extraction, thus augmenting the precision of their interpretations.

During the late twentieth century, the progression of technology led to the emergence of noninvasive techniques like ground penetrating radar (GPR) and magnetometry. These approaches played a crucial role in the identification and mapping of subterranean structures, tombs, and various archaeological elements, eliminating the need for extensive excavation procedures. These strategies were crucial in the preservation of fragile archaeological sites and the strategic use of resources for excavation. The technological and innovative research work undertaken by Fondazione Lerici[2] in Etruria in 1950–1970 introduced new methods in archaeology and Etruscan studies, with the idea that "science" could support field archaeology and more. The first maps of underground[3] sites such as Vulci, Tarquinia, and Cerveteri generated an international echo supporting noninvasive technologies, and the Digital Revolution, spanning from the late twentieth century to the present, brought forth a multitude of revolutionary technologies that have had a profound impact on the field of Etruscan archaeology. The utilization of geographic information systems (GISs) has facilitated the development of comprehensive spatial datasets, hence supporting academics in conducting site analysis and landscape studies. Furthermore, the utilization of three-dimensional scanning technology and virtual reconstructions has facilitated the revitalization of artifacts and sites, hence enabling improved preservation, study, and public involvement.

The field of archaeological science, from the late twentieth century to the present, has witnessed the utilization of scientific methodologies, including radiocarbon dating, DNA analysis, and stable isotope analysis.[4] These techniques have been shown to be instrumental in unraveling significant knowledge pertaining to various aspects of Etruscan civilization, such as their dietary practices, patterns of migration, and networks of commerce. The utilization of these methodologies has contributed to

[2] Fondazione Ing. See Lerici, C. M. (2015), "The Fondazione Lerici: Pioneering the application of new technologies to archaeology," *Digital Heritage* 2: 71–72; and Meskell, L. (2022), "Atomic archaeology: Italian innovation and American adventurism," *American Anthropologist* 124: 655–669, https://doi.org/10.1111/aman.13745.

[3] Lerici, C. M. (1960), *Alla scoperta delle civiltà sepolte: Lerici e le prospezioni archeologiche*. Lerici Editori.

[4] Posth C., V. Zaro, M. A. Spyrou, S. Vai, G. A. Gnecchi-Ruscone, A. Modi, Alexander Peltzer, et al. (2021). "The Origin and Legacy of the Etruscans through a 2000-Year Archeogenomic Time Transect." *Science Advances* 7 (39): eabi7673, https://doi.org/10.1126/sciadv.abi7673.

the enhancement of chronological frameworks and provided insights into the cultural dynamics of the Etruscan civilization.

Geophysical prospections, remote sensing, three-dimensional modeling, bioarchaeology, material analysis, excavation technologies, digital epigraphy, and linguistics are all crucial tools in the field of Etruscan archaeology. Geophysical prospection uses techniques like ground-penetrating radar (GPR), magnetometry, and electrical resistivity tomography (ERT) to survey Etruscan sites without intrusive digging, revealing the layout of entire towns. Remote sensing technologies, such as aerial photography and satellite imagery, have allowed the mapping of Etruscan landscapes, identifying burial sites and necropolises hidden beneath the Earth's surface. Aerial photography has been essential in detecting subtle differences in crop growth or soil marks, which often indicate the presence of subterranean archaeological features. Three-dimensional modeling software has transformed the way archaeologists visualize ancient sites, allowing for the analysis of construction techniques and offering a platform for public engagement and educational outreach.

Bioarchaeological analysis provides valuable information about the Etruscan population, including diet, health, social structure, and migration patterns. Techniques like stable isotope analysis reveal information about agriculture and food consumption, offering insights into trade and socioeconomic status.

Material analysis has significantly impacted the study of Etruscan metallurgy, pottery, and other craft productions. Techniques like X-ray fluorescence (XRF)[5], neutron activation analysis (NAA), and mass spectrometry allow researchers to determine the composition of materials without causing damage to artifacts.

Excavation technologies, such as laser scanning and photogrammetry, provide precise measurements of excavation layers and artifact placement, enabling more targeted and efficient excavations. Digital epigraphy and linguistics have become key tools in the interpretation of Etruscan texts, with high-resolution imaging and computational linguistics aiding in understanding Etruscan language structure and its relationship with other ancient languages. Conservation technologies have also improved the conservation of Etruscan artifacts, with microscopic and chemical analyses and novel restoration materials and methods ensuring the longevity of these cultural treasures. Public archaeology and data sharing are also significant aspects of modern Etruscan archaeology, with virtual museums, online databases, and interactive GIS maps making Etruscan heritage accessible to a global audience.

In brief, the historical trajectory of Etruscan archaeology demonstrates a transition from initial casual investigation to the incorporation of sophisticated technologies and rigorous scientific methodologies. Nowadays, the archaeological research pipeline entails detailed data collection and innovative recontextualizations in space and time. Also, methodologies to document archaeological landscapes, sites, and

---

[5] Chiti, M., D. Chiti, F. Chiarelli, R. Donghia, A. Esposito, M. Ferretti, and A. Gorghinian (2024). "Design and Use of Portable X-ray Fluorescence Devices for the Analysis of Heritage Materials" *Condensed Matter* 9(1): 1, https://doi.org/10.3390/condmat9010001.

excavations differ substantially from those of the past, making archaeological research an interdisciplinary and collaborative endeavor. Chronologies are revised because of the combination of C14 methods, paleoenvironmental analyses, and very accurate stratigraphic recontextualizations of archaeological finds.

Those methods have expanded our interpretation and understanding of the Etruscan world. For instance, the combined use of virtual reality, remote sensing, and three-dimensional modeling generated detailed diachronic reconstructions of archaeological landscapes, including three-dimensional visualization of artifacts and archaeological excavations.[6] Moreover, recent analyses of settlement organization increased our knowledge of varying geomorphological and environmental impacts across Etruria. Also, the application of cognitive science and neuroscience to funerary context led to new interpretations on experiential nature of Etruscan rituals.[7]

How can these new approaches enrich our knowledge of the Etruscans? Can different methodologies generate alternative hermeneutic outcomes and, if so, how? How can the study of the Etruscan past be related to our contemporary society? How do different scales of representation, from kilometers to microns, change our perception of a site, an artifact, or a landscape? How can new comprehensive "big data" for the reconstruction of the past be most appropriately handled? How can comparative studies of paleoenvironmental analyses help us to better understand climate change and other phenomena in contemporary societies? Can we envision the Etruscan mind?

This volume is addressed to a broad public composed of, but not limited to, researchers, students, and readers interested in classical studies, archaeology, archaeometry, anthropology, history, art history, digital humanities, and more. The combined use of different technologies and methods can attract a large audience interested in the relationships between the hard sciences, archaeology, and the humanities. Ultimately, our aim for this volume is to highlight the most recent advances in archaeological methods in the field of Etruscology to move the discipline beyond its traditional scope to a new era of technological innovation and multidisciplinary collaboration.

Chapter 1, by P. Gregory Warden, Michael L. Thomas, and Alessandro Nocentini, focuses on the use of digital technologies for the study, reconstruction, and dissemination of texts and inscriptions. Digital technologies have created new methods for representing, reconstructing, and disseminating ancient texts, whether inscribed, painted, or eventually written on manuscripts. However, epistemological issues remain, such as the singular materiality of the original, the nature of the material itself, and the context. Three case studies raise issues of contexts and interpretation.

---

[6] Forte, M., and A. Siliotti (1997) *Virtual Archaeology: Re-creating Ancient Worlds*. New York, H. N. Abrams; Forte, M. (2011) Cyber-Archaeology: Notes on the simulation of the past. *Virtual Archaeology Review*, 2(4), 7–18, https://doi.org/10.4995/var.2011.4543. Forte, M., De Castro F. I., Pkhovelishvili I. (2023) "AI for IA: Artificial Intelligence for Interpretative Archaeology", in *Proceedings of the International Workshop on AI for Cultural Heritage CINECA Supercomputing Center*, 43-56.

[7] Forte, M. (2024) Perceiving Etruscan Art: AI and Visual Perception. *Humans*, 4, 409–429, https://doi.org/10.3390/humans4040027.

Digital technologies can provide greater accuracy or fidelity, but important episte-mological issues remain. Traditional approaches to Etruscan inscriptions, even those that have taken an interdisciplinary approach, have been primarily text-based and focused on translation and interpretation, thus neglecting the spatial relationship between inscription and object, something that can be recreated and visualized through digital methods. This has meant that both comparative linguists and epigra-phers are involved in understanding the inscription in its original context. Inscribed objects have a "voice" that raises questions about the emic and etic aspects of a par-ticular object, what it communicates, and the nature of context.

Contemporary epigraphic studies have become increasingly more interested in context, which is often defined as the relation of the inscription to its physical space, but also, and as important, the conceptual space and the wide variety of other contexts (social, visual, historical, and experiential). Inscriptions are both text and images; they can communicate as text but can also be visually processed as an image. They have materiality that results not only from the object on which they are painted or incised but also as part of the process: the making of the inscription, the actual bite of a sharp instrument.

Chapter 2, by Stefano Campana, discusses Etruscan cityscapes, focusing on the challenges of studying urbanized societies in the Mediterranean region. Techniques differ for one-time townscapes versus historical urban landscapes. Remote sensing, when combined with excavation and surface survey, has revolutionized the under-standing of ancient cities. Magnetometry has been particularly successful in map-ping Roman towns and cities. Research questions include discovering the emergence of urban cultures, mapping infrastructure, identifying activity areas, and under-standing urban–rural relationships.

Magnetometry (predominantly fluxgate radiometry) has produced impressive results, mapping complete towns and transforming the fund of evidence available for urban studies. Gradiometric survey is a method used to explore urban areas, with more than 85 percent of the projects focusing on Roman towns and cities. Research questions include defining the emergence of the first urban cultures, trac-ing their paths of development, mapping the urban infrastructure, locating foci of particular activities and production sites, outlining suburban zones, and identifying social groups. It is important to remember that there is a close relationship between the historical and archaeological questions and the research methods implemented to answer them. A good strategy must be based on careful choice and the integra-tion of methods and sources, consistent with the archaeological questions under investigation.

Specific questions are addressed through urban geophysical surveys, such as set-tlement extent, occupation patterns, activity areas, and defensive walls. The relation-ships between urban and rural contexts are important because written sources refer to organic connections between the city, suburbs, and countryside. Urban geophysical survey is often used to detect and depict the overall plan or detailed physical layout of a town.

The Emptyscapes initiative at Veii and Rusellae employed magnetometry and electrical resistivity to fill in superficially "empty" areas of the landscape, identifying previously unknown features like Roman vineyards, street systems, funerary complexes, and medieval settlements, thus dramatically altering the understanding of territorial occupation density and continuity.

Chapter 2 demonstrates overall the importance of expanding site territories and the effectiveness of remote sensing for efficiently understanding cityscapes. It also exemplifies the integration of remote sensing with traditional surveys and excavations for enhanced chronology and feature interpretation.

Chapter 3, by Antonio LoPiano and Katherine McCusker, discusses how remote sensing technologies have revolutionized archaeological research in Etruria, supplementing traditional excavation methods with broad-scale, contextualizing data acquisition. Etruria has been a testbed for survey methodologies, from the development of landscape studies using aerial photography following World War II to the advent of GPR, magnetometry, and light detection and ranging (lidar) in the twenty-first century. These technologies are divided into airborne tools (satellite imagery, unmanned aerial vehicles [UAVs]) and ground-based tools (magnetometry, electrical resistivity surveys, GPR), each with unique strengths and limitations based on terrain, geology, and research focus.

Several case studies in Etruria demonstrate the utility of these technologies. At San Giovenale, the combination of aerial and satellite imagery, lidar data, infrared thermographic images, and near-infrared and normal-colored images identified new archaeological features and habitation patterns. The Vulci 3000 project used magnetometry, GPR, and aerial surveys to understand the city's urban layout and development, revealing a thriving city with increasing wealth and power during the Imperial period.

By utilizing electrical resistivity and magnetometry, the Emptyscapes initiative at Veii and Rusellae identified previously unidentified features such as Roman vineyards, street networks, funerary complexes, and medieval settlements that appeared to be "empty" regions of the landscape. This significantly altered the modern understanding of the density and continuity of territorial occupation.

At Falerii Novii, an extensive GPR survey mapped the urban plan in high detail, identifying public structures, a unique monumental building, and evidence of continual development and prosperity.

These case studies highlight the importance of using remote sensing technologies in concert with each other and with traditional excavation methods to create a holistic understanding of a site. The optimal combination of methodologies depends on the research focus and the need for extensive or intensive data. However, the complexity of data collection and analysis presents new challenges related to "big data," including processing, analyzing, archiving, and publishing large digital datasets. In this context, archaeologists must balance old and new methods to optimize data use and publication from these complex approaches while grappling with the shifting nature of data infrastructures, research methods, and knowledge transformation in the era of "big data."

Fabiana Battistin, in Chapter 4, debates the significant contributions to the field of spatial analysis, particularly as it concerns the study of Etruscan state formation and geopolitical patterns in Etruria. She argues that Simone Stoddart's research on geopolitical patterns and land use in Etruria, published in *Power and Place in Etruria*, demonstrated the advanced applications of spatial analyses in managing incomplete and fragmented information.

Spatial analysis techniques as applied in urban areas focus on processing, interpretation, and categorization of data. The best results are achieved at extensively documented sites like Pompei and Ostia. In Pompei, space syntax analysis highlights trends in the distribution of activities, showing that the buildings' integration is linked to activities within them. In Ostia, the visibility graph analysis (VGA) method was applied, revealing that the location of urban elements coincides with the points of greatest visual integration. Although not all cities follow the "Pompeii premise," spatial analysis has led to interesting results even when applied to limited datasets like geophysical maps.

A significant issue is that urban boundaries in Etruscan city sites frequently lack information regarding street networks. Methodological concerns plague geophysical data and marks identified through aerial and satellite imagery, including the presence of fragmented data and the absence of direct chronological footholds. Nevertheless, approaches to spatial analysis can be employed to assess and contrast hypotheses pertaining to potential alterations in urban configuration. By employing space syntax, which was utilized in the Roman city of Falerii Novi, it is feasible to compare and contrast hypotheses regarding potential alterations to the urban layout. During the planning phase, an exploratory analysis of the available dataset can be conducted to identify its strengths and limitations, generate additional inquiries, and establish research priorities. Concerning Etruscan urbanization, the most urgent challenges are the procurement, administration, and exploitation of data. To distinguish their methodology for site analysis, archaeologists must amass a diverse array of data and validate it via a variety of analyses. In fact, spatial analysis can aid in the process of interpretation by providing relational and spatial data that are more manageable to compute using IT tools.

Jacqueline Ortoleva, in Chapter 5, explains the relevance of cognitive sciences in the study of the performance space in Etruscan tombs. Cognitive archaeology, a processual field of inquiry, recognizes that human cognition is rooted in perceptual and physical engagement with the material world. In fact, archaeological science has increasingly incorporated cognitive science to understand the material record of past cultures, particularly in the context of painted tombs in Etruria. These tombs have been largely understood in iconographic and textual terms, with the aural nature of the space often overlooked. This chapter explores sound propagation inside the painted tomb in Tarquinia, focusing on the acoustic nature of the burial chamber and dromos and its implication with respect to the funerary experience.

Etruscan archaeology has progressed in recent years, but chambered tombs in the Etruscan record are largely understood in visual terms. Most studies involving painted tombs rely on tomb iconography, epigraphic evidence, and architectural typologies, with little discussion on the experienced dromos, particularly from the standpoint of sound. This chapter seeks to recontextualize the Etruscan chambered tomb space with respect to the physical and cognitive experience of funerary ritual. The painted tomb space is situated as a point of origin with respect to the cognitive experience of sound and space during the funerary event. Music and dance are the second most common narrative in Etruscan tomb paintings, providing a visual tapestry of music without any corresponding sound. The recreation of musical instruments in Etruria is valuable for visualizing their overall construction, but musings involving musical composition in Etruria must be viewed with caution.

The tomb paintings depict musical performance and acoustic effects, with male vocal frequencies being more likely to stimulate low-frequency reverberatory effects. This study highlights the complex nature of sound and the need for a comprehensive approach that considers all structural aspects of the tomb space.

Recent neuroscience studies have shown that when an observer hears a task-related sound, the same part of the brain fires as though the listener was personally enacting the activity even if only hearing the sound. The acoustic data suggest that sound crosses the visual and structural boundaries of the tomb in terms of its entrances, burial chamber, and dromos. This suggests that funerary rituals for Etruscan elites involved musical instruments.

Chapter 6, by myself and my colleagues, investigates the aesthetic impact of art on the brain, including subjective, conscious, and unconscious consequences in relation to Etruscan artifacts. This research is part of the NeuroARTifact project, which aims to study cognitive and performing affordances between artifacts reproduced through virtual simulations and empirical observations. In particular, the project aims to understand the neural and affective regions responsible for object perception and how they influence emotional involvement, well-being, learning, and cognitive development. This combines an empirical neuroscientific approach with a visual/narrative one, focusing on the performing activities of material culture users as an aesthetic process. Interdisciplinary researchers from Sapienza University of Rome and Duke University collaborated on the project, employing methodologies such as electroencephalography, pupil movement tracking, visual thinking strategies (VTS), and eye-tracking to investigate novel research protocols. VTS aims to foster a deeper understanding of artifacts, enhance critical thinking abilities, and improve communication skills by engaging students in meaningful discussions and encouraging them to support their interpretations with evidence from the artwork.

The Sarcophagus of the Spouses serves as a case study, with the project examining the aesthetic process that underpins its development, from conception to spatial modeling and "consumption" as a symbolic object.

Statistical analysis of the gathered data is essential for resolving the research questions. Eye-tracking data reveal patterns in observations, with differences based on gender and educational background. The emotional index derived from an electroencephalogram (EEG) is correlated with eye tracking data to ascertain emotional arousal at different time points.

The NeuroARTifact project also compares visitors' observations of the Sarcophagus of the Spouses with a virtual reality reproduction. Portable EEG devices and sensors are used to measure mental workload, attention, and emotional response. The project found that museum observation demanded a higher level of cognitive engagement and elicited a more intense and positive emotional reaction compared to virtual reality observation.

The case study of the Sarcophagus of the Spouses is highly relevant, investigating the conscious and subliminal associations individuals have with artifacts alongside their kinesthetic learning and aesthetic appreciation. The results have implications for various fields, including neuroaesthetics, museum studies, Etruscan art, the evaluation of public perception of cultural heritage, and applications in the realm of wellness promotion.

Chapter 7, by Teresa Carta and Fondazione Vulci, is focused on conservation practices and new methods for the preservation of archaeological structures. The conservation of archaeological structures in Italy has faced numerous challenges, including abandonment, invasive excavations, and inappropriate restoration methods. The use of modern construction materials, such as Portland cement, led to harmful interventions in the 1960s and 1970s. It was not until the 1990s that a shift toward minimally invasive techniques, compatibility with original materials, and the importance of in situ conservation gained traction.

Conserving archaeological sites involves managing heterogeneous systems with varying degrees of material robustness. The changed chemical and physical status of finds during excavation poses initial difficulties. Methods of "active conservation" (rapid intervention, restoration, and maintenance) and "preventive conservation" (action on the surrounding environment) are employed to slow down degradation. Temporary and permanent protective roofing plays a crucial role in conservation during excavation and for visitor access. Specific tools of active conservation include mechanical supports, temporary fixing, and injections of desalinated mortar or "lean lime" cements.

The author presents specifically the case of Vulci, an ancient Etruscan city, which deals with conservation challenges due to the use of tuff, a fragile material with reactive minerals and high porosity. In this case, early interventions of conservation focused on consolidating tuff with ethyl silicate and protecting it with fluoroelastomer, mainly applied to monumental tombs.

The Tomb of the Carved Ceilings (ETP Tomb) underwent interventions in 2002 to address water infiltration, microbiological attacks, and surface deterioration. Excavations revealed deep cracks and rock breakage necessitating sealing, consolidation, and the use of mortars with characteristics similar to siltstone.

The Tomb of the Sphinx, discovered in 2011, presented severe degradation, including cracks, flaking, and loss of material. The restoration involved constructing protective roofing and conducting consolidation tests using nano silica, a water-based dispersion of nanometric silica that has low environmental impact and excellent compatibility with the substrate. Nano silica was used as a bonding agent to create an inorganic mortar for filling and repairing missing parts. Repositioning large detached rock fragments required structural consolidation, thinning, reinforcement, and fixing with clamps and rods.

The development of colloids and other materials has led to significant advancements in conservation science, providing new and safe methods such as nanoparticle dispersions, microemulsions, gels, nanocomposites, and nanosensors. These systems offer improved properties, compatibility, and control compared to traditional conservation methods. The market for conservation of historical and artistic heritage in Europe, estimated at around €5 billion per year, could increase with the wider use of nanomaterials.

Monitoring the Tomb of the Sphinx has confirmed the success of the intervention, with the degradation process slowed, and has show-cased the improved stability and compatibility of nano silica cements. However, regular checks and maintenance are crucial to address issues such as microbiological attacks and to ensure proper, long-lasting conservation of the monument. Future projects aim to complete conservation interventions within the underground chambers and apply innovative methods and materials to other important monuments in the Osteria Necropolis.

Chapter 8, by Daniele Federico Maras, Adele Cecchini, and Antonio Giglio, introduces another research topic concerning the conservation of Etruscan painting in Tarquinia and Caere. In fact, the conservation of Etruscan painting, in the form of wall paintings in tombs and terracotta plaques, is a complex and multidisciplinary task that requires the collaboration of archaeologists, conservators, scientists, public authorities, and law enforcement agencies. The painted tombs of Tarquinia, included in the UNESCO World Heritage List, are considered masterpieces of creative art and provide insights into the life, death, and religious beliefs of the Etruscans. The terracotta plaques from Caere, recently recovered from the illicit market, offer a unique opportunity to study and appreciate this form of art.

The main challenges in conserving these painted surfaces include sudden variations in temperature and humidity, inadequate conformation of the overlying terrain, penetration of roots, presence of biodeteriogenic microorganisms and insects, and inappropriate lighting systems. These factors can lead to chemical-physical, biological, mechanical, and anthropic damage.

Monitoring the conservation status of the hypogea is crucial for planning interventions and preventing degradation. Regular inspections, twice a year, are carried out by the personnel of the Soprintendenza, accompanied by a restorer who evaluates the status of the paintings and chambers.

The production of terracotta plaques involved pressing clay into squared frames, applying a refined slip, and painting the polychrome decoration vertically using a limited palette of clays and metallic oxides. The plaques were arranged in series to compose pictorial friezes with mythological or other subjects.

The conservation of fragmentary and incomplete plaques requires a systematic approach, including documentation, diagnostic analysis, cleaning, consolidation, and reassembly. The cleaning phase aims to remove earth deposits, accretions, and other formations developed during the burial period while preserving the original material and pictorial decoration. Consolidation is performed when necessary to ensure adherence between fragments and the mechanical resistance of the terracotta.

Recent conservation projects, such as the restoration of the Tomba dei Vasi Dipinti at Tarquinia and the recovery of painted plaques from the illicit market, demonstrate the importance of collaboration between various stakeholders. Innovative techniques, such as multispectral reflectometry and ultraviolet fluorescence, are being applied to detect faded pigments and reconstruct lost pictures.

In conclusion, the integration of multidisciplinary approaches and the collaboration between public and private institutions are essential for ensuring the preservation of this unique cultural heritage for future generations.

Chapter 9, by Meryl Shriver-Rice, Anna Maria Mercuri, Angela Trentacoste, Assunta Florenzano, and Simon Stoddart, concerns the study of landscape archaeology and paleoenvironments in Etruscan archaeology. Paleoenvironmental studies have been slow to take hold in Etruscan archaeology despite their potential to provide valuable insights into the complex relationships among environment, biological need, and society in ancient Etruria. Recent efforts by interdisciplinary teams have begun to shed light on these topics, using methods such as geoarchaeology, palynology, and zooarchaeology.

Geomorphological studies, for example, have focused on the implications of structural geology on settlements, the impact of erosion and alluviation on landscapes, comparative sea level studies, and the interpretation of modern soil distributions. Key findings include the influence of volcanic eruptions on settlement patterns, the localized effects of Etruscan urbanism on erosion and alluviation, and the use of modern soil distributions to infer past land use.

Palynological studies have revealed that the Etruscan landscape was characterized by a richer flora and a scarcity of olive trees compared to modern Tuscany. Etruscans actively managed their local landscapes, practicing short-term coppicing to sustain their economy and obtain fuel for iron metallurgy. Pollen records also suggest that Etruscans encouraged the spread of chestnut and possibly walnut trees. Future palynological research should focus on careful sampling strategies and the integration of micro- and macrobotanical analyses to obtain reliable paleoenvironmental reconstructions.

Despite the importance of agriculture in Etruscan society, archaeobotanical evidence for agricultural strategies is scarce. The few sites where macro archaeobotanical remains have been recovered suggest a diverse cereal and pulse crop repertoire similar to that of the mid- to late Bronze Age in central Italy. Zooarchaeological analyses have demonstrated a rise in pork consumption and an increase in domestic livestock size over the first millennium BCE. Future research will employ techniques such as geometric morphometrics (GMM), stable isotope analysis, and genetics to reveal details of Etruscan management practices and explore questions related to cuisine, consumption, and human–environment interactions.

The future of Etruscan environmental studies is promising, but challenges include destructive and inadequate sampling. Systematic environmental sampling, including the use of large-volume flotation machines, is essential for obtaining sufficient data. Destructive sampling for isotopic and genetic analyses should be balanced with the preservation of cultural heritage and the potential for nondestructive techniques like GMM.

Collaboration between archaeologists, local stakeholders, and scientific experts is crucial for developing sound sampling strategies and disseminating results. By embracing interdisciplinary approaches and participating in broader scientific discussions, Etruscan environmental archaeology can contribute to our understanding of the complex relationships among people, their environment, and the processes of urbanization, mobility, and historical development in ancient Italy and beyond.

Chapter 10, by Margarita Gleba, is aimed at studying ancient textiles according to a multidisciplinary perspective. For example, new attention to various sources of evidence, analytical techniques, and theoretical approaches has begun to change the status quo of textile studies in Etruscan archaeology. Evidence includes textiles, textile tools, zooarchaeological data, archaeobotanical remains, iconography, and occasional written sources. Etruscan textiles rarely survive in an organic state, but mineralized textiles on metal objects and in calcium-rich environments are more common. The uneven geographical and chronological distribution of textile finds is a result of peculiarities in burial customs, excavation, and conservation practices.

Textile structural analysis provides data on raw materials, production techniques, and function, allowing for the reconstruction of regional and chronological trends. Scientific methods such as scanning electron microscopy, DNA and protein analysis, high-performance liquid chromatography, accelerator mass spectrometry, and strontium isotope analysis can help answer questions about textile materials, technology, dating, and provenance. Textile tool analysis, particularly functional analysis, can provide insights into textile production areas, intensity, and the range of textile qualities produced. Experimental archaeology has helped us to better understand tool function and production processes. Zooarchaeological analysis of sheep bones can indicate a site's specialization in wool production and provide evidence for animal husbandry practices. Iconography has been used to study ancient dress, corroborate archaeological finds, and investigate the relationship between textiles and social factors.

Recent data suggest that Etruscan textile technique was characterized by plain weave linen textiles, wool twills with tablet-woven borders, and the use of sophisticated dyeing methods. Textile production in Etruria primarily used locally available raw materials and was largely a household-level, female occupation. Textiles were used for clothing, furnishings, wrapping, sails, tents, and linen armor, with luxury textiles playing a significant role in elite status display. The accumulation of data and the development of analytical techniques are allowing for a more synthetic approach to the history of textiles in Etruria.

However, more analyses are needed to increase the statistical robustness of the data and investigate intra-site variation, the correlation of textiles with adornments, flax cultivation, and sheep husbandry. Ancient DNA analysis combined with wool fiber quality analysis has the potential to trace the development of various sheep breeds.

Chapter 11, by myself and Felipe Infante de Castro, presents an overview on one of the most revolutionary technology in the humanities, generative AI. The field of generative AI has made significant strides in recent years, with the potential to revolutionize various domains, including Etruscan archaeology. This chapter introduces the topic and presents preliminary applications of generative AI in this field. The development of AI algorithms and parallel processing technology has enabled the creation of AI systems capable of generating original content, such as images, videos, and models. Generative AI art, pioneered by OpenAI's DALL-E in 2021, has become a reality in people's daily lives. The launch of Stable Diffusion, a compact and open-source AI, has sparked widespread interest among developers, artists, and researchers. However, AI models have limitations, particularly in specialized applications like archaeological interpretation. Underrepresentation or overrepresentation of specific archaeological images in training datasets and insufficient or inaccurate text captions can impact the AI's ability to generate accurate representations. To mitigate these limitations, fine-tuning processes using curated datasets and manual text captions can improve the AI's understanding of domain-specific concepts.

Initial studies involving AI techniques in Etruscan archaeology focused on examining Etruscan tumuli, creating environmental reconstructions, and generating AI characters for an Etruscan temple reconstruction. The rapid advancements in AI technology, such as image-to-image creation techniques and ControlNet, are expected to enhance the capabilities and applications of AI in archaeology. The phenomenological study of generative AI is complex because it intersects with technological revolutions and philosophical dilemmas. Virtual archaeology, cyber-archaeology, and AI archaeology mark significant junctures in the evolution of digital representation of the past. AI archaeology offers new perspectives in interpretation and reconstruction, with the ability to generate visualizations, models, and complex simulations using simple coding or textual instructions.

The concept of the past as a "multiverse" challenges our understanding of history and archaeology, emphasizing the relativistic notion that the past is mutable and perceived differently across space and time. Initial experiments using Stable Diffusion and Deforum demonstrate the success of AI in simulating ancient locations, artifacts, and landscapes. The multiplication of contents through AI generates new information and encourages the consideration of various alternatives, worlds, and contexts. Deep learning AIs have the potential to revolutionize the processing and analysis of large datasets in generative archaeology, opening up unexplored research avenues in visualization and simulation. While still in its early stages, the systematic incorporation of deep learning AIs into the archaeological process could lead to significant advancements in the field.

In chapter 12, I discussed how Etruscan archaeology Etruscan archaeology has undergone profound changes through the integration of new research methodologies that emphasize a multidisciplinary approach and dynamic forms of study. The incorporation of diverse fields such as cognitive science, artificial intelligence, and environmental studies has allowed scholars to move beyond traditional analyses, fostering a deeper understanding of the Etruscan world. By combining spatial, material, and cognitive perspectives, researchers can now examine Etruscan society not only through its artifacts but also through the sensory and symbolic experiences that shaped its cultural identity. This shift enables a more holistic reconstruction of ancient environments, social structures, and artistic expressions, bridging gaps between archaeology, neuroscience, and digital humanities. Multidisciplinary collaborations have expanded the interpretative scope of research, highlighting the Etruscans' adaptive strategies, resource management, and ritual practices in ways that were previously inaccessible. The ability to process vast amounts of archaeological data has transformed the way patterns and relationships are identified, allowing scholars to generate new hypotheses and recontextualize material culture within a broader historical and environmental framework. This evolving research paradigm also enhances public engagement, providing immersive and interactive ways to experience Etruscan heritage while ensuring its preservation for future generations. As archaeology increasingly intersects with technological and scientific disciplines, it reinforces the necessity of collaborative efforts to develop more nuanced narratives about the past.

Maurizio Forte, *Introduction: Beyond Time and Space: Digital Frontiers, Cognitive Perspectives, and AI in Etruscan Archaeology* In: *A New Etruscan Archaeology: Twenty-First Century Techniques and Methods.*
Edited by: Maurizio Forte, Oxford University Press. © Oxford University Press 2025.
DOI: 10.1093/9780197582053.003.0001

1

Representation to Reproduction

Digital Phenomenology and Hermeneutics of Inscriptions

P. Gregory Warden, Michael L. Thomas, and Alessandro Nocentini

Introduction

Digital technologies have created new methods for representing, reconstructing, and disseminating inscriptions, providing processes that present us with seemingly more realistic representations. Digitalization can provide greater accuracy or fidelity but important epistemological issues remain.[1] Part of the question is semantic. What do we mean by more realistic? What exact kind of fidelity is intended? Any representation of an inscription is just that—a representation—and thus by definition interpretative. Different technologies interpret in different ways. The traditional drawing of an inscription uses the eye and hand of the draftsman to provide what we believe is a faithful reproduction. The degree of fidelity depends on the ability of the draftsman. A photograph seems more real, perhaps, because a machine now replaces the seemingly more interpretative eye and hand, but any photograph is also subject to infinite variations of lighting, angle, and even medium, such as alteration through traditional processes of "wet" photography or, more recently, through possibly even greater alteration in the various modes of digital processing that we call "photoshopping."

Traditional approaches to Etruscan inscriptions,[2] even those that have taken an interdisciplinary approach, have been primarily text-based and focused on translation and interpretation. Less attention has been paid to the spatial relationship between inscription and object that can be recreated and visualized through digital methods.[3] Until now innovation has meant that both comparative linguists and epigraphers are involved or, as postulated at a recent symposium that used broad

---

[1] "What we need is a realistic approach to what technology can do for us, explicitly defining how we think it improves our work and enables us to answer questions otherwise unanswerable" (Lanjouw, 2016).

[2] For instance, Wallace (2010), or Becker and Wallace (2010). An excellent example of full and thorough publication of inscriptions, in this case non-Etruscan, is Crawford et al., *Imagines Italicae* (2011). Reviewed by Benjamin W. Fortson IV and Michael Weiss (*BMCR* June 6, 2013).

[3] A good example would be the publication of an inscription on a three-dimensional object such as a spindle whorl. See Bagnasco Gianni's innovative article "L'acquisizione della scrittura" (1999, fig. 5) for a spindle whorl reproduced in a drawing from 1965. Both publications (1965 and 1999) obviously predate the technology necessary to reproduce and publish an inscribed object that needs to be considered three-dimensionally.

approaches, that "The linguist and epigrapher are concerned with issues of orthography, paleography, literacy, and language structure and function. But all share the common goal of understanding the inscription in its original context and this makes inscribed objects documents that allow scholars a point of entry into aspects of daily life in the ancient world that ancient literary texts cannot provide. Inscribed objects have a 'voice.' "[4] The metaphor of "voice" raises questions of the emic and etic aspects of a particular object, what it communicates, and the nature of context. Contemporary epigraphic studies have become increasingly more interested in context. Context is often defined as the relation of the inscription to its physical space[5] but, just as important perhaps, is the conceptual space and the wide variety of other contexts (social, visual, historical, and experiential, to name just a few possibilities) that come into play in understanding an inscription. Also pertinent is the much-debated issue of literacy, raising questions of elite control and display, social access, degrees of literacy, and visuality. Inscriptions are both text and image. They are text and context. They can communicate as text but can also be visually processed as an image. Beyond "voice" there are visibility and visuality—two quite different things—but which create the realm where an image/object becomes a "thing."[6]

Inscriptions have materiality that results not only from the object on which they are painted or incised but is also part of the process: the making of the inscription, the actual bite of a sharp instrument into the baked clay of a sherd or into the granular surface of local sandstone (as we shall see in the particular case studies discussed below). Inscriptions result from a process that is both conceptual and material. The result is an entity that we broadly term an "inscription," something that has three important parts: the text, which is conceptual as well as visual; the image or sign, which may have myriad meanings for the viewer; and materiality. Traditional methods of reproduction are primarily interested in the first part, the text, and digital technologies have created greater fidelity in this component.[7] Visuality and materiality are more contextual and more difficult to convey, perhaps because a multiscalar interpretation that depends on broader, phenomenological methodologies is more difficult to realize with traditional modes of representation. The problem was well-stated by di Fazio in the context of situating inscriptions within the locus of cultural memory.

> Several factors combined together to build this sociocultural context: to limit discussion to those factors which are "embedded" with writing, particular importance is attached to the place in which the inscriptions are located, *the environment*

---

[4] The conference was entitled "The Etruscan Objects Speak: New Linguistic and Socio-historical Approaches to Etruscan Epigraphy," and was held in Philadelphia as part of the 2009 annual AIA meetings. Selected contributions were published in *Etruscan Studies* (Becker and Wallace, 2010, 107–108).

[5] Grzesik (2020). "Epigraphy is never exclusively a study of texts, nor is it limited to the reconstruction of texts carved in stone. Rather, most inscriptions are artistic monuments, which are designed to achieve a certain effect within their architectural context."

[6] For thingness, see Brown (2003), Kopytoff (1986), and Olson (2010).

[7] For a balanced evaluation of text and image in funerary inscriptions, see Lomas (2015).

and the context. These aspects, in most cases lost to our comprehension, were an *integral part of the meaning of the inscription*: the visual impact of the writing . . . may have been as important as its content. In addition we should also remember the importance of factors such as the choice of material, lighting, and colours of an inscription. (Di Fazio, 2020, 140; emphasis added)

The impact described here is what we have defined as *visuality*, something that encompasses and transcends concepts of word, image, and materiality. The broader context, often lost, as di Fazio has noted, is the larger perception embedded in time and place, something that might be partly recaptured through phenomenological approaches that interrogate the relationships between text, object, creator, and viewer(s).[8]

This cultural aspect (human interaction with an object, the object's "thingness," and myriad cultural meanings) is by definition intimately contextual and would seem to defy mechanical interaction, although some of the challenges are clear. What kind of agency does the object exert? Can objects be said to have identity and, if so, in what way?[9] There are also semantic questions that impact epistemological aspects: Is a "thing" different from an object? How can technology help us move from the physical object to a broader understanding of the "thing?" The question of understanding the "thing" at second hand, whether as a drawing, a photograph, or a complex 3D digital reconstruction, becomes of even greater importance when we consider that the nature of the medium will de facto influence interpretation.[10]

Three case studies from the Etruscan site of Poggio Colla will illustrate the challenges.

Case Study 1: The Ostrakon

Our first case study, a ceramic fragment from the Etruscan sanctuary of Poggio Colla[11] is inscribed with four letters that are centrally placed (Figure 1.1). The ceramic itself, a brownish bucchero of local manufacture, clearly dates to the Archaic period, thus sixth or very early fifth century BCE. The inscription reads *cavi*, clearly the name of an individual, and the fragment was published by Maggiani as a possible

[8] Some of these relationships are already being investigated in novel ways, for instance by Bagnasco Gianni (2012) for the culture of epigraphy; and Biella (2012), who considers the relationship between text and the inscribed object (the "sostego epigrafico"). Also relevant is Bortolotto et al. (2012), with the intent of analyzing and processing multifaceted archaeological evidence in a context-oriented environment.

[9] The assumption in this chapter is that agency can exist for an inanimate object—the *inanimate agency proposition* (IAP). A broad definition is intended, for which see Johannsen (2012), especially 340. See also Hodder (2012).

[10] As shown, for instance, by Henderson (1999) in her analysis of computer graphics and the production by engineers.

[11] Inventory no. PC 2008-031. For Poggio Colla, see Warden (2012), "Giving the gods their due," and Warden, "Monumental embodiment" (2012).

Figure 1.1 Inscribed sixth-century bucchero sherd. Poggio Colla inv. no. 08-031. (Mugello Valley Archaeological Project)

ostrakon.[12] Ostraka are common in the eastern Mediterranean, Egypt, and the Middle East, but relatively rare in Italy, and, in fact, Maggiani's study was innovative. *Cavi* is the name of a male individual, and the form of the first letter of the inscription is clearly a gamma rather than a kappa, indicating that the person inscribing the object was following the "orthographic norms" of southern Etruria rather than of the region of Poggio Colla, which is located in far northern Etruria. The date of the inscription is quite certain; both the stratigraphic context and the nature of the orthography suggest a date in the last decades of the sixth century BCE. Thus, a southern Etruscan seems to have visited the sanctuary in the sixth century BCE and left his calling card, so to speak. We cannot be sure about the process and the exact contextual meaning of the bucchero fragment, but we can surmise that Cavi inscribed it himself. But was the sherd part of a vase that was used/dedicated[13] by Cavi and then inscribed, or did he merely pick an appropriate fragment and inscribe it?

---

[12] Maggiani (2016), "Ostraka."
[13] The fragment was part of a bucchero hemispherical bowl, a body sherd with the edge of the foot ring inscribed on exterior with *post cocturam* graffito. We are grateful to Phil Perkins for this information.

Maggiani's careful reading of the object included more than the orthography. He also noticed that the second letter, the alpha, is idiosyncratic, and that the bite of the stylus (or whatever sharp instrument was used to create the graffito) was notable: "la lettera è stata incisa esercitando una forte pressione sullo stilo in corrispondenza della parte centrale delle aste e della traversa, mentre la parte finale di esse è tracciato molto più leggermente; cosicché la lettera prende una singolare forma a bandiera che se pur esiste nella documentazione, è certamente una forma assai rara." In fact the idiosyncratic "handwriting" provided a clue not only for the date, but also, given the regionality of the Etruscan alphabet, for the regional identity of Cavi: "The Poggio Colla fragment can be approximately dated on the basis of the gamma in front of the alpha, an orthographic usage that became normal in southern Etruria from the last decades of the sixth century BCE. But this inscription cannot, on the basis of the alpha, have been incised by someone from Cerveteri; better candidates are the other cities of southern Etruria: Tarquinia, Vulci, and most of all, Orvieto." This important insight results from an analysis of the "texture" of the second letter, the alpha, clearly visible in a photograph but not reproducible in a drawing.

The materiality of the sherd allows this nuanced reading, but the nuances cannot be understood from a drawing (Figure 1.2). A photograph (Figure 1.1) renders the particularities of the second letter more exactly and shows the hesitant crossbar of the alpha. A three-dimensional reconstruction would allow the object to be seen from a number of viewpoints. It could be moved and rotated three dimensionally (albeit on a two-dimensional screen), giving the viewer what is unarguably a better sense of the whole.

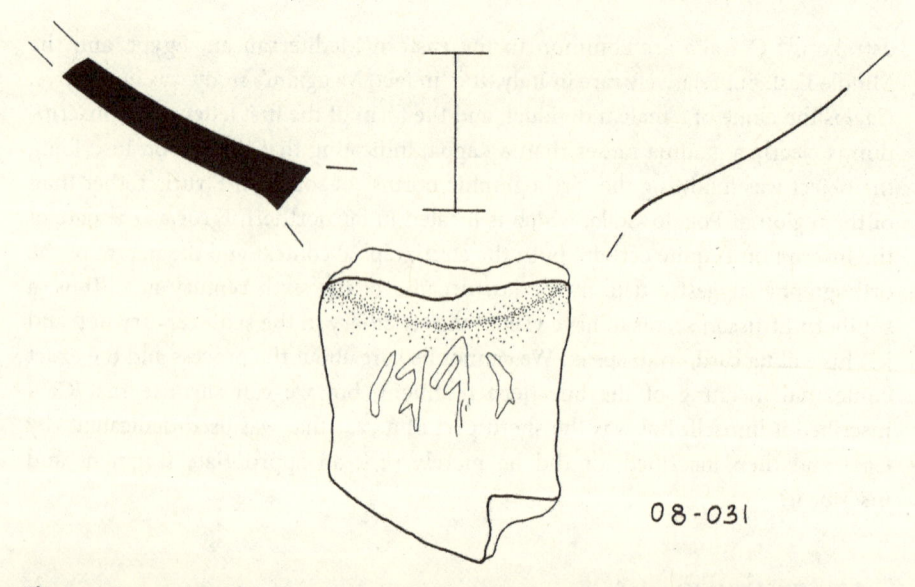

08-031

Figure 1.2 Drawing of the inscription. Poggio Colla inv no. 08-031. (Mugello Valley Archaeological Project)

But what about the object itself and the relationship to the viewer, to the body of the person who inscribed and/or dedicated it, or to a viewer today? A three-dimensional virtual reconstruction could allow the object to be "printed," not unlike the way a squeeze would have been used to study inscriptions in the past, but now we would have an object that is a reproduction of the entire object rather than just the inscription. If the sherd is an ostrakon, a very rare thing in an Etruscan context, our identification is based on two things. First is the size of the sherd, about 4 × 5 centimeters, which fits comfortably and snugly in the palm of a human hand. Second is the perfect centering of the inscription and the regularity of the fragment. Its weight and heft are important. It asks be held in hand. It creates an intimate connection with the viewer, just as it must have created an intimate connection between Cavi and the divinity of the sanctuary. The sherd is thus a "thing" in the Heideggerean sense of something that is not bounded, which is not complete in itself. The sherd became a "thing" when the vase was broken. It further evolved when Cavi picked it up and inscribed it with his name. It may have even exercised agency as Cavi dedicated it in its sacred setting, although we might debate whether that agency was that of Cavi, of the inscription, of the sherd, or of all three. And it continues, if we can push this idea its limit, to exercise a kind of agency as it is interpreted, archaeologically or anthropologically, today, through different means of reproduction or explanation. Each mode of reproduction, including its explanation through this textual narrative, brings out a different aspect of its thing-ness.

This intimacy, this act of becoming a "thing," is further borne out by the materiality of the ceramic object, the black surface of a bucchero vase, an elite vessel that was used to celebrate the divine nature of this particular place. It is made of local earth and thus connects to the chthonic cult that characterizes this particular sanctuary. That vital connection was made by the very personal act of inscribing one's name.[14] To have a name is to exist, and Cavi created the most personal type of bond between himself and the divinity. He introduced himself and invited himself to be part of the cult, to be part of the place. By inscribing an already broken sherd, Cavi has created a gift to the divinity that may mirror the connections of elite guest and elite host, the kind of *tessera hospitalis* familiar from other Archaic Italic contexts. It is tempting to consider that the most important aspect of the inscription is the way in which it was inscribed, the act of cutting into ceramic with a sharp instrument those simple four letters form a name and thus represent so much, an act that was conceptual before it became material. The process involves *anticipation* that precedes the materiality, as Tim Ingold calls the cogitation that comes *before sight* and that was postulated by Derrida, who had to "resort to the same idea in reference to the art of drawing in which, he claims, the inscribing hand continually overtakes the cogitation of the head."[15] It is a kinetic creative process where action embodies concept or, as de Kerangal aptly describes in her fictional account of trompe l'oeil painting: "*to see* is

---

[14] For the importance of an individual's name, see Whitehouse (2020).
[15] Ingold (2013), 69, quoting Derrida (1993), *Memoirs of the Blind*, and referencing Sennett (2008), *The Craftsman*.

to engage in pure action, create an image . . . that resembles the one the eyes have created on the brain" (2021, 39). Cavi's inscription is both a sign and a text whose process reveals its meaning—for process in this case is ritual, and the meaning is physical and contextual. What technology can reproduce or even describe this? Can digital technology or artificial intelligence allow for processual interpretation rather than mere reproduction? Can they more fully realize the haptic and intimate qualities of an object that was meant to be cradled in the palm of the offerer?

While the haptic quality may need modern digital methods to be properly understood, simpler technology—drawing—at least for the moment might be more useful for the dissemination of certain kinds of analysis. A case in point is Wallace's study of Orientalizing inscribed ivories from Poggio Civitate (Murlo), where five different inscriptions were compared and analyzed in terms of traditional paleography (Wallace, 2010, 114–115, fig. 10). As was the case with Maggiani's analysis of the Poggio Colla ostracon, the crossbar of the alpha seems to be the telltale. In this case, it allowed the identification of three different hands. These results can then inform the stylistic analysis of the carved ivories. They are presented clearly in tabular format by drawings of each individual letter. We have to rely on the accuracy of the draftsperson and/or the keen eye of the archaeologist, but the results can always be checked against the original. The presentation is convincing.

The ostrakon, a seemingly humble fragment, tells a complex story that can only be understood through the connection of the inscription to the material nature of the object and then to the broader contexts of both the liminal sanctuary of Poggio Colla and the Etruscan belief system. A southern Etruscan came to Poggio Colla, perhaps on his way over the Apennines or, just as likely, returning from Etruria Padana; he gave thanks to the local divinity (or divinities?). A three-dimensional reconstruction, such as a printed version of the sherd, comes closest to communicating a particular reality but still cannot convey the tactile interpretation that comes from the object itself, nor the particular ancient ideological process through which an object became a "thing."

Case Study 2: An Inscribed Statue Base

A very different case is presented by a sandstone statue base from Poggio Colla (Figure 1.3). It is much larger, almost 40 centimeters in height, quite heavy, and well finished.[16] While stone statue bases are known from Etruscan sacred contexts, the Poggio Colla base is unusual for its trapezoidal shape and fine finish. The hole at the top still preserves the lead setting for what, judging by the diameter, would have been an impressively large figurine.[17] The base was an object of display, almost

[16] Poggio Colla Inv. 2005-105.

[17] A statuette of comparable size is the exquisite female *ex voto* from the water sanctuary at nearby Marzabotto. It is approximately 30 centimeters in height. Illustrated in Govi (2007), 29, and discussed in Malnati et al. (2005), 97–99, pl. 4.

Figure 1.3 Inscribed sandstone statue base. Poggio Colla inv. no. 2005-105. (Mugello Valley Archaeological Project)

certainly in the monumental temple that was built at Poggio Colla ca. 500 BCE and possibly destroyed by the end of the fifth century. Warden originally published the base and its context in 2005; subsequent excavation at Poggio Colla in 2014 and 2015 discovered other important aspects of its context within the sanctuary.[18] Warden posits that the inscription base was part of an array of carefully placed objects that included another smaller, pentagonal sandstone base (without an inscription); a sandstone cylinder that may represent the top of a votive column or small circular altar; some bronze fragments; gold wire; and a bronze bowl (Figure 1.4). He interprets this deposit as the physical remains of a ritual activity. Subsequent excavation seasons after Warden's initial publication suggest that the two statue bases and presumably the statues they supported stood on display in the first monumental temple at Poggio Colla, and the fifth-century dating of the inscription supports this hypothesis.

These excavations delineated the remains of the presumed cella area of the temple. They also led to the discovery of four bronze statuettes that also belong to the

---

[18] Warden (2009), with previous bibliography.

Figure 1.4 Poggio Colla. The "Inscription Deposit" with the statue base. (Mugello Valley Archaeological Project)

same context. These include two archaic-period female figures found in 2014, as well as another female figure and a male Kouros discovered during excavations in 2015. Though all of these figures are too small to be assigned to the inscription base, they nonetheless point to a context of purposeful display within the confines of the temple, possibly within the cella itself. Within this assemblage, the base is the only surviving artifact with an inscription. The entire assemblage is a collection of objects that were displayed in an Etruscan temple; hence the inscribed base needs to be conceptualized in that unique context.

One face of the base is inscribed with a text that runs from left to right, from top center, downward in a gentle curve. The relation of inscription to object is deliberate, and the layout of the letters is thoughtful. Two incised lines cutting diagonally from left to right, over which individual letters have been cut, seem to have served as guides for the general direction of the inscription. These "guide lines" can be seen quite clearly in the drawing (Figure 1.5) that was published by Camporeale (2012, 187–188). Camporeale, who was able to study the original object, interpreted the inscription as the name of an elite Etruscan who had donated the base and its figurine: *nakaske velns*.[19]

---

[19] While the praenomen is unusual, the gentilicial belongs to a family well known in the Mugello through inscriptions on pottery of later date. For those inscriptions, see Cappuccini et al. (2009), 115–119, with the suggestion by G. de Marinis that the Velasnas were the ruling family of Frascole (Dicomano) a few kilometers from Poggio Colla.

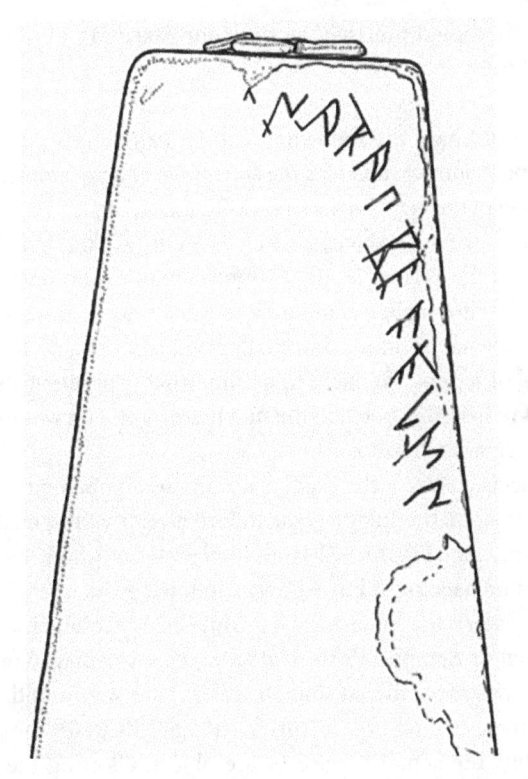

Figure 1.5 Drawing of the inscribed on the sandstone statue base. Poggio Colla inv. no. 2005-105. (Mugello Valley Archaeological Project)

The inscription was discussed again only three years later when Colonna, working solely from the photograph and not having seen the original, came up with an ingenious alternative reading. Colonna makes it clear that he is entirely basing his "reading" on a photo, and his argument is worth quoting.

"La foto . . . mostra che il segno tralasciato consta di un'asta cui è addossata e in parte sovrapposta una linea curva verticale. Una sorta di segno *c*, identificabile a mio avviso con una *k* mal riuscita, assai diversa dalle altre due altre presenti nell'iscrizione e da attribuire a un lapicida assai meno esperto di chi ha inciso la prosecuzione del testo, iniziando a una certa distanza e a una quota leggermente più bassa, con un cambio di mano motivato a quanto pare proprio dalla cattiva prova data da chi aveva in inciso il segno in questione. (Colonna, 2015)"

The photo ... shows that the omitted mark consists of a vertical stroke to which a curved vertical line is attached and partially superimposed. A kind of c mark, which in my opinion can be identified as a poorly executed k, significantly different from the other two present in the inscription and attributable to a stonecutter far less skilled than the one who engraved the continuation of the text. The latter began at a certain distance and at a slightly lower level, with a change of hand seemingly prompted precisely by the poor execution of the mark in question. (Colonna, 2015)

Thus we would have the following text: *kn akaske velsn*. In some ways, this is a more satisfying reading, with *kn* as the accusative of a praenomen, and *akaske* a documented version of the verb "to donate" or "to make," depending on context (Colonna, 2014, 47, n. 15). The statue base, after all, is an important donation to the divinity of the temple from the Velsnas family. Colonna's reading, however, is based on nuances observed in a photograph, a small nick to the left to the initial kappa, and complex explanation for what he admits is a malformed letter too far to the left in a carefully spaced series of letters. We have to assume that a different individual, a different hand, started to inscribe, botched the first letter, and then was replaced by a different individual, a "cambio di mano."[20]

The final decision about the exact text remains an open question, but what is pertinent in terms of methodology is the different reality presented by a drawing and a photo. The drawing (Figure 1.5) is an interpretation made by an artist/technician who is not an archaeologist but who was following the intent of the site's directors, who did not discern the initial kappa postulated by Colonna. Clearly there is something to the left of Camporeale's initial letter, partly damaged (a nick in the surface) along with a small incision that could be interpreted as one of the guide lines. Should the drawing include it and other surface damage as well? The photograph shows a different reality, the actual surface of the object, allowing the viewer to judge for themselves. But two different photographs, depending on lighting, will show different details and differences of surface. In this case a three-dimensional digital scan would be preferable and would allow the object or part of it to be printed. It would certainly better represent the object—in this case its "thing-ness"—but what about the color, what about the gritty texture of the local sandstone? Would it be as "real" as the actual object? Here we are in danger "of falling into the fallacy of authenticity," as Huvila has put it, and even more interestingly doing so "by suggesting that it is a visualization of not only an interpretation, but of the past itself" (Huvila, 2018, 108).

In the case of the inscribed statue base, we would have to acknowledge that even when examining the base itself, given the state of preservation, we may not be able to answer the questions raised by Camporeale and Colonna. An interesting corollary of this line of thought is whether, in looking at an artifact produced by digital means (whether a model or some other virtual form) we might be able to see or perceive something that cannot be seen in the original artifact, thus raising epistemological issues about whether a reproduction is in some way more real than the "original." The matter becomes even more complex when we consider that this is an object that was displayed in antiquity, meant to be seen most likely in a dimly lit temple, in a

---

[20] Warden has repeatedly examined the actual object in the flesh, in raking light from different angles, and, to his eye, Colonna's hypothetical first letter is not evident. Absolutely fascinating, in terms of what we see and interpret, is that in photographs the hypothetical letter can be "seen."

particular context, placed at a certain height (on the column/altar base found with it), and viewed with a bronze statuette on top of it. Would the inscription have been viewed from above or below? A photograph will usually show it from a frontal view, at eye height. Will digital technology that allows a viewer to rotate the object on a screen permit a better understanding? Perhaps the most important aspect is not the exact meaning of the inscription but what would have been readily understood by anyone looking at it, whether they could read the inscription or not, the message that an elite Etruscan had donated it, a message that, by being inscribed, commemorated an action whose meaning would have been evident to the cult and the divinity of place.

In fact, the Poggio Colla statue base has been studied using three-dimensional digital technology. Its digital acquisition through three-dimensional reality-based technologies, such as digital photogrammetry, has tested the potential of *structure from motion* (SfM) strategy for capturing the three-dimensional nature of the base and its peculiar inscription (see Nocentini and Warden, 2017). This represents a significant case study to evaluate the benefits provided from the three-dimensional recording activity and especially from three-dimensional imaging techniques for those archaeological objects with inscriptions. Thanks to the optical approach (Montani et al., 2021, 5), the dimensional, formal, material, and chromatic attributes of the artifact are acquired without physical contact and using the reflected light radiation of its sandstone surfaces. This class of three-dimensional techniques reconstructed through digital output in a virtual environment the real aspect of the statue base and how this appears during the acquisition phase, through mathematical and informatic procedures (see, e.g., Barazzetti et al., 2009, 12). Image feature detection and matching algorithms created a dense numerical model—the so-called *point cloud*, which is a discrete set of points with known spatial position (x, y, z coordinates) and defined accuracy—that provided an "objective" replica that can easily be displayed, navigated, and measured as well as understood in virtual space. From the discrete model, meshing and texturing procedures created a three-dimensional continuous polygonal model reconstructing the colored surface of the base and its inscription. Enriched with geometrical and chromatic details, this output shows the three-dimensional artifact's "body" in a virtual environment (e.g., the informatic windows of three-dimensional online platforms, with modeling and editing software) where shading and rendering tools[21] allow the viewer to vary the lighting parameters of the scene. Simulating and orienting light effects on the mesh of the model enhance the real-time visualization of the statue base thus facilitating the reading of its inscription. A model of this sort presents an important reality, but, in this case, it is one of four realities that include the physical object, the interpretative drawings, and the photographs. It may also be worth noting that the model is based on photogrammetry. Are we surprised that it is not a question of medium, that we see what we want to see?

---

[21] For instance, the "scale radiance parameters" and "ambient occlusion" options in the open source MeshLab software, https://www.meshlab.net/

Case Study 3: The Vicchio Stele

Our third case study is more complex. The Vicchio Stele,[22] found at Poggio Colla in 2015, was discovered in a secure archaeological context, carefully placed in the foundations of the podium of a fifth-century temple. It had been displayed in an earlier phase when the sanctuary was a characteristic "hut" village of the Italian Iron Age, thus in the second half of the sixth century. This date matches the paleographic evidence that also firmly places it in the archaic period. The stele is one of the three longest religious texts found to date, the earliest, and the only one from a secure archaeological context. It seems to have been a *lex sacra* or *lex arae*, and its secure date in the second half of the sixth century makes it, we would argue, the earliest extant example of a law code in Europe.

The stele is 1.2 meters high; about two-thirds of its length would have been above ground. It is made of fine-grained sandstone that presents difficulties for the reading of the long sequences of letters. Parts are lost, but the entire text may have been more than 200 characters in length. It was inscribed four times, twice on the edges and twice on its face, and one of the inscriptions covers an earlier text. It is a palimpsest. The texts are still being studied, and only one of the four texts, inscribed on the lower left face, has been read with some certainty.[23] The identification of the names of Tinia and Uni and the possibility that Uni is the titular divinity of at least one part of the sanctuary fits the published evidence for ritual at the site.

While the Vicchio Stele is unique,[24] it is locally produced and can be contextualized in local stone-carving traditions; it has formal connections to other lapidary monuments from northern Etruria, especially the so-called *pietre fiesolane*[25] that are widely dispersed throughout the Sieve and Arno river valleys. The Vicchio Stele is very similar in shape and usage (inscribed but otherwise undecorated) to the stele of Laru Arianas from Panzano.[26] The Panzano stele is a particularly convincing parallel because of its shape as well as the form of its letters and especially the use of interpunctuation of three superimposed dots. It is datable from 525 to 510 BCE, and thus contemporary with the Vicchio Stele. Most of the *pietre fiesolane* depict human figures. The Panzano stele thus shows us that an inscription as well as an image could portray and define an individual. Text in this case is costume.

The texts of the Vicchio Stele would have been difficult to read even if the individual letters had been enhanced with pigments. Because of the size and three-dimensionality of the object, the poor state of conservation, and the fact that one of

---

[22] Poggio Colla Inv. PC 2015-001. Maximum preserved height, 1.20 meters; width, 0.64 meters.

[23] Maggiani (2016), "The Vicchio stele"; Warden (2016), "The Vicchio stele and its context"; Warden (2016), "Una scoperta recente"; and, most recently, Warden and Maggiani (2020), "Authority and display."

[24] It is the only Etruscan stele or cippus from north Etruria that is not funerary. For the general category of stelai, cippi, etc., see Steingräber (2017).

[25] See Cappuccini (2009) for a useful summary; see also Amman (2017). For detailed discussion and thorough illustrations, see also Perazzi et al. (2016).

[26] Maggiani (2016), "La scrittura a Fiesole in età arcaica," 75 and fig. 6.

the inscriptions erases and covers up part of another one, today the text is extraordinarily difficult to interpret. Like the *pietre fiesolane*, the stele is relatively small; only 70 to 80 centimeters would have been above ground. In terms of proxemics, the stele required the viewer to come very close to the object. To read the pseudo-boustrophedic text, someone would have to bend down, almost as if genuflecting; move the eye over and around; and then shift position (unless you could read upside down) to repeat the process in the other direction. Small has noted that (Greek or Roman) "inscriptions on public display were intended to be pleasing to the eye rather than to the reader" (Small, 1993, 53). Thus visuality versus readability. Ruth Whitehouse (2013) has taken things a step further in discussing the physical difficulty of reading both Etruscan and Venetic stelae, a gymnastic challenge—not just the question of being able to read, but of being fit enough to read. The object insists on specific actions from the viewer/reader, a kind of intimacy. It both communicates and dominates. It would have been less easily comprehensible than a funerary stele decorated with an image of an elite Etruscan. How much of this is intentional? The texts were not meant to be read by one and all but only by the elite few who had the ability and authority to unravel the "scroll" that wound its way around the edges.

Digitizing the heavy sandstone slab was a key challenge for the three-dimensional recording activity (Aterini et al., 2017, 60–69; Nocentini, 2017) and for analyzing, understanding, and interpreting this exceptional object and the fragile text inscribed on its irregular surface. Future publication will assess the aspects of visibility and visuality, the relation of object to viewer. The digital model is a first step. Application of three-dimensional technologies aimed to document the stele at high resolution but without physical contact, and, especially, the use of advanced optical sensors allowed the acquisition of surface geometry and the submillimeter depth of the inscriptions, thus ensuring the capture of high density three-dimensional information. The processing of information acquired by triangulation-based laser scanner produced a three-dimensional model that is accurate for both geometry and measurement. Through reverse modeling procedures the irregular surface was reconstructed as a polygonal mesh, defining a continuous three-dimensional model able to fully present the stele in the virtual environment. This digital replica is both a dimensionally exact output that can be the basis for analysis by specialists and an extraordinary informative matrix that can be explored as well as easily transmitted and shared (Figure 1.6). The large number of points acquired could make model management and inspection difficult (depending on the performance parameters of the hardware used) within three-dimensional software and platforms. Postproduction phases that focused on the dense polygonal mesh decimation procedures to reduce the digital model weight would be necessary while preserving the main geometry of the numerous inscriptions on the slab surface. Subsequent render-to-texture procedures would allow recovery of the geometrical features lost during the decimation process and the mapping of these on to the simplified meshes of the "lightweight" model of the stele (see Forte and Danelon, 2015, 46).

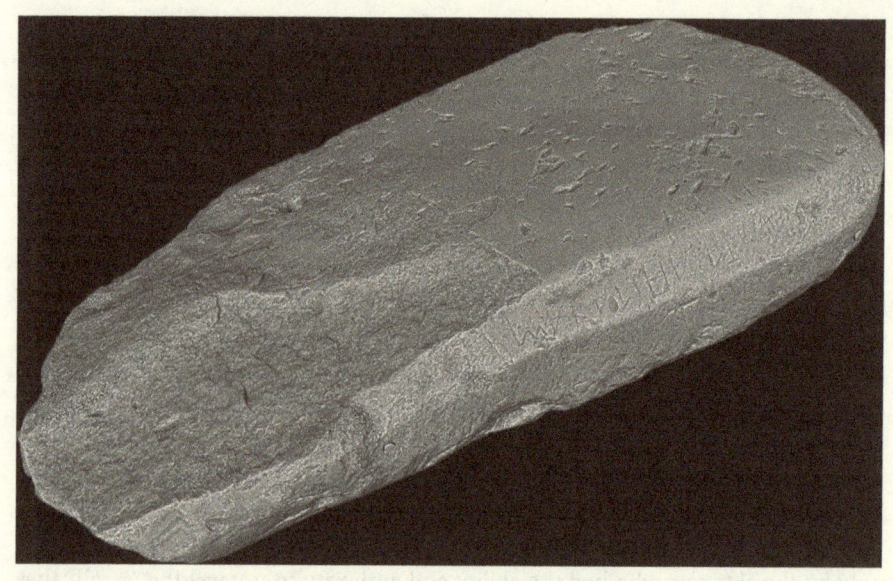

Figure 1.6 The Vicchio Stele. Poggio Colla inv. no. 2015-070. Digital model by Alessandro Nocentini. (Mugello Valley Archaeological Project)

Figure 1.7 Hologram of the Vicchio Stele. Poggio Colla inv. no. 2015-070. (Mugello Valley Archaeological Project)

Surveying a complex artifact with surface inscriptions by three-dimensional optical technologies means accessing the object's three-dimensional nature, including its physical, dimensional, and geometrical details. Obtained with carefully planned and rigorous procedures, the digital model exhibits objective data that satisfy the needs of documentation while also providing a key device not only for obtaining knowledge of the stele and its physicality, but also for their valorization, preservation, and communication, as well as dissemination (Nocentini and Sarti, 2020, 325–326). Finally, publishing the digital model of the Vicchio Stele through a holographic display (Figure 1.7) has revealed the fascinating potential of three-dimensional documentation in the cultural heritage domain. The Stele's holographic copies are produced through three-dimensional output (e.g., digital prints on holographic sheets or digital projections by LCD and OLED panels), and these not only enhance the user's visual and perceptual experiences with the artifact but also can be used to overlay additional information, such as highlighting the relevant text inscribed on the Stele's surface.

Conclusion

We have argued that context is of paramount importance in understanding the meaning of inscriptions that are often treated more as single-dimension artifacts than as things or visual experiences whose full effect depends on myriad contexts. A lesson might be learned from modern studies of text and visuality in urban landscapes that consider "linguistic landscapes" and "semiotic landscapes." Physical context affects perception. A good example is the landscape context of rock art (e.g., Polkowski, 2020), while a pertinent Etruscan example is the Crocifisso del Tufo in Orvieto, where a series of inscriptions are placed on the architraves of individual family tombs, thus creating a linguistic landscape that imparts meaning (and memory) in a funerary setting. A phenomenological analysis rather than a list of texts is required to understand the visuality of place, starting with the placement of texts. Location is power, and the inscriptions define space and territory: "The places of inscriptions are just as important as their visual and textual components and can produce powerful contentions over permissions and entitlements. . . . Signs are part of material and communicative surface networks. . . . In fact, it is often the case that the physical presence itself is the message, and simply being visible on a certain surface is the most powerful content one can send across" (Andron, 2017, 76). Position is privilege, and in Etruria inscriptions were the very substance of privilege.

Etruscan archaeologists have treated text and image differently,[27] and, in fact, there is a fundamental difference even if the two categories are not mutually exclusive semantically or in practice.[28] In this sense, Mitchell's conception of pictures and all media as image-texts, while theoretically interesting, may be impractical in suggesting that bifurcating writing and image is nothing more than an "ideology, a complex of desire and fear, power and interest."[29] It may be best to focus on the

[27] And have even differentiated between *semata* and text; see Bonghi Jovino (2017).
[28] A particularly interesting example is that of texts that are in fact nonsensical and thus images. Sometimes they are referred to as "pseudo-inscriptions" (e.g., Napolitano, 2021), but perhaps they should more precisely be considered "pseudo-texts."
[29] Mitchell (1995). A text-image is far different from a text that is also an image.

concept of an inscription as an artifact that, in its "thing-ness," creates a relationship that is essentially transactional. Reading and viewing are thus a social transaction, an interaction that takes on its own meaning, whatever meaning was originally intended or is now being received.[30]

Different technologies are appropriate for different contexts and for different scientific purposes. Advanced photographic technologies may even be able to reconstruct inscriptions that are barely visible or even indicate when something was inscribed.[31] But the crux of the matter is that a visual–material approach requires us to move beyond reproduction and consider conceptualization. Consideration of visuality broadens the definition of a context that can analyzed using multimodal and semiotic approaches (Andron, 2017, 71). A solution to the challenges of understanding inscribed contexts in their full complexity would be to separate the study of inscriptions from a purely epigraphical semantic approach—in other words, to study the visuality of inscriptions with broader digital visualization methodologies.[32] Contextual approaches of this kind, that situate the text/image in its broader context, will have the greatest potential to reveal multivalent meanings.

We argue that a best-practices approach for the documentation, interpretation, and dissemination of Etruscan inscriptions would attempt to situate an inscription in its broader contexts. Digital technology certainly enhances this process. Online databases have become an integral tool for the organization of archaeological information. In the case of the sandstone stele, laser scanning offers a precise documentation of the current condition and acts as a virtual conservation of this fragile artifact. Modeling through photogrammetry affords the ability to study objects such as the Vicchio Stele in a virtual environment, with the opportunity to enhance aspects of the inscription. In terms of exploring context, archaeologists can utilize a wide range of virtual reality, augmented reality, and mixed reality applications and softwares (such as Sketchfab, Unity, Blender, Cinema4D, Autodesk 3DS Studio and Maya) to provide navigable platforms and design suites able to create unlimited interpretive and immersive scenarios through digital reconstruction.

While the benefits of digital publication for archaeology are enticing (Clarke, 2016), there are likewise challenges for both the long and short terms. Although born-digital publications seem poised to replace print, limits to data size can potentially restrict the ability to disseminate high-definition digital models through the internet.[33] As the publication of digital information expands, we must also take into account the long-term sustainability of digital platforms: Will the programs we use

---

[30] Appadurai (2006), 15: "the idea that persons and things are not radically different categories and that the transactions that surround things are invested with the properties of social relationships."

[31] For instance, advanced polarized photography. Wang et al. (2019).

[32] For instance, the recent three-dimensional vector-based visibility study of the Forum Romanum, which analyzes space as "a medium of political, and representative messages." See Braun (2020), 189. A more specialized analysis of inscribed surfaces within the spatial context could be valuable. Broader contextual approaches that combine complex built structures with three-dimensional modeled object are also promising: see Paliou et al. (2011).

[33] For some of these problems, see Chen et al. (2008) and Kostic et al. (2008).

today be available in fifty or even one hundred years? We must also confront the issue of cost for the maintenance and storage of digital information.[34] Do such costs become the responsibility of the researcher, their institution, or their publisher? Despite such challenges, it is clear that digital tools allow for a new and engaging level of archaeological documentation and its interpretation.

Placing an inscription within a visual context moves beyond the simple study of language to a full phenomenological understanding of human interaction with word and object. A virtual interpretation of the complete physical environment provides an unrivaled opportunity to visualize possible receptions of both object and word in the ancient world.

Bibliography

Amman, P. "Le 'pietre fiesolane': Repertorio iconografico e strutture sociali." In *Cippi, stele, statue-stele, e semata: Testimonianze in Etruria, nel mondo italico e in Magna Grecia dalla prima Éta del Ferro fino all'Ellenismo*, edited by S. Steingräber, 63–79. Pisa: Edizioni ETS, 2017.

Andron, S. "Interviewing walls: Toward a method of reading hybrid surface inscriptions." In *Graffiti and Street Art: Reading, Writing, and Representing the City*, edited by K. Avramidis and M. Tsilimpoumidi, 71–88. London: Routledge, 2017.

Appadurai, A. "The Thing Itself." *Public Culture* 18.1 (2006), 15–22.

Aterini, B, A. Nocentini, and P. G. Warden. "Digital technologies for the documentation, analysis and dissemination of the Etruscan 'Stele di Vicchio.'" In *New Activities for Cultural Heritage: Proceedings of the International Conference HeritageBot 2017*, edited by M. Ceccarelli, M. Cigola, and G. Recinto, 60–69. Cham: Springer, 2017.

Bagnasco Gianni, G. "L'acquisizione della scrittura in Etruria: Materiali a confronto per la ricostruzione del Quadro storico e culturale." In *Scritture mediterranee tra il IX e il VII secolo a.C*, edited by G. Bagnasco Gianni and F. Cordano, 80–105. Atti del Seminario di Studio (Milano 23–24 febbraio). Milano: Edizioni ET, 1999.

Bagnasco Gianni, G. "L'incidenza della rete di relazioni sulla cultura epigrafica." *Aristonothos* 4 (2012), 15–36.

Barmpoutis, A., E. Bozia, and R. S. Wagman. "A novel framework for 3D reconstruction and analysis of ancient inscriptions." *Machine Vision and Applications* 21 (2010), 989–998. https://doi.org/10.1007/s00138-009-0198-7

Barazzetti, L., F. Remondino, and M. Scaioni. "Combined use of photogrammetric and computer vision techniques for fully automated and accurate 3D modeling of terrestrial objects." In *Videometrics, Range Imaging and Applications X*, Processing of SPIE Optics+Photonics, vol. 7447. San Diego, 2009.

---

[34] For the problem, see Wright et al. (2009).

Beagrie, N., and D. Greenstein. *A Strategic Policy Framework for Creating and Preserving Digital Collections*. British Library Research and Innovation Report 107. London: British Library, 1998.

Becker, H., and R. Wallace. "Historical approaches to Etruscan epigraphy." *Etruscan Studies* 13 (2010), 107–108.

Biella, M. C. "Oggetti iscritti e tradizioni artigianali di età orientalizzante in Agro Falisco." *Aristonothos* 4 (2012), 37–58.

Bonghi Jovino, M. " 'Semata': Spunti e riflessi a proposito di tre casi di studio tra configurazione e significato." In *Cippi, stele, statue-stele, e semata: Testimonianze in Etruria, nel mondo italico e in Magna Grecia dalla prima Éta del Ferro fino all'Ellenismo*, edited by S. Steingräber, 213–222. Pisa: Edizioni ETS, 2017.

Bortolotto, S., G. Bagnasco, S. Valtolina, P. Favino, A. Garzulino, M. Marzullo, R. Simonelli, and B. R. Barricelli. "An ecosystem of tools and methods for archaeological research." In *VSMM 2012 Virtual Systems in the Information Society*, edited by G. Guidi and A. C. Allison, 133–140. New York: IEEE, 2012.

Braun, A. "Shau Augustus (?): Visueile Kommunikation Veränderungen auf dem Forum Romanum zwischen der späten Republik und der frühen Kaiserzeit. Ein cuputergestützter Ansatz." *Kölner und Bonner Archaeologica* 9/10 (2020), 189–202.

Brown, B. *A Sense of Things: The Object Matter of American Literature*. Chicago: Chicago University Press, 2003.

Camporeale, G. "Ager Faesulanus, Poggio Colla." *Studi Etruschi* 75 (2012), 187–188.

Cappuccini, L. "Le 'pietre fiesolane.'" In *Museo Archeologico Comprensoriale del Mugello e della Val di Sieve*, edited by L. Cappuccini, C. Ducci, S. Gori, and L. Paoli, 82–93. Firenze: Aska, 2009.

Cappuccini, L., C. Ducci, S. Gori, and L. Paoli, eds. *Museo Archeologico Comprensoriale del Mugello e della Val di Sieve*. Firenze: Aska, 2009.

Chen, M., M. Ponec, S. Sengupta, Jin Li, and P. Chou. "Utility maximization in peer-to-peer systems." *Sigmetrics Performance Evaluation Review – SIGMETRICS* 36 (2008), 169–180.

Colonna, G. "Firme di artisti in Etruria." *Annali della Fonazione per il Museo Claudio Faina* 21 (2014), 45–74.

Colonna, G. "Ager Faesulanus: Poggio Colla (Vicchio)." *Studi Etruschi* 78 (2015), 223–224.

Clarke, J. R. "3D model, linked database, and born-digital e-book: An ideal approach to archaeological research and publication." In *3D Research Challenges in Cultural Heritage II: How to Manage Data and Knowledge Related to Interpretative Digital 3D Reconstructions of Cultural Heritage*, edited by S. Münster, M. Pfarr-Harfst, P. Kuroczyński, and M. Ioannides, 136–148. Berlin: Springer, 2016.

Crawford, M. H., W. M. Broadhead, J. P. T. Clackson, F. Santangelo, S. Thompson, and M. Watmough, eds. *Imagines Italicae: A Corpus of Italic Inscriptions (3 vols.)*. Bulletin of the Institute of Classical Studies, Supplement 110. London: Institute of Classical Studies University of London, 2011.

de Kerangal, M. *Painting Time*. Translated by J. Moore. New York: Farrar, Strauss, and Giroux, 2021.

Derrida, J. *Memoirs of the Blind: The Self-Portrait and Other Ruins*. Translated by P.-A. Brault and M. Nauss. Chicago: Chicago University Press, 1993.

Di Fazio, M. "Writing time and space in ancient Etruria. In *Etruscan Literacy in Its Social Context*, edited by R. Whitehouse, 135–144. London: Accordia Research Institute, 2020.

Forte, M., and N. Danelon. "Regium@Lepidi 2200 project." *Archeomatica* 1 (2015), 374–398.

Govi, E. *Marzabotto una città etrusca*. Bologna: Ante Quem, 2007.

Grzesik, D. "Review of Dirksen, Svenja, and Lena Krastel. Epigraphy through five millennia: Texts and images in context." Sonderschrift/Deutsches Archäologisches Institut, Abteilung Kairo, 43. Wiesbaden: Harrassowitz Verlag, 2020. *Bryn Mawr Classical Review* April 5, 2021. Retrieved from https://bmcr.brynmawr.edu/2021/2021.04.05/

Henderson, K. *On Line and on Paper: Visual Representations, Visual Culture, and Computer Graphics in Design Engineering*. Boston: MIT Press, 1999.

Hodder, I. *Entangled: An Archaeology of the Relationships between Humans and Things*. Malden, MA: Wiley-Blackwell, 2012.

Huvila, I. "The subtle difference between knowledge and 3D knowledge." *Hamburger Journal für Kulturanthropologie* 7 (2018), 99–111. Retrieved from https://journals.sub.uni-hamburg.de/hjk/article/view/1196

Ingold, T. *Making. Anthropology, Archaeology, Art, and Literature*. London and New York: Routledge, 2013.

Johannsen, N. "Archaeology and the inanimate agency proposition: A critique and a suggestion." In *Cross-Sections through Culture, Cognition, and Materiality*, edited by N. Johannsen, M. D. Jensen, and H. J. Jensen, 305–347. Arhus: Arhus University Press, 2012.

Kopytoff, I. "The cultural biography of things: Commoditization as process." In *The Social Life of Things: Commodities in Cultural Perspective*, edited by A. Appadurai, 64–91. Cambridge: Cambridge University Press, 1986.

Kostic, D., A. Snoeren, A. Vahdat, R. Braud, C. Killian, J. Anderson, J. Albrecht, A. Rodriguez, and E. Vandekieft. "High-bandwidth data dissemination for large-scale distributed systems." *ACM Transactions in Computer Systems* 26 (2008), 1–61.

Lanjouw, T. "Discussing the obvious or defending the contested: Why are we still discussing the 'scientific value' of 3D applications in archaeology?" In *The Three Dimensions of Archaeology*, edited by H. Kamermans, W. de Neef, C. Piccoli, A. G. Posluschny, and R. Scopigno, 1–12. Oxford: Archeopress, 2016.

Lomas, K. "Hidden writing: Epitaphs within tombs in Early Italy." In *L'écriture et l'espace de la mort: Épigraphie et nécropoles à l'époque pré-romaine*, edited by M. L. Haack. Rome: École française de Rome, 2015. Retrieved May 2021, from https://books.openedition.org/efr/2777?lang=en

Maggiani, A. "The Vicchio Stele: The inscription." *Etruscan Studies* 19.2 (2016), 220–24.

Maggiani, A. "La scrittura a Fiesole in età arcaica." In *L'ombra degli etruschi: Simboli di un popolo tra pianura e collina*, edited by P. Perazzi, G. Poggesi, and S. Sarti, 73–81. Florence: Edifir, 2016.

Maggiani, A. "Ostraka iscritti dall'Etruria." *Studi Etruschi* 78 (2016), 145–155.

Malnati, L., P. Desantis, A. Losi, and C. Balista. "Nuove testimonianze cultuali a Marzabotto: L'area sacra nord-orientale." In *Culti, forma urbana e artigianato a Marzabotto: Nuove prospettive di ricerca*, edited by G. Sassatelli and E. Govi, 89–100. Atti del Convegno di Studi. Bologna, S. Giovanni in Monte, June 3–4, 2003. Bologna: Ante Quem, 2005.

Mitchell, W. J. T. *Picture Theory: Essays on Verbal and Visual Representation*. Chicago: University of Chicago Press, 1995.

Montani, C., C. Rocchini, and R. Scopigno. *Tecnologie 3d Scanning: Introduzione e Valutazione Comparativa*. Pisa: Consiglio Nazionale delle Ricerche, 2001.

Napolitano, E. *Arabic Inscriptions and Pseudo-Inscriptions in Italian Art*. Thesis. Bamberg: Otto-Friedrich Universität, 2021.

Nocentini, A. *La Stele etrusca di Vicchio: Metodologie di rilievo per un'iscrizione da svelare*. Thesis. Florence: Università degli Studi, Department of Architecture DIDA, 2017.

Nocentini, A., and S. Sarti. *Le Giornate degli Etruschi (2016–2019): Esperienze di valorizzazione e Archeologia Belle Arti e Paesaggio per la Città Metropolitana di Firenze e le Province di Pistoia e Prato*, 325–326. Sesto Fiorentino: All'Insegna del Giglio, 2020.

Nocentini, A., and P. G. Warden. "Il santuario di Poggio Colla: Dalla ricerca archeologica alla rappresentazione digitale, testimonianze per il rituale etrusco [The Etruscan sanctuary at Poggio Colla: From archaeological research to digital representation, evidence for Etruscan ritual]." In *Territori e Frontiere della Rappresentazione – Territories and Frontiers of Representation*, edited by A. Di Luggo, et al., 1028–1032. 39° Convegno Internazionale dei docenti delle discipline della Rappresentazione. Rome: Gangemi Editore, 2017.

Olson, B. *In Defense of Things. Archaeology and the Ontology of Objects*. Lanham, MD: Alta Mira Press, 2010.

Paliou, E., D. Wheatly, and G. Earl. "Three-dimensional visibility analysis of architectural spaces: Iconography and visibility of the wall paintings of Xeste 3 (Late Bronze Age Akrotiri)." *Journal of Archaeological Science* 38 (2011), 375–386.

Perazzi, P., G. Poggesi, and S. Sarti, eds. *L'ombra degli etruschi: Simboli di un popolo fra pianura e collina*. Firenze: Edifir, 2016.

Polkowski, P. 2020. "World of mages or imaginary world? Rock art, landscape, and agency in the Western Desert of Egypt." In *Epigraphy through Five Millennia: Texts and Images in Context*, edited by S. Dirksen and L. Krastel, 255–284. Sonderschrift/Deutsches Archäologisches Institut, Abteilung Kairo, 43. Wiesbaden: Harrassowitz Verlag, 2020.

Robb, J. "Tradition and agency: Human body representations in later Prehistoric Europe." *World Archaeology* 40.3 (2008), 332–353.

Sennett, R. *The Craftsman*. London: Penguin, 2008.

Small, J. P. *Wax Tablets of the Mind: Cognitive Studies of Memory and Literacy in Classical Antiquity*. London and New York: Routledge, 1993.

Steingräber, S. *Cippi, stele, statue-stele, e semata: Testimonianze in Etruria, nel mondo italico e in Magna Grecia dalla prima Éta del Ferro fino all'Ellenismo*. Pisa: Edizioni ETS, 2017.

Wallace, R. "Alphabet orthography and paleography at Poggio Civitate (Murlo)." *Etruscan Studies* 13 (2010), 109–121.

Wang, H., Y. Luo, C. An, S. Chu, Z. Shen, L. Huang, and D. Zhang. "Application of imaging polarimeters to enhanced detection of stone carving." *Journal of Cultural Heritage* 40 (2019), 92–98.

Warden, P. G. "Remains of the ritual at the sanctuary of Poggio Colla." In *Votives, Places, Rituals in Etruscan Religion. Studies in Honor of Jean MacIntosh Turfa*, edited by M. Gleba and H. Becker, 121–127. Leiden: Brill, 2009.

Warden, P. G. "Monumental embodiment: Somatic symbolism and the Tuscan temple." In *Monumentality in Etruscan and Early Roman Architecture: Ideology and Innovation*, edited by M. L. Thomas and G. Meyers, 82–110. Austin: University of Texas Press, 2012.

Warden, P. G. "Giving the gods their due: Ritual evidence from Poggio Colla." In *Francesco Nicosia. L'archeologo e il soprintendente: Scritti in memoria*, edited by G. Camporeale, et al., 249–257. Notiziario della Soprintendenza per i Beni Archeologici della Toscana Supplemento 1 al n. 8/12. Sesto Fiorentino: All'Insegna del Giglio, 2012.

Warden, P. G. "The Vicchio Stele and its context." *Etruscan Studies* 19.2 (2016), 208–219.

Warden, P. G. "Una scoperta recente: La stele iscritta del santuario etrusco di Poggio Colla (Vicchio)." In *L'ombra degli etruschi: Simboli di un popolo tra pianura e collina*, edited by P. Perazzi, Gabriela Poggesi, and Susanna Sarti, 83–85. Florence: Edifir, 2016.

Warden, P. G., and A. Maggiani. "Authority and display in sixth-century Etruria: The Vicchio Stele." In *Roman Law before the Twelve Tables: An Interdisciplinary Approach*, edited by S. Bell and P. Du Plessis, 41–54. Edinburgh: Edinburgh University Press, 2020.

Whitehouse, R. "'Tombstones' in the North Italian Iron Age: Careless writers or athletic readers?" In *Writing as Material Practice: Substance, Surface, and Medium*, edited by K. E. Piquette and R. D. Whitehouse, 271–278. London: Ubiquity Press, 2013.

Whitehouse, R. "Personal names in Early Etruscan Inscriptions: An anthropological perspective." In *Etruscan Literacy in Its Social Context*, edited by R. D. Whitehouse, 181–192. London: Accordia Research Center, 2020.

Wright, R., A. Miller, and M. Addis. "The significance of storage in the 'cost of risk' of digital preservation." *International Journal of Digital Curation* 3.4 (2009), 105–122.

P. Gregory Warden, Michael L. Thomas, and Alessandro Nocentini, *Representation to Reproduction: Digital Phenomenology and Hermeneutics of Inscriptions* In: *A New Etruscan Archaeology: Twenty-First Century Techniques and Methods.* Edited by: Maurizio Forte, Oxford University Press. © Oxford University Press 2025. DOI: 10.1093/9780197582053.003.0002

2

A Paradigm Shift in the Investigation of Etruscan Former Townscapes

A View from Veii

Stefano Campana

Introduction

Urbanized societies have been characteristic of most of the Mediterranean region from at least the latter part of the fourth millennium BCE in the Levant, from around 2000 BCE in the Aegean, and for the last two and a half millennia in the rest of the Mediterranean area. In Roman times, there were as many as 430 known urban centers dotted across the whole of the Italian Peninsula, around a third of them displaying substantial evidence that they were once inhabited by Etruscans to one extent or another. According to legend, among the most important cities an alliance was formed between 600 BCE and 500 BCE by twelve Etruscan towns, the so-called Etruscan League, Etruscan Federation, or Dodecapolis. Etruscan culture flourished within cities and in confederacies of cities; indeed, Etruscan civilization was from the outset primarily urban based.

Architecture and urbanism in the ancient cities of the Mediterranean lend themselves very well to investigation. By virtue of their complex social, economic, and political background; their historical and monumental importance; their artistic value; and (in many cases) their easy accessibility, the ruined remains of their monuments and related structures have always attracted fascination and study by those who lived or undertook cultural tours around the Mediterranean area.

Today, from an archaeological perspective, it is possible to distinguish two contrasting types of past urban settings. First, there are cities that have long been abandoned and that are now defined through such terms as "former urban areas" or "one-time townscapes." Numerous examples of Etruscan cities fall into this category, including Veii, Vulci, Vetulonia, Populonia, Roselle, Marzabotto, and Spina. Second, there are cities that have remained continuously occupied and that have become major centers of population in the present day as so-called historical urban landscapes, including Arezzo, Chiusi, Cortona, Perugia, Volterra, Orvieto, Florence, and Bologna among their number.

It is important to emphasize the distinction between the development and implementation of archaeological research within one-time townscapes as compared with the study of historical urban landscapes. The most valued techniques in cities still under occupation can be distinguished in several respects from those that are appropriate for deployment in once-urban contexts that become wholly or partially buried following their abandonment. In ancient cities that have never lost their original urban function, one can count on an ample supply of documentary information or archival material that preserve the memory of the past and accounts of previous archaeological discoveries. Among the major problems encountered in such contexts, however, are the inevitable impediments of past and recent urban development. The systemic presence of buildings, especially those of some antiquity, can, through their standing facades, cellars, and foundations, provide an important source of information, but, at the same time, they constitute a grave obstacle for the application of many of our standard diagnostic methods, thus not altogether excluding their use but certainly reducing, complicating, and slowing down the possibility of carrying out survey work within the area of the buildings themselves and thereby interrupting the continuity of any analyses that can be made. The open areas free of buildings are limited to often-busy streets, squares, and parks along with private and public gardens but little else. In these spaces, it is equally difficult to deploy many of our usual investigative techniques. The great majority of the public spaces are covered in hard surfaces of one kind or another, which precludes direct observation of the underlying deposits and therefore also prevents the use of nondestructive methods such terrestrial or aerial survey, even though this last technique has been shown to have value in certain circumstances and situations. Even the methods of geophysics suffer in the urban context: magnetometry in particular struggles in the face of the strong magnetic interference that is inevitable in living towns and cities.

That said, the rest of this chapter focuses on abandoned cities, on how we can study them today, on what new questions we can try to answer, and how this was attempted in the study of one of the most important Etruscan cities: Veii.

Former Townscapes in the Mediterranean Area: Archaeology and "State of the Art" in Etruscan Urban Surveys

Following World War II, a fresh interest in archaeological studies developed in the Mediterranean area. It is possible to identify several reasons, however, one of the first purposes of survey projects was the desire to place excavated urban sites in the context of their rural settings (Bintliff and Snodgrass, 1988).

Some decades earlier a highly influential role in landscape archaeology had been played in Greece and around the Mediterranean more generally by the Messenia Expedition of the University of Minnesota. This project was particularly interesting because of its pioneering attempts, in the late 1930s, to resolve problems in the Homeric geography of the southwestern Peloponnese (McDonald, 1942). Over time this line of research developed into a more general search for Mycenaean sites, then for sites of all periods from the Neolithic to the Middle Ages (Cherry, 2003).

In the western Mediterranean during the postwar years, John Ward-Perkins and the British School at Rome provided a major stimulus and played a key role in Italy as a whole, carrying out, over the course of two decades between the 1950s and the 1970s, a systematic survey of Southern Etruria with the aim of exploring and understanding the past landscape of the area through the discovery, documentation, and interpretation of surface artifact scatters. The Southern Etruria Survey was particularly notable in that the work involved the systematic survey of landscape areas that showed no distinction between the cities themselves and their surrounding countryside—for example, the work undertaken in the "vanished" city of Veio and its rural surroundings by Ward-Perkins when he was Director of the British School (Ward, 1961).

From the 1970s, a new generation of increasingly intensive work brought about striking achievements in rural areas, refining the methods used but, in some senses, carrying out the work "in isolation" from the urban contexts that lay at their core. These so-called New Wave surveys marked a break with the pioneering projects of earlier years that had been based for the most part on identifying the largest urban and suburban settlements through "intuitive" search procedures. Now the focus moved to the introduction of new methodological approaches to enhance the scope and reliability of the resulting information, especially regarding the open countryside (Bintliff, 2000). This new phase of archaeological exploration, based almost exclusively on field-walking surveys, played a leading role over virtually all of the Mediterranean area, invigorated by a keen attention to methodological approaches that sought to improve the reliability of the collected data while inevitably reducing the size of the landscape blocks that could be incorporated within the survey work (Terrenato, 2004).

Between the mid-1970s and end of 1990s, this new wave of intensive survey work spread throughout the whole of the Mediterranean area, with particularly important projects undertaken in Greece and Italy but also, somewhat later, in Spain and France (Macready and Thompson, 1985). On the other hand, the southern flank of the Mediterranean Basin, as well as parts of the Levant, followed a rather different approach based on the compilation of inventories and catalogs of sites and monuments (Cherry, 2003).

A peculiarity—or, better perhaps, a paradox—of this new phase of survey work was highlighted in a key paper on "Mediterranean survey and the city," published in *Antiquity* by John Bintliff and Anthony Snodgrass (Bintliff and Snodgrass, 1988). The authors argued that field-walking survey as practiced at that time in a number of Mediterranean countries involved intensive, multiperiod investigations closely associated with rural landscapes and the rural sector of the economy. They pointed out that a clear gap had developed between urban research, mainly conducted through archaeological excavation, and the study of the rural landscape through intensive survey work. In practice, the contextualization of urban areas had from the outset been one of the major aims of regional survey; indeed, without including these urban areas the picture of the rural landscape remains in many senses incomplete. In that context, this schism between the methodologies employed in urban versus rural areas, along with the progressive contraction in the size of the chosen study area, made comparison of the collected information from the two different environments problematic and its overall interpretation extremely difficult. As a result, new means had to be found for collecting and then reconciling the results from a variety of urban areas (former townscapes and historical urban landscapes) by integrating the results from the urban areas with those from the open countryside.

The upshot was that, from the late 1970s or early 1980s, a number of archaeologists who were prominent in the development of survey methods adapted to the rural context turned their attention, quite independently of one another, to applying those "rural" methods of investigation in once-urban areas as well. After about two decades of intensive survey work of this kind, a series of unresolved problems and limitations began to attract attention and debate in the archaeological literature (Alcock and Cherry, 2004; Francovich and Patterson, 1999; Papadopoulos and Leventhal, 2003). By the end of the 1990s, leading experts in the field of landscape archaeology had begun to highlight some of these limitations, focusing their attention on basic improvements that they felt ought to be implemented in the following years. In summary, among the major limitations, most of the writers subscribed to the general idea that field-walking survey and surface collection were affected by inherent problems that could only be reduced or partially resolved by integrating them with other survey methods. Particular hopes in this respect fell on nondestructive techniques such as remote sensing, geophysical prospection, and geochemical studies (Keay et al., 2004). Moreover, the increasing role of computer and spatial technology, in particular geographic information systems (GISs) and global positioning systems (GPSs), was considered crucial within the sphere of landscape research. The improvements that they could make to data collection, analysis, synthesis, and presentation were considered almost from the beginning as much more than new tools but rather as an opportunity to bring the archaeology of surface collection and observation to a qualitatively higher level (Cherry, 2003; Gillings, 2000).

Around the turn of the millennium impatience with this situation, combined with discussion within the academic community about possible new approaches, was matched by a general improvement within the hard sciences. Among other influences, geophysical prospection played a central role. The efficacy of this technique improved dramatically in the 1990s, but the authentic revolution has only materialized in the past few years with the application of very-large-scale geophysical prospection in both landscape and once-urban contexts. In this context, Simon Keay, Martin Millett, and Frank Vermeulen, among others, played a primary role within the Mediterranean area.

As a consequence, there has been a significant upsurge in the use of nondestructive survey, notably in the formerly urban context of "vanished" historical towns. From the very first years of their application it became clear that the opportunities and potential gains offered by these new techniques and instrumentation were enormous. Large and complex once-urban sites previously studied for their monumental importance and historical or artistic value through field-walking survey, surface collection, and exploratory or targeted excavation could now be studied in the first instance through geophysical prospection, sometimes revealing the entire plan of the town before any intrusive method of investigation was put in hand. This was a truly significant transformation, allowing archaeologists to address specific questions in a way that had not been possible previously. Unsurprisingly, important improvements in the understanding of urbanism followed many of these survey projects. In particular, understanding of urbanism in the Roman Empire benefitted hugely from the integration of remote sensing methodologies in partnership with GIS-based archaeological mapping and, of course, field-walking survey, artifact collection, and excavation. An important contribution was also made in a variety of cases by aerial photography, from both targeted exploratory flights and through the analysis of "historical" photographs already available in regional and national archives (Musson et al., 2009). The combined application of these essentially nondestructive techniques has greatly enhanced our knowledge of the scale, structure, and chronology of specific buildings and the overall infrastructure within formerly urban contexts, allowing us to look at the wider phenomenon of urbanism from a valid and comparative viewpoint (Vermeulen et al., 2012).

It would be worthwhile at this point to provide a general overview of the incidence of large-scale geophysical surveys on urban contexts, as implemented so far within the Mediterranean area and other parts of Europe. The summary presented in Figure 2.1 has been compiled through a systematic scanning of relevant national and international journals and publications in the fields of archaeological prospection, urbanism, and topographic studies, with the author's own work on this aspect being aided and enriched by generous assistance from colleagues throughout Europe and in the United States. The map does not, of course, claim to be a comprehensive representation of the full geographical spread of survey-based research in urban studies. No doubt there are omissions, in some cases perhaps important ones, but the picture is probably a fair representation of the current state of affairs. Even a cursory glance at the figure leaves a clear impression of the diffusion all around the Mediterranean Sea of the application of this approach.

However, to extract a general meaning, the present sample would first need to be made more comprehensive and then normalized. But that is not the aim here. It is more relevant at this stage to focus on a different point: the chronological range and the geophysical methods implemented so far. Starting from the latter, it should be recognized that over the past twenty years our understanding of ancient towns has been revolutionized by the use of remote sensing techniques (Doneus et al., 2014; Linck et al., 2012; Vermeulen et al., 2012). These have enhanced our knowledge of the overall topography of these sites, especially when combined with excavation and surface survey. For example, magnetometry (predominantly fluxgate gradiometry) has produced impressive results, mapping complete towns and

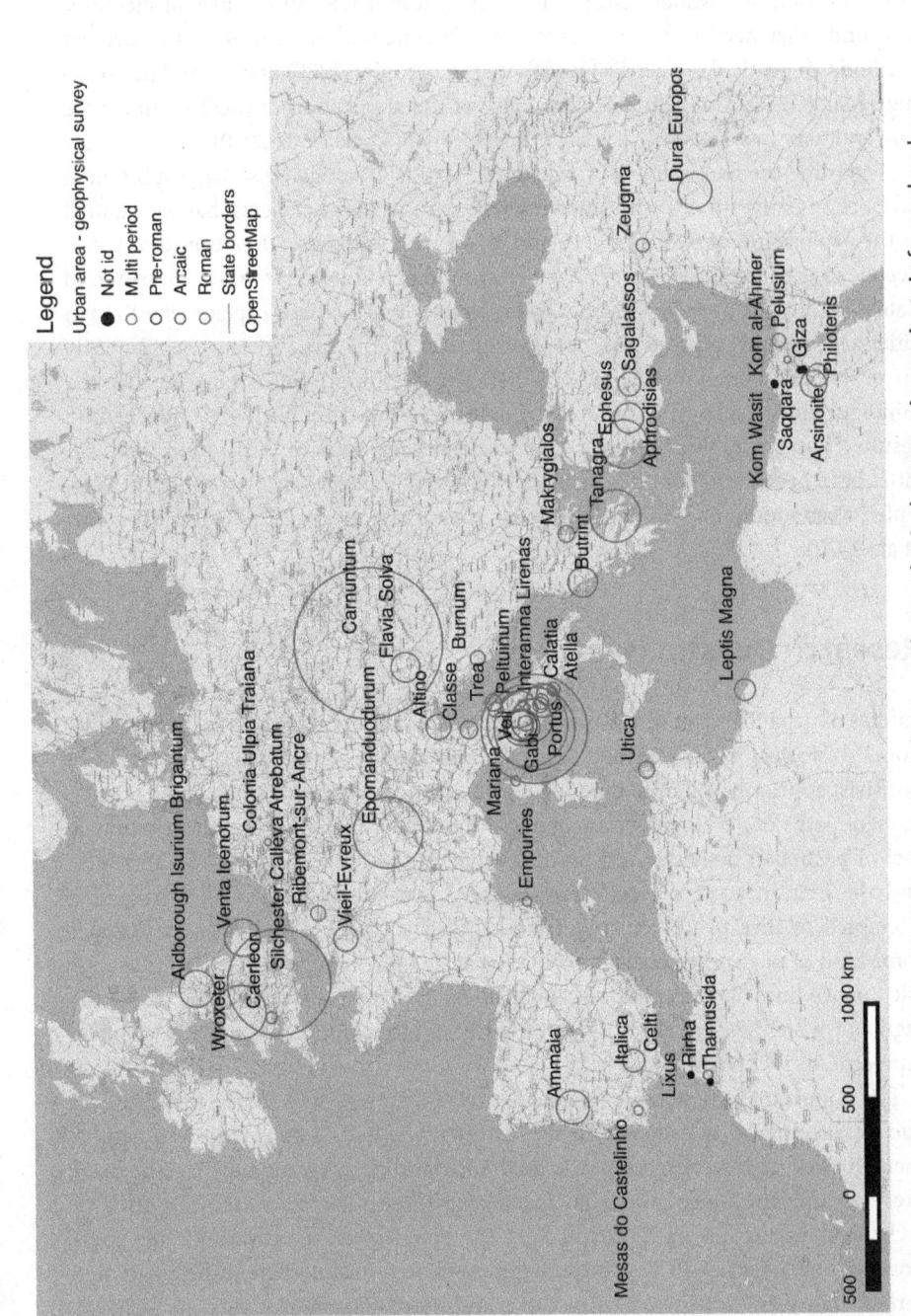

Figure 2.1 Distribution around the Mediterranean Sea of large-scale geophysical prospection projects in formerly urban contexts. The size of the circles is proportional to the size of the survey in hectares.

transforming the fund of evidence available for urban studies (Campana, 2018; Johnson and Millett, 2013). However, gradiometric survey, like all methods, has limits that need to be counterbalanced by integration with other prospecting methods, in particular electrical resistivity tomography (ERT) and ground penetrating radar (GPR). Unfortunately, examples of the application of these methods are rare and have involved very few sites (Boschi, 2016; Forte et al., 2020).

Regarding the chronological range of the targets investigated so far, a substantial proportion of the survey work (more than 85 percent of the projects) has been aimed at the exploration of Roman towns and cities, with less than 10 percent devoted to deeply stratified contexts across a wider chronological range from the Iron Age to Late Antiquity or even beyond. Several reasons might perhaps explain why Roman cities are so highly represented, not least the fact that Roman society was primarily an urban phenomenon (Launaro, 2014). An additional factor may be that the buildings and street systems of Roman cities are inherently likely to produce good results from geophysical survey. However, at the moment, only four Etruscan cities have been surveyed on a large scale by aerial or geophysical prospection: Veio, Vulci, Marzabotto, and Spina (Campana, 2019; Forte et al., 2020; Govi, 2014; Kay et al., 2020).

Research Questions

Studies of urbanism can be focused on a variety of different objectives, from "traditional" historical, economic, and topographical analyses (usually within a basically positivist approach) aimed at defining the emergence of the first urban cultures, subsequent paths of development, mapping of the urban infrastructure, the location of foci of particular activities and production sites, the outlining of suburban zones, and the identification of social groups etc. Occasionally such studies have also attempted to investigate and understand the social use of space, usually through some kind of post-processual approach. Recently some scholars have tried to reconcile the two lines of data collection and analysis, in some cases developing new paradigms in which the plurality and complexity of city contexts are more adequately represented (Filippi, 2022).

It is important to remember that a close relationship exists between the historical and archaeological questions and the research methods implemented to answer them; indeed, to a certain extent the methodological framework may in some cases predetermine the outcome. As an instance, written sources on subjects such as archeology or the history of architecture can be effective in answering *some* questions but certainly not all. A good strategy, therefore, must necessarily be based on a careful choice and integration of methods and sources, consistent with the archaeological questions under investigation.

In essence, the most common objective of urban geophysical survey is to detect and depict the overall plan or detailed physical layout of the town under study.

However, treating this as the final goal should be seen as an inherently reductive approach, at its most basic level little better than "wall chasing" (Johnson, 2013). For a more productive approach, specific questions need to be asked, for instance about the full extent of the settlement area and, of course, across a wide passage of time. Questions need to be asked about aspects that are fundamental to the understanding of an urban entity: the varying pattern of occupation over time, the location of discrete areas of activity within the urban whole (public and private building areas, sacred spaces, workshops, etc.), and the identification of a defensive wall or other boundary feature as it persisted or varied across time. Long-term continuity of occupation, matched by periodic changes or radical transformations, are common characteristics of urban areas, at least in Italy, so all of the elements described above (and more) need to be analyzed in light of the collected data if any true understanding is to be achieved about variations in settlement size, contraction or expansion of the walled circuit, and internal patterns of occupation and activity, in all cases as revealed across the passage of time.

Another crucial point in the understanding of cityscapes, with particular regard to their economy, social organization, and cultural background, along with the inherent nature of urban and rural life and its development over time, is the relationships between urban and rural contexts. For a whole series of conceptual, ideological, and structural reasons, including the differing methodologies generally applied to the study of the two contexts, "city" and "countryside" have often been dealt with separately from one another, generating a serious gap or disjunction in our understanding of either. Written sources, by contrast, refer frequently to an organic relationship between city, suburban areas, and the open countryside, their unity and interdependence being to all intents implicit.

Within this complex theoretical framework, in the past decade we have seen—or taken part in—a revolution in the archaeological methodologies used to study the ancient landscape. These now offer a wide and continuously expanding variety of "new" remote sensing methodologies, increasingly widely deployed for archaeological exploration and mapping. In addition to the improvements in technical capabilities, we can also recognize the beginnings of a conceptual change. Archaeology has traditionally been focused on individual locations—"sites"—which we have sought to identify and then explore through excavation and the analysis of the finds and other dating evidence recovered from them. Although pragmatically understandable, the division of the world into a series of isolated dots is conceptually problematic since human beings do not just exist at particular points in the landscape but rather utilize the whole of their surroundings in a wide variety of different ways (Campana, 2018; Powlesland, 2011). Given that the same was true in the past, and that today we increasingly have technologies capable of exploring whole tracts of the landscape, our aim should not "just" be to put more spots on the map but also, for instance, to defuse the traditional division between urban, suburban, and rural landscapes. Archaeology, thanks to the development of remote sensing methods and instrumentation, is hopefully moving toward paradigms that represent a "practical, theoretical, and philosophical" approach to the exploration and understanding of the reality and interconnectivity of past landscapes, whether in or around the city or in the open countryside (Clarke, 1973).

The Archaeological Topography of the Ancient Veii

The city of Veii, situated about 15 kilometers north of Rome, occupied what is now a broad plateau of gently rolling countryside about 190 hectares in extent. The best way to begin discussion of this sample area is perhaps to quote from the introduction by Christopher Smith to the volume dedicated by scholars of the British School at Rome to a reconsideration of the survey work conducted by John Ward-Perkins in the 1950s: "To understand Veii is in part to understand both what Rome might have been, had history not favoured her rise to power, and to understand better what made Rome the success she was, for in many respects Veii is Rome through a sort of looking glass. In their early history there were more similarities than differences between the two settlements, and Veii was more like Rome than she was like other Etruscan cities" (Smith, 2012). That comparison faces us with a great challenge in undertaking further work at Veii.

However, Veii also occupies a privileged position in the history of archaeology itself. Investigation within the city really began with the work of a number of distinguished scholars from the second quarter of the nineteenth century onward: Gell, Nibby, Canina, Dennis, Stefani, Lanciani, Colini, and Giglioli. The beginning of intensive and systematic research, however, did not come until after World War II, through the initiative of John Ward-Perkins, then Director of the British School at Rome. He realized that the rapid mechanization of agriculture under way at that time would bring about widespread destruction of archaeological resources but, at the same time, create unprecedented opportunities for investigating what was inevitably at risk of destruction. His response was to initiate a survey at Veii that radically changed our understanding of the city and its surrounding countryside while at the same time revolutionizing the methods and practice of what has subsequently become known as "landscape archaeology" within the Mediterranean world (Potter, 1979; Ward-Perkins, 1961).

In more recent times, the University of Rome, "La Sapienza," has been undertaking the "Veii Project," first under the leadership of G. Colonna, then G. Bartoloni and, more recently, M. T. D'Alessio. This project has brought together committed research teams under the supervision of G. Bartoloni, A. Carandini, and M. Fenelli and has also involved the Archaeological Superintendency through F. Boitani and the Consiglio nazionale delle ricerche (CNR) in the person of M. Guaitoli. To Guaitoli in particular has fallen the task of systematic research in the collection and analysis of large numbers of aerial photographs taken between 1929 and 2010, involving the accurate mapping of all of the features identified during air photo interpretation (Guaitoli, 2015). The overall result of the work undertaken so far has brought about a very substantial improvement in our understanding of the city and its surroundings.

Within this framework, I was invited by Guaitoli and the CNR, in the spring of 2009, to undertake trials in the application of magnetic survey within the area once occupied by the ancient city. The first results demonstrated the high potential of this technique at Veii, and it was therefore decided to extend the survey to cover the whole of the plateau, eventually amassing almost 170 hectares of magnetic measurements between the spring of 2011 and the winter of 2016.

At the beginning of this work the aims and underpinning archaeological questions were set out as follows:

1. Although a very substantial amount of information has been collected over the past two centuries and a wide range of methodologies have been employed, the plateau of Veii still presents large areas where apparently no information is yet available. It is expected that new information from these gaps may provide a clearer understanding of the transformation of the city across time and a better appreciation of post-depositional processes.

2. Magnetic survey, preferably integrated in specific areas with ETR and/or GPR, may provide a detailed layout, or layouts, of Veii across the Iron Age and Etruscan and Roman periods, making it possible to contextualize, integrate, and combine this new information with that collected in the past and thereby substantially improve understanding of the topography of the city, better defining its limits, its fortification structures, the location of its gateways, the length and orientation of its streets, and the differentiation between built-up and open areas, etc.

3. In some cases, it is expected that opportunities will present to go beyond the concept of "wall-following" and, in addition, to begin analyzing economic and social patterns within transformations of the urban layout and expansions and contractions in the topography of economic activity: workshop areas, the religious center, public areas, agricultural activity, stock areas, etc.

4. The implementation of this new approach and array of survey methods may make it possible to identify unexpected features that will shed new light on chronological phases that, on the basis of current evidence, appear to be "empty"; for instance, in the case of Veii, there is at present no evidence of Bronze Age or earlier cultural material having been found.

5. The influence of the environmental background should be further investigated (the geo- and bio-archaeological context) as well as the relationships between the city and the broader landscape across time.

Although a magnetic survey has almost been completed, with just two fields yet to be surveyed, the search for a better understanding of the environmental context is still ongoing. However, it is possible at this stage to present a first interpretation of the magnetic data within the framework of current understanding of the site provided by the long-standing research work described above.

At the time of writing, toward the end of 2021, a total of 169.7 hectares of magnetic measurements have been collected within the city of Veii. The interpretation work is still ongoing but has been based up to this stage on the identification of 1,998 archaeological and other features. Figure 2.1 shows quite clearly the complexity and density of the information provided by the magnetic data. The extraordinary density of the information makes it at first glance somewhat daunting. To achieve a good understanding of such a highly stratified context requires a strictly systematic approach and, above all, a well-defined starting point. The first step has therefore been the identification of those features that could be considered relatively stable across the long time span of settlement activity.

Building on previous experience it was decided to start by identifying the urban road system and in particular the two main axes of communication, one running from northwest to southeast and the other from west to east, both suggested by previous studies to have been developed in the first instance during the Iron Age (Guaitoli, 2015).

It can be seen on the magnetic map and on the graphic representation of the features in Figures 2.2 and 2.3 that the main axes present clear evidence of what may be called "arterial roads," in one instance crossing the plateau from a gate at the north to another at the south and in the other case from an access point at the west to another at the east. Likewise, it is easy to recognize a fairly regular pattern of linear features that start from the arterial roads and run for the most part in straight lines to cover

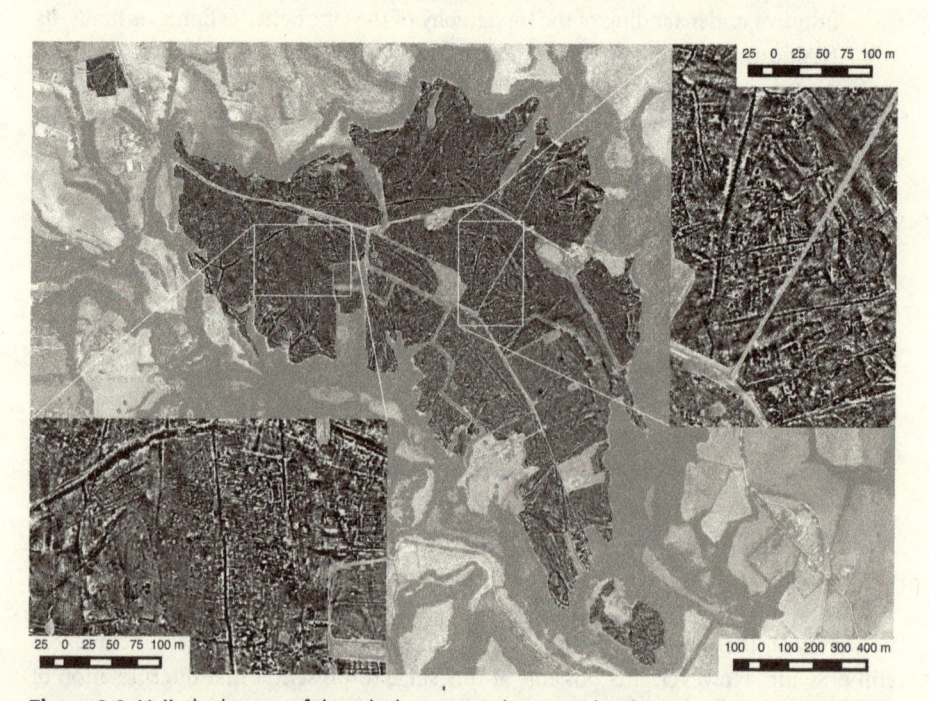

Figure 2.2 Veii: the layout of the whole surveyed area and a close-up showing the detail and density of the archaeological features.

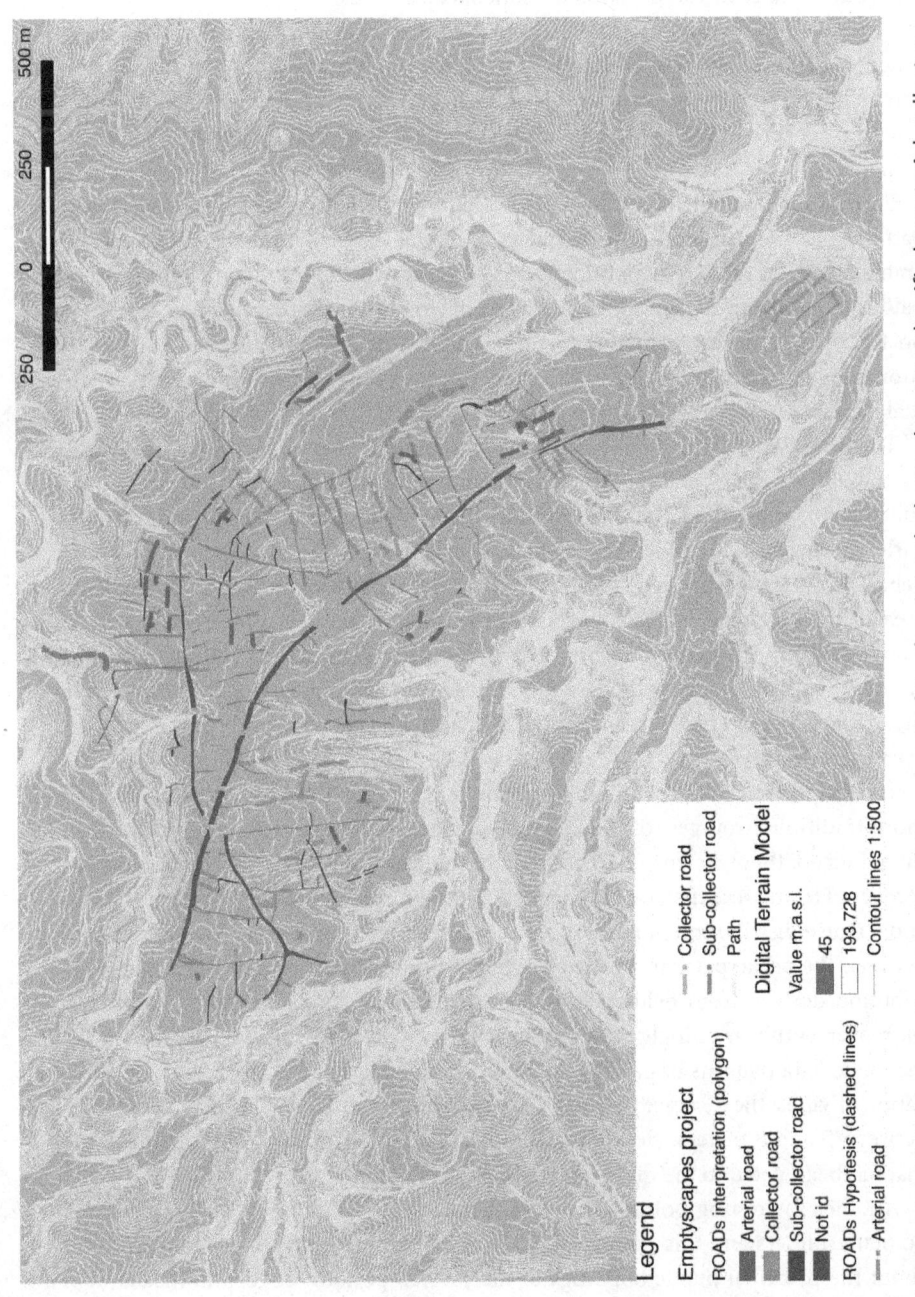

Legend

Emptyscapes project

ROADs interpretation (polygon)
- Arterial road
- Collector road
- Sub-collector road
- Not id

ROADs Hypotesis (dashed lines)
- Arterial road

- - - Collector road
- - - Sub-collector road
- - - Path

Digital Terrain Model

Value m.a.s.l.
- 45
- 193.728

Contour lines 1:500

Figure 2.3 Veii: interpretative mapping of the magnetic data showing only the road system, classified as arterial, collector and sub-collector roads.

most of the plateau with what have been designated as "collector roads." In addition, it has in places also been possible to identify features connecting two or more collector road, hence their classification as "subcollector roads."

Overall, the Veii road system fairly closely reflects the physiography of the landscape. It also indicates the high level of sophistication in the layout of the city; this can be interpreted as the result of a long-term process of gradual development that nonetheless preserved a strong consistency across the long history of the urban center.

From visual analysis of the features it seems possible to recognize a single basic pattern that, in terms of its finer detail, probably developed gradually over a considerable length of time. Only a limited number of discontinuities within this general pattern have been detected so far. A reasonable hypothesis is that the main axes took on their shape during a first occupation some time between the end of the late Bronze Age and the beginning of the Iron Age, the period for which the first artifactual evidence is available (Cascino et al., 2015).

The overlay of the field-walking data and magnetic map makes it probable that, by the end of the Archaic period the road system, including collector and even subcollector roads, had already been fully developed. Indeed, it is known from the early survey by the British School at Rome and from the more recent work on behalf of CNR that the greatest development of the city took place and the built-up area of the city reached its fullest extent in the Archaic period; artifact scatters from that time are present across the whole of the plateau. By contrast, after the conquest by Rome during the late Republican and the Imperial Age, the extent of the artifact scatters reduces substantially in accord with historical sources and the excavation data.

The magnetic data provide quite strong support for the view, developed from more traditional sources, of the city's expansion and subsequent contraction over time. Indeed, there are large parts of the plateau where no Roman material has been recovered from areas that, on the magnetic maps, display a pattern of collector roads and a dense distribution of buildings or other features (Figure 2.4). The consistency between the urban pattern revealed by geophysical prospection and the pottery distribution derived from field-walking survey leaves no room for doubt about this. Moreover, within seemingly built up parts of the city it is possible to recognize in the magnetic data patterns of parallel ditches that can readily be attributed to the cultivation of vines; the distance between the rows varies, from one allotment to another, between 5 and 8 meters, closely matching excavation evidence from around Rome that has been dated to the mid and late Republic (Volpe, 2009).

Another interesting point is the extraordinary longue durée of the road system. To better understand this point it might be useful to focus on what is known so far about the principal public buildings of the Roman period: the forum, theater, and thermal baths. None of these shows any consistent orientation with one another to form any kind of orthogonal or regular pattern. In fact, all of them clearly adopt orientations based on the system of roads laid out during the Etruscan period.

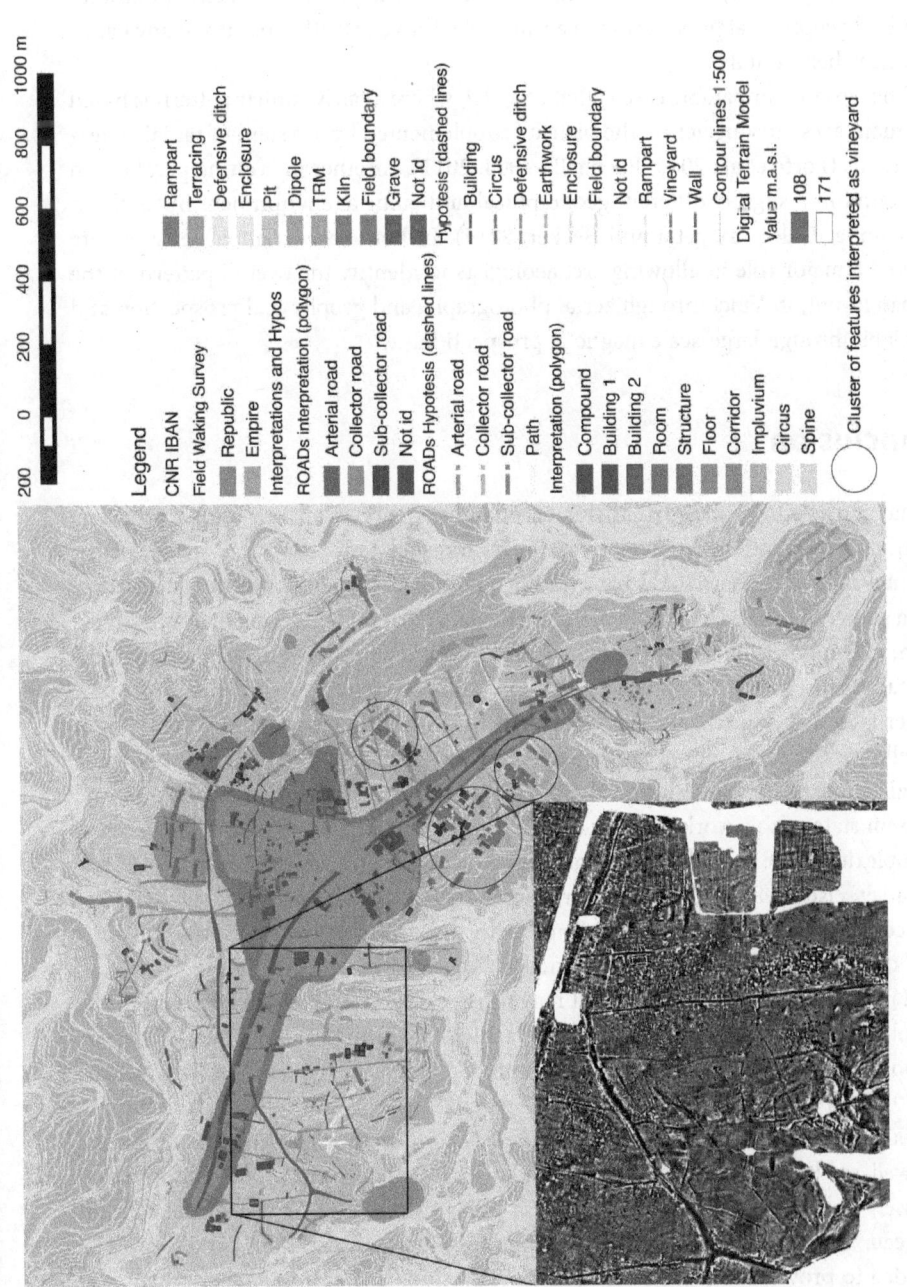

Legend

CNR IBAN

Field Waking Survey

Republic
Empire

Interpretations and Hypos

ROADs interpretation (polygon)
Arterial road
Collector road
Sub-collector road
Not id

ROADs Hypotesis (dashed lines)
Arterial road
Collector road
Sub-collector road
Path

Interpretation (polygon)
Compound
Building 1
Building 2
Room
Structure
Floor
Corridor
Impluvium
Circus
Spine

Rampart
Terracing
Defensive ditch
Enclosure
Pit
Dipole
TRM
Kiln
Field boundary
Grave
Not id

Hypotesis (dashed lines)
Building
Circus
Defensive ditch
Earthwork
Enclosure
Field boundary
Not id
Rampart
Vineyard
Wall

Contour lines 1:500
Digital Terrain Model
Value m.a.s.l.
108
171

◯ Cluster of features interpreted as vineyard

Figure 2.4 Veii: the Late Republican and Imperial Age distribution of artefact scatters (red and green areas respectively) is clearly less extensive compared with the Etruscan period when artefacts covered the whole of the plateau, including parts of the magnetic map that have clear evidence of structures that can be interpreted as dwellings, roads, workshops, temples and so on.

Among the first results of this phase of the work, therefore, one of the main achievements is that almost the entire road layout of the largest and most important Etruscan city in Italy has been depicted through the application of aerial photography and geophysical prospection in a way and with a clarity that has few if any parallels elsewhere in Italy.

The closest comparable case is that of Vulci, where a fairly similar pattern is based on main axes curving across the plateau, supplemented by a system of radial collector roads (Forte et al., 2020; Pocobelli, 2004, 2011). Another interesting parallel can be found in a slightly different geographical and cultural environment in southern Lazium, at Gabii (Mogetta and Becker, 2014). In both cases, remote sensing data played a major role in allowing archaeologists to identify the overall pattern of the urban layout, in Vulci through aerial photography and geophysical prospection and in Gabii through large-scale magnetic prospection.

Conclusion

It has already been noted that this case study is very much a work in progress. Further investigation, particularly through targeted test excavation and environmental analyses, are needed to extend the quantity and quality of the archaeological data gathered so far. In particular, magnetic data currently under further interpretation, in combination with the results of previous and current research by more traditional means, promise, on the basis of preliminary results, to shed light on many other issues, such as the pattern of settlement distribution across time, the types of dwellings, the fortification system, previously unknown public buildings, and the ruralization and exploitation of the plateau during the Roman period. Even at the present state of this work in progress, however, it is worth emphasizing the extreme complexity of the overall situation at Veii involving an Etruscan layout that finds few parallels elsewhere, combined with a long-lasting development and taphonomic process from the Iron Age onward and with the added difficulty of distinguishing the chronology of most of the detected features. Together with the interpretation and mapping of the magnetic data it may be necessary to employ GPR survey on the whole or substantial parts of the site to achieve three-dimensional data of subsoil deposits that will hopefully resolve a number of crucial issues (Verdonck et al., 2020). Furthermore, the clarification of specific issues could perhaps be achieved through the application of high-resolution ERT on carefully chosen areas of the site as well as the use of high-resolution lidar aimed at revealing information about densely vegetated areas within the site or along the wooded border of the summit plateau. A parallel series of targeted but minimalist excavations would also be needed to provide critical stratigraphical, artifactual, and chronological evidence at critical points in the layout of the city. The invaluable contribution of the air-photographic and geophysical data can be seen in the fact that it is now possible to identify at least some of these key locations in which minimally invasive excavation could hopefully provide answers to chronological and perhaps functional questions that would otherwise remain unresolved despite many years of previous archaeological study of the ancient city.

Acknowledgments

The research for this chapter would not have been possible without the financial support of the Marie Curie action for the Emptyscapes project (FP7-PEOPLE-2013-IEF n. 628338) and the Culture 2007 ArchaeoLandscpes Europe project (Grant Agreement nr. 2010/1486/001-001).

I am particularly grateful to Professor Martin Millett, scientist in charge of the Marie Curie project, for his constant support, valuable advice, and critical attitude. I would like to thank Ken Saito for his tenacity, rigor, and outstanding work done in the field and in the laboratory while gathering and processing vast amounts of magnetic measurements at Veii. Important advice was also received from Dr. Simon Stoddart.

I am indebted to "Progetto Veio," at the University of Rome "La Sapienza," coordinated initially by Giovanni Colonna, later by Gilda Bartoloni, and currently by Maria Teresa d'Alessio. The project involves several research teams, including the group led by Gilda Bartoloni, Maria Teresa d'Alessio, and Marcello Guaitoli (CNR and the University of Salento). All of them have collaborated freely and generously with their time and ideas. For the same reasons I am most grateful to the British School at Rome and particularly to Roberta Cascino and Director General Christopher Smith.

Particular thanks are offered to Salvatore Piro (CNR-ITABC), Michel Dabas (Geocarta), and Gianfranco Morelli (Geostudi) for their valuable support in the survey, processing, and interpretation of the geophysical measurements.

The University of Siena spin-off company Advanced Technology Systems (ATS) played a crucial role, generously sharing use of the Foerster magnetometer system used in the survey work.

Special thanks are also due to two good friends who have followed and inspired so much of the writer's research work since early in his career, Chris Musson and Dominic Powlesland. As ever, they have helped with constructive criticism and comments throughout all stages of the project.

Finally, my thoughts turn inevitably to my mentor, the late Riccardo Francovich, who gave me the cultural background and the intellectual vigor to face, time after time, new research challenges.

Bibliography

Alcock, S., and J. Cherry, eds. *Side-by-Side Survey: Comparative Regional Studies in the Mediterranean*. Oxford: Oxbow Books, 2004.

Bintliff, J. "Beyond dots on the map: Future directions for surface artefact survey in Greece." In *The Future of Surface Artefact Survey in Europe*, edited by J. Bintliff, M. Kuna, and N. Venclova, 3–20. Sheffield: Sheffield Academic Press, 2000.

Bintliff, J., and A. Snodgrass. "Mediterranean survey and the city." *Antiquity* 62 (1988): 57–71.

Bintliff, J., M. Kuna, and N. Venclova, eds. *The Future of Surface Artefact Survey in Europe*. Sheffield: Sheffield Academic Press, 2000.

Boschi, F. "Reading ancient cities: The contribution of the non-invasive techniques." In *Looking to the Future, Caring for the Past. Preventive Archaeology in Theory and Practice*, edited by F. Boschi, 85–100. Bologna: Bonomia University Press, 2016.

Campana, S. *Mapping the Archaeological Continuum: Filling "Empty" Mediterranean Landscapes*. New York: Springer, 2018.

Campana, S. "Filling gaps in space and time at Veii. 'Emptyscapes' project." In *Veii: An Etruscan City*, edited by J. Tabolli, 29–33. Austin: University of Texas Press, 2019.

Cascino, R., U. Fusco, and C. Smith, eds. *Novità nella ricerca archeologica a Veio: Dagli studi di John Ward-Perkins alle ultime scoperte*. Rome: Sapienza University Press, 2015.

Cherry, J. "Archaeology beyond the site: Regional survey and its future." In *Theory and Practice in Mediterranean Archaeology: Old World and New World Perspectives*, edited by J. Papadopoulos and R. Leventhal, 137–159. Los Angeles: University of California, 2003.

Clarke, D. "Archaeology: Loss of innocence." *Antiquity* 47 (1973): 7–18.

Doneus, M., G. Verhoeven, C. Atzberger, M. Wess, and M. Ruš. "New ways to extract archaeological information from hyperspectral pixels." *Journal of Archaeological Science* 52 (2014): 84–96.

Filippi, D., ed. *Rethinking the Roman City: The Spatial Turn and the Archaeology of Roman Italy*. Oxon: Routledge, 2022.

Forte, M., N. Danelon, D. Johnston, K. Mccusker, E. Newton, Gianfranco Morelli, and Gianluca Catanzariti. "Vulci 3000: A digital challenge for the interpretation of Etruscan and Roman cities." In *Digital Cities: Between History and Archaeology*, edited by M. Forte and H. Murteira, 13–41. Oxford: Oxford Scholarship Online, 2020.

Francovich, R., and H. Patterson, eds. *Extracting Meaning from Ploughsoil Assemblages*. Oxford: Oxbow, 1999.

Gillings, M. "The utility of the GIS approach in the collection, management, storage and analysis of surface survey data." In *The Future of Surface Artefact Survey in Europe*, edited by J. Bintliff, M. Kuna, and N. Venclova, 105–120. Sheffield: Sheffield Academic Press, 2000.

Govi, E. "Etruscan urbanism at Bologna, Marzabotto and in the Po valley." In *Papers on Italian Urbanism in the First Millennium B.C.*, edited by E. Robinson, *Journal of Roman Archaeology* Supplementary Series 97 (2014): 81–112.

Guaitoli, M. "La città tra nuove metodologie e tradizione." In *Novità nella ricerca archeologica a Veio: Dagli studi di John Ward-Perkins alle ultime scoperte*, edited by R. Cascino, U. Fusco, and C. Smith, 83–97. Rome: Sapienza University Press, 2015.

Johnson, P. "Conceptualising townscapes: Perceptions of urbanism and their Influence on Archaeological Survey Strategies." In *Archaeological Survey and the City*, edited by P. Johnson and M. Millett, 8–23. Oxford: Oxbow Books, 2013.

Johnson, P., and M. Millett, eds. *Archaeological Survey and the City*. Oxford: Oxbow Books, 2013.

Kay, S., E. Pomar, and S. Hay. "Spina revisited: The 2008 geophysical prospection in the light of the excavation results." *Groma* 5 (2020), 1–16.

Keay, S., M. Millett, L. Paroli, and K. Strutt, eds. *Portus: An Archaeological Survey of the Port of Imperial Rome*. Archaeological Monograph of the British School at Rome, 15. Oxford: Alden Group, 2005.

Launaro, A. "Survey archaeology in the Roman world (history, approach, methodology)." In *Encyclopaedia of Global Archaeology*, edited by C. Smith, 7146–7155. Berlin: Springer, 2014.

Linck, R., J. Fassbinder, and S. Buckreuss. "Integrated geophysical prospection by high-resolution optical satellite images, synthetic aperture radar and magnetometry at the example of the UNESCO World Heritage Site of Palmyra (Syria)." *Proceedings of Archaeology and Geoinformatics* 7 (2012): 1–26.

Macready, S., and F. Thompson. *Archaeological Field Survey in Britain and Abroad. Occasional Paper (New Series) VI*. London: Society of Antiquaries of London, 1985.

McDonald, W. "Where did Nestor live?" *American Journal of Archaeology* 46 (1942): 538–545.

Mogetta, M., and J. Becker. "Archaeological research at Gabii, Italy: The Gabii Project excavations 2009–2011." *American Journal of Archaeology* 118, 1 (2014): 177–188.

Musson, C., R. Palmer, and S. Campana. "Flights into the past: Aerial photography, photo interpretation and mapping for archaeology." http://archiv.ub.uni-heidelberg.de/propylaeumdok/2009/1/flights_into_the_Past_2013.pdf. Accessed June 20, 2022.

Papadopoulos, J., and R. Leventhal, eds. *Theory and Practice in Mediterranean Archaeology: Old World and New World Perspectives*. Los Angeles: University of California, 2003.

Pocobelli, G. "Vulci: Il contributo della fotografia aerea alla conoscenza dell'area urbana." *Archeologia Aerea* 1 (2004): 127–142.

Pocobelli, G. "Vulci ed il suo territorio: Area urbana, necropolis e viabilità. Applicazioni di cartografia archeologica e fotogrammetria finalizzata." *Archeologia Aerea* 4/5 (2011): 117–126.

Potter, T. *The Changing Landscape of South Etruria*. London: Elek, 1979.

Powlesland, D. "Identifying the unimaginable: Managing the unmanageable." In *Remote Sensing for Archaeological Heritage Management*, edited by D. Cowley, 17–32. Budapest: Archeolingua, 2011.

Smith, C. "Historical introduction." In *Veii: The Historical Topography of the Ancient City*, edited by R. Cascino, H. Di Giuseppe, and H. Patterson. London: Archaeological Monographs of the BSR, 2012.

Terrenato, N. "Sample size matters! The paradox of global trends and local surveys." In *Side-by-Side Survey: Comparative Regional Studies in the Mediterranean*, edited by S. Alcock and J. Cherry, 36–48. Oxford: Oxbow Books, 2004.

Verdonck, L., A. Launaro, F. Vermeulen, and M. Millett. "Ground-penetrating radar survey at Falerii Novi: A new approach to the study of Roman cities." *Antiquity* 94, 375 (2020): 705–723.

Vermeulen, F., G.-J. Burgers, S. Keay, and C. Corsi, eds. *Urban Landscape Survey in Italy and the Mediterranean*. Oxford: Oxbow Books, 2012.

Volpe, R. "Vino, Vigneti ed Anfore In Rome Repubblicana." In *Suburbium II: Il suburbio di Rome dalla fine dell'età monarchica alla nascita del sistema delle ville (V-II secolo a.C.)*, edited by V. Jolivet, C. Pavolini, M. A. Tomei, and R. Volpe. 3–6. Rome: École française de Rome, 2009.

Ward-Perkins, J. "Veii: The historical topography of the ancient city." *Papers of the British School at Rome* 29 (1961).

Stefano Campana, *A Paradigm Shift in the Investigation of Etruscan Former Townscapes: A View from Veii* In: *A New Etruscan Archaeology: Twenty-First Century Techniques and Methods*. Edited by: Maurizio Forte, Oxford University Press.
© Oxford University Press 2025. DOI: 10.1093/9780197582053.003.0003

3

The Remote Revolution

Recent Remote Sensing Projects in Etruria

Antonio LoPiano and Katherine McCusker

Remote Sensing Methodologies

"Remote sensing" is a broad term referring to any method to obtain information in a noninvasive, remote manner. The more general field of remote sensing can be divided into two categories: airborne tools (sometimes subdivided into "space" and aerial) and ground-based tools. The field of remote sensing thus includes an array of technologies including satellite imagery, unmanned aerial vehicles (UAVs), light detection and ranging (lidar), magnetometry, electrical resistivity surveys, and ground penetrating radar (GPR). This array of sensors enables scholars to examine beyond what is visible to the human eye.

Satellite remote sensing uses information gained from the various sensors on a satellite, often in the form of a raster image. The other type of airborne remote sensing uses UAVs (drones) to gather information using a range of camera-mounted light sensors, such as normal color (RGB), red-edge, near-infrared, thermal, and multispectral. UAVs can be divided into two categories: *copters*, which can hover in the air, stationary over a specific location, and *continuous flight* devices, which have fixed wings and must maintain continuous motion. The expanding development of drones has led to the easier use of the technology both as a hobby and for scholars. Increased access to this technology has created more affordable models and the easier applicability of them to various projects. The specifications and quality of a drone determine the quality of the results, and this is reflected in the cost of the tool, illustrating that there are some financial barriers that affect results. While new technological developments have made drones easier to fly, shifting national and local laws make the requirements for conducting an aerial survey a moving target. These changing regulations thus cause the execution of surveys to be difficult and prone to unpredictable circumstances.

Magnetometry is a ground-based remote sensing method that uses an instrument to measure changes in the magnetic field within the layers of earth beneath, thus making it capable of easily and quickly covering large areas. Minute changes in the magnetism of an area can be used to detect ditches, structures made of wood or other organic materials, burned areas, and ferrous objects. Electrical resistivity surveys measure vertical and horizontal changes in the electrical resistivity of the

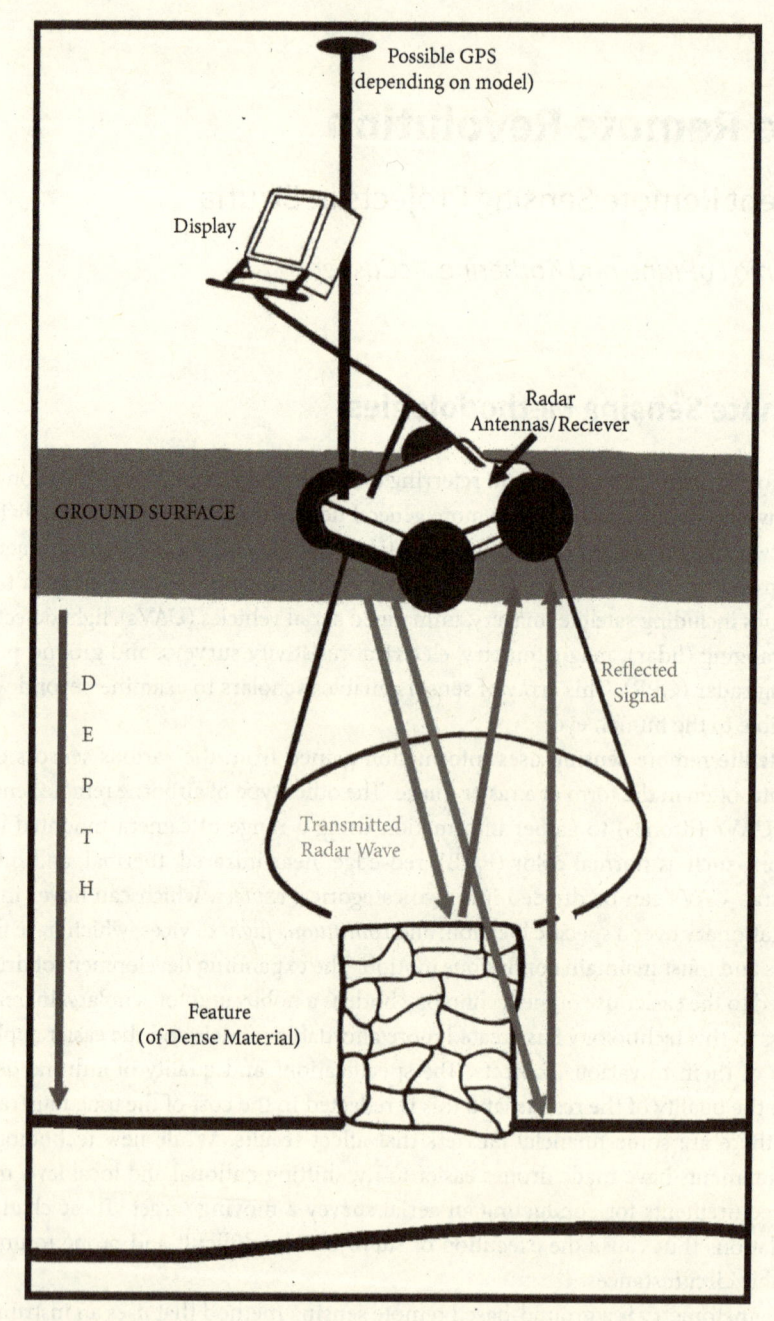

Figure 3.1 Diagram visualizing the process of ground penetrating radar (GPR) (McCusker 2021).

subsurface. This method is often used to sense groundwater and similar features. The last method, GPR, sends electromagnetic radar pulses into the ground, with the frequency of the signal varying depending on the machine and the specifics of the survey (Figure 3.1). This radar signal is reflected by dense materials, and it continues on until it dissipates, the time for that frequency's length has passed, or it hits an impassably dense material. An antenna reads the returning signal, recording the time elapsed and its returning strength. GPR machines can send a range of frequencies as a signal and often record two at a time. The differing results that the various frequencies provide expand the range of information gathered. Although a lower frequency will penetrate further into the ground, it will not record minute changes in density as a higher signal would. A high frequency will only reach shallower depths, but it is able to "see" smaller changes in density, thus offering higher-resolution detail. Together, the different signals provide a more accurate picture depending on the needs of the survey.

The success of ground-based remote sensing methods heavily depends on the geology of the area, and one method may not be suitable for a site or a particular part of it. The terrain of the area can also preclude the use of some methods.

Vulci Case Study

Vulci is an Etruscan-Roman city in Southern Etruria, located near modern-day Montalto di Castro. A long-enduring site and one of the cities in the Etruscan League of Twelve Cities, Vulci held a position as an important spatial, political, and economic crossroads.

The ancient city remains largely unexcavated after its rediscovery in the late 1700s (Buranelli, 1995) Initial excavations during the 1800s largely focused on the necropolises surrounding the city (Bonamici, 1980; Buranelli, 1992, 1994; Campanari, 1836; Dennis, 1884 Falconi Amorelli, 1983; Sciacca, 2017; Scullard, 1967; Sgubini Moretti, 1993; Torelli, 2008). The first quarter of the twentieth century saw numerous excavations, still focused on burials outside the city, although Ferraguti offered the first photographs of the city walls of Vulci in 1930 (Falconi Amorelli, 1983, 1987; Mengarelli, 1929). Crucial excavations inside the city occurred between 1956 and 1958, overseen by Benato Bartoccini and Sergio Paglieri with assistance from the Lerici Foundation (Lerici, 1960). These years focused on the city walls, a votive deposit, access roads to the city, the Great Temple, and exploration of several possible public and religious buildings probably dating to the Roman Republican period. Paglieri focused on excavating a large remaining portion of the House of Cryptoporticus (a Roman-era domus) in 1957 (Paglieri, 1959). The years from 1957 to 1961 saw a return to a focus on the necropolises, with a large number of investigations carried out in various locations: Osteria Necropolis, Cavaluppo Necropolis, Cuccumella area, Cuccumelletta area, Poggio Maremma, Pelicone, Agnesina, the Necropolis of Fosso dell'Osteria, and several other surrounding lands.

While topographical and aerial surveys of Vulci's gained traction in the late twentieth and early twenty-first centuries, in 1962, the Lerici Foundation attempted to survey the area around Cuccumella with geoelectrical devices as the first major ground-based remote sensing survey of the site. Late surveys completed by Sgubini Moretti, Pacciarelli, and Pocobelli remain formative studies of the site (Pacciarelli, 1991; Pocobelli, 2004, 2007, 2011; Sgubini Moretti, 1988, 1990, 1993, 1994, 2001, 2003, 2008; Sgubini Moretti and Ricciardi, 2001). Vulci remained undeveloped during modern times and was designated an Archaeological and Nature Park in 2001. Most of the recent excavations at Vulci have focused by necessity on necropolis areas that were either partially looted or damaged by natural forces. In 2014, Marchetti used magnetic susceptibility and electrical resistivity tomography to create a detailed geological map of the area (Marchetti et al., 2014).

The series of limited, older excavations within the city revealed only a handful of structures, including the Great Temple, the House of Cryptoporticus, the House of the Fisherman, the gates, the apsidal church, and the medieval-era church (Forte and Campana, 2016; Forte et al., 2020). These few structures are the only direct urban evidence available to work with the plethora of burial studies to inform our opinion about the development of urban life and space at Vulci.

The first systematic excavation and digital exploration in Vulci's urban context began in 2015, undertaken by Maurizio Forte and Duke University through the Vulci 3000 project. The team conducted magnetometry (in 2014), GPR (2015 and 2018), and aerial surveys (2015–2019). The magnetometry results were largely inconclusive, likely due to the magnetic nature of the volcanic soil and geology of the plateau. The first aerial surveys during the same year focused on collecting normal-colored images of the center of the city. Subsequent surveys were conducted in conjunction with the Duke Marine Lab with an eBee drone and collected normal-color (RGB), red-edge, and near-infrared images for the entire plateau area of the city.

The first GPR survey was conducted by Gianfranco Morelli from Geostudi Astier srl in 2015, which covered around four hectares using a 250-MHz frequency, focusing on the area that would have been the center of the city. The success and clear results of this first survey prompted another survey in 2018, in collaboration with a team from the Ludwig Boltzmann Institute for Archaeological Prospection and Virtual Archaeology led by Dr. Inno Trinks. The team brought a highly specialized GPR unit—a sixteen-channel MALÅ imaging radar array (MIRA) using a 400-MHz antenna—which is one of the highest-resolution and best-quality GPR machines currently available. Two smaller motorized SPIDAR units were also utilized to collect additional and cross-information using six-channel systems at 500 MHz and another using a four-channel system at 400 MHz. While the two surveys overlapped in coverage, each covered some areas that the other did not. Both surveys began in the area around the Western Forum of Vulci, due to both the importance of the area as well as the easy access to the area.

A combined, layered spatial analysis using all of the remote sensing datasets allowed for new understandings about Vulci's urban layout and development (McCusker, 2021) (Figure 3.2). The research presented a relative chronology for the development of the urban spaces of the city. Vulci, like many southern Etruscan cities, began during the Villanovan Period (tenth-ninth centuries BCE) on a hillside next to the plateau. It was not until the late ninth and early eighth centuries BCE that the pattern shifted to the

Figure 3.2 Map indicating the general development of Vulci's urban plan based on relative chronology derived from excavation and the superposition of features and structures apparent in the remote sensing data. (McCusker 2021).

plateau proper. McCusker concluded that the first area likely settled was the northeast area and the Northeastern Acropolis, followed by an expansion southward along Road C to the Southern Acropolis. The plan illustrates the new phase of expansion during the sixth century to the central plateau area, to the later titled "Western Forum" (Figure 3.3). The Western Forum of Vulci is an area located along the main *decuamanus*, with the Great Temple (Etruscan-Roman) being the only excavated building along with a posited "basilica" first proposed by Giorgio Pocobelli (Pocobelli, 2004, 2007). This new analysis provides a clear, more detailed layout of the suggested basilica-like feature, which these authors argue is an Augusteum. GPR results point to a paved plaza surrounded by other public, governmental buildings. Evidence also supports an initial phase of development during the sixth century BCE, with a major transformation of space during the early Imperial period after Vulci was under Roman control.

The remote sensing surveys also led to the discovery of a residential structure just east of the Western Forum between the Great Temple and the House of Cryptoportico (Figure 3.4). This feature began as a single *domus*, possibly dating

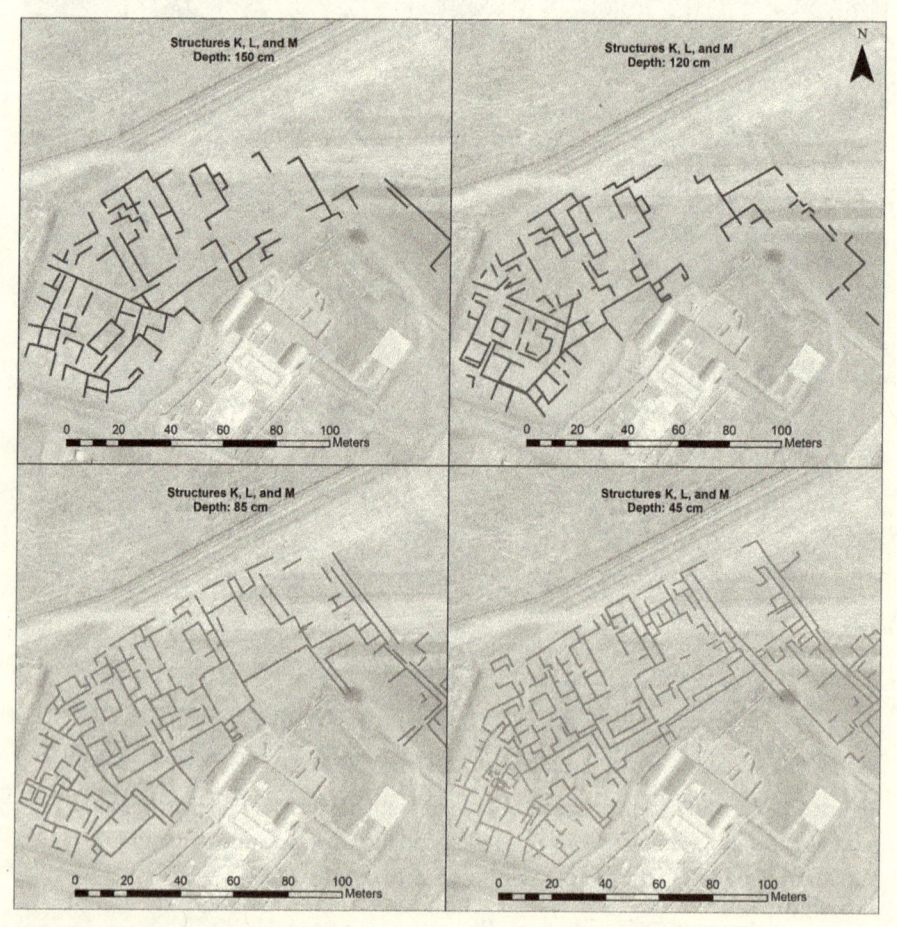

Figure 3.3 Vectorization of archaeological features of two residential structures (Structure K-To the SW and Structure L-To the NE) visualizing the transformation of the space over time as seen though several depth slices via GPR (McCusker 2021).

to the sixth-century Etruscan expansion in the city. A second *domus* with a different orientation was then constructed to the north of the first area. These two *domus* were then combined into one, larger Roman *domus*, pointing to a period of increasing wealth and power for the city during the Imperial period. This chronological narrative suggests a thriving city even after Roman conquest, with an influx of wealth and social power alongside renovations and additional public structures, particularly during the Imperial period.

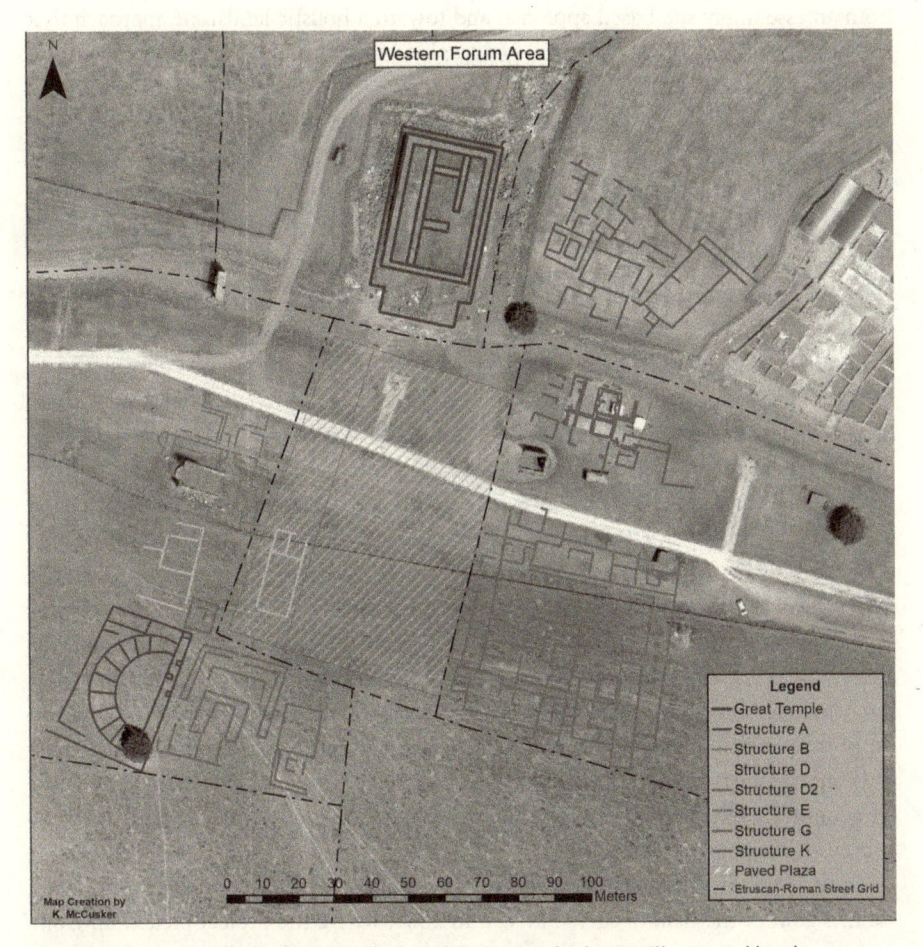

Figure 3.4 The importance attributed to the city can be better illustrated by the development of the Western Forum with an open, paved plaza space, an Augusteum/ basilica (Structure B), a governmental/public speaking building (possibly a curia and a comitium) (Structure A and E), at least one additional Temple (Structure D) besides the Great Temple, and several other large public buildings of multi-purpose use (Structures E and G).

The Emptyscapes Initiative at Veii and Rusellae

The Emptyscapes initiative is an ongoing remote sensing survey project led by Stefano Campana of the University of Siena that is analyzing the landscapes of Veii and Rusellae. Its mission is to the fill in the superficially "empty" areas of the landscape of these two cities and develop a methodology that can be applied to other Mediterranean landscapes to form a more comprehensive understanding of the archaeological record (Campana, 2015, 2016, 2017a, 2018a). The project aims to contribute to a shift away from an essentially site-based approach and toward a holistic landscape approach that encompasses both urban and rural geography within the interpretation of cultural territories. Specifically, the project is interested in what these researchers refer to as the "connective tissue" of the archaeological landscape: agricultural fields, roads, and minor settlements (Campana, 2009; 2017b, 1224). These features, taken together, are what allow the project to establish the "archaeological continuum" of a given territory. This continuity is conceptualized as both spatial and chronological (Campana, 2018b, 31–42).

Thus the integrated remote sensing approach that the Emptyscapes initiative is developing is intended to reveal elements of the archaeological record that connect sites through space and time by identifying constructed features and cultural phases of the ancient landscape that are not easily detected by traditional field survey methodology. For example, negative features such as pits and ditches are not easily identifiable at the surface, and some cultural products such as ceramics made from friable fabrics are less likely to survive the processes that bring artifact scatters to the surface. This means that certain typologies of structures and cultural phases that are represented by these features are easily underrepresented by traditional field surveying methodology. One excellent example of this being borne out by excavation is the work carried out by the Roman Peasant Project in the area of ancient Rusellae and modern-day Grosseto, where meager surface scattering belied the presence of a rural production center (Vaccaro 2012; Vaccaro et al., 2013). The Emptyscapes initiative hopes to identify such features using remote sensing and thus repopulate those aspects of the archaeological record that may initially seem to be geographically and chronologically "empty" from the results of field walking surveys (Campana, 2018b, 87–114).

The project's first practical attempts at developing a methodology that would realize this goal in the field occurred at Veii in 2009, where the project picked up from earlier aerial surveys (Campana, 2019; Guaitoli, 2003; 2015). The magnetometry survey continued from 2011 to 2017, during which time the team covered 170 hectares. The focus of the project's work at Veii so far has been within the urban area of the Etruscan city, but today this landscape gives the impression of being quite empty as the primarily agricultural fields are mostly devoid of visible structures. In fact, this rural appearance seems to have developed during the Roman period. One of the most interesting discoveries of the magnetometry survey conducted at Veii is the identification of Roman vineyards overlying areas of the city that were densely occupied during the Etruscan phase (Campana, 2018b, 111; 2019, 30). This demonstrates that while these areas of the city may have changed use and were less densely occupied, they were certainly not empty. They were evidently still under intensive use that required the presence of caretakers, cultivators, and harvesters.

The other main contribution that the Emptyscapes team has made at Veii is the identification of the street system and its development through time. (Campana, 2009, 29; 2018b, 110). They reasonably argue that the earliest phase of the street net work dates to the Iron Age based on artifact assemblages and that it developed gradually over time until its ultimate elaboration in the Archaic period as there are few discontinuities. Additionally, the project has demonstrated that the orientation of later Roman buildings conforms to the layout of the earlier Etruscan streets, thus implying the continued visibly of and respect for the Etruscan urban plan. By identifying these connective road and field features with their differing occupation through time, the project is able to provide spatial and temporal continuity to the site. Looking toward the future, the team would like to employ GPR, ERT, and possibly targeted excavation to refine the interpretation of certain areas.

A combined magnetometry and electrical resistivity survey conducted at Rusellae by the Emptyscapes initiative has also proved highly productive in establishing geographic and chronological continuity throughout a landscape where there initially appeared to be major breaks (Campana, 2017b). Previous research into the landscape of Rusellae has relied on field walking and aerial surveys (Bianchi et al., 2014; Campana, 2009; Campana and Francovich, 2005; Campana and Piro, 2009; Carandini and Cambi, 2002; Citter and Arnoldus, 2007; Francovich, 1985). These projects have managed to furnish a substantial amount of information concerning the landscape of Rusellae, but, when placed as points on a map, it is evident that significant "empty space" seems to exist between these contexts. Indeed, the majority of the map would seem to be occupied by "empty space." In the approximately 400-hectare transect around the ancient city that the project is now intensively studying, these previous surveys have identified around 80 archaeological contexts, while the Emptyspaces project has identified 1,886 archaeological features (Campana, 2017b, 1227). This clearly gives the impression of a far more densely populated landscape than traditional survey methodologies would suggest.

The team has thus far detailed two major areas of previously unknown features that significantly alter our understanding of the city's landscape. The first is directly to the south of Rusellae, where the team has identified a large previously unrecorded funerary complex (Campana, 2017b, 1229). Based on the typology of tomb design, this large cemetery appears to have been occupied continuously from the seventh or sixth centuries BCE throughout the Roman period. Just to the south of this area the team also identified a medieval settlement in an unexpected location (Campana, 2017b, 1230). The prevailing theory of *incastellamento* argued that the medieval period saw the wholesale movement of populations to fortified hill towns, whereas this settlement and two others found by the survey in the lowlands of Grossetto imply a pattern of rather more densely populated hinterlands (Campana, 2017b, 1231–1232; Francovich and Hodges, 2003). During the 2017 field season, the project excavated test trenches in the medieval settlement to confirm the features found in the survey and to provide more refined chronological and space use interpretations. These excavations confirmed the previous interpretations, finding ditch fortifications, roads, burials, medieval ceramics, and anthropogenic soils. (Campana, 2018b, 100–104). They also found geomorphic evidence for the presence of standing water in Etruscan and Roman times.

Finally, the project was able to clarify the organization of a massive Roman villa complex that was previously recognized via field scatter and aerial photography in the southwest of the transect. The new data allow Campana to argue convincingly for a relative chronology that places the northern structure of this complex earlier than the southern structures, which are oriented along what is likely the mid-Imperial centuriation system visible in the argentometry data (Campana, 2017b, 1236–1238). On the subject of this centuriation system, the survey results identified a system of field division closely matching the Roman *iugerum* but not aligned with the previously hypothesized centuriation patterns for this region (Mazzolai, 1960; Prisco, 1998). Through all of these discoveries and the sheer number of other features that the survey has discovered but not yet fully analyzed and published, the Emptyscapes initiative has dramatically shifted our understanding of the density and continuity of territorial occupation at Rusellae.

The outstanding work being carried out by the Emptyscapes initiative at Veii and Rusellae has demonstrated that archaeologists need to expand their geographic consideration of sites to encompass territories at large and that remote sensing technologies are ideally suited to relatively rapidly delivering a much fuller picture of a city's territorial landscape. It is clear that much of what has been determined to be "empty" by traditional survey methodology may well have been occupied by features or cultural phases that are simply undetectable to those approaches. Furthermore, the project has furnished an excellent example of how remote sensing technologies are still best utilized in conjunction with traditional surface surveys and excavations to provide essential chronological data and refined interpretations of important features.

Falerii Novii

The most recent major remote sensing project in the region to date is the survey undertaken by the joint team from the Ghent University and the University of Cambridge. This project has extensively and in high detail mapped the urban plan of the city of Falerii Novii (Verdonck et al., 2020). Because the city was founded in

241 BCE, following the defeat and destruction of Falerii Veteres, the plan detailed by the survey is of course related to the long-lived Roman phase of the city. That it is not to say that there was no influence exerted by local culture on its form (Millett, 2007). Indeed, the survey has identified at least one major monumental structure seemingly without parallel from other Roman cities, and the project pushes against the idea of a "standardized" Roman town. However, the authors are primarily interested in Roman urban planning and seek to put forth their project as a case study for the investigation of Roman cities through GPR.

The argument they present is that the traditional conceptualization of Roman urban planning is inherently skewed geographically and temporally because we have extensive excavation data from only a handful of Roman cities, primarily the atypical sites of Pompeii and Ostia. With that in mind, they commend the recent use of magnetometry surveys that have revolutionized our understanding of Roman cities, including the Emptyscapes initiative discussed above. Indeed, Falerii Novii itself has been the site of recent magnetometry surveys that have had some success in identifying aspects of the city's layout, especially its streets and public buildings (Hay et al., 2010; Keay et al., 2000; Wallace-Hadrill, 2013). The authors argue that GPR is able to provide a higher-resolution image of subsurface features and that the main limitation preventing site-wide GPR surveys is the mobility of the antenna units (Verdonck et al., 2020, 706). Until very recently, these have been manually pushed, single-antenna packages, but multi-antenna arrays towed by all-terrain vehicles are now available, and they greatly enhance the user's ability to rapidly cover large areas. However, it should be noted that using these new units remains a very expensive proposition.

Another advantage, which the authors point out, that GPR has in comparison to magnetometry is its ability to produce a three-dimensional dataset or model. Magnetometry is strictly two-dimensional, but the nature of GPR allows it to record a series of depth slices that can detect the presence of features at given depths. This is useful not only for providing greater structural detail, in that it captures height as well as width and length, but it also allowed the team to clarify areas obstructed by rubble in the magnetometry survey and even provide a relative chronology to building phases (Verdonck et al., 2020, 710). That being said, the authors have found that certain structures and features are more readily identifiable via magnetometry due to either the nature of their composition or the composition of the soil overlying them. Therefore, they have incorporated the earlier magnetometry dataset into their analysis (Verdonck et al., 2020, 715).

The results of the GPR survey conducted by the team at Falerii Novii are very convincing in their clarity, extent, and depth. To demonstrate the effectiveness of the GPR survey, the authors have highlighted several important discoveries in their data. First, the authors were able to identify several previously unknown public structures in the data. These include a temple, macellum, and bath complex. While structures of these types might be expected, the size and elaboration of these particular examples may be greater than would be expected for a town of Falerii Novii's presumed significance (Verdonck et al., 2020, 710). A more surprising find was a large monumental structure of a form that seems to have no known comperanda. This structure is located just inside the city walls, directly to the east of the north gate, and is comprised of a large *porticus duplex* along three sides of a central space approximately 90 × 40 meters in size. Inside the central space is a pair of opposed rectangular structures with niches along their long eastern and western faces (Verdonck et al., 2020, 711). The authors also call attention to two insulae whose separating street has been overbuilt in the southern half of the city and in which a medium-sized bathing complex, several atrium houses, and a series of pipes have been clearly identified. This busy section of the urban plan suggests continual development of the structures and alterations to the street network of the city. It is also interesting to note that the pipes crisscross the insulae and do not adhere to the sides of the streets as might be expected (Verdonck et al., 2020, 711–713). Even though the survey largely confirmed the previous understanding of the city's organization, the finds and the clarity the survey has produced gives the impression of a city altogether more dynamic, monumentally embellished, and evidently economically prosperous than previous scholarship has anticipated.

The team also attempted to find novel approaches to circumventing the main difficulty of their results: the sheer size of the dataset. It contains approximately 28.68 billion data points, and the authors estimate that for a trained archaeologist it would take around twenty hours to analyze one hectare. Given the size of the city at about 30.5 hectares, this situation quickly becomes untenable. To address this situation the team experimented with algorithmic approaches to computer-aided recognition of features based on length, width, and reflectance. They found some success with this methodology, but it still required manual input from the analyzer to accept or revise the computer's suggested feature identifications. Ultimately, this limited its time savings, but the authors are hopeful that future developments in processing power and software sophistication will increase accuracy and speed of processing, thus increasing this approach's utility (Verdonck et al., 2020, 716–719).

Conclusion

The case studies presented in this chapter illustrate multiple technological approaches available using remote sensing methodologies for archaeological studies. These various remote sensing approaches are best used in concert with each other because the different technologies will offer unique perspectives that create a more holistic picture when viewed together as well as with traditional excavation methods. Remote sensing does not replace traditional excavation, which is necessary to determine chronological data and define archaeological features; however, remote sensing can enhance scholarly knowledge about a site prior to excavation or where excavation is not possible. The best combination of methodologies depends on the focus of the study—extensive or intensive data.

While the increased utilization of these new technologies and multimodal methods offers new opportunities, the complexity of data collection and analysis presents additional problems intrinsic to "big data," including the processing, analyzing, archiving, and publishing of such "big data" datasets. The increased amount and detail of data have shifted a bottleneck in the archaeological process from data collection to the amount of time necessary to fully analyze it. Archaeologists grapple with new issues arising from "big data" as well as old issues that are exacerbated by the complexities and new factors introduced by "big data," especially with the heavy weight of *digital* data. For example, both digital technology and applications produce larger amounts of data than they used to, requiring more storage space, RAM and processing power, and method adaptations. The increasing quantity, variety, and context of digital data complicate the issue of data storage space and organization as well as platforms or software programs that support the multitude of file types that make up the dataset.

The period of big data has also led, however, to new questions about data infrastructures, data-driven research methods, and the transformation process of characteristics of data into knowledge. The field of archaeology began shifting toward multidimensional, multimedia data and away from the previous data minimizing or data-poor methods before the emergence of "big data." The field still struggles with the archiving and publishing of such large digital datasets, leaving many surveys and projects under- or not optimally published. Archaeologists must continue to search for a balance between old and new methods, creating a path forward that allows for the optimal use and publication of data from these complex approaches.

Bibliography

Bianchi, G., M. Benvenuti, J. Bruttini, M. Buonincontri, L. Chiarantini, Dallai, G. Di Pasquale, A. Donati, F. Grassi, and V. Pescini. "Studying the Colline Metallifere mining area in Tuscany: An interdisciplinary approach." In *Research and preservation of ancient mining areas, Yearbook of the Institute Europa Subterranea 2014.* edited by *Jacquo Silvertant,* 261–287. Trento, Italy, June 5–8, 2014. Valkenburg a/d Geul: Silvertan Erfgoedprojecten, 2014.

Bonamici, M. "Sui primi scavi di Luciano Bonaparte a Vulci." *Prospettiva: Rivista di storia dell'arte antica e moderna* 21 (1980), 6–24.

Buranelli, F. *Gli scavi a Vulci della società Vincenzo Campanari: Governo pontificio (1835–1837).* Rome: L'Erma di Bretschneider, 1992.

Buranelli, F. *Ugo Ferraguti, l'ultimo archeologo-mecenate: Cinque anni di scavi a Vulci (1928–1932) attraverso il fondo fotografico Ugo Ferraguti.* Rome: G. Bretschneider, 1994.

Buranelli, F. "Gli scavi di Vulci (1828–1854) di Luciano ed Alexandrine Bonaparte Principi di Canino." *Luciano Bonaparte/a cura di Marina Natoli: Con contributi di Mina Gregori* (1995), 81–218.

Campana, S. "Archaeological site detection and mapping: Some thoughts on differing scales of detail and archaeological 'non-visibility.'" In *Seeing the Unseen*, edited by S. Campana and S. Piro, 5–26. Leiden: Taylor & Francis, 2009.

Campana, S. "Emptyscapes: Filling "empty" mediterranean landscapes, mapping the archaeological continuum." *Archaeologia Polona 53 (2015)*, 149–152.

Campana, S. "Towards mapping the archaeological continuum: New perspectives and current limitations in Planning Led Archaeology in Italy." In *Preventive Archaeology: Urban Sites and Landscapes*, edited by F. Boschi, 27–40. Ravenna, Italy (July 1–12, 2013), 2016.

Campana, S. "Empty spaces and empty phases within Mediterranean landscapes: The 'Emptyscapes' project." In *La prospezione archeologica: Metodi tecnico-scientifici e approccio storico in Germania e in Italia/Survey-Archaeologie: Naturwissenschaftlich-technische versus historische Methode in Italien und Deutschland*, edited by O. Belvedere and J. Bergemann, 41–56. Rahden/Westf: Verlag Marie Leidorf GmbH, 2017a.

Campana, S. "Emptyscapes: Filling an 'empty' Mediterranean landscape at Rusellae, Italy." *Antiquity* 359.91 (2017b), 1223–1240.

Campana, S. "Emptyspaces: Towards filling gaps in Mediterranean landscape archaeology." In *Humans and Environmental Sustainability: Lessons from the Past Ecosystems of Europe and Northern Africa*, edited by Emptyspaces: Towards filling gaps in Mediterranean landscape archaeology, 8–15. Modena, Italy, February 26–28, 2018. Modena: University of Modena and Reggio Emilia, 2018a.

Campana, S. *Mapping the Archaeological Continuum: Filling "Empty" Mediterranean landscapes*. Cham: Springer, 2018b.

Campana, S. "The Emptyscapes project: Filling gaps in space and time at Veii." In *Veii*, edited by J. Tabolli and O. Cerasuolo, 9–16. Austin: University of Texas Press, 2019.

Campana, S., and R. Francovich. "Seeing the unseen. Buried archaeological landscapes in Tuscany." In *Recording, Modeling, and Visualization of Cultural Heritage*, edited by E. Baltsavias, A. Gruen, L. Van Gool, and M. Pateraki, 67–76. Leiden: Taylor & Francis, 2005.

Campana, S., and S. Piro, eds. *Seeing the Unseen*. London: Taylor & Francis, 2009.

Campanari, D. *Sepolcri Vulcenti – Scavi di Vulci*, 1836.

Carandini, A., and F. Cambi. *Paesaggi d'Etruria. Valle dell'Albegna, Valle d'Oro, Valle del Chiarone, Valle del Tarone: Progetto di ricerca italo-britannico seguito allo scavo di Settefinistre, Roma*. Rome: Edizioni di storia e letteratura, 2002.

Citter, C., and A. Arnoldus, eds. *Archeologia urbana a Grosseto: Origine e sviluppo di una città medievale nella "Toscana delle città deboli." Le ricerche 1997–2005*. Firenze: All'Insegna del Giglio, 2007.

Dennis, G. *The Cities and Cemeteries of Etruria* (abridged edition). Princeton, NJ: Princeton University Press, 1848.

Falconi Amorelli, M. T. *Vulci: Scavi Bendinelli (1919–1923)*. Rome: Paleani Editrice, 1983.

Falconi Amorelli, M. T. *Vulci: Scavi Mengarelli (1925–1929)*. Rome: Borgia Editrice, 1987.

Forte, M., and S. Campana. *Digital Methods and Remote Sensing in Archaeology: Archaeology in the Age of Sensing*. Cham, Switzerland: Springer, 2016.

Forte, M., N. Danelon, D. Johnston, K. McCusker, E. Newton, G. Morelli, and G. Catanzariti. 2020. "Vulci 3000: A digital challenge for the interpretation of Etruscan and Roman Cities." In *Digital Cities*, editec by M. Forte and H. Murteira, 13–36. Oxford: Oxford University Press, 2020.

Francovich, R. *Scarlino I. Storia e Territorio*. Firenze: All'Insegna del Giglio, 1985.

Francovich, R., and R. Hodges. *Villa to Village: The Transformation of the Roman Landscape in Italy*. London: Duckworth, 2003.

Guaitoli, M. *Lo sguardo di Icaro*. Rome: Campisano, 2003.

Guaitoli, M. "La città tra nuove metodologie e tradizione." In *Novità nella ricerca archeologica a Veio: Dagli studi di John Ward-Perkins alle ultime scoperte*, edited by R. Cascino, U. Fusco, and C. Smith, 83–97. Rome: La Sapienza University Press, 2015.

Hay, S., P. Johnson, S. Keay, and M. Millett. "Falerii Novi: Further survey of the northern extra-mural area." *Papers of the British School at Rome* 78 (2010), 1–38.

Keay, S. J., M. Millett, S. Poppy, J. Robinson, J. Taylor, and N. Terrenato. "Falerii Novi: A new survey of the walled area." *Papers of the British School at Rome* 68 (2000), 1–93.

Lerici, C. M. "Prospezioni geofisiche nella zona archeologica di Vulci." In *I nuovi metodi di prospezione archeologica alla scoperta delle civilta sepolte*, edited by M. Carlo Lerici, 216–258. Milan: Lerici Editori, 1960.

Marchetti, M., V. Sapia, A. Garello, D. De Rita, and A. Venuti. "Geology and geophysics at the archaeological park of Vulci (central Italy)." *Annals of Geophysics* 57.1 (2014), 1–11.

Mazzolai, A. *Roselle e il suo territorio*. Grosseto: s.n., 1960.

McCusker, K. *Visualizing Vulci: Reimagining an Etruscan-Roman City*. Durham: Duke University, 2021.

Mengarelli, R. "Un anno di scavi a Vulci." *Studi etruschi* (1929), 103–110.

Millett, M. "Urban topography and social identity in the Tiber Valley." In *Roman by Integration: Dimensions of Group Identity in Material Culture and Text (Journal of Roman Archaeology Supplementary Series 69)*, edited by R. Roth and J. Keller, 71–82. Portsmouth, RI: Journal of Roman Archaeology, 2007.

Pacciarelli, M. "Ricerche topografiche a Vulci: Dati e problemi relativi all'origine delle citta medio-tirreniche." *Studi etruschi* 56 (1991), 11–48.

Paglieri, S. "Vulci: Scavi stratigrafici." *Notizie degli Scavi di Antichita* (1959), 102–111.

Pocobelli, G. F. "Vulci: Il Contributo della Fotografia Aerea alla Conoscenza dell'Area Urbana." In *Archeologica Aerea: Studi Di Aerotopografia Archaeologica I*, edited by G. Ceraudo and F. Piccarreta, 127–143. Rome: Istituto Poligrafico E Zecca Dello Stato, 2004.

Pocobelli, G. F. "Il territorio di Vulci attraverso le evidenze aerofotografie. Viabilità e necropolis." In *Archeologia Aerea II. Studi di Aerotopografia Archaeologica*, edited by G. Ceraudo, and F. Piccarreta, 167–185. Rome: Instituo Poligrafico e Zecca dello Stato S.p.A., 2007.

Pocobelli, G. F. "Vulci ed il suo territorio: Area urbana, necropolis e viabilità. Applicazioni di cartografia archeologica e fotogrammetria finalizzata." In *Archeologia Aerea IV. Studi di Aerotopografia Archeologica*, edited by G. Ceraudo. 117–126. Foggia, Italy: Claudio Grenzi Editore, 2011.

Prisco, G. *Castelli e potere nella Maremma grossetana nell'alto medioevo.* Grosseto: Innocenti, 1998.

Sciacca, F. "Materiali etrusco-italici e greci da Vulci (scavi Gsell) e di provenienza varia." *Etruscan Studies* 22 (2017), 182–185.

Scullard, H. H. *The Etruscan Cities and Rome.* Ithaca, NY: Cornell University Press, 1967.

Sgubini Moretti, A. M. "Note di topografia vulcente." In *Un arista etrusco e il suo mondo: Il pittore di Micali*, edited by M. A. Rizzo, 111–116. Rome: De Luca, 1988.

Sgubini Moretti, A. M. "Ricerche archeologiche a Vulci 1985–1990." In *Atti della Giornata di studio organizzata dalla Facoltà di Conservazione dei Beni Culturali dell'Università degli Studi della Tuscia in occasione della mostra "il mondo degli Etruschi. Testimonianze dai Musei di Berlino e dell'Europa orientale, Viterbo, Italy, October 13, 1990*, edited by M. Martelli. Brussels: Société d'Études Latines de Bruxelles, 1990.

Sgubini Moretti, A. M. *Vulci e il suo territorio.* Rome: Editori Quasar, 1993.

Sgubini Moretti, A. M. "Ricerche archeologiche a Vulci 1985–1990." In *Tyrrhenoi philotechnoi: Atti della giornata di studio organizzata dalla Facoltà di Conservazione dei Beni Culturali dell'Università degli Studi della Tuscia in occasione della mostra Il mondo degli Etruschi. Testimonianze dai Musei di Berlino e dell'Europa orientale, Viterbo 1990*, edited by M. Martelli, 9–49. Brussels: Société d'Études Latines de Bruxelles, 1994.

Sgubini Moretti, A. M. *Veio, Cerveteri, Vulci: Citta d'Etruria a Confronto*, edited by Museo nazionale di Villa Giulia. Rome: L'Erma di Bretschneider, 2001.

Sgubini Moretti, A. M. "Ultime scoperte a Vulci." In *Tra Orvieto e Vulci: Atti del X Convegno Internazionale di Studi sulla Storia e l'Archeologia dell'Etruria (2002)*, edited by G. M. Della Fina, 10–53. Rome: Editori Quasar, 2003.

Sgubini Moretti, A. M. "Le mura di Vulci. Un aggiornamento sullo stato della ricerca." In *Etruschi: Le antiche metropoli del Lazio: Catalogo della mostra*, edited by M. Torelli and A. M. Moretti Sgubini, 171–189. Rome, October 21, 2008–January 6, 2009. Milan: Electa, 2008.

Sgubini Moretti, A. M., and L. Ricciardi. "Prime puntualizzazioni sulla cinta muraria di Vulci." *Orizzonti: Rassegna di archeologia* 2 (2001), 63–74.

Torelli, M., and A. M. Sgubini Moretti. *Etruschi le antiche metropolis del Lazio.* Rome: Mandadori Electa S.p.A., 2008.

Vaccaro, E. *Sites and Pots: Settlement and Economic Patterns in Southern Tuscany (AD 300–900).* Oxford: Archaeopress, 2012.

Vaccaro, E., K. Bowes, M. Ghisleni, C. Grey, A. Arnoldus-Huyzendveld, M. MacKinnon, A. M. Mercuri, A. Pecci, M. A. Cau Ontiveros, E. Rattigheri, and R. Rinaldi. "Excavating the Roman peasant II: Excavations at Case Nuove, Cinigiano (GR)." *Papers of the British School at Rome* 81 (2013), 129–179.

Verdonck, L., A. Launaro, F. Vermeulen, and M. Millett "Ground-penetrating radar survey at Falerii Novi: A new approach to the study of Roman cities." *Antiquity* 94.375 (2020), 705–723.

Wallace-Hadrill, A. "Planning the Roman city: Grids and divergences at Pompeii and Falerii Novi." In *Living and Working in the Roman World: Essays in Honour of Michael Fulford (Journal of Roman Archaeology Supplementary Series 95)*, edited by H. Eckardt and S. Rippon, 75–93. Portsmouth, RI: Journal of Roman Archaeology, 2013.

Antonio LoPiano and Katherine McCusker, *The Remote Revolution: Recent Remote Sensing Projects in Etruria* In: *A New Etruscan Archaeology: Twenty-First Century Techniques and Methods*. Edited by: Maurizio Forte, Oxford University Press. © Oxford University Press 2025. DOI: 10.1093/9780197582053.003.0004

4

Spatial Analysis and Etruscan Cities

Past Experiences and Future Challenges

Fabiana Battistin

The Etruscan civilization developed through a long and articulated urban experience. The process that led to the formation of Etruscan culture began in the ninth century BCE, when a number of villages started to take over other neighboring centers. The so-called *synoecism processes* gradually led to the formation of the great metropolises of the historical age. Conversely, by the eighth century BCE, all the characteristic components of life in the Archaic Age on the ideological, sacral, and institutional levels had taken form. This period saw the rise of a landed aristocracy, manifest in cases such as Tarquinia and Veii. The Etruscan cities, like Marzabotto and Musarna, had fully established themselves by the sixth century BCE, occasionally arranged in orthogonal grid patterns and featuring public buildings and infrastructure (Izzet, 2007; see also Colonna, 2004; De Sanctis, 2015; Gottarelli, 2003; Mansuelli, 1998a; Michetti, 2013). During this period, major centers conquered most smaller villages, transforming them into oppida, vici, or castella to better control the vast territories of the burgeoning city-states (Cerasuolo et al., 2008; Cerasuolo and Pulcinelli, 2008; Pulcinelli, 2012). Pliny (Pliny Nat. Hist. 3, 8, 50–52) lists more than fifty Etruscan towns and cities. According to Strabo (5, 2, 2–9), the Etruscan dodecapoli was a group of twelve cities. He then lists a number of Etruscan centers, including those on the coast (Tarquinia, Chiusi, Caere, Luna, Lucca, Pisa, Volterra, Populonia, Cosa, Gravisca, Pyrgi, Alsio, Fregene, Regisvilla), in the middle of the country (Arezzo, Perugia, Volsinii, Sutri), and in smaller towns (Blera, Ferentino, Falerii, Falisci, Nepita, Statonia, Veii, Fidene, Feronia). Livius (V, 33) and Plutarch (Vita Romuli) both mention a dodecapolis in the Po Valley area.

In the fifth century BCE, the aristocratic system began to falter. Throughout Etruria, a repopulation of the countryside occurred during the same period as Rome began to press on its borders and major urban centers (Blake, 2013; Cifani et al., 2012; Holloway, 2005; Iaia and Mandolesi, 1993; Izzet, 2007; Mansuelli, 1985; Osanna and Verger, 2018; Rasmussen, 2005; Steingräber, 2000, 2008; Stoddart, 2020a; Torelli, 2000; Zamboni et al., 2020). From the fourth century BCE, the Etruscan cities gradually fell under Roman rule. The Romans reorganized the territory (Biella, 2020; Carandini, 1985; Castagnoli, 1993; Gualtieri, 2002; Pulcinelli, 2016), and each city's fate took a distinct course. The Etruscan culture merged with the Roman, generating a new phenomenon with cities still at the heart of social, political, and economic life (Ceccarelli, 2016; Mansuelli, 1998b; Munzi, 2001; Papi, 2000; Pulcinelli, 2016; Stek, 2018; Witcher, 2006). The Roman Empire's long history saw the survival of some urban centers and the abandonment of others. Some of these urban centers experienced repopulation during the Middle Ages and remain inhabited to this day.

Even though it is possible to trace the general trends of Etruscan urbanism, Etruscan studies suffered a delay compared to those centered on Greek and Roman city sites. For a long time, in fact, Etruscan urban centers played a marginal role in the field of Etruscology, overshadowed by the study of necropolis—the cities of the dead—more accessible and better preserved than urban contexts, these last characterized by longer and more complex histories. Moreover, excavations often focus more on monumental areas than on residential sectors and the general urban layout, regardless of whether the Etruscan cities are located in rural areas or hidden beneath living towns. We should not underestimate the scarcity of literary sources, which are primarily indirect and suggest that the study of Etruscan cities belongs to the field of prehistoric studies (Stoddart, 2020a, 1). In recent decades, there has been more research into Etruscan cities. This is because new technologies, like satellite, aerial, and ground-based remote sensing methods, make it possible to do in-depth studies of the ground without having to do any invasive fieldwork. Also, geographical information systems (GIS) make it simple to manage, combine, display, and analyze large amounts of spatial data at different scales. Today, several ongoing research projects in Etruria are making use of new technologies, in particular geophysics (see Chapters 2–3 in this volume), and managing their documentation through GIS (see, e.g., *Caere* in Moscati, 2001 and Vulci in Forte et al., 2020). Their goal is to bridge the many gaps in our current understanding of urban areas, gain a more profound understanding of Etruscan urbanization, and elevate it to the forefront of comparative studies that typically exclude the Etruscan urban experience (Stoddart, 2020a, 1). Considering that the results of this research will be available in the coming years, it may be useful to start approaching Etruscan urbanism from a global perspective, looking for available theories and methods applicable to the analysis of urban space. For precisely this reason, this chapter focuses on spatial analysis techniques, especially those methods that allow for the analysis of certain aspects of urban structure and city life.

State of the Art

Cities and Spatial Analysis Techniques

In any analysis, the first step is to define the object, which in this case is the city. Currently, there is a vast body of literature on the subject, and the definition of a city varies depending on the adopted perspective and context (Forte and Murteira, 2020; Smith, 2020). In general terms, cities are highly complex, multifaceted, and dynamic objects, changing form and character over time by adapting to a myriad of different political, social, religious, and contingent economic factors, making each an individual case in terms of spatial configuration and development. However, all cities have "something in common across time and place," leaving scholars with similar questions about societies (Raja and Sindbæk, 2020, 9). By identifying these aspects, we can find a common methodology and simultaneously develop new tools for analysis. We must study cities from various perspectives, including the city as a physical entity, the city as a population, and the city as the center of political, administrative, economic, and religious functions, as recently mentioned (Liverani, 2020, 139). In other words, there are several "dimensions of urbanism," including settlement size and form, urban functions, society, spatial meaning, and urban growth and decline (Smith, 2020, 17–18). A city's definition must encompass the territory it controls for resource exploitation and production, which it defends as an extension of its own boundaries. These factors must be considered of equal importance if we are to understand the urban experience, not to mention the strong interrelation that spatial analysis can help assess and visualize.

For an updated overview of the most widely used spatial analysis techniques in archaeology, see Gillings, Hacigüzeller, and Lock (2020). Researchers can perform these techniques at intra- and inter-site (or landscape) levels, and they are constantly evolving (Gaydarska, 2014). All the techniques adhere to the principle of measuring the spatial dimension of human actions through relational graphs and maps, which describe location, distance, distribution, connection, and access control. Indeed, a reciprocal influence between space and human behavior imbues spatiality with social meaning. Collective and individual needs determine spatial organization, while spatial configuration can influence people's movements and social trends. Spatial analysis can help reveal spatial aspects that reflect social meaning, thus providing support for the archaeological interpretation of urban dynamics. Therefore, network science, or analysis, can conceptualize a system with numerous interconnected parts as a network. We refer to these parts as *nodes* or *vertices* and the connections between them as *edges* or *links* (see Brughmans, 2014; Prignano et al., 2017). Analysis tools can be coupled with other techniques, such as statistics and social network analysis (Verhagen, 2018, 13), and are frequently updated and available in open-access websites (i.e., QGIS), thus facilitating their use in all disciplines involved in understanding spatial dynamics.

These new opportunities rapidly drew archaeologists plagued by issues of spatial order and the management of complex datasets (Clarke, 1977; Hodder and Orton, 1976). The adoption of GIS in the early, 1990s marked the beginning of a new era in landscape studies (Moscati, 2017, 52; see also Forte and Campana, 2016; Moscati, 1998; Wheatley and Gillings, 2002). This made it possible to "go beyond the spatial-temporal scale restrictions traditionally imposed by paper maps" (Moscati, 2017, 49) and look at issues that happen over time, like urban development, in a whole new way. This sparked the growth of research theory and practice, facilitating the formulation of fresh inquiries into the spatial distribution of people, objects, and activities as well as the perception of natural and man-made spaces.

Archaeology represents a test bed for spatial analysis techniques; the latter is usually developed for present-day activities in which data collection can take place in real time and therefore does not present the same difficulties, anomalies, and unevenness as an archaeological dataset. As a result, existing techniques frequently fail to address specific research questions or align with the available dataset, necessitating their adaptation to the unique requirements of the research (Brughmans, 2014, 21). It is critical to assess the suitability of methods using the scale adopted for analysis, research questions, and the characteristics of the available dataset. It is not a coincidence that most archaeology books on spatial analysis are collections of articles, each one focusing on a different case study (Gillings et al., 2020; Harari, 2010; Hietala and Larson, 1984; Knappett, 2013; Knitter et al., 2021; Leidwanger and Knappett, 2018; Paliou et al., 2014; Robertson et al., 2006; Siart et al., 2018). Archaeologists were also pioneers in applying these methods to investigate extensive landscape issues (Brughmans, 2014, 23–24; Verhagen, 2018), including excavated cities, where researchers gained extensive knowledge about their cultural and historical context. This is not the case for the Etruscan city sites, which have seen a limited use of spatial analysis techniques due to the poor archaeological record.

Archaeologists typically use techniques to model urban intra-site dynamics, including the distribution of finds and features (in terms of density and location), the visibility level (which provides a sense of the urban space), the urban configuration (i.e., the city layout and building locations), and the relationship between these elements and sociocultural meaning. Distribution analyses focus on characterizing specific classes of objects (Prignano et al., 2017, 127) to highlight patterns of land use and better understand socioeconomic dynamics such as resource production and consumption (see, e.g., Navas et al., 2008 on faunal remains). Typically, researchers combine these with statistical methods to provide quantitative data, such as the concentration of objects. These types of analyses saw early use in archaeology (Carr, 1984; Djindjian, 1988; Hietala and Larson, 1984) at both inter- and intra-site scales.

Since vision is the easiest (if not the only) sense to reproduce and model, it aids in understanding space from the inside using a perceptual approach. The gaze guides movement and settlement-related choices, such as the location of buildings and other urban features. The visibility of an object or space is intimately connected to control and power because "the visible area may not be related to specific territorial boundaries, but visible/non-visible duality creates a natural boundary in the landscape" (Rajala, 2004, 396). This is valid for both inter-site visibility and the urban landscape. Figuring out visibility is hard because it depends on things like light, vegetation, and how the landscape changes over time. To do a good job of analyzing this, you need a lot of archaeological and environmental data (Rajala, 2004, 397). Therefore, when the organization of space and architecture is well documented and reproducible in three dimensions, we can achieve the best results (Paliou, 2014, 2017). This leads to a decreasing adoption of spatial analysis in GIS, while three-dimensional virtual reconstructions present more opportunities (see Forte and Murteira, 2020), particularly in small-scale contexts. An additional spatial analysis technique, namely *space syntax*, can instead calculate visibility in a two-dimensional space.

Archaeologists are increasingly using space syntax, a social network analysis technique, to study the built environment, including urban street networks and buildings. You can carry out several types of spatial analysis, such as axial analysis, segment analysis, convex analysis, and visibility graph analysis (VGA), using specifically designed open-source, professional software and tools (such as DepthmapX and the QGIS toolkit; visit https://spacesyntax.com for more information). This technique allows for the production of information on the social use of space, such as meeting places or segregated areas, as well as the modeling of movement dynamics, which is particularly useful when studying urban layouts. For instance, one can determine the connectivity of streets and rooms, the centrality (integration) of various buildings and urban sectors, and the most efficient routes to various locations within the analyzed space (Figure 4.1). (For more information on this method, see Cutini, 2010; Hillier, 1996; Hillier and Hanson, 1984; Penn and Turner, 2002; Van Nes and Yamu, 2021). Space syntax allows researchers to figure out things that have to do with space (not culture), and it shows those parts of the relationship between people and the built environment that are considered to be spontaneous. Understanding any urban setting is crucial even when considering cultural and temporal differences in data analysis and interpretation. This is what is known as *natural movement* (Hillier et al., 1993), defined as the instinctive behavior that causes people, as they experience space, to prefer to walk in a straight line, avoiding as many changes in direction as possible, to congregate and socialize in larger spaces and to look for privacy in places located far from a more intense social life, whether in a city or inside a building. By contrast, *attracted movement*, which space syntax cannot calculate, results from the presence of socially significant attraction points within the community. Even if the area is not naturally suitable for traffic, people will still visit these points.

Using space syntax, archaeologists have studied towns, cities, and buildings from various times and cultures (see Bermejo Tirado, 2015), demonstrating the method's versatility and ability to work with both planned and unplanned layouts, sometimes utilizing geophysical maps (Battistin, 2021; Benech, 2003, 2007, 2010; Carpentiero and Tessaro, 2015; Gondet and Benech, 2009; Paliou and Corsi, 2013).

The success of space syntax in archaeology is due to several reasons. First, it provides an integrated set of user-friendly techniques that allow one to model numerous aspects of space related to social behavior, combining a phenomenological view of space with the science of space (Hillier, 2014, 45). Second, it is also suitable for sparsely detailed datasets because it analyzes space in geometric terms even on the basis of two-dimensional maps. Initially, this last aspect faced strong criticism, but space syntax eventually gained full acceptance (Cutini, 2007, 2010, 129) and was partially resolved by applying the method to digital elevation models in GIS (Cutini, 2011; Cutini et al., 2004; Ratti, 2005).

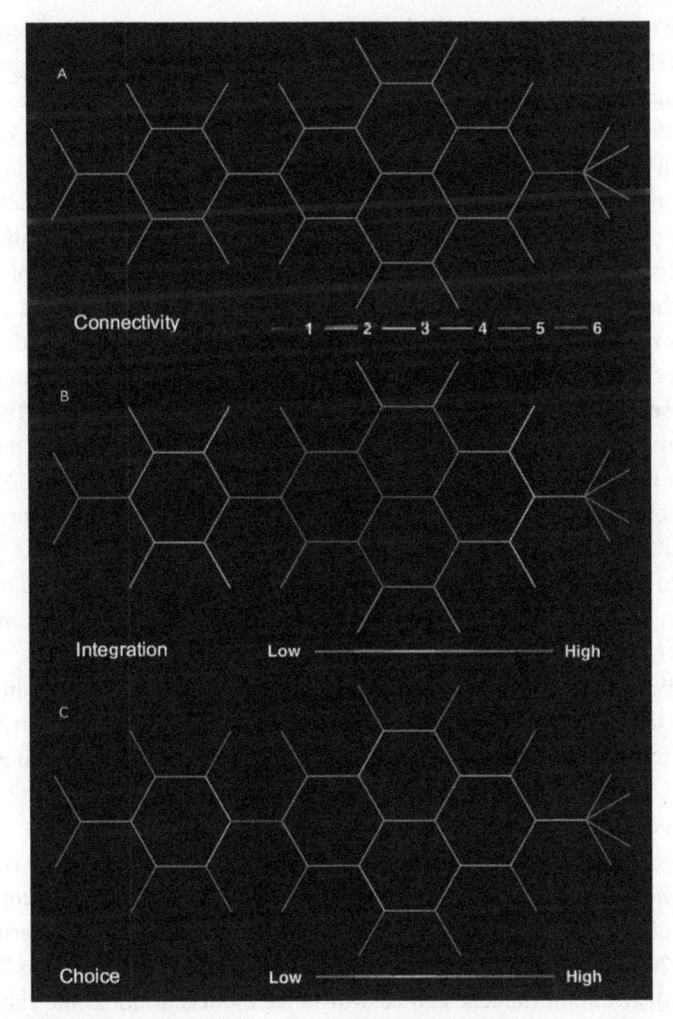

Figure 4.1 Illustration of the three Space Syntax measures in a sample network. Note each measure identifies different streets as having the highest value. A) The highest degree centrality street is the one having more streets connected to it. B) The highest integrated streets are the ones topologically closest to all other streets in the network. C) The highest choice indicates that this street would be travelled most frequently when travelling from any one street to another (from Javadi et al. 2017). The original coloured image can be found in the cited source.

Spatial Analysis and Etruscan Urbanism

Since the 1980s, researchers have used spatial analyses to gain a territorial perspective on pre-Roman urbanism in Etruria and central Italy. One of these first studies applied Thiessen's polygons to the area of South Etruria and Umbria to define settlement patterns and their development during the Bronze and Iron Ages (di Gennaro,

1982). The results highlighted trends in settlement patterns, noting the recurrence of certain territorial modules during the Final Bronze Age and the Iron Age. The frequent coincidence of boundary lines and waterways makes the correspondence between the ideal territories defined by Thiessen's polygons and the real ones more realistic (di Gennaro, 1982, 110). However, di Gennaro avoided modifying the map to make boundaries coincide because knowledge of settlement identification was still incomplete. Di Gennaro carefully described the available dataset, highlighting its limitations, particularly the knowledge gaps apparent for a portion of the territory and the unresolved identification of numerous settlements. Despite the provisional nature of the results, di Gennaro stressed the importance of using the maps as a guide for future research efforts because they identified border boundaries as potential settlement locations for future field surveys (di Gennaro, 1982, 105). Angelo Amoroso also used Thiessen's polygons to compare settlement patterns in South Etruria and Latium Vetus during the Early Iron Age (Amoroso, 2016). The geomorphology of the region as well as the location, morphology, and size of central and satellite settlements were the parameters considered. The results provided insight into whether territories grew or disappeared over time in relation to the size of the site, territorial management, and resource exploitation, as well as pattern anomalies (Amoroso, 2016, 95–97).

This approach has been criticized (Rendeli, 1993), arguing that the influence of a city could be better defined by its visual control on the surrounding territories, as suggested by Aristotle, who stated that the control of a city extended as far as the eye could see (Aristotle. Pol., 7.5.4), and emphasized by work carried out in the settlement areas of Gabi and Nepi (Rajala, 2004).

Viewshed and cost-distance analyses have also been used to look at the communication network, figure out the strategic goals of hilltop settlements, and confirm the existence of an intervisibility-based system along the coast of Northern Etruria (Iacopini, 2011). Researchers have also used a variety of methods, such as Thiessen's polygons, distribution models, and cost-distance models, to look into the possible economic relationship between large and small settlements in the so-called Etruria Padana (which is part of the Po Valley area). They did this by measuring the distance between the main centers and calculating what land might be relevant to each settlement (Quirino, 2014). A further study focused on movement, with the goal of understanding how communities cooperated or competed in Southern Etruria between 950 and 500 BCE (Prignano et al., 2019).

Simon Stoddart recently made a significant contribution to this field, completing with spatial analysis Etruscan state formation research that began in the 1980s with his PhD thesis (Stoddart, 1987; see also Redhouse and Stoddart, 2011). His research on Etruria's political patterns and land use is a clear and organized look at the data gathered from excavations, surveys, and archaeometry. It helps us understand the history of this area and the rise of Etruscan cities between 1200 and 500 BCE (Stoddart, 2020a, 2020b; Stoddart et al., 2020). His book, *Power and Place in Etruria* (Stoddart, 2020a), shows the outcomes of using a spatial analysis program (GIS integrated with the so-called XTENT model, a computational analytical tool that calculated hypothetical territories around a set of input points) to look into how states form and how power changes in the area north of the Tiber River. As with Spivey and Stoddart (1990), the book focuses on the archaeological record. Stoddart (2020a, 2–3) says that "the dynamic spatial organization, the regionality of the Etruscans, and, more specifically, the settlement component and its associated infrastructure, are an essential corollary to the rich evidence of material culture." Based on spatial analyses, Stoddart identifies "five regions of contrast" (Figure 4.2): South Etruria, the Albenga Valley, the Maremma and its hinterland, and the areas of Perugia and Gubbio (see Stoddart, 2020a, 129–185), and these were ruled by a few large centers that oversaw larger networks of smaller towns and territories. This research is an example of the advanced applications of spatial analyses, demonstrating how they allow for the management of incomplete and fragmented information gathered through different methodologies and forms of classification. It also shows the importance of knowing and understanding the strengths and limits of the available dataset and techniques and how this understanding is critical for the proposal of new research queries and for identifying the appropriate analysis techniques to employ and correctly read the data produced.

The territorial relationship between Etruscan cities and settlements is the focus of all the studies cited so far, which aids in understanding the dynamics of power and land control in large territories. However, what if one looks for intra-site spatial analysis applications within the Etruscan cities?

Although the spatial issue is widely considered, not all studies address it using digital tools (Zamboni and Buoite, 2017). On the contrary, there are only a few examples in literature. Caere is likely the first historical location where researchers utilized GIS to accurately position archaeological data in space, thereby reconstructing the timeliness of structures and their spatial and temporal relationships. At the site level, researchers used GIS to put the structures' spatial and topological parts in context. They determined what the structures were meant to do by looking at information from excavations and the amount and location of pottery (Ceccarelli, 2001, 110). They applied viewshed analysis to assess the visual relationship between the excavated area at the Vigna Parrocchiale site (Cristofani, 1988) and the plateau and its surrounding area (Ceccarelli, 2001, 105–106; see also Moscati, 2001).

Researchers have used spatial analysis techniques to interpret aspects of Marzabotto's urban layout, which is likely the best preserved and most thoroughly investigated Etruscan urban center. Musarna, a Tarquinia colony in Southern Etruria, also attested to the late sixth-century trend of regular pattern layout, albeit for a later period (fourth century BCE) (Broise and Jolivet, 1997; Cinque et al., 2017). Marzabotto was founded on astronomical and geometrical principles based on the sun's movement (Govi, 2014, 97–102; Guarino, 2011, 221–224), resulting in a complete integration of sacred and urban spaces in the urban layout (Govi, 2017, 89). Excavation data from the site are abundant, while a geophysical survey revealed the entire street network of the urban center (Boschi, 2016). Despite this, the literature

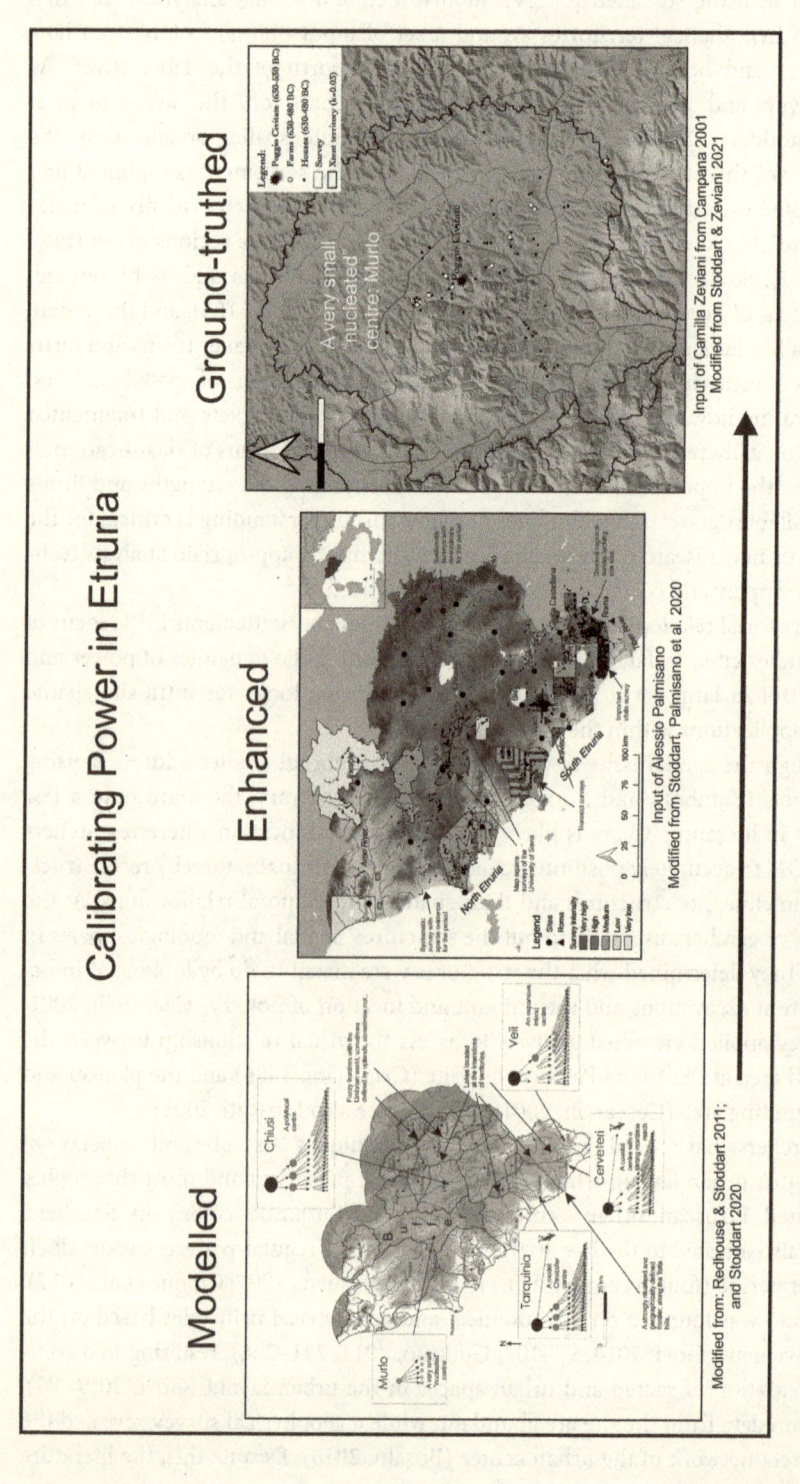

Figure 4.2 Three stages in the modelling of settlement data from Etruria. Left: Abstract modelling of site hierarchy and territory. Centre: Incorporation of published survey data within the modelled territories. Right: Detailed analysis of the territory of Murlo (image by S. Stoddart).

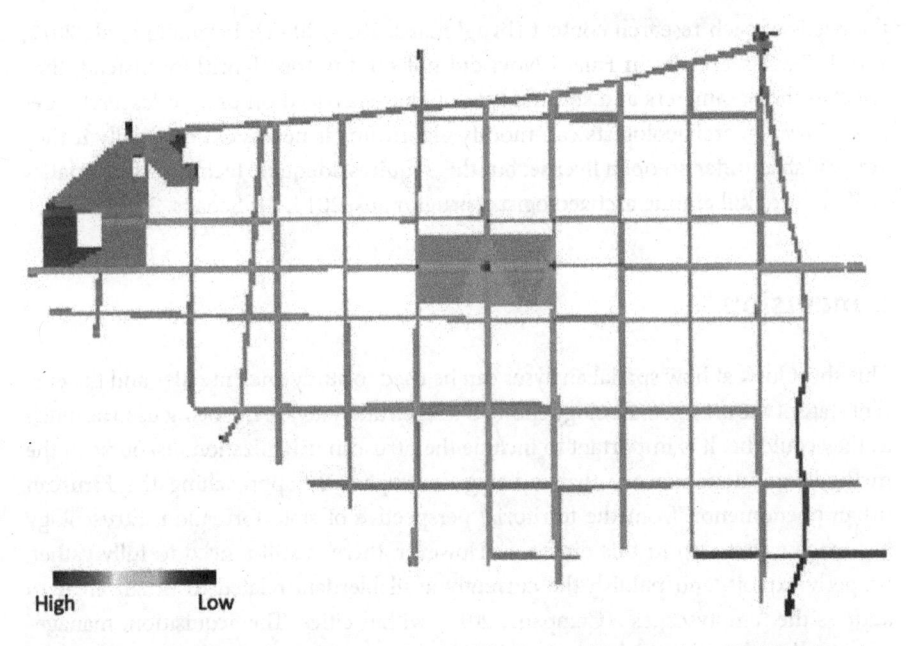

High　　　　Low

Figure 4.3 Space Syntax application in Falerii Novi: visual integration. Visibility Graph Analysis of a reconstructive urban layout (Battistin 2021, scenario 2ab, on the base of Keay et al. 2000) (image by the author). The original coloured image can be found in the cited source.

on Marzabotto only discusses space syntax and viewshed analysis in a limited manner, focusing on the main roads and the acropolis's location (Govi, 2017, 93–94). The scarcity of data primarily contributes to the narrow use of spatial analysis in urban contexts. This has likely discouraged the use of such analytical techniques, which are preferably employed in more well-documented contexts. For example, in urban and architectural contexts of the Roman period, where data are more readily available and accurate, the application of the space syntax method has yielded interesting results, both in Pompeii (van Nes 2009, 2014; Kaiser 2011; Fridell Anter and Weilguni 2002), and in other cases that do not adhere to the so-called "Pompeii premise" (Allison, 1992; Binford, 1981), such as Ostia (Stöger, 2011; Newsome, 2005), Augusta Raurica (Straumann, 2018), and Emona (Mlekuž and Županek, 2017).

Figure 4.3 shows the space syntax application in Falerii Novi using visual integration and visibility graph analysis of a reconstructive urban layout (Battistin, 2021, scenario 2ab; based on Keay et al., 2000). This example demonstrates the exploratory use of spatial analysis on the available dataset (Gillings et al., 2020, 13). The planning phase inherently involves analysis because it involves selecting the most suitable technique and preparing data for application, all while observing the dataset from various angles. This helps define its strengths and limits, highlighting additional questions and establishing research priorities. Even though the available algorithms often limit the application of formal methods of spatial and network analysis, considering the contents of the dataset also demonstrates how techniques can adapt to the needs of each research context (Brughmans, 2014, 20–22; Prignano et al., 2017, 126–127). Researchers in Falerii Novi did not modify the algorithm; instead, they selected the parameters and specific type of analysis based on precise research queries. However, archaeologists can modify algorithms if necessary, especially if they are available under an open license, but this requires adequate technical-informatics skills, a rare skill among archaeologists (Brughmans, 2014, 21; Schaps, 2010, 94).

Conclusion

This short look at how spatial analyses can be used to study ancient cities and the current state of the art in Etruscology shows that such analyses are not being used as much as they could be. It is important to include the Etruscan urbanization discourse in the methodological framework that is being developed. By approaching the Etruscan urban phenomenon from the territorial perspective of state formation, Etruscology has made a first step in this direction. However, there is still a need to fully gather, properly exploit, and publish the currently available data related to urban areas to address the "emptyscapes" (Campana, 2017) within cities. The acquisition, management, and exploitation of data is therefore the most pressing problem when approaching Etruscan urbanism, even if Etruscologists are gradually nearing a more all-encompassing analysis of cities through landscape studies and surveys in urban areas. Recent research has given us a chance to look at Etruscan city studies and develop with "future agendas." These can be summed up in two main points: do more open-area excavations in primary, nonmonumental, and rural centers and improve the statistical analysis of existing datasets, especially in urban areas (Stoddart, 2020b, 115).

Archaeologists have learned to use a variety of tools over time, often incorporating them into the discipline in accordance with the context's characteristics as well as the type and volume of data available. They apply traditional tools when available and seek out new ones when the former are either insufficient or ineffective. Here, the archaeologist resembles the "bricoleur" described by Lévi-Strauss in "La pensée sauvage" (Lévi Strauss, 1962), who is capable of using any available tool to solve a problem. Although *bricolage* is not a risk-free operation (Manacorda, 2008, 26), it is also true that the contexts of the past represent a continuous challenge for archaeologists. Archaeologists can only recover the remains of extinct cultures and societies, and the preservation conditions of finds and materials can fluctuate over time. It is therefore essential that archaeologists differentiate their approach to site analysis by gathering as wide an assortment of data as possible and verifying it through a variety of different analyses (Vermeulen, 2016).

Spatial analysis can aid in the interpretation process by providing spatial and relational information that is easier to compute using information technology (IT) tools. Each type of analysis allows for different questions and approaches to data, highlighting the characteristics of the space examined. The preparatory phase of the analysis is a fundamental interpretive moment because it allows for a more in-depth understanding of the context, highlighting aspects that would otherwise have escaped notice without considering the operational requirements of the method(s) and software used. For these reasons, it is always interesting to apply diversified methods. Even if the results are not satisfying, they nevertheless offer an opportunity to better understand the dataset available, its strengths and its needs. As a result, even on limited datasets, spatial analysis can help define more specific research queries, supporting the planning of future on-site activities.

This brief review aims to lessen the skepticism often associated with these techniques, promoting their use not only in well-documented contexts but also in situations involving incomplete and fragmented datasets. Complementary approaches and the resulting data can aid in gaining extensive knowledge and constructing an appropriate methodological framework.

Bibliography

Allison, P. M. "Artefact assemblages: Not the Pompeii premise." In *Papers of the Fourth Conference of Italian Archaeology, London 1990*, edited by E. Herring, R. Whitehouse, and J. Wilkins, 49–56. London: Accordia Research Centre, 1992.

Amoroso, A. "Settlement patterns in South Etruria and Latium Vetus." In *Early States, Territories and Settlements in Protohistoric Central Italy*, edited by P. Attema, J. Seubers, S. Willemsen, P. A. J. Attema, F. di Gennaro, E. Jarva, 83–100. Proceedings of a Specialist Conference, Groningen Institute of Archeology, University of Groningen, 2013. Eelde: Barkhuis, 2016.

Battistin, F. "Space Syntax and buried cities: The case of the Roman town of Falerii Novi (Italy)." *Journal of Archaeological Science: Reports* 35 (2021), 102712. https://doi.org/10.1016/j.jasrep.2020.102712

Benech, C. "The study of ancient city planning by geophysical methods: The case of Dura-Europos, Syria." *5th International Conference on Archaeological Prospection. Archaeologia Polona* 40 (2003), 124–127.

Benech, C. "New approach to the study of city planning and domestic dwellings in the ancient Near East." *Archaeological Prospection* 14.2 (April/June 2007), 87–103. https://doi.org/10.1002/arp.306

Benech, C. "The use of 'space syntax' for the study of city planning and household from geophysical maps: The case of Dura-Europos (Syria)." *Städtisches Wohnen im östlichen Mittelmeerraum 4. Jh. v. Chr.–1. Jh. n. Chr. Archäologische Forschungen* 18, 403–416. Vienna: Austrian Academy of Sciences Press, 2010.

Bermejo Tirado, J. "Aplicaciones de sintaxis evisionl en Arqueología: Una evisionn de algunas tendencias actuales." *Arqueología de la Arquitectura* 12 (2015), 1–23.

Biella, M. C., ed. *Displacements continuità e discontinuità urbana nell'Italia centrale tirrenica*. Rome: Prima Italia, 2020.

Binford, L. R. "Behavioral archaeology and the Pompeii premise." *Journal of Anthropological Research* 37.3 (1981), 195–208.

Blake, E. "Social network, path dependence, and the rise of ethnic groups in pre-Roman Italy." In *Network Analysis in Archaeology: New Approaches to Regional Interaction*, edited by Society for American Archaeology and C. Knappett, 203–221. Oxford: Oxford University Press, 2013.

Boschi, F. "Reading ancient cities: The contribution of the non-invasive techniques." In *Looking to the Future, Caring for the Past. Preventive Archaeology in Theory and Practice*, edited by F. Boschi, 85–100. Bologna: Bologna University Press, 2016.

Broise, H., and V. Jolivet. "Une colonie étrusque en territoire tarquinien." *Comptes rendus de l'Académie des Inscriptions et Belles Lettres* 141.4 (1997), 1327–1350.

Brughmans, T. "The roots and shoots of archaeological network analysis: A citation analysis and review of the archaeological use of formal network methods." *Social Network Perspectives in Archaeology* 29.1 (2014), 18–41.

Campana, S. "Emptyscapes: Filling an 'empty' Mediterranean landscape at Rusellae, Italy." *Antiquity* 91.359 (2017), 1223–1240.

Carandini, A. *La romanizzazione dell'Etruria: Il territorio di Vulci*. Milan: Electa, 1985.

Carpentiero, G., and C. Tessaro. "Multi-scale approach for the reconstruction of a past urban environment: From remote sensing to space syntax: The case of Dionysias (Fayum, Egypt)." In *Proceedings of the 43rd Annual Conference on Computer Applications and Quantitative Methods in Archaeology*, edited by S. Campana, R. Scopigno, G. Carpentiero, and M. Cirillo, 803–814. Oxford: Archaeopress Archaeology, 2015.

Carr, C. "The nature of organization of intrasite archaeological records and spatial analytic approaches to their investigation." *Advances in Archaeological Method and Theory* 7 (1984), 103–222.

Castagnoli, F. "La centuriazione di Cosa." In *Topografia Antica: Un metodo di studio, vol. III, Italia*, edited by F. Castagnoli, 785–803. Rome: Istituto Poligrafico e Zecca dello Stato, 1993.

Ceccarelli, L. "Progetto Caere: Dallo scavo al territorio. Una soluzione per la distribuzione dei dati tramite un GIS on-line." *Archeologia e Calcolatori* 12 (2001), 105–122.

Ceccarelli, L. "The romanization of Etruria." In *A Companion to the Etruscans*, edited by S. Bell and A. A. Carpino, 28–40. Chirchester: Wiley Blackwell, 2016.

Cerasuolo, O., L. Pulcinelli, and F. Rubat Borel. "Rofalco (Farnese, VT). Una fortezza vulcente tra la metà del IV e i primi decenni del III secolo a.C." In *La città murata in Etruria: Atti del XXV Convegno di Studi Etruschi e Italici*, edited by Giovannangelo Camporeale, 533–538. Chianciano Terme Sarteano-Chiusi, March 30–April 3, 2005. Rome: F. Serra Editore, 2008.

Cerasuolo, O., and L. Pulcinelli. "Fortezze di confine tardo-etrusche nel territorio tra Caere e Tarquinia. Note di topografia e architettura." In *La città murata in Etruria: Atti del XXV convegno di studi etruschi ed italici*, edited by G. Camporeale, 527–532. Chianciano Terme, Steano, Chiusi, March 30–3 April, 2005. Pisa-Rome: Fabrizio Serra Editore, 2008.

Cifani, G., S. Stoddart, and S. Neil. *Landscape, Ethnicity and Identity in the Archaic Mediterranean Area*. Oxford: Oxbow Books, 2012.

Cinque, G. E., H. Broise, and V. Jolivet. "Civita Musarna (Vt), il suo territorio e la *chora* di Tarquinia in età ellenistica: Uno spazio ritualmente suddiviso?" *Archeologia e Calcolatori* 28.2 (2017), 223–232.

Clarke, D. L. *Spatial Archaeology*. London: Academic Press, 1977.

Colonna, G. "*La "disciplina"* etrusca e la dottrina della città fondata." *Studi Romani* 52 (2004), 303–311.

Cristofani, M. "Cerveteri." In *Caere 1. Il Parco archeologico*, edited by M. Cristofani, G. Nardi, and M. A. Rizzo, 29–42. Rome: Consiglio Nazionale delle Ricerche, 1988.

Cutini, V. "Axial line and contour lines: Climbing up the center." *Proceedings of the Sixth Space Syntax Symposium* 2 (2007), 49.1–49.14.

Cutini, V. *La rivincita dello spazio urbano: L'approccio configurazionale allo studio e all'analisi dei centri abitati*. Pisa: Plus University Press, 2010.

Cutini, V. "Ripide griglie urbane: Per una analisi configurazionale delle città su terreno acclive." Paper presented at the *XXXII Conferenza scientifica annuale dell'Associazione Italiana di Scienze Regionali: Il ruolo delle città nella economia della conoscenza*, Torino, September 15–17, 2011. Unpublished Conference program available at https://www.aisre. it/images/call_for_paper/Programmi_vecchi/ProgrammaAISReTorino2011_stampa.pdf.

Cutini, V., M. Petri, and A. Santucci. "From axial map to Mark Point Parameter Analysis (Ma. P.P.A.): A G.I.S. implemented method to automate configurational analysis." *Computational Science and Its Applications – ICCSA 2004 – Lecture Notes in Computer Science* 3044 (2004), 1107–1116.

De Sanctis, G. *La logica del confine. Per un'antropologia dello spazio nel mondo romano*. Rome: Carocci, 2015.

Di Gennaro, F. "Organizzazione del territorio nell'Etruria Meridionale Protostorica. Applicazione di un modello grafico." *Dialoghi Di Archeologia* 4.2 (1982), 102–112.

Djindjian, F. "Improvements in intra-site spatial analysis techniques." *Computer and Quantitative Methods in Archaeology 1988 (CAA88)*, edited by Sebastian Rahtz. BAR International Series 446 (1988), 96–106.

Forte, M., and S. Campana, eds. *Digital Methods and Remote Sensing in Archaeology*. Cham: Springer, 2016.

Forte, M., N. Danelon, D. Johnston, K. McCusker, E. Newton, G. Morelli, and G. Catanzariti. "Vulci 3000. A digital challenge for the interpretation of Etruscan and Roman cities." In *Digital Cities: Between History and Archaeology*, edited by M. Forte and H. Murteira, 13–41. Oxford: Oxford University Press, 2020.

Forte, M., and H. Murteira, eds. *Digital Cities: Between History and Archaeology*. Oxford: Oxford University Press, 2020.

Fridell Anter, K., and M. Weilguni. "Public space in Roman Pompeii." *Nordisk Arkitekturforskning* 3 (2002), 87–97.

Gaydarska, B. "Spatial analysis in field archaeology." In *Encyclopedia of Global Archaeology*, edited by C. Smith, 6976–6980. New York: Springer, 2014.

Gillings, M., P. Hacigüzeller, and G. Lock, eds. *Archaeological Spatial Analysis: A Methodological Guide*. New York: Routledge, 2020.

Gondet, S., and C. Benech. "Application of the space syntax to the study of city planning from Syrian Late Bronze Age circular cities." *ArcheoSciences* 33 (suppl. 2009), 217–219.

Gottarelli, A. "*Auguraculum, sedes inaugurationis* e *limitatio* rituale della città fondata. Elementi di analogia tra la forma urbana di Marzabotto ed il *templum* augurale di Bantia." *Ocnus* 11 (2003), 135–150.

Govi, E. "Etruscan urbanism at Bologna, Marzabotto and in the Po valley." In "Papers on Italian urbanism in the first millennium B.C." *Journal of Roman Archaeology* Supplementary Series 97 (2014), 81–111.

Govi, E. "Kainua-Marzabotto: The archaeological framework." *Archeologia E Calcolatori* 28 (2017), 87–97.

Gualtieri, M. "Cosa, the Roman city, and 'Romanization.'" *Journal of Roman Archaeology* 15 (2002), 397–400.

Guarino, A. "Croce, crux interpretum: Alcune note sulla croce celeste etrusca, sull'orientamento dei templi etrusco-italici e sul fegato di Piacenza." In *Munuscula: Omaggio degli allievi napoletani a Mauro Cristofani*, edited by F. Roncalli, 183–235. Pozzuoli: Naus, 2011.

Harari, M. "Gli Etruschi Nella Valle Del Po: Il paesaggio agrario italiano protostorico e antico. Storia e didattica." *Quaderni/Istituto Alcide Cervi, Museo Cervi* 6 (2010), 51–57.

Hietala, H. J., and P. A. Larson. *Intrasite Spatial Analysis in Archaeology.* Cambridge/New York: Cambridge University Press, 1984.

Hillier, B. *Space Is the Machine: A configurational Theory of Architecture*, 2nd ed. Cambridge: Cambridge University Press, 1996. https://spaceisthemachine.com

Hillier, B. "Spatial analysis and cultural information: The need for theory as well as method in space syntax analysis." In *Spatial Analysis and Social Spaces: Interdisciplinary Approaches to the Interpretation of Prehistoric and Historic Built Environments*, Topoi Berlin Studies of the Ancient World 18, edited by E. Paliou, U. Lieberwirth, and S. Polla, 19–48. Berlin: De Gruyter, 2014.

Hillier, B., and J. Hanson. *The Social Logic of Space.* Cambridge: Cambridge University Press, 1984.

Hillier, B., A. Penn, J. Hanson, T. Grajewski, and J. Xu. "Natural movement: Or configuration and attraction in urban pedestrian movement." *Environment Planning B* 20.1 (1993), 29–66.

Hodder, I., and C. Orton. *Spatial Analysis in Archaeology.* Cambridge: Cambridge University Press, 1976.

Holloway, R. R. "Urbanism, Etruscan, Italic and Latin in the light of recent developments." *Papers in Italian Archaeology VI: Communities and Settlements from the Neolithic to the Early Medieval Period: Proceedings of the 6th Conference of Italian Archaeology*, edited by P. Attema, A. Nijboer, A. Zifferero, O. Satijn, L. Alessandri, M. Bierma and E. Bolhuis, 32–38. University of Groningen, Groningen Institute of Archaeology, The Netherlands, April 15–17, 2003. BAR International Series 1452 (1). Oxford: Oxford University Press, 2005.

Iacopini, E. *Indagini topografiche nell'Etruria settentrionale costiera: Analisi statistico-spaziali su piattaforma GIS*. Scuola di Specializzazione in Beni archeologici, Facoltà di lettere e filosofia, Università di Pisa, thesis, 2011.

Iaia, C., and A. Mandolesi. "Topografia dell'insediamento dell'VIII secolo a.c. in Etruria meridionale." *Journal of Ancient Topography* 3 (1993), 17–33.

Izzet, V. *The Archaeology of Etruscan Society: Identity, Surface and Material Culture in Archaic Etruria*. Cambridge: Cambridge University Press, 2007.

Javadi, A.-H., B. Emo, L. R. Howard, F. E. Zisch, Yichao Yu, R. Knight, J. P. Silva, and H. J. Spiers. "Hippocampal and prefrontal processing of network topology to simulate the future." *Nature Communication*, 8.14652 (2017), 1–11. doi:10.1038/ncomms14652

Kaiser, A. *Roman Urban Street Networks*. New York/London: Routledge, 2011.

Keay, S., M. Millett, S. Poppy, J. Robinson, J. Taylor, and N. Terrenato. "Falerii Novi: A new survey of the walled area." *Papers of the British School at Rome* 68 (2000), 1–93.

Knappett, C., ed. *Network Analysis in Archaeology: New Approaches to Regional Interaction*. Oxford: Oxford Scholarship Online, 2013. doi:10.1093/acprof:oso/9780199697090.001.0001

Knitter, D., W. Schier, and B. Schütt. *Spatial Environment and Conceptual Design: The Concept of Social Ecology as a Means to Integrate Humanities and Science in Landscape Archaeological Research*. Berlin: Edition Topoi, 2021.

Leidwanger, J., and C. Knappett. *Maritime Networks in the Ancient Mediterranean world*. Cambridge: Cambridge University Press, 2018.

Lévi Strauss, C. *La Pensée sauvage*. Paris, 1962/English ed., Chicago: University of Chicago Press, 1962.

Liverani, P. "Displacements: Riflessioni conclusive di metodo." In *Displacements continuità e discontinuità urbana nell'Italia centrale tirrenica*, edited by M. C. Biella, 135–141. Rome: Edizioni Quasar, 2020.

Manacorda, D. *Lezioni di Archeologia*, Rome-Bari: Laterza, 2008.

Mansuelli, G. A., ed. *La formazione della città preromana in Emilia Romagna: Atti del Convegno di studi Bologna-Marzabotto 7–8 Dicembre 1985*. Bologna: Istituto per la storia di Bologna, 1985.

Mansuelli, G. A. 1998a. "Etrusca disciplina e pensiero scientifico." *Annali della Fondazione per il Museo Claudio Faina* 5 (1998a), 105–118.

Mansuelli, G. A. 1998b. *L'ultima Etruria, aspetti della romanizzazione del paese etrusco: Gli aspetti culturali e sacrali*. Bologna: Pàtron, 1998b.

Michetti, L. M. "Riti di fondazione nell'Italia antica: Riflessioni su altri contesti di area etrusca." *Scienze dell'antichità* 19.2-3 (2013), 333–357.

Mlekuž, D., and B. Županek. "The town as a machine: Space syntax analysis of Emona." In *Emona MM, Urbanization of Space, Beginning of a Town*, edited by B. Županek, B. Vičič, A. Maver, R. Miović, and B. Smith-Demo, 91–110. Ljubljana: Zavod za varstvo kulturne dediščine Slovenije, 2017.

Moscati, P. "Methodological problems and future perspectives in the application of GIS in archaeology in GIS applications in Italian archaeology." *Archeologia e Calcolatori* 9 (1998), 191–236.

Moscati, P. "Progetto Caere: Questioni di metodo e sperimentazioni." *Archeologia e Calcolatori* 12 (2001), 47–53.

Moscati, P. "Archaeological computing and ancient cities: Insights from the repository of 'Archeologia e Calcolatori.'" *Archeologia e Calcolatori* 28.2 (2017), 47–66.

Munzi, M. "Strategies and forms of political Romanization in central-southern Etruria (third century BC)." In *Italy and the West: Comparative Issues in Romanization*, edited S. Keay and N. Terrenato, 39–53. Oxford: Oxbow Books, 2001.

Navas, E., J. A. Esquivel, and F. Molina. "Butchering patterns and spatial distribution of faunal animal remains consumed at the Los Milllares chalcolithic settlement (Santa Fe de Mondújar, Almería, Spain)." *Oxford Journal of Archaeology* 27.4 (2008), 325–339.

Newsome, D. *Ostia Antica: Spatial Structure and Social Dynamics: A Preliminary Discussion of the Spatiality of Urban Identities in a Major Roman Port.* Unpublished master's thesis, University of York, 2005.

Osanna, M., and S. Verger. *Pompei e gli Etruschi: Exposition, Pompei, Palestra Grande, Du 12 Décembre 2018 Au 2 Mai 2019.* Rome: Electa, 2018.

Paliou, E. "Visibility analysis in 3D spaces: A new dimension to the understanding of social space." In *Spatial Analysis and Social Spaces: Interdisciplinary Approaches to the Interpretation of Prehistoric and Historic Built Environments*, Topoi Berlin Studies of the Ancient World 18, edited by E. Paliou, U. Lieberwirth, and S. Polla, 277–296. Berlin: De Gruyter, 2014.

Paliou, E. "Visual perception in past built environments: Theoretical and procedural issues in the archaeological application of three-dimensional visibility analysis." In *Digital Geoarchaeology: New Techniques for Interdisciplinary Human Environment Research*, edited by C. Siart and M. Forbriger, 65–80. Berlin: Springer, 2017.

Paliou, E., and C. Corsi. "'The whole is more than the sum of its parts': Geospatial data integration, visualisation and analysis at the Roman Site of Ammaia (Marvão, Portugal)." In Archaeology in the Digital Era (Volume 2), edited by E. Graeme, T. Sly, A. Chrysanthi, P. Murrieta-Flores, C. Papadopoulos, I. Romanowska, and D. Wheatley, 592–607. Papers from the 40th Annual Conference of Computer Applications and Quantitative Methods in Archaeology (CAA), Southampton, 26–29 March 2012. Amsterdam: Amsterdam University Press, 2013.

Paliou, E., U. Lieberwirth, and S. Polla, eds. *Spatial Analysis and Social Spaces: Interdisciplinary Approaches to the Interpretation of Prehistoric and Historic Built Environments.* Topoi Berlin Studies of the Ancient World 18. Berlin: De Gruyer, 2014.

Papi, E. *L'Etruria dei Romani: Opere pubbliche e donazioni private in età imperiale.* Rome: Quasar, 2000.

Penn, A., and A. Turner. "Space syntax based agent models." In *Pedestrian and Evacuation Dynamics*, edited by M. Schreckenberg and S. Sharma, 99–104. Heidelberg: Springer-Verlag, 2002.

Prignano, L., I. Morer, S. Lozano, J. P. Gonzàlez, F. Fulminante, and A. Dìaz-Guilera. "The weird, wired past: The challenges of applying network science to archaeology and ancient history." *Economía romana: Nuevas perspectivas/The Roman Economy: New Perspectives* (2017), 125–148.

Prignano, L., I. Morer, F. Fulminante, and S. Lozano. "Modelling terrestrial route networks to understand inter-polity interactions (southern Etruria, 950–500 BC)." *Journal of Archaeological Science* 105 (2019), 46–58. https://doi.org/10.1016/j.jas.2019.02.007

Pulcinelli, L. "Le fortificazioni di confine: L'organizzazione del territorio tarquiniense al tempo della conquista romana." In *Il ruolo degli oppida e la difesa del territorio in Etruria: Casi di studio e prospettive di ricerca*, edited by Franco Cambi, 69–120. *Aristonothos*: Scritti per il Mediterraneo antico 5. Trento: Tangram Edizioni Scientifiche, 2012.

Pulcinelli, L. *L'Etruria meridionale e Roma: Insediamenti e territorio tra IV e III secolo a.C.* Rome: L'Erma di Bretschneider, 2016.

Quirino, T. *Sistema informativo territoriale dell'Etruria Padana: Creazione di un archivio topografico e analisi dei modelli insediativi della Pianura Padana fra VI e IV secolo a.C.* Scuola di Dottorato in Humanae Litterae, Dipartimento di Scienze dei Beni Culturali e Ambientali, Dottorato di ricerca in antichistica: Curriculum storico-archeologico, Università degli Studi di Milano, thesis. Milan, 2014.

Raja, R., and S. M. Sindbæk. "Urban archaeology: A new agenda – editorial." *Journal of Urban Archaeology* 1 (2020), 9–13.

Rajala, U. "The landscapes of power: Visibility, time and (dis)continuity in central Italy." *Archeologia e Calcolatori* 15 (2004), 393–408.

Rasmussen, T. "Urbanization in Etruria." In *Mediterranean Urbanization 800–600 BC*, edited by R. Osborne and B. Cunliffe, 71–90. *Proceedings of the British Academy* 126. Oxford: Oxford University Press, 2005.

Ratti, C. "The lineage of the line: Space syntax parameters from the analysis of urban DEMs." *Environment and Planning B: Planning and Design* 32 (2005), 547–566.

Redhouse, D. I., and S. Stoddart. "Mapping Etruscan state formation." In *State Formation in Greece and Italy*, edited by N. Terrenato and D. C. Haggis, 162–178. Oxford: Oxbow Books, 2011.

Rendeli, M. *Città Aperte: Ambiente e paesaggio rurale organizzato nell'Etruria meridionale costiera durante l'età orientalizzante e arcaica*. Rome: GEI Gruppo Editoriale Internazionale, 1993.

Robertson, E. C., J. D. Seibert, D. C. Fernandez, and M. U. Zender, eds. *Space and Spatial Analysis in Archaeology*. Calgary: University of Calgary Press, 2006.

Schaps, D. "Systems network analysis and the study of the ancient world: Review of *Greek and Roman Networks in the Mediterranean*, by Irad Malkin, Christy Constantakopoulou and Katerina Panagopoulou (eds.)." *Scripta Classica Israelica* 29 (2010), 91–97.

Siart, C., M. Forbriger, and O. Bubenzer, eds. *Digital Geoarchaeology: New Techniques for Interdisciplinary Human-Environmental Research*. Springer: Natural Science in Archaeology, 2018.

Smith, M. E. "Definitions and comparisons in urban archaeology." *Journal of Urban Archaeology* 1 (2020), 15–30.

Spivey N. J., and S. Stoddart. *Etruscan Italy*. London: Batsford, 1990.

Steingräber, S. "Etruscan urban planning." In *The Etruscans*, edited by M. Torelli, 291–311. New York: Rizzoli, 2000.

Steingräber, S. "The process of urbanization of Etruscan settlements from the Late Villanovian to the Late Archaic Period (end of the eight to the beginning of the fifth century B.C.): Presentation of a project and preliminary results." *Etruscan Studies: Journal of the Etruscan Foundation* 8 (2008), 7–33.

Stek, T. D. "The impact of Roman expansion and colonization of ancient Italy in the Republican period. From diffusionism to network opportunity." In *The Peoples of Ancient Italy*, edited by G. D. Farney, and G. Bradley, 269–294. Boston: De Gruyter, 2018.

Stoddart, S. *Complex Polity Formation in North Etruria and Umbria 1200-500 BC*. Unpublished PhD thesis, University of Cambridge, 1987.

Stoddart, S. 2020a. *Power and Place in Etruria*. Cambridge: Cambridge University Press, 2020a.

Stoddart, S. 2020b. "An Etruscan urban agenda." *Journal of Urban Archaeology* 1 (2020b), 99–121.

Stoddart, S., A. Palmisano, D. Redhouse, G. Barker, G. di Paola, L. Motta, T. Rasmussen, T. Samuels, and R. Witcher. "Patterns of Etruscan urbanism." *Frontiers in Digital Humanities* 7.1 (2020), 1–30. doi:10.3389/fdigh.2020.00001

Stöger, J. *Rethinking Ostia: A Spatial Enquiry into the Urban Society of Rome's Imperial Port-Town*. Leiden: Archaeological Studies Leiden University 24, 2011.

Straumann, S., U. Rosemann, and H. Sütterlin. "Viele Wege führen durch Augusta Raurica. Das Strassennetzwerk neu betrachtet mit Space Syntax." *Augusta Raurica Magazine* 2 (2018), 15–18.

Torelli, M. "The Etruscan city-state." In *A Comparative Study of Thirty City-State Cultures*, edited by M. H. Hansen, 189–203. Copenhagen: Kongelige Danske Videnskabernes Selskab, 2000.

van Nes, A. "Measuring the degree of street vitality in excavated towns: How can macro and micro spatial analyses tools contribute to understandings on the spatial organization of urban life in Pompeii?" In *Proceedings of the 7th International Space Syntax Symposium*, edited by D. Koch, L. Marcus, and J. Steen, 120, 1–11. Stockholm: KTH-TRITA-ARK-Forskningspublikationer, 2009.

van Nes, A. "Indicating street vitality in excavated towns: Spatial configurative analyses applied to Pompeii." In *Spatial Analysis and Social Spaces: Interdisciplinary Approaches to the Interpretation of Prehistoric and Historic Built Environments*, Topoi Berlin Studies of the Ancient World 18, edited by E. Paliou, U. Lieberwirth, and S. Polla, 277–296. Berlin: De Gruyter, 2014.

van Nes, A., and C. Yamu. *Introduction to Space Syntax in Urban Studies*. Cham: Springer, 2021.

Verhagen, P. "Spatial analysis in archaeology: Moving into new territories." In *Digital Geoarchaeology: New Techniques for Interdisciplinary Human-Environmental Research*, Natural Science in Archaeology, edited by C. Siart, M. Forbriger, and O. Bubenzer, 11–25. Berlin: Springer, 2018.

Vermeulen, F. "Towards an holistic archaeological survey approach for ancient cityscape." In *Digital Methods and Remote Sensing in Archaeology*, edited by M. Forte and S. Campana, 91–112. Cham: Springer, 2016.

Wheatley, D., and M. Gillings. *Spatial Technology and Archaeology: The Archaeological Applications of GIS*. New York: Taylor & Francis, 2002.

Witcher, R. "Settlement and society in early imperial Etruria." *Journal of Roman Studies* 96 (2006), 88–123.

Zamboni, L., and C. Buoite. "Le officine mutevoli. Analisi spaziale e riesame delle evidenze produttive nel porto adriatico di Spina (VI-III sec. A.C.)." In *Gli artigiani e la città. Officine e aree produttive tra VIII e III sec. a.C. nell'Italia centrale tirrenica* (Atti della giornata di studio British School at Rome, 11 gennaio 2016), edited by M. C. Biella, R. Cascino, A. Ferrandes, and M. Revello Lami. *Scienze dell'Antichità* 232 (2017), 377–386.

Zamboni, L., M. Fernández-Götz, and C. Metzner-Nebelsick. *Crossing the Alps: Early Urbanism between Northern Italy and Central Europe (900–400 BC)*. Leiden: Sidestone Press, 2020.

Fabiana Battistin, *Spatial Analysis and Etruscan Cities: Past Experiences and Future Challenges* In: *A New Etruscan Archaeology: Twenty-First Century Techniques and Methods*. Edited by: Maurizio Forte, Oxford University Press. © Oxford University Press 2025. DOI: 10.1093/9780197582053.003.0005

5

Sounds Beneath the Surface

A New Cognitive Approach to the Etruscan Funerary Space

Jacqueline K. Ortoleva

Introduction

During the past few decades, archaeological science has increasingly drawn on evolving fields such as neuroscience and experimental psychology to further understand the material record of past cultures. While utilized in fields such as prehistory, pre-Roman scholarship has more slowly adopted approaches involving human cognition. This is especially clear when considering painted tombs in Etruria. Etruscan painted tombs have often been assessed according to social constructs, with the presentation of tomb paintings as symbolic of gender, status, and the general identity of the deceased (Amman, 2000; Avramidou, 2009; Bonfante, 1981; Pallottino, 1952, 1955a; Rathje, 1990; Roncalli, 1997; Roth, 2012; Weber-Lehrmann, 1986). The lack of primary textual sources and the prevalence of Greek and Roman texts has further led scholars to present specific motifs as connected to Greek or Roman traditions (Rouveret, 1974; Pfiffig, 1975; Holloway, 1986; Steingräber, 1986; Cristofani, 1987; Naso, 1996, 2017; Torelli, 1999; Brandt, 2020). These approaches emphasize the presumed meaning of visuals inside the tomb space rather than considering *how* the tomb space was experienced.[1] As a result, crucial areas of the tomb, such as the dromos, have been eclipsed, and funerary ritual remains unclear. Approaching the painted tomb from a cognitive perspective addresses this lack of clarity by recontextualizing the tomb space as a physically and sensorially experienced space. Although the word "cognitive" may induce visions of "theory over substance," an approach that accurately draws on empirical research in the field of cognitive science is the antithesis of such a reading.

In 1982, Renfrew framed cognitive archaeology as a processual field of inquiry.[2,3] Renfrew's stance intersected processual aims with post-processual concerns,

[1] The experiential nature of material remains is of primary note across multiple theoretical approaches including cognitive archaeology (Renfrew, 1994; Renfrew et al., 2009), sensory archaeology (Betts, 2017; Graham, 2011, 2021; Skeates, 2010), phenomenological and other bodily approaches (Taylor, 2020; Warden, 2009), and neuroarchaeology (Malafouris, 2008; 2013; Stout and Chaminade, 2007).

[2] Colin Renfrew discussed the potential of a "cognitive-processual" form of inquiry in 1982. during his inaugural address at Cambridge University and thereafter across multiple publications. See Renfrew (1983).

[3] I am grateful to Simon Stoddart who served as my sponsor at Cambridge, in 2019. While there, I met Lord Prof. Colin Renfrew to thus discuss Etruria, cognitive archaeology, the Etruscan language, and the

essentially forging a theoretical perspective that considers the archaeological record from a material and "immaterial" perspective.[4] Such a stance recognizes that cognitive processes are rooted in perceptual and physical engagement with the material world, not one or the other (Craighero, 2014). Human beings perceive the world as a result of external sensory data (visual, somatosensory, auditory, and so forth) that are transformed by the brain to ultimately construct a snapshot of the physical world. Audition is perhaps one of the most overlooked sensory experiences, particularly when considering the Etruscan record.

While multiple scholars have aptly considered music and funerary performance in Etruria, the behavior of sound has never been documented in any Etruscan setting (Colonna, 1993; Carrese, 2010; Jannot, 1974, 1979; Lawergren, 1993, 2007; Maras, 2016, 2018; Martinelli and Melini, 2010; Warden & Thomas 1999). Indeed, the entirety of the Etruscan record has only recently to be studied in terms of *how* sound may have played a role in religious worship and other cultural practices.[5] When reflecting on sound propagation inside the painted tomb, it is important to note that audition is the sum product of what and particularly how one perceives sound. Many things dictate this process, including language (speech not literacy) and cultural constructs. In sum, we "hear" because our brain tells us that we are perceiving specific sounds, even if such sounds are not present (Waller, 2002). The transactional nature of sound between the brain and external cues influences how the external world is cognized. Hence, sound can shape how a space feels, how it appears, and how it is emotionally recalled.

This chapter explores sound propagation inside the painted tomb space. A new methodology is illustrated using the Tomba del Gallo (c. 450–430 BCE), from the Necropoli dei Monterozzi in Tarquinia, to discuss the acoustic nature of the burial chamber and dromos with respect to the interment experience.

Nature of the Problem

Although Etruscan archaeology has progressed in recent years with studies involving sanctuary and/or urban settings, chambered tombs in the Etruscan record, particularly painted tombs, are largely understood in visual terms.[6] Indeed, most studies

bridging of processual and postprocessual approaches in archaeology. His stories of being introduced to Etruria as a young boy in Tarquinia and Cerveteri exemplify his passion for the archaeological sciences, and I am grateful for his feedback and inspiring candor.

[4] Paul Garwood (personal communication, 2020); Dominik Maschek (personal communication, 2020).

[5] The first publication involving an acoustic analysis of an Etruscan tomb is found in Ortoleva (2021).

[6] Analyses involving urban and settlement contexts, roadways, and sanctuary settings are now extensive. For example, Bonghi Jovino and Chiaramonte Trerè, 1997; Colonna, 1986, 2012; de Grummond, 2009; Forte and Murtiera, 2020; Maggiani, 1999; Stoddart, 2020; Stopponi, 2007, 2009; Torelli, 1977; Warden, 2009, 2012, 2018. In the present publication, see Chapter 2, by Stefano Campana; Chapter 3, by Antonio Lo Piano and Katherine McCusker; and Chapter 4, by Fabiana Battistin.

involving painted tombs tend to heavily rely on tomb iconography, epigraphic evidence, and/or architectural typologies (Marzullo, 2017, 2018; Morandi, 1983; Prayon, 1975; Serra Ridgway, 2004; Steingräber, 1986; Weber-Lehmann, 1986). The latter is especially clear when considering architectural structures inside the tomb space such as the entrance corridor (Cavagnaro Vanoni, 1972, 1977; Linington and Ridgway, 1997; Roncalli, 1997; Torelli, 1999). Entrance corridors (dromoi) were included in chambered (unpainted) tombs in Tarquinia as early as the seventh century and continued well after the region's absorption by the Romans.[7] Most studies involving dromoi have focused on scale, with only minimal discussion in terms of the experienced dromos, particularly from the standpoint of sound (Cavagnaro Vanoni, 1997; Izzet, 2007). Several research questions are pertinent to the present discussion. How was the dromos perceived during the burial event? What can an assessment of sound tell us regarding the relationship of the tomb with its exterior setting? Moreover, can an analysis involving sound shed light on the use of the dromos during each funerary event? This chapter seeks to recontextualize the Etruscan chambered tomb space with respect to the physical and cognitive experience of funerary ritual. Rather than privileging tomb paintings, the painted tomb is considered from a more emic perspective by focusing on bodily movement and sensory phenomena involving sound and space.

The Study of Cognition in Archaeology and Its Application to the Etruscan Record

There are multiple ways in which the material record has been approached from a cognitive perspective in archaeology. Experimental protocols have been developed using modern test subjects to study aspects of tool use, numeracy, and rock art. Such studies are often self-identified as "neuroarchaeology" (d'Errico et al., 2003; Hodgson, 2012; Malafouris, 2013; Overmann, 2016; Renfrew et al., 2009). In terms of the Etruscan record, recent approaches include sensory and phenomenological perspectives (Izzet, 2001; 2007; Ortoleva, 2021, 2022, 2023, 2024; Taylor, 2020; Warden, 2009, 2012; see also Warden et al. and Forte et al. in this volume). This chapter springs from the perspective of *cognitive archaeology*, which emerged during the late twentieth century, in part as a response to strict processual methodologies. Since then, the improvement of technologies that document the human brain, such as

---

[7] After decades of conflicts and peace treaties, details leading to the final "fall" of Tarquinia are unclear. However, the date is usually identified as either 281 or 268 BCE. A triumph celebrated by Q. Marcius Philippus in 281 is often identified as an indication of Tarquinia falling under Roman rule. In sum, we do not have an exact date documented in any textual source. Livy later details the takeover of Gravisca (originally Tarquinian territory) in 181 BCE (40.29.1). Although we do not have an exact date for Tarquinia's absorption, a later third-century CE inscription translated by Torelli describes the populace of Tarquinia as unequal to Roman citizens (Torelli 1981, 251–78). Ultimately, Southern Etruscan regions established a series of treaties with Rome entitling them to Roman protection in exchange for their support of Roman military campaigning (Liv. 28.45.14). See Torelli (1975, 162).

magnetic resonance imagery (MRI) and positron emission technology (PET) scans in addition to studies involving neurological disease and injuries, have led to a new track in cognitive archaeology. It is important to note here that a cognitive approach is best served by drawing on the expertise of those in the field of cognitive science. Therefore, it is recommended that scholars without a background in cognitive science, neuroscience, or the behavioral sciences personally train and/or consult with scholars who have expertise in such fields (Laughlin, 2015).

There are many reasons why Etruscan archaeology can benefit from a perspective that considers sensory perception, many of which fall outside the scope of this chapter. However, one is worth noting here. Cognitive science is a multidisciplinary field that draws on neuroscience, experimental psychology, linguistics, genetics, and other similar fields to explore human cognition (Henley et al., 2020). Such an approach provides the opportunity to assess the archaeological record across different contexts in Etruria. In terms of the present methodology, the cognitive experience of sound and space during the funerary event is our focus, as perceived inside and outside of the painted tomb space.

Cognition of Sound and the Archaeological Record

Human sensory experience of sound is processed via pressure waves moving through the air, water, or other substances. However, sound is also perceived at frequencies below 200 Hz via bone conduction. Lower-frequency sounds also stimulate nerve endings in the skin, such as the Pacinian corpuscles, and further affect bodily organs.[8] Therefore, what is experienced as "sound" is more accurately understood as a form of physical touch, and this in turn shapes bodily movement through space (Tchumatchenko and Reichenbach, 2014). Whether the listener is six years old, with the ability to hear a wide range of sound frequencies between 20 and 20,000 Hz, or a mature adult able to perceive frequencies more so up to 8,000–10,000 Hz, some frequencies provide a way for all human beings—even those who are hearing impaired—to sense or 'feel' sound (Tchumatchenko and Reichenbach, 2014). The manner in which sound can be studied in the archaeological record is wide ranging.

The study of sound in the archaeological record ("archaeoacoustics") has often centered on prehistoric sites featuring rock art (Diaz-Andreu et al., 2017; Reznikoff, 2006; Reznikoff and Dauvois, 1988; Waller, 2002). Others, such as Watson and Keating and Till have analyzed acoustics in architectural structures (Till, 2019; Watson and Keating, 1999). The extent to which sound propagation may have played a role across landscape settings is also of note (see, e.g., Jordan, 2021). More recently, scholars such as Díaz-Andreu and Kolar have begun to focus on the

---

[8] Technically, "sound," as we know it does not exist. Instead, sound emerges as a result of changes in atmospheric conditions that affect human beings and other living creatures with auditory capabilities (Johnson, 2001).

cognition of sound as part of archaeoacoustic research (Diaz-Andreu et al., 2017; Kolar, 2017). *Audition* is the sum of interactions between external auditory data and internal constructs (Clark, 2013). Therefore, aural experience is not always conscious. An interesting example of this involves music.

Studies have shown that when classical music is streamed for patients under anesthesia they require less analgesia and sedation than those not exposed to such sounds. Moreover, when a surgeon listens to the same sound bite, the surgical process tends to be faster and more accurately completed. Interestingly, anesthesiologists are negatively affected by the exact same instrumentals and contexts (Linos, 2012). These intriguing findings regarding the inherent cognitive effects of music were surely not understood in the ancient world. However, the Etruscan record as well as secondary textual sources do illustrate an observance of sonic phenomena in Etruria, such as thunder and bird calls.[9]

Representation of Sound in the Etruscan Record

The representation of sound in the Etruscan record ranges from surviving musical instruments to more obtuse visual representations (Bonghi Jovino, 1987). One example of the latter involves a terracotta antefix from Vulci that dates to the fourth century BCE (Figure 5.1) (Colonna, 2009; de Grummond, 2016). The antefix displays a male head, suggested by Colonna to represent the Etruscan deity Suri and conversely identified by de Grummond as Tinia. In terms of the piece's connection to sound, the identity of the head is not the most relevant part of the piece, but rather what is held inside the mouth. While Colonna has postulated that the stalk-like object represents lightning, as seen on multiple bronze mirrors and other objects, de Grummond suggests it could even represent thunder (Colonna, 2009; de Grummond, 2016). Whether symbolic of lightning or thunder, both phenomena are clearly connected in that lightning prefaces the strong low-frequency sounds of thunder. Therefore, the present antefix visually signifies the importance of thunder and sound in Etruscan religious worship. Moreover, if de Grummond is correct and the piece does visually 'depict' thunder, then an implication to speech and/or verbal incantations inside the temple space in Vulci is possible. Although debate will continue in terms of this intriguing piece, the most overt representation of sound in Etruria involves the use and depiction of various musical instruments.

Music and dance are the second most common narrative in Etruscan tomb paintings, in essence providing visual representations of music without any corresponding sound.[10] The question is why. When considered together with the material

---

[9] Multiple Roman and Greek textual sources attest to the recognition of different natural acoustic phenomena in Etruria, for example, see: Cic. *Div.* 2.38.80; Plin. *HN.* 2.51.136; J. Lydus De Ostentis, 27–38.
[10] Banqueting scenes are the most common illustration in Etruscan tomb paintings; see Rathje (1990); Weber-Lehmann (1986).

Figure 5.1 4th-3rd century BCE temple antefix from Vulci. After: de Grummond, 2016, Fig. 15.

remains of instruments from areas such as Cortona and Tarquinia, it is clear that music was important across Etruria. Its commonality has led to the recreation of instruments that were originally used in Etruscan contexts.[11] While the recreation of musical instruments in Etruria is a valuable exercise in terms of our visualizing their overall construction, musings involving musical composition in Etruria cannot be accurately assessed because no Etruscan scores have survived. However, further understanding the *behavior* of sound (particularly in the enclosed space of the tomb) is attainable via a systematically developed acoustic method.

Painted Tombs in Tarquinia: Acoustic Method

The acoustic protocol for this study was developed around a series of safeguards established to protect the delicate nature of each tomb's structure and any present tomb paintings.[12] In total, Sixteen tombs were documented in Tarquinia, outside

[11] See Jannot (1974, 1979, 1988), Martinelli (2007), Martinelli and Melini (2010), Sarti (2010); the European Music Project (EMAP) has recreated several Etruscan instruments such as the lituus (see: http://www.emaproject.eu). A basic review of scholarly reviews of Etruscan musical instruments is Li Castro (2017).

[12] Thank you to the Soprintendenza ABAP per l'area metropolitana di Roma, la provincia di Viterbo e l'Etruria Meridionale and the Soprintendenza Archeologia, Belle Arti e Paesaggio dell'Umbria, for providing access to the documented tombs in Tarquinia, the Commune of Porano, and Cerveteri.

of Orvieto, and Cerveteri. Before visiting the tombs, a digitalized sound sample was created after considering musical instruments in the painted tomb record. Ultimately, sounds from three instruments were included in the sound source: the double-pipes, the most depicted instrument displayed in Tarquinian tomb paintings; the lituus; and the concert kithara.[13] A female *a capella* song and handclaps were also incorporated into the final sound source. The sound source was projected from designated placements inside each chamber and dromos using a loudspeaker that accurately reproduced frequencies between 64 and 24,800 Hz (Figure 5.2).[14] An omnidirectional sound receiver set at a 48 kHz sample rate and 16-bit depth was placed in three to six areas of each chamber and dromos on a tripod whose height was averaged from male and female osteological evidence from Tarquinia (ISO 3382).

The study's goal to utilize cognitive science to further understand sound propagation during the funerary event inspired the creation of a second protocol that further considered the human actors involved in each funerary event. This second acoustic protocol was conducted on subsequent visits to five of the previously documented tombs to consider live musical performance and speech inside each tomb's burial chamber and dromos.[15] Each visit involved the placement of a musician skilled in playing chordophone instruments (in this case, the musician played a chelys lyra) in different areas of the tomb to understand sound in terms of bodily movement.[16]

Subsequent to the fieldwork conducted inside each tomb, the resulting acoustic data were studied using the software program EASERA. In addition, an acoustic engineer who provided consultation for the study made assessments using the MATLAB program to verify the emerging data.[17] Moreover, a scaled acoustic model was built of each burial chamber and dromos using the acoustic modeling program Odeon to consider such things as original building material (vs. modern), acoustic absorption and scattering rates in conjunction with the surface area, and overall volume of each tomb. Each final model allows visual observation of sound propagation inside a specific space, which is especially useful in terms of structural details such as the size of each dromos, entrances, and so forth.

---

[13] The concert kithara is depicted only two times inside Tarquinian painted tombs, in the Tomba della Pulcella and the Tomba della Fustigazione. However, the musical segment of the concert kithara was deemed important to use because it contrasted well, in terms of its presumed frequency range, with the chelys lyra, which was chosen for the second acoustic protocol (live performance protocol).

[14] Based on BOSE data specifications and field testing of the BOSE sound device by the author.

[15] Thank you to Rory Stalwick who volunteered his time and talent to provide live acoustic assessment inside five Tarquinian tombs.

[16] Etruscan depictions of lyre instruments, such as the chelys lyra, concert kithara, and barbiton show musicians holding the instrument higher than typically shown in Greek iconography; see Lawergren (2007).

[17] Thank you to Andrew Barnard, PhD, at Michigan Technical University, who provided invaluable feedback regarding the study's acoustic data, the scattering rates of specific material, and the acoustical effects of modern building materials.

Material Constructs and Sound in Space

There are multiple ways in which audition is affected inside a fully enclosed space such as the chambered tomb. Spatiality and architectural features affect sound propagation across all frequency bands, while environmental conditions including humidity and temperature as well as the number of people present in a given space manipulate sound at higher frequencies (4,000 Hz and above).[18] Building materials further shape the behavior of sound in space. The lengthy tradition of painted tombs in Tarquinia, which persisted between the seventh and third centuries, was in part driven by the bedrock local to the area. Etruscan painted tombs are geologically distinct across central Italy, and tombs in Tarquinia were constructed from "macco" or biocalcarenite limestone from the Upper Pliocene interbedded with a weaker fossiliferous biocalcarenite (Caneva et al., 2021 D'Agostino et al., 2010). The combination provided an appropriate surface for the application of an underlay and paint with a level of stability from the macco that is not always found in other regions of central Italy.[19] In Orvieto, where just three painted tombs have been found, such tombs were carved from a softer welded tuff with large trachyte-phonolite deposits. Additional treatments to tomb walls, ceilings, and floors, including the dromos, further contributed to sound propagation. For example, the Tomba Golini I in Orvieto and the Tomba dell'Orco in Tarquinia were prepared with a thin layer of marble dust applied to the walls on top of the plaster underlay for painting, and this likely accentuated reverberant properties inside the tomb.[20]

One of the most well-researched measures in acoustic science is reverberation, or the accumulation of sound within a confined or semi-confined space that reflects across all surfaces until ultimately ceasing (Till, 2019). Reverberation is assessed from a room impulse response (RIR) across different time-based metrics (early decay time [EDT], reverb time [RT]20, RT30, and so forth). The metric of focus here, EDT, is transposable to the cognition of reverberation because it measures how sound is

[18] Malleable burial objects (e.g., textiles) would have blunted reverberation, while objects made of stone and metal could have accentuated reverberation times depending on their placement. Vitruvius details the use of vases in Roman theaters to assist with sound quality. See *De arch.* 5.5.1. Contemporary music studios used for music rehearsals are designed to enhance reverberation times using strategically placed objects. The musician who assisted with the present study even relayed that he has previously used surf boards to assist with reverberation times in his rehearsal studio. The strategic placement of different objects inside smaller tomb spaces could have made reverberation stronger or weaker depending on the size and material of such objects and specific frequency bands. This dynamic is being considered as part of the author's doctoral thesis.

[19] The application of paint on the walls and sometimes the ceilings of chambered tombs adapted from the initial application of paint directly on rock walls to the creation of more complex overlays. Each surface was prepared for the paint by flattening and smoothing each rectilinear wall to allow a smoother application of paint. During the seventh century BCE, when tomb paintings first emerged in Tarquinia, paint was directly applied to the hewn walls. As early as the sixth century BCE, an underlay was applied to the walls (and sometimes the floors) made from 1–3 millimeters of clay mixed with ground stone created from the rock removed from the walls. See Borrelli (1986), Naso (1995, 1996).

[20] Andrew Barnard (personal communication, 2020).

perceived at different positions in a given space (Till, 2019). "Sound" is produced with multiple frequencies supporting a fundamental frequency, which ultimately corresponds to the perceptual breadth of pitch (Till, 2019). Therefore, reverberation and all acoustic metrics are assessed across specific frequencies. Although the perception of modern structures is not easily transferred to those from the past, a series of clues involving reverberation can assist with understanding how reverberation can tailor audition. If reverberation is too long, surrounding reflections can be perceived as distinct echoes. A modern orchestral hall with RTs of between 1.5 and 2.4 seconds is considered ideal. When falling below 1.5 seconds, such a space may seem acoustically flat (Reinhart and Souza, 2018). Alternatively, spaces with long RTs, longer than 2.4 seconds, can interfere with sound localization and therefore make it very difficult to identify the origins of a specific sound. A simple example of the latter is found in theater contexts.

When performing musical theater, the modern performer learns each song and/or scene according to strictly choreographed movements in connection with the space. If performing in an especially reverberant space, without such structure, the performer has difficulty localizing sound cues.[21] Interestingly, this does not seem to be the case with skilled musicians. Studies have found that professional musicians can cognitively withstand high levels of reverberation and are two to four times more capable of deciphering speech in a highly reverberant space than are nonmusicians (Bidelman and Krishnan, 2010). Even a smaller space can include areas that seem aurally magnified thus creating a space that is sonically varied (Reybrouck, 2017). Such facts illustrate the complex nature of sound and necessitate an approach that considers all structural aspects of the tomb space. To explore reverberation more fully inside the painted tomb, a study of one tomb is presented, with particular focus on the tomb's dromos.

Sounds Beneath the Surface Case Study: The Tomba del Gallo

The Tomba del Gallo (Figures 5.2 and 5.3; c. 450–430 BCE) is a tripartite tomb that is carved from biocalcarenite limestone (macco) and is located in the Secondi Archi area of the Necropoli dei Monterozzi in Tarquinia.[22] The burial chamber located at the bottom of the tomb's dromos is tiny, measuring just 3.31 meters in length and 2.50 meters wide; it includes a gabled roof and large *loculus* on the left rear wall of the burial chamber, in the area of the tomb hypothesized by Torelli and Roncalli to have been reserved for the dead (Roncalli, 1997; Torelli, 1983, 1999). The tomb paintings inside the Tomba del Gallo include a banqueting scene on the right wall and double-pipes players pictured on the

---

[21] Based on the author's personal experience performing in theater settings. See also Goldstein and Goldstein Bloom (2011).

[22] Steingräber identifies a date of 400 BCE, and more recent analyses based on the architecture of the tomb and the identification of additional painted tombs designate an earlier date, between 450 and 425 BCE. See Marzullo (2017, 147).

left wall as well as on both entrance walls (right and left). Although its name was inspired by the small rooster pictured in the pediment atop the right entrance wall, the tomb is perhaps most well-known for its highly animated dance scene picturing a male figure (identified by some scholars as the Etruscan figure of Phersu—or, more likely, a male performer masked as Phersu) dancing alongside a female dancer with a clapper in each hand (*crotalum*) and one double-pipes player.[23]

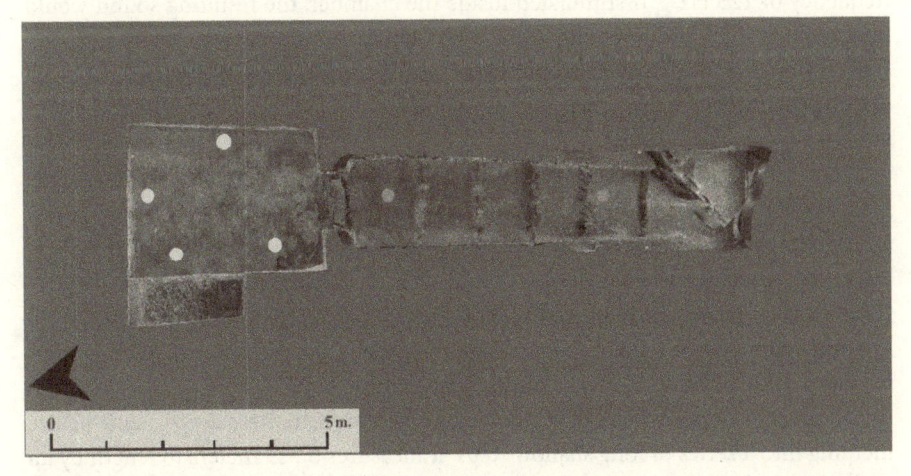

Figure 5.2 Scaled model of the Tomba del Gallo showing sound source placements in red & sound receiver placements in blue. Model: JK Ortoleva.

Figure 5.3 Scaled model of Tomba del Gallo, c. 450–430 BCE, showing the dromos from inside the burial chamber. Model: JK Ortoleva 2022, Fig. 6.22.

[23] The tendency of most scholars has been to assess images of Phersu through Greek and Roman textual sources. For example, see Avramidou (2009). Rather than seeing Phersu as a specific being, the figure may be akin to a musical instrument or perhaps more likely, a costume. See Bonfante (1989).

When considering RTs (EDTs); Early Decay Time inside the burial chamber, only frequencies of 125 Hz and below produced strong reverberation, with times ranging between 6.31 seconds at 100 Hz and 2.34 seconds at 125 Hz. Very few instruments could have stimulated such low frequencies, and, interestingly, one of them is pictured inside del Gallo's burial chamber on the left-hand wall (a clapper is shown in both hands of the female dancer).

Studies have shown that a clapper can produce a B_2 note corresponding with a frequency of 125 Hz.[24] If stimulated inside the chamber, the resulting sound would have seemed loud and booming while other sounds would have faded in comparison. Although vocal frequencies can range widely, depending on language, age, and sex, in general, the female voice has a fundamental frequency of 210 Hz while males tend to hover around 120 Hz.

Lower frequencies have been documented in multiple languages. For example, male Mandarin speakers have been found to exhibit fundamental frequencies as low as 108 Hz, while English speakers have been identified as low as 101 Hz (Chen, 1974). Female fundamental frequencies have been documented as low as 182 Hz (Chen, 1974). Therefore, male, rather than female vocals, would have also stimulated low-frequency reverberatory effects inside the present burial chamber. With respect to sound, another intriguing part of the tomb is its dromos.

The dromos of the Tomba del Gallo begins with an extremely deep incline before merging into a series of long shallow steps; it measures 6.749 meters in length by an average width of 1.368 meters (Figure 5.3). On modeling the entire tomb space using the accrued acoustic data along with scattering rates and the overall volume of the tomb, several patterns emerged. The placement of the first sound source approximately 1 meter inside the dromos resulted in a huge amount of sound escaping the dromos and extending into the tomb's immediate surroundings. Even when placing the sound source at the *bottom* of the dromos, sound scattered outside of the tomb's exterior (Figure 5.4). In fact, sound emerging from the tomb was modeled as extending some 5 meters outside of the tomb space. Interestingly, many of the studied tombs in Tarquinia had dromoi with extremely long EDTs across multiple frequencies, with the dromos seemingly functioning as a sort of "conduit" for sound propagation (Figure 5.5). The subterranean tunnel-like shape of many dromoi contributed to these effects more so than building material or length. Therefore, similar sound effects were identified in longer dromoi as

[24] It is difficult to assess the exact frequency range of the Etruscan double-pipes as few fragments have survived in Etruscan contexts, and almost all iconography depicts the instrument being played making it difficult to deduce information regarding the instrument's mouthpiece in Etruria. However, based on iconography, the instrument was composed of two double-tube reed aerophones, an instrument seen throughout the ancient Mediterranean. Although Etruscan archaeological evidence, iconography, and Greek and Roman texts do not always align, with respect to the double-pipe, there are remarkable consistencies across all three types of evidence. According to Pliny the Elder, the Etruscans used boxwood to create pipes for religious ritual and bone from an ass with silver or nettle wood for theatrical performance (*NH*, 16.172). With respect to archaeological remains, the double-pipe survives via bone fragments from Chianciano from a domestic settlement, possibly supporting Pliny's claim that nonreligious settings used double-pipes made from bone (*NH*, 16.172; Figure 5.4). It is worth noting here that the well-known shipwreck dating to 600 BCE at the Bay of Campese, in the Isola del Giglio, is often mentioned when discussing the Etruscan double-pipe (Sutkowska, 2010). However, the ship is purported to have been from Ionia, and the eleven recovered double-pipes are likely Greek manufactured (Martinelli and Melini, 2010). The frequency range of the Greek aulos has been found to range across frequencies of 460–5,000 Hz. See Jannot (1974) and Hagel (2014).

well (Ortoleva, 2021, 2023; Ortoleva and Barnard, 2021). When considering eleven of the acoustically documented tombs, one of the most reverberant areas across lower frequencies (125–250 Hz) was indeed the dromos (Figure 5.6).

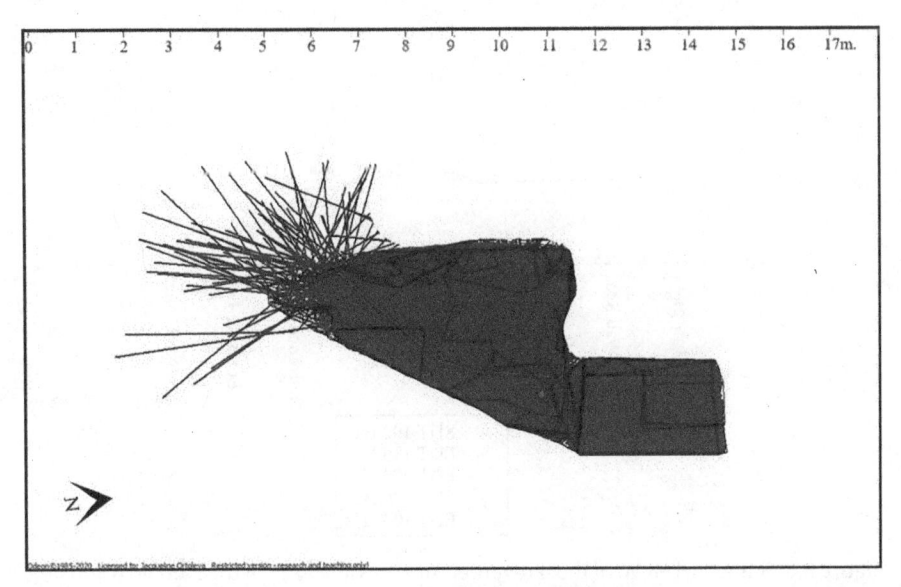

Figure 5.4 Acoustic model of the Tomba del Gallo showing the pattern of sound propagation inside the dromos/burial chamber with a sound source at the bottom of the dromos (shown in red). Model: JK Ortoleva. Created with Odeon acoustic modeling software.

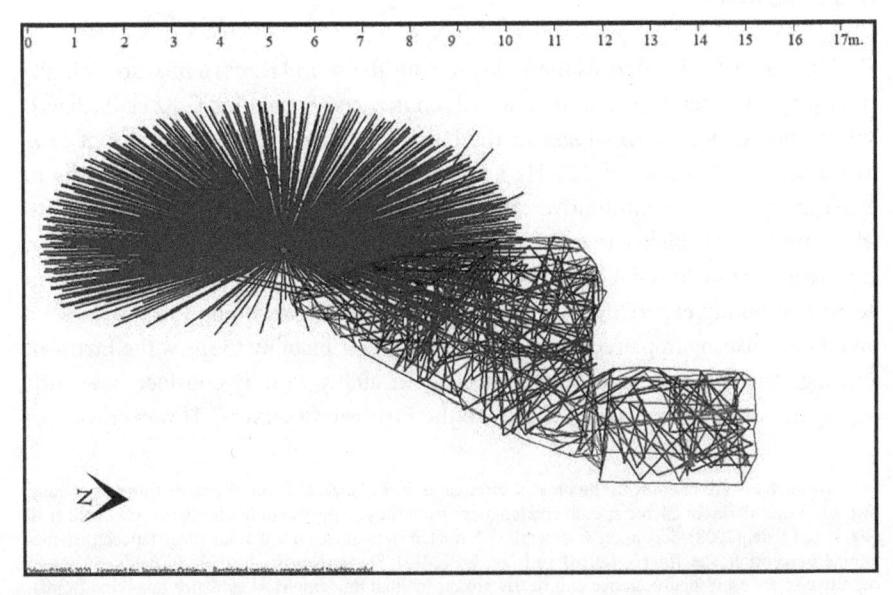

Figure 5.5 Acoustic model of the Tomba del Gallo sound propagation from a sound source placed to the left outside of the tomb. Model: JK Ortoleva. Created using Odeon acoustic modeling software.

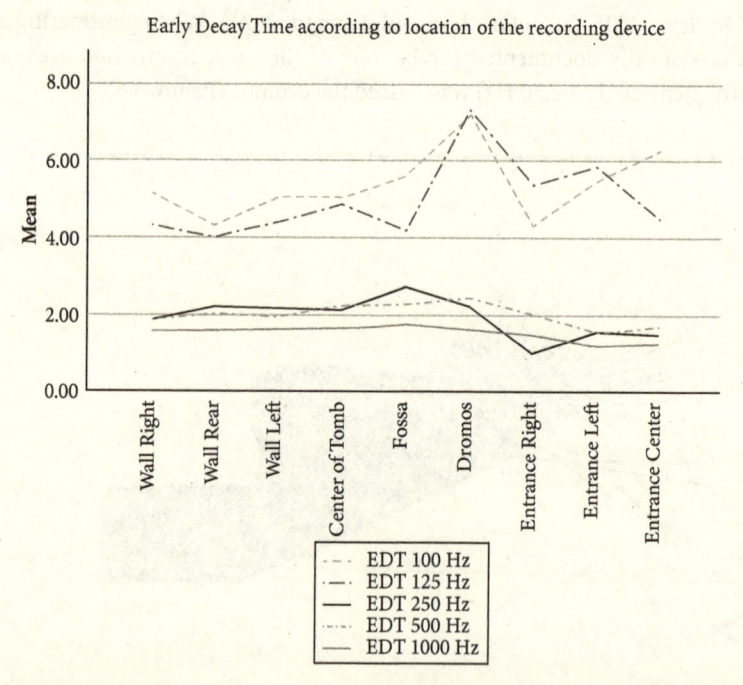

Figure 5.6 Statistical Mean of most reverberant areas inside 11 of the studied tombs across frequencies of 100–1000 Hz. Created using SPSS software by J.K. Ortoleva.

Discussion

The Tomba del Gallo offers us the ability to consider sound across a mixture of highs and lows and material versus "immaterial" constructs (Fernández-Götz et al., 2020). When contrasting the small size of the burial chamber with the intensity of low-frequency reverberation at 125 Hz and lower, the tiny chamber aurally seems to "expand" beyond its diminutive structure. During the Etruscan funerary event, while most vocals higher than 125 Hz would have diminished inside the chamber, low-frequency male vocalizations were enhanced. Such an effect would have been heard and bodily experienced by funerary participants, including those who were potentially hearing impaired (Reybrouck, 2017). Our inability to *speak* the Etruscan language (not read or write it) diminishes our ability to fully consider how such experiences would have actually "felt" to the Etruscan observer.[25] However, we can

[25] Two debates are relevant to the present discussion. First, "speech" is not the same thing as literacy. Two good summaries involving speech and language from the perspective of neuroscience are Diehl et al. (2004) and Patel (2008). Second, it is generally postulated in neuroscience that language (speech) shapes human perception; see Thierry (2016) and Lupyan (2012). Some theorists (usually in fields outside of cognitive science and neuroscience and nearly always without any empirical evidence involving human perception) have postulated that language (speech) does *not* shape human perception. Casasanto (2008) summarizes why such a perspective is lacking.

accurately discern how different processes involving sound are cognitively processed, and this in turn elucidates various clues regarding the Tarquinian burial process.

Interment actions across cultures are immersed in different sounds, whether religious chant, song, or sounds of mourning, and each type of sound affects the observer in different ways. For example, music can influence emotion and physical movement and stimulate cultural connections (Reybrouck et al., 2018). Because music is processed in the same areas of the brain as speech, the structure of music performed during the funeral in Tarquinia had the potential to emotionally affect those native to Tarquinia who learned the language before five or six years of age more so than native speakers from other cultures (e.g., Romans, Sabines, and so forth) and potentially even those from other regions of Etruria.[26] In terms of sounds connected to specific funerary actions, recent studies in neuroscience have shown that when an observer sees and/or hears a task-related sound, the same part of the brain fires as though the observer were personally enacting the activity, even if only hearing the sound (Aglioti and Pazzaglia, 2010). This suggests that if the aural isolation of one voice over others was combined with physical tasks inside the burial chamber of the Tomba del Gallo, the deposition process would have been cognitively framed (to Tarquinian observers) as a collective experience, even if only hearing or viewing such activities. The implications regarding musical instruments at the tomb site are of particular importance here.

Musical instruments such as the cornu and lituus have been discovered in funerary contexts in Tarquinia. The organic nature of lyres limits their preservation inside tombs.[27] However, plectra used to play chordophone instruments have been found in eighth- to seventh-century BCE funerary contexts.[28] Inside the Tomba dei Demoni Azzurri, tortoise (carapace) fragments were found that could indicate the presence of a chelys lyra (Cataldi Dini, 1986). The latter, while in fragments, is unusual among painted tombs and was probably found because the burial chamber was looted once rather than multiple times, as is typical with painted tombs throughout Etruria (Adinolfi et al., 2005). Indeed, the fact that all painted tombs were not intact on discovery suggests that additional instruments may have originally existed in chambered tombs and were either destroyed or removed during clandestine activities (Maras, 2018). The combination of surviving musical instruments across Etruria and tomb paintings depicting musical performance suggests that funerary rituals for Etruscan elites involved musical instruments.

[26] Although Rix has argued that there is little evidence of divergent regional dialects in Etruria, regional differences are clear with the use of consonants and vowels, and this in turn would have affected how speech was perceived (Rix, 1989, 1300–1302; 2004, 147–148). For more on early language development from the perspective of neuroscience, see Rogers et al. (2006).

[27] Lyres were largely constructed from wood, animal intestine, and, in the case of the, chelys lyra, tortoise carapaces were used for the sound box of instrument. See Sarti (2010).

[28] Intact ivory and bone plectra, used to strum string instruments, survive from eighth–seventh century tombs in Tarquinia, Vulci, and Caere (Cataldi Dini, 1986; Petrizzi, 1986; Rizzo, 1987).

Although the subterranean location of the tomb makes it easy to envision sounds inside the tomb space as isolated below the surface of the bedrock, the present acoustic data suggest otherwise. In fact, with respect to the Tomba del Gallo, sound *crosses* the visual and structural boundaries of the tomb in terms of its entrances, burial chamber, and dromos. Constructs of boundaries and thresholds in Etruria are well-documented across various contexts (Edlund-Berry, 2006; Sassatelli and Govi, 2005). However, boundaries are rarely considered from the perspective of nonvisual paradigms. Even analyses that consider presumed boundaries across the sociopolitical landscape of Etruria are often led by visual readings (Torelli, 1990). For example, the placement of necropolises in Etruria bordering urban areas, such as Tarquinia and Cerveteri, create what Riva and Stoddart describe as a "halo-like" effect, separating (and yet also linking) the living and the dead (Riva and Stoddart, 1996). Such constructs, if indeed present, were not solely guided by the visual nature of the necropolis because that is simply antithetical to how human sensory experience works.[29]

Ancestral cult rituals performed at funerary sites was a common practice throughout Etruria. So much so that some scholars have suggested that tombs may have been akin to temples and/or other devotional settings (Camporeale, 2009; Rouveret, 1974; Warden, 2016). Evidence of performative events and ritual enacted outside of multiple tomb spaces in areas such as Tarquinia, Sarteano, Cortona, and Pisa support such a conclusion. In Tarquinia, altars were physically placed inside painted tombs, as seen in the Tomba del Tifone (c. 280 BCE) and illustrated on tomb walls. Small niches flanking some dromoi in Tarquinia and in other regions such as Sarteano, were probably used to honor the dead after the inhumation process (Steingräber, 2006).

Because sound escaped the Tomba del Gallo during the burial event, the bounded nature of the tomb space expanded across physical boundaries to aurally connect those outside of the tomb with activities practiced therein. Conversely, activities practiced outside the tomb had the potential to be aurally experienced well inside del Gallo's physical entrance. This in turn suggests that the exterior of the tomb served a primary role in the funerary event, culminating with the final deposition. Funerary sounds emanating from the tomb's interior, or alternatively from the exterior of the tomb, would have aurally extended the tomb's structural boundaries, essentially funneling sound from one physical space to another and, in turn, reinforcing a perceived exchange between funerary participants, the tomb space, and the dead. The aforementioned effects of aural data, with its ability to induce the same cognitive response as if participating in associated activities, is relevant here.

Rather than the dromos simply creating a spatial "divide" between the living and the dead, as often suggested by scholars, its acoustic nature actually provided a way

---

[29] As previously intimated, human sensory cognition is not segmented into detached perceptual experiences, but rather the result of multiple sensory percepts that collectively construct perception; see Sugiyama et al. (2018) and Libby and Buschman (2021).

to aurally connect to the dead, with the dead perhaps even perceived as "speaking" in the form of intense and far-reaching reverberant effects (e.g., see Izzet, 2007). The value of a methodology that assesses sound is further supported when considering other structural devices inside the tomb space.

Steingräber and others have suggested that some structures, such as fosse, inside some burial chambers were constructed after the tomb was in full use.[30] The importance of aural phenomena in Etruria, together with the present acoustic data, suggests that we should at least contemplate whether structural devices such as wall niches may have been built to honor especially strong aural properties emerging from specific tombs or perhaps constructed to enhance the aurality of the tomb space. For example, wall niches inside dromoi are not commonly included inside Tarquinian tombs. Interestingly, the tombs that were discovered to be the most reverberant as part of the present study all have niches inside each dromos, while less reverberant tombs do not. This could be a mere coincidence considering that only fourteen tombs in Tarquinia were acoustically documented. However, we must ask ourselves if this finding indicates something more purposeful in nature. As the present study continues and new data emerge, one thing seems abundantly clear: to solely consider the painted tomb space, or any site in Etruria, entirely from a visual perspective provides a fragmented and indeed incomplete view of Etruscan cultural activities. The aural nature of the funerary event, as well as potential exchange with its exterior setting, clearly merits further investigation (Ortoleva, 2021; 2022; 2023).

Conclusion

The aural analysis, as presented here, represents the first Archaeoacoustic analysis ever attempted in pre-Roman archaeology. Emerging data from the study shed light on acoustic patterns inside chambered tombs (painted or not) with respect to architectural structures such as dromoi and wall niches and asks new questions pertaining to how we tend to envision boundaries in the Etruscan record. Future scholarship involving sound and auditory perception can assume many forms. In terms of the funerary record, the assessment of further chronologies and funerary contexts across Etruria would provide valuable data regarding sound propagation across contrasting regions.

One of the challenges encountered as part of the present study pertains to the highly delicate nature of tomb paintings and burial chambers as a whole. The limited time allowed inside each burial chamber required that a highly portable protocol be implemented to thus preserve the archaeological record during future acoustic studies involving painted and unpainted chambered tombs.[31] This was achieved with the use of portable equipment as well as sound cues, such as claps. While effective, this

---

[30] See Adinolfi et al. (2005) regarding the trench inside the Tomba dei Demoni Azzurri.
[31] Per the dictates of the Soprintendenza, 15–20 minutes was allowed inside each burial chamber. Such constraints are intended to preserve the delicate nature of surviving tomb paintings.

made many other sound cues unviable.[32] To further employ additional impulse response options, such as white or pink noise, a more specialized system is required. This ultimately led to the design and construction of a new portable wireless sound device to use inside future tomb sites that would allow quicker setup and assessment of a sound field while fully protecting especially delicate contexts such as painted tombs (Figure 5.7).[33]

If we truly want the field of Etruscan archaeology to expand, we must extend across more diverse audiences and therefore outside of more traditional forums involving Roman and pre-Roman archaeology (see Potts and Smith, 2021; Stoddart, 2020; Warden, 2016). It is thus worth noting that collaboration between Etruscan specialists and acoustic as well as mechanical engineers and those in fields such as cognitive science and neuroscience provides a viable way to broaden pre-Roman

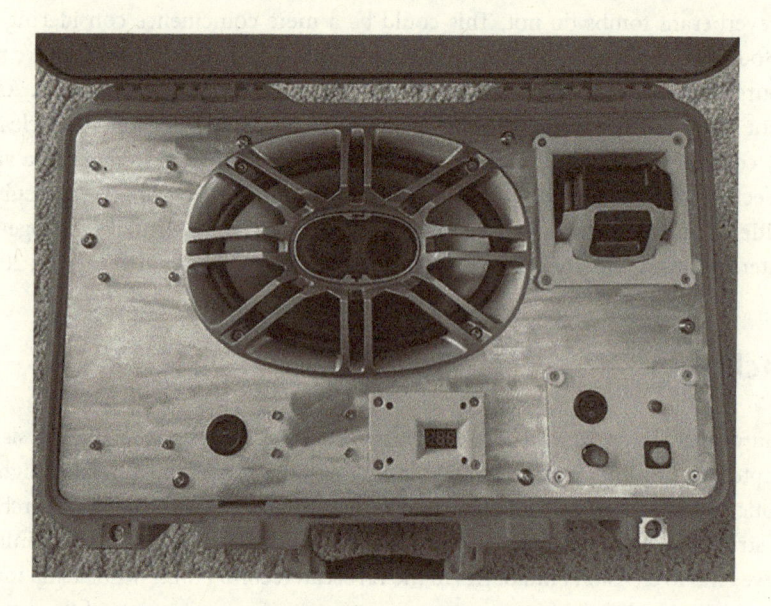

Figure 5.7 Wireless sound system built as a result of the present study. Device designed by Tyler Ryynanen under the supervision of Dr Andrew Barnard at Michigan Technical University upon consult with J.K. Ortoleva.

[32] In acoustic science, reverberation is defined as the accumulation of sound within a confined or semi-confined space that reflects across all surfaces, magnifying the initial sound energy until ultimately ceasing (Diaz-Andreu et al., 2017). Reverberation therefore amplifies sound as though a microphone is used, and the longer reverberation spans, the more startling the effect may seem. Reverberation can only be measured with a valid impulse response (IR). This can be as simple as hand claps or white noise. Other IR involve the sound of a starter pistol, bursting balloon, and other sounds that generate a quick burst of energy and gradual de-escalation of sound across a wide range of frequencies. A good summary regarding impulse responses is Guidorzia et al. (2015).

[33] Wireless speaker system built as a result of the present study. I am grateful to Tyler Ryynanen and multiple other graduate students who, after consultation with J. K. Ortoleva, designed and tested each device under the supervision of Andrew Barnard at Michigan Technological University, Houghton, Michigan, USA (Ortoleva and Barnard, 2021).

scholarship across new fields of inquiry. Another completely untapped application of acoustic and cognitive science involves burial objects.

Although the aurality of burial objects was minimally reviewed in this chapter, clarifying how different objects may have enhanced or stymied the acoustic nature of chambered tombs is important, particularly with higher-frequency sounds.[34] For example, we know a great deal regarding the visual nature of the terracotta slabs placed inside tombs in Cerveteri and other regions, and yet what do we know regarding their aurality? As noted here, while the recognition of boundaries is well known across different Etruscan regions, it is interesting how rarely scholars have considered the extent to which sound(s) were projected (or not) across different contexts and chronologies (Colonna, 1985; Edlund-Berry, 2006, 2018; Potts, 2015). Acoustic modeling tools, as shown here with the Tomba del Gallo, provide an additional way to further assess such interactions while also modeling sites that have been transformed as a result of modern and/or environmental changes (e.g., through the integration of modern building materials). The use of acoustic modeling to study different landscape settings is also potentially fruitful.[35]

Modern assessments of tomb paintings involve visual analyses of ancient images based on what we presume tomb paintings may "mean." An aural analysis, particularly one explored through a cognitive lens, provides replicable aural data involving the tomb structure itself. When adhering to a scientifically sound acoustic protocol, the resulting data are driven by physics, not our own perceptions regarding what different images may have presumably "represented" to the Etruscan observer.[36] Such interpretation, especially when applied alongside more traditional approaches (e.g., epigraphic studies), provides a more balanced understanding of Etruscan funerary experiences.

Extensive evidence exists of sonic recognition in Etruria—ranging from the documentation of bird calls, thunder, and other natural phenomena to the incorporation of musical performance across different contexts—portrays a society that clearly emphasized specific types of sounds.[37] A cognitive approach that acknowledges the importance of sound in Etruria provides a more direct link to such observation. As recently noted elsewhere, perhaps it is now our turn to pause and indeed listen (Ortoleva, 2021, 1191).

Acknowledgments

Thank you to Maurizio Forte for the kind invitation to participate in the present volume. This present study was supported by a fellowship from the Etruscan Foundation. Thank you to MiBACT—Soprintendenza Archeologia, Belle Arti e

---

[34] Reviewed in extensive detail in Ortoleva (2022).

[35] See Ortoleva (2022); currently being studied at the University of Oxford as part of a Leverhulme Trust funded study (Leverhulme Early Career Fellowship.

[36] Discussant comments delivered by P. Gregory Warden at the American Institute of Archaeology's 123rd annual meeting, January 6, 2022.

[37] Cic. *De Div.* 1.41.92; 2.38.80; Sen. *QNat.* 2.32.2; Ov., *Fast.* 4.812–18; Livy 1.34.3–10.

Paesaggio per l'area di Roma, e di Viterbo e l'Etruria Meridionale—for kindly providing access to the Tomba del Gallo.

Dedication

This chapter is dedicated to the memory of Louise Ortoleva, whom we lost in June 2021. Your light lives on, Lou.

Ancient Sources

Corocan, T. H. *Seneca: Naturales quaestiones.* London: Heinemann, 1971.

Falconer, W. A. *Cicero: De Senectute de Amicitia de Divinatione.* Cambridge, MA: Harvard University Press, 1923.

Foster, B. O. *Livy in Fourteen Volumes.* London: Heinemann, 1924.

Frazer, J. G. *Ovid: Fasti.* Loeb Classical Library Volume. London: Heinemann, 1931.

Granger, F. *Vitruvius on Architecture.* Cambridge, MA: Harvard University Press, 1931.

Rackham, H. *Naturalis historia.* Cambridge, MA: Harvard University Press, 1938.

Scholfield, A. F. *De Natura Animalium.* Cambridge, MA: Harvard University Press, 1958.

Turfa, J. M. *Divining the Etruscan World: The Brontoscopic Calendar and Religious Practice.* Cambridge: Cambridge University Press, 2012.

Bibliography

Adinolfi, G., R. Carmagnola, and M. Cataldi. "La tomba dei Demoni Azzurri: Lo scavo di una tomba violate." *Atti del XXXIII Convegno di Studi Etruschi e Italici.* Pisa: Studi Etruschi, Oct. 1, (2005), 431–447.

Aglioti, S. M., and M. Pazzaglia. "Representing actions through their sound." *Experimental Brain Research* 206.2 (2010), 141–51.

Amann, P. *Die Etruskerin. Geschlechterverhdltnis und Stellung der Frau im frilhen Etrurien. (9.-5.jh.v.Chr.).*Vienna: Osterreichische Akademie der Wissenschaften, 2000.

Avramidou, A. "Attic vases in Etruria: Another view on the divine banquet cup by the Codrus Painter." *American Journal of Archaeology* 110.4 (2006), 565–579.

Avramidou, A. "The Phersu game revisited." Etruscan Studies, 12:1, (2009), 73–88.

Betts, E., ed. *Senses of the Empire: Multisensory Approaches to Roman Culture.* London: Routledge, 2017.

Bidelman, G., and A. Krishnan. "Effects of reverberation on brainstem representation of speech in musicians and non-musicians." *Brain Research* 1355 (2010), 112–125.

Bonfante, Larissa. "Etruscan couples and their aristocratic society." *Women's Studies: An Interdisciplinary Journal* 8.1-2 (1981): 157–187.

Bonfante, L. "Nudity as a costume in classical art." *American Journal of Archaeology* 4 (1989), 543–570.

Bonghi Jovino, M. "Gli scavi nell'abitato di Tarquinia e la scoperta dei "bronzi" in un preliminare inquadramento." In *Tarquinia: Ricerche scavi prospettive (atti del convegno internazionale di studi La Lombardia per gli Etruschi*, edited by M. Bonghi Jovino and C. Chiaramonte Treré. 59–70. Rome: L'Erma di Bretschneider (1987).

Bonghi Jovino, M. "Tarquinia, testimonianze archeologiche e Ricostruzione storica". Scavi sistematici nell'abitato, Campagne 1982–1988." I materiali 2, Roma. Bonghi Jovino (ed.). Roma: L'Erma di Bretschneider (2001).

Borrelli, L. V. "Techniques and conservation of Etruscan painting." In *Etruscan Painting: Catalogue Raisonné of Etruscan Wall Painting*, edited by S. Steingräber. New York: Johnson Reprint, 1986.

Brandt, J. R. "Emotions in a liminal space: A look at Etruscan tomb paintings." In *Reading Roman Emotions*, edited by H. von Ehrenheim and M. Prusac-Lindhagen, 41–68. Stockholm: Stockholm University, 2020.

Camporeale, G. *The Deified Deceased in Etruscan Culture: New Perspectives on Etruria and Early Rome*, edited by S. Bell and H. Nagy. Madison: University of Wisconsin Press, 2009.

Caneva, G., S. Langone, F. Bartoli, A. Cecchini, and C. Meneghini. "Vegetation cover and tumuli's shape as affecting factors of microclimate and biodeterioration risk for the conservation of Etruscan tombs (Tarquinia, Italy)." *Sustainability* 13.6 (2021), 3393.

Carrese, M. "La documentazione degli strumenti e oggetti sonori in Etruria alla luce della classificazione organologica." In *La musica in Etruria: Atti del convegno internazionale, Tarquinia, 18–20.9.2009*, edited by M. Carrese, E. Li Castro, and M. Martinelli, 229–268. Tarquinia: Assessorato alla Cultura, 2010.

Casasanto, D. "Who's afraid of the big bad Whorf? Crosslinguistic differences in temporal language and thought." *Language Learning* 58 (2008), 63–79.

Cataldi Dini, M. "Tarquinia nel Mediterraneo." In *Gli Etruschi di Tarquinia. Catalogo della Mostra Milano*, edited by M. Bonghi Jovino: 203–206. Modena: Edizioni Panini, 1986.

Cavagnaro Vanoni, L. "Tarquinia: Sei tombe a camera nella necropoli dei Monterozzi, localita Calvario." *NSc* 97 (1972), 148–194.

Cavagnaro Vanoni, L. "Tarquinia (Viterbo): Sei tombe intatte nella necropoli dei Monterozzi in localita Calvario." *NSc* 102 (1977), 157–204.

Cavagnaro Vanoni, L. 1997. "Dromoi non completati e l'utilizzo dello spazio nella necropoli dei Monterozzi." In Etrusca et Italica, Scritti in Ricordo di Massimo Pallottino. Roma, (1997), 117–130.

Chen, G-T. "The pitch range of English and Chinese speakers." *Journal of Chinese Linguistics* 2 (1974), 159–171.

Clark, A. "Whatever next? Predictive brains, situated agents, and the future of cognitive science." *Behavioral and Brain Sciences* 36.3 (2013), 181–204.

Colonna, G. "Le Forme ideologich della citta." In *Civilta degli Etruschi*, edited by M. Cristofani, 249–289. Milan: Electa, 1985.

Colonna, G. "Strutture Teatriformi in Etruria." In *Spectacles Sportifs et Scéniques dans le Monde Étrusco-Italique*, Collection de l'École française de Rome, 321–347. Rome: École Française de Rome, 1993.

Colonna, G. "Ancora su Śur/Śuri: L'attributo del fulmine." *Studi Etruschi* 75 (2009), 9–32.

Colonna, G. "I santuari comunitari e il culto delle divinità catactonie in Etruria." *Annali della Fondazione per il Museo Claudio Faina* 19 (2012), 203–226.

Craighero, L. "The role of the motor system in cognitive functions." In *The Routledge Handbook of Embodied Cognition*, edited by L. Shapiro, 51–58. Boston: Routledge, 2014.

Cristofani, M. "Il banchetto in Etruria." In *L'Alimentazione nel mondo antico: Gli Etruschi*, edited by C. Ampolo et al., 123–132. Rome: Istituto Poligrafico dello Stato, 1987.

D'Agostino, S., G. Lombardi, R. Gianpiero, and C. Viggiani "Structural engineering and geology applied to the static problems of the Etruscan Tomba dell'Orco." *Journal of Cultural Heritage* 11.1 (2010), 107–112.

d'Errico, F., Henshilwood, C., Lawson, G., Vanhaeren, M., Tillier, A-M., Soressi, M., Julien, M. "Archaeological evidence for the emergence of language, symbolism, and music - An alternative multidisciplinary perspective." Journal of World Prehistory, 17, (2003), 1–70.

de Grummond, N. T. "*The Sanctuary of the Etruscan Artisans at Cetamura del Chiant: The Legacy of Alvaro Tracchi.*" Florence: Edifir, 2009.

de Grummond, N. T. "Thunder versus lightning in Etruria." *Etruscan Studies* 19.2 (2016), 183–207.

Diaz-Andreu, M., G. Atienzar, C. G. Benito, and T. Mattioli. "Do you hear what I see?: Analysing visibility and audibility in the rock art landscape of the Alicante mountains of Spain." *Journal of Anthropological Research* 73.2 (2017), 181–213.

Diehl, R. L., A. Lotto, and L. Holt. "Speech perception." *Annual Review of Psychology* 55 (2004), 149–79.

Edlund-Berry, I. "Ritual space and boundaries in Etruscan religion." In: The Religion of the Etruscans, edited by N. T. de Grummond and E. Simon, 116–131, Austin: University of Texas Press, 2006.

Edlund-Berry, I. "Acque Sacre nel territorio etrusco." In *Acque Sacre, culto etrusco sull'Appennino toscano, 28 settembre 2017–28 febbraio 2018, Palazzo del Pegaso, Firenze*, edited by A. Nocentini, S. Sarti, and P. G. Warden, 33–40 Firenze: Tipografia del Consiglio regionale della Toscana, 2018.

Fernández-Götz, M., D. Maschek, and N. ,Roymans, N. "The dark side of the Empire: Roman expansionism between object agency and predatory regime." *Antiquity* 94.378 (2020), 1630–1639.

Forte, M., and H. Murteira. *Digital Cities between History and Archaeology*. Oxford: Oxford University Press, 2020.

Goldstein, T. R. , and P. Goldstein Bloom. "The mind on stage: Why cognitive scientists should study acting." *Trends in Cognitive Sciences* 15 (2011), 4.

Graham, E-J. "Memory and materiality: Re-embodying the Roman funeral." In, Memory and mourning: studies on Roman death. edited by V. Hope and J. Huskinson, 21–39. Oxford: Oxbow, 2011.

Graham, E-J. "Interactional sensibilities: Bringing ancient disability studies to its archaeological senses." In *The Forgotten Other: Disability Studies and the Classical Body*, Studies in Ancient Disabilities, edited by E. Adams, London: Routledge, 165–191. 2021.

Guidorzia, P., L. Barbaresia, D. D'Orazioa, and M. Garaia. "Impulse responses measured with MLS or Swept-Sine signals applied to architectural acoustics: An in-depth analysis of the two methods and some case studies of measurements inside theatres." *Science Direct, Energy Procedia* 78 (2016), 1611–1616.

IIagel, S. "Better understanding the Louvre Aulos." *Studien zur Musikarchäologie* 9 (2014), 131–142.

Hamilton, S., and R. Whitehouse. *Neolithic Spaces: Social and Sensory Landscapes of the First Farmers of Italy*. Specialist Studies on Italy 19.1 London: Accordia Research Institute, University of London, 2020.

Henley, T. B., M. J. Rossano, and E. P. Kardas. *Handbook of Cognitive Archaeology, Psychology in Prehistory*. Boston: Routledge, 2020.

Hodgson, D. "Emanations of the Mind: Upper Paleolithic Art as a Visual Phenomenon." Time and Mind 5:2, (2012), 185–193.

Holloway, R. "The bulls in the 'Tomb of the Bulls' at Tarquinia." *American Journal of Archaeology* 90.4 (1986), 447–452.

Izzet, V. "Form and meaning in Etruscan ritual space." *Cambridge Archaeological Journal* 11.2 (2001), 185–200.

Izzet, V. *The Archaeology of Etruscan Society*. Cambridge: Cambridge University Press, 2007.

Jackson, L. "The poverty of structuralism: Literature and structuralist theory." (1991), New York: Longman.

Jannot, J. "L'aulos étrusque." *ArchCl* 43 (1974), 118–142.

Jannot, J. "La lyre et la cithare, les instruments à cordes de la musique étrusque." *ArchCl* 48.2 (1979), 469–507.

Jannot, J. "Musiques et musiciens étrusques." *Comptes rendus des séances de l'Académie des Inscriptions et Belles-Lettres* 132.2 (1988), 311–334.

Johnson, K. O. "The roles and functions of cutaneous mechanoreceptors." *Current Opinions in Neurobiology* 11 (2001), 455–461.

Jordan, P. "Searching for ancient sonic experience in present-day landscapes." *Archeologia e Calcolatori* 32.1 (2021), 439–456.

Kolar, M. A. "Sensing sonically at Andean Formative Chavín de Huántar, Perú." *Time and Mind* 10 (2017), 39–59.

Laughlin, C. D. "Neuroarchaeology." *Time and Mind* 8.4 (2015), 335–349.

Lawergren, B. "Lyres in the West (Italy, Greece) and the East (Egypt, the Near East) ca. 2000–400 B.C." *OmRom* 19.6 (1993), 55–76.

Lawergren, B. "Etruscan musical instruments and their wider context in Greece and Italy." *Etruscan and Italic Studies* 10 (2007), 119–138.

Libby, A., and T. J. Buschman. "Rotational dynamics reduce interference between sensory and memory representations." *Nature Neuroscience* 24 (2021), 715–726.

Li Castro, E. "Etruscan music." In *Etruscology*, edited by A. Naso. Boston: De Gruyter, 2017, 505–21.

Linington, R., and F. R. Serra Ridgway. *Lo scavo nel Fondo Scataglini a Tarquinia, Vol. I: Testo and Vol. II: Tavole*. Milan: Fondazione Ing. Carlo M. Lerici del politecnico di Milano, 1997.

Linos, D. "Music meets surgery: Two sides to the art of healing." *Surgical Endoscopy* 27.1 (2012), 2525–2528.

Lupyan, G. "Linguistically modulated perception and cognition: The label-feedback hypothesis." *Frontiers in Psychology* 3 (2012), 54.

Maggiani, A. "Modello etico o antenato eroico? The plea of suicidal Ajax in Felsinee stele," *StEtr*, 63, (1999), 149–165.

Malafouris, L. "Before and beyond representation: Towards an enactive conception of the palaeolithic image." In *Image and Imagination a Global Prehistory of Figurative Representation*, edited by C. Renfrew and I. Morley, 287–300. Cambridge: McDonald Institute for Archaeological Research, 2007.

Malafouris, L. "Beads for a plastic mind: The "Blind Man's Stick" (BMS) hypothesis and the active nature of material culture." *Cambridge Archaeological Journal* 18 (2008), 401–414.

Malafouris, L. *How Things Shape the Mind: A Theory of Material Engagement*. Cambridge, MA: MIT Press, 2013.

Maras, D. F. "Gods, men, turtles: Terracotta lyre-players in Etruscan votive deposits." In *Representations of Musicians in the Coroplastic Art of the Ancient World: Iconography, Ritual Contexts and Functions, Proceedings of the Conference*, edited by A. Bellia and C. Marconi, 163–178. Telestes: Studi e ricerche di archeologia musicale nel Mediterraneo 2, New York, 2015. Rome: Istituti Editoriali e Poligrafici Internazionali, 2016.

Maras, D. F. "Dancing myths: Musical performances with mythological subjects from Greece to Etruria." In *The Study of Musical Performance in Antiquity: Archaeology and Written Sources*, edited by C. Tavolieri, L. Verderame, and A. Garcia-Ventura, 137–154. Newcastle upon Tyne: Cambridge Scholars, 2018.

Martinelli, M. *Spettacolo e sport in Etruria: Musica, danza, agonismo e rappresentazioni tra Italia e Mediterraneo*. Florence: Regione Toscana, 2007.

Martinelli, M., and R. Melini. "L'aulos etrusco di Chianciano: Indagini attraverso la comparazione archeologica ed iconografica." In *La musica in Etruria: Atti del convegno internazionale, Tarquinia, 18–20.9.2009*, edited by M. Carrese, E. Li Castro, and M. Martinelli, 93–120. Tarquinia: Assessorato alia Cultura, 2010.

Marzullo, M. *Spazi sepolti e dimensioni dipinte nelle tombe etrusche di Tarquinia*. Tarchna suppl. 7. Milan, Ledizioni, 2017.

Marzullo, M. *Grotte Cornetane: Materiali e apparato critico per lo studio delle tombe dipinte di Tarquinia*. Tarchna suppl. 6. Milan: Ledizioni Ledi Publishing, 2018.

Morandi, A. *Le pitture della tomba del Cardinale: Monumenti della pittura antica scoperti in Italia sez*. Rome: I Tarquiniifasc, vi, 1983.

Naso, A. "All'origine della pittura etrusca: Decorazione parietale e architettura funeraria in Etruria meridionale nel VII sec. a.C." *JRGZM* 37.2 (for 1990; 1995), 439–499.

Naso, A. *Architetture Dipinte*. Roma: L'Erma di Bretschneider, 1996.

Naso, A. "Death and dying." In *Etruscology*, edited by A. Naso, 317–39. Berlin: De Gruyter, 2017.

Ortoleva, J. K. "Sounds of Etruria: Aural characteristics of the Tomba dell'Orco, Tarquinia." Antiquity 95.383 (2021), 1179–1194.

Ortoleva, J. K. "Making sense of landscape: A new study of sound propagation between Tarquinian funerary and habitation settings." *Journal of Etruscan and Italic Studies* 25.1–2 (2022), 79–112.

Ortoleva, J. K. "Visions of light: An investigation of visual perception inside the Etruscan painted tomb space." *Journal of Archaeological Science* 160.105887 (2023), 1–18.

Ortoleva, J.K. 2023. "Sounds of the blue daemon: a new aural study of the Etruscan Tomba dei Demoni Azzurri, 450–430 BCE." *Journal of Archaeological Science: Reports*, 49: 104000, 1–11. 2023.

Ortoleva, J. K. "Light and vision inside the Tomba degli Hescanas, Orvieto (Porano), c.350–325 BCE." *Journal of Archaeological Science Reports* Special Edition 53 (2024), 104286.

Ortoleva, J. K., and A. Barnard. "Sound properties of painted tombs." *Journal of the Acoustical Society of America*, 150 (4_Supplement), A249–A249. 2021.

Overmann, K. A. "The role of materiality in numerical cognition." Quaternary International. 405. (2016), 42–51.

Pallottino, M. "Tarquinia." *Monumenti Antichi* 36 (1937), 5–594.

Pallottino, M. *Etruscan Painting*. Lausanne: Skira Color Studio, 1952.

Pallottino, M. *Art of the Etruscans*. New York: Vanguard Press, 1955a.

Pallottino, M. *Etruscologia*, 3rd ed. Milan: Hoepli, 1955b.

Patel, A. *Music, Language, and the Brain*. New York: Oxford University Press, 2008.

Petrizzi, C.V. "Il tumulo monumentale di Poggio Gallinaro." In: Gli Etruschi di Tarquinia. Catalogo della Mostra, edited by Jovino, M. Bonghi, 206–15. Milano: Modena, Edizioni Panini. 1986.

Pfiffig, A. J. *Religio Etrusca*. Graz: Akademische Druck- u. Verlagsanstalt, 1975.

Potts, C. R. *Religious Architecture in Latium and Etruria, c.900–500 BC*. Oxford Monographs on Classical Archaeology. Oxford: Oxford University Press, 2015.

Potts, C. R., and C. Smith. "The Etruscans: Setting new agendas." *Journal of Archaeological Research* 30, (2022), 597–644.

Prayon, F. *Frühetruskische Grab- und Hausarchitektur*. Heidelberg: F. H. Kerle, 1975.

Prew, G. "How to dress a corpse: Funerary dress and the construction of the funeral at Gabii and Osteria dell'Osa." 122nd Joint Annual Meeting of the Archaeological Institute of America and the Society for Classical Studies. Virtual, January 3–7, 2021.

Rathje, A. "The adoption of the Homeric banquet in central Italy in the Orientalizing period." In *Sympotica: The Papers of a Symposium on the Symposium, Oxford 1984*, edited by O. Murray, 279–288. Oxford: Oxford University Press, 1990.

Reinhart, P. N., and P. E. Souza. "Listener factors associated with individual susceptibility to reverberation." *Journal of the American Academy of Audiology* 29.1 (2018), 73–82.

Renfrew, C. "Divided we stand: Aspects of archaeology and information." *American Antiquity* 48.1 (1983), 3–16.

Renfrew, C. "Towards a cognitive archaeology." In *The Ancient Mind: Elements of Cognitive Archaeology*, edited by C. Renfrew and E. B. W. Zubrow, 3–12. Cambridge: Cambridge University Press, 1994.

Renfrew, C., C. Frith, and L. Malfouris. *The Sapient Mind: Archaeology Meets Neuroscience*. New York: Oxford University Press, 2009.

Reybrouck, M. "Perceptual immediacy in music listening: Multimodality and the in time/outside of time dichotomy." *Versus* 124 (2017), 89–104.

Reybrouck M., T. Eerola T., and P. Podlipniak. "Editorial: Music and the functions of the brain: Arousal, emotions, and pleasure." *Frontiers in Psychology* 9 (2018), 113.

Reznikoff, I. "On the sound dimension of prehistoric painted caves and rocks." In *Musical Signification*, edited by E. Taratsi. 541–558, Berlin: Mouton de Gruyter, 1995.

Reznikoff, I. "The evidence of the use of sound resonance from Palaeolithic to Medieval times." In *Archaeoacoustics*, edited by C. Scarre and G. Lawson, 77–84. Cambridge: McDonald Institute Monographs, 2006.

Reznikoff, I., and M. ,Dauvois. "La dimension sonore des grottes ornées." *Bulletin de la Société Préhistorique Française* 85 (1988), 238–246.

Riva, C., and S. Stoddart. "Ritual landscapes in archaic Etruria." In *Approaches to the Study of Ritual: Italy and the Mediterranean*, edited by J. B. Wilkins, 91–109. London: Accordia, 1996.

Riva, C. *The Urbanisation of Etruria: Funerary Practices and Social Change, 700–600 BC*. Cambridge: Cambridge University Press, 2010.

Rix, H. "Per una grammatica storica dell'etrusco." In *Secondo Congresso Internazionale Etrusco, Firenze 26 Maggio–2 Giugno 1985, vol. 3: 1293–1306*. Rome: Bretschneider, 1989.

Rix, H. "Etruscan." In *The Ancient Languages of Europe*, edited by R. Woodard, 943–966. Cambridge: Cambridge University Press. 2004.

Rizzo, M. A. "La Ceramica a Figure Nere, and La Ceramica a Figure Rosse." In *La Ceramica degli Etruschi*, edited by M. Martelli, 31–42. Rome: L'Erma di Bretschneider, 1987.

Robbs, J. "Beyond agency." *World Archaeology* 42.4 (2010), 493–520.

Rogers, C., J. Lister, and D. Febo. "Effects of bilingualism, noise, and reverberation on speech perception by listeners with normal hearing." *Applied Psycholinguistics* 27 (2006), 465–485.

Roncalli, F. "Iconographie Funéraire Et Topographie De L'au-delà En Étrurie." Les Plus Religieux Des Hommes, 1997, 37–54.

Roth, R. "Regionalism: towards a new perspective of cultural change in central Italy, c. 350–100 BC," Roselaar, 2012, 17–34.

Rouveret, Agnès. "La Tombe du Plongeur et les fresques étrusques: Témoignages sur la peinture grecque." *Revue Archéologique* 1 (1974), 15–32.

Sarti S. "Gli strumenti a corda degli etruschi: uso e iconografia." In: La Musica in Etruria, atti del convegno internazionale Tarquinia 18-20 settembre 2009, edited by M. Carrese, E. Li Castro & M. Martinelli, Tarquinia, 185–204, (2010).

Sassatelli, G., and E. Govi. *Culti, forma urbana, e artigianato a Marzabotto: Nuove prospettive di ricerca*. Bologna: Ante Quem, 2005.

Serra Ridgway, F. R. "Revisiting the Etruscan underworld." *Accordia Research Papers* 10 (2004), 127–141.

Skeates, R. *An Archaeology of the Senses: Prehistoric Malta*. Oxford: Oxford University Press, 2010.

Spivey, N. *Etruscan Art*. London: Thames and Hudson, 1997.

Steingräber, S. *Etruscan Painting: Catalogue Raisonné of Etruscan Wall Painting*. New York: Johnson Reprint, 1986.

Steingräber, S. "Abundance of life: Etruscan wall painting." Translated by Russell Stockman. Los Angeles: J. Paul Getty Museum. (2006).

Stoddart, S. *Power and Place in Etruria: The Spatial Dynamics of a Mediterranean Civilization, 1200–500 BC*. Cambridge: Cambridge University Press, 2020.

Stopponi, S. "Notizie preliminari dallo scavo di Campo della Fiera." *AnnFaina* 14 (2007), 493–530.

Stopponi, S. "Campo della Fiera di Orvieto: Nuove acquisizioni." *Annali della Fondazione per il Museo Claudio Faina*, 16 (2009), 425–478.

Stout, D., and T. Chaminade. "The evolutionary neuroscience of tool making." *Neuropsychologia* 45 (2007), 1091–1100.

Sugiyama, S., N. Takeuchi, and K. Inui. "Effect of acceleration of auditory inputs on the primary somatosensory cortex in humans." Science Reports 8 (2018), 12883.

Sutkowska, O. "Etruscan and Greek Double Pipes. An Iconographical Comparison of Their Organology." Ln: La musica in Etruria. Atti del convegno internazionale, Tarquinia 18-20.9. 2009, M. Carrese, E. Li Castro & M. Martinelli (eds.), Tarquinia: Assessorato alla Cultura, 79–92. (2010).

Taylor, L. "Reading the ritual: Representation and meaning on an Etruscan funerary monument in Perugia." *Etruscan and Italic Studies* 23.1–2 (2020), 3–28.

Tchumatchenko, T., and T. Reichenbach. "A cochlear-bone wave can yield a hearing sensation as well as otoacoustic emission." *Nature Communications* 5 (2014), 1–10.

Thierry, G. "Neurolinguistic relativity: How language flexes human perception and cognition." *Language Learning* 66.3 (2016), 690–713.

Till, R. "Sound archaeology: A study of the acoustics of three world heritage sites, Spanish prehistoric painted caves, Stonehenge, and Paphos theatre." *Acoustics* 1 (2019), 661–692.

Torelli, M. "Tre studi di storia etrusca." *DArch* 8.1 (1975), 3–78.

Torelli, M. "Il santuario Greco di Gravisca." *La parola del passato*, 32 (1977), 398–458.

Torelli, M. "Storia degli Etruschi." Bari: Laterza, (1981).

Torelli, M. "Ideologia e rappresentazione nelle tombe tarquiniesi dell'Orco I e II." Dialoghi di Archeologia, 2, (1983), 7–17.

Torelli, M. "Funera Tusca: Reality and representation in archaic Tarquinian painting." In *The Art of Ancient Spectacle*, edited by B. Berman and C. Kondoleon. 146–161, New Haven: Yale, 1999.

Waller, S. J. "Rock art acoustics in the past, present and future: American Indian rock art." In special issue edited by P. Whitehead, W. Whitehead, and L. Loendorf, 11–20. *1999 IRAC Proceedings* 2 (1999), 26. Tucson: American Rock Art Research Association, 2002.

Watson, A., and D. Keating. "Architecture and sound: An acoustic analysis of megalithic monuments in prehistoric Britain." *Antiquity* 73 (1999), 325–336.

Warden, P. G. "The blood of animals: Predation and transformation in Etruscan funerary representation." In *New Perspectives on Etruria and Rome: Papers in Honor of Richard D. DePuma*, edited by S. Bell and I. Nagy, 198–219. Madison: The University of Wisconsin Press, 2009.

Warden, P. G. "The temple is a living thing: Fragmentation, enchainment, and the reversal of ritual at the acropolis sanctuary of Poggio Colla." In *The Archaeology of Sanctuaries and Ritual in Etruria*, edited by N. T. de Grummond and I. Edlund-Berry. 55–67. Portsmouth, RI: Journal of Roman Archaeology, 2010.

Warden, P. G. "Monumental embodiment: Somatic symbolism and the Tuscan temple." In *Monumentality in Etruscan and Early Roman Architecture: Ideology and Innovation*, edited by M. Thomas and G. Meyers, 82–110. Austin: University of Texas Press, 2012.

Warden, P. G. "Communicating with the gods: Sacred space in Etruria." In *A Companion to the Etruscans*, edited by A. Carpino and S. Bell. 162–178. Malden, MA: John Wiley & Sons, Inc., 2016.

Warden, P. G. "Devoti in bronzo." In *Acque Sacre, culto etrusco sull'Appennino toscano, 28 settembre 2017–28 febbraio 2018, Palazzo del Pegaso, Firenze*, edited by A. Nocentini, S. Sarti, and P. G. Warden, 21–32. Firenze: Tipografia del Consiglio regionale della Toscana, 2018.

Warden, P. G. "Discussant comments: Dynamics of scale: Manipulation, perception and agency in Pre-Roman Italy." 123rd Joint Annual Meeting of the Archaeological Institute of America and the Society for Classical Studies. Virtual, January 5–7, 2022.

Warden, P. G., A. Nocentini, and S. Sarti. *Acque Sacre, culto Etrusco sull'Appennino Toscano.* Florence: Consignio Regionale della Toscana, 2018.

Warden, P. G., A. Nocentini, and S. Sarti. "The Etruscan way of death" In *The Temple and the Tomb*, edited by P. G. Warden, From the Temple and the Tomb, Meadows Museum, SMU, 95–113.

Warden, P. G., and M. Thomas. *Archaic Etruscan Tomb Painting: Five Tarquinian Tombs.* Dallas, TX: Southern Methodist University, 1999.

Weber Lehmann, C. 1986 "The Archaic period." In *Etruscan Painting*, edited by S. Steingräber, 44–53. Harcourt Brace-Johnson Reprint, New York, 1986.

Jacqueline K. Ortoleva, *Sounds Beneath the Surface: A New Cognitive Approach to the Etruscan Funerary Space* In: *A New Etruscan Archaeology: Twenty-First Century Techniques and Methods.* Edited by: Maurizio Forte, Oxford University Press. © Oxford University Press 2025. DOI:10.1093/9780197582053.003.0006

6

The NeuroARTifact Project

Seeing with the Mind

Maurizio Forte, Vincenza Ferrara, Marco Mingione, Pierfrancesco Alaimo Di Loro, Andrea Giorgi, Stefano Menicocci, Fabio Babiloni, and Marco Iosa

When an artifact is observed, a complex interplay of cognitive, emotional, and perceptual processes takes place within the observer's mind (Freedberg and Gallese, 2007).

From a neuroaesthetic perspective, the observation of an artifact involves the activation of various brain regions associated with visual processing, attention, memory, and emotion. The conscious experience of observing an artifact may include the recognition of its physical properties, such as shape, color, and texture, as well as the cognitive processing of its cultural and historical context. Thus, during observation, a complex interplay of cognitive, affective, and perceptual processes occurs in the observer's consciousness when an artifact is scrutinized.

In addition, subjective and subliminal responses may be elicited during the observation of an artifact that are not readily apparent to the observer. Individual experiences, time and space during the exposure, and preexisting knowledge of the observer may exert an impact on these responses. For instance, an artifact may elicit emotions of inquiry or astonishment in one observer while evoking sentiments of nostalgia or familiarity in another. The subjective reactions described are facilitated through the engagement of brain regions that are responsible for processing emotions, including the amygdala and the insula.

The act of observing an artifact can be comprehended as a cognitive process of meaning-making, wherein the observer actively constructs an interpretation of the object by drawing on their preexisting knowledge and experiences. The integration of bottom-up perceptual information with top-down cognitive processes, including attention, memory, and reasoning, constitutes the core process. Individual beliefs and aesthetic inclinations may all impact the observer's analysis and interpretation of the artifact.

Within the realm of material culture, the term "art object" possesses a multifaceted and intricate definition. An art object, as defined from a neuroaesthetic standpoint, encompasses any artifact that provokes an aesthetic reaction in the observer, be it a functional object, sculpture, or painting. Brain regions implicated in reward processing, including the orbitofrontal cortex and nucleus accumbens, as well as those involved in affective processing and self-referential thought become activated during this response.

The definition of an art object is, nevertheless, influenced by historical and cultural factors. In certain cultural contexts, artifacts might serve utilitarian functions like storage or transportation, whereas in others their primary function might be decorative or symbolic. It is possible for the cultural environment in which an artifact is produced and utilized to have an impact on how much people value and consider it to be an artistic work.

The cognitive characterization of an art object might rely on the subjective assessment of the observer regarding its aesthetic attributes, including but not limited to beauty, originality, or technical proficiency. The assessment is subject to the observer's personal preferences and biases in addition to their previous knowledge and experiences. The assessment of a technical quality, the interpretation of its symbolic or metaphorical significance, and the comparison of the object to prior experiences or expectations are all potential cognitive processes that contribute to the evaluation of an artwork.

In essence, the act of scrutinizing an artifact entails an intricate interplay of subjective, subliminal, and conscious processes that are facilitated by the stimulation of diverse cerebral regions and cognitive mechanisms. Similarly intricate is the definition of an art object within the realm of material culture, which incorporates cultural and historical influences in addition to neuroaesthetic and cognitive elements. The comprehension of these processes can furnish significant knowledge regarding how individuals perceive and interpret their environment as well as contribute to the investigation of material culture, aesthetics, and art.

Experiments in museums and archaeology that straddle the disciplines of neuroscience and archaeology are considerably less frequent despite neuroaesthetics' extensive methodological and theoretical history. Such investigations frequently involve challenging research inquiries that the instruments at hand fail to adequately address.

The NeuroARTifact project[1] can be characterized in this fashion (Forte, 2024). An empirical examination of the aesthetic and performance relationships between artifacts replicated via virtual simulations and those observed in the real world is the aim of this endeavor. The study is premised on the fact that vision significantly engages both the conscious and subconscious levels of the brain. The underlying reasons and mechanisms that contribute to the profound subjectivity of an experience that we know to be aesthetic pleasure remain unknown. Are universal structures present in the domain of neuroaesthetic techniques? Could cognitive processes evident in modern neuroaesthetics and that also existed during ancient times and in ancient cultures (such as Etruscan) be identified?

The most cutting-edge investigations in the domain of cultural heritage are focusing on endeavors that incorporate neuroscience to create interdisciplinary

---

[1] The project, directed by M. Forte, was born thanks to the collaboration between Duke University (US), Sapienza University (IT) and the National Museum of Villa Giulia in Rome.

applications that can resolve specific concerns regarding the enhancement of cultural object accessibility, utilization, and reutilization. By employing qualitative analysis and technological tools that detect biometric and neurophysiological data during the observation of an artifact—in this case, archaeological artifacts from the National Etruscan Museum—the NeuroARTifact project aims to examine the emotional engagement, well-being, learning, and cognitive development of individuals in relation to museum objects, beginning with archaeological artifacts (Figure 6.1).

This investigation is conducted in both a physical museum setting and a virtual environment to compare the outcomes.

In light of the research inquiries and methodological presumptions, the objective is to gain an understanding of the neural and affective regions accountable for object perception and their corresponding responses. However, when viewed solely through the lens of a museum, this research could help determine the optimal way to present exhibits and provide context for them.

The integration of methodologies such as electroencephalography (EEG), pupil movement tracking, recording with portable devices, and eye tracking (cortical activity measurement of the frontal regions of the brain) has compelled the investigation of new research protocols (Figures 6.2–6.4).

Furthermore, insights into the degree to which the perceiver experiences positive emotions have been gleaned from the responses of participants to particular questionnaires. Conversely, investigation into the stimulation of particular neural regions could potentially enhance comprehension regarding reactions to an activity linked to the "perception" of a work of art or museum specimen. As an aesthetic process, the neuroaesthetic observation of the project focuses on the performing activities of material culture consumers.

Figure 6.1 EEG and eye-tracking recording session of the Sarcophagus of the Spouses at the National Etruscan Museum of Villa Giulia, Rome.

At its inception, the definition "neuroarchaeology" (Malafouris, 2013; Renfrew, 2008) denoted a theoretical framework that transcended disciplines and aimed to comprehend the cognitive aspects of material culture and the past. The majority of these studies have placed greater emphasis on the anthropology of material culture rather than the thought processes that generated it. The NeuroARTifact project and this chapter both pertain to a heuristic application methodology that integrates a visual/narrative component with an empirical neuroscientific approach (i.e., one based on brain activity acquisition tools).

Archaeology, anthropology, and the material culture disciplines have placed greater emphasis on the narrative and cognitive dimensions of artifacts since the 1970s. It is preferable to consider an object in the context of its spatiotemporal transformation and as a process with a performative and multivocal identity, as opposed to formally classifying it. In this regard, an artifact emerges prominently in numerous interactions with the environment; the society that manufactured, consumed, and transformed it; its interlocutors; and the contexts in which it was utilized and reused—it is no longer merely a "product." To put it briefly, a taxonomic description of material culture alone is inadequate for situating its interpretation; therefore, the process that constructs a multivocal identity and representation takes precedence over "what it is" and emphasizes "how it became what it is." It is an innovative methodological approach that places greater emphasis on the object's interaction with its environment rather than its inherent characteristics.

To employ a more technical term, the interpretation of an artifact is predicated on its *affordances*, which denote the connections it forges with both its primary and secondary environments. Consequently, it is critical to evaluate the performance of an object in a multivocal sense, which leaves interpretation greater latitude. By utilizing contextual simulation and/or endeavoring to comprehend the two sides of vision—what we look at or contemplate when observing an artifact and what the artifact itself is at the moment of observation—it is possible to reconstruct the symbolic value of an object. Simply stated, statues respond to our gaze with "look at us." When considered from the perspective of the artist or creator, a statue or figurative representation does not exist in isolation or in an abstract vacuum, but rather occupies a contextual space deliberately oriented toward its intended audience.

In this project, three different methods of data capture have been adopted: visual thinking strategies (VTS), based on what's going on in an image/model; EEG; and eye tracking (sensor technology that can detect a person's presence and follow what they are looking at).

VTS is an instructional approach that promotes critical thinking, communication abilities, and visual literacy through the use of art (Housen, 2002). VTS, which was created by museum educator Philip Yenawine and cognitive psychologist Abigail Housen, encourages participants to observe, analyze, and discuss works of art (Yenawine, 2013). Three essential inquiries comprise the method: "What is happening in this image?", "What do you observe that leads you to that conclusion?", and "What else can we discover?" (Housen & Yenawine, 2000). Facilitators provide support to participants by paraphrasing their answers and establishing connections between concepts to enhance the depth of the dialogue (Hailey et al., 2015; Shifrin, 2008). VTS is a valuable aid for both educators and learners, as evidenced by studies showing that it enhances visual literacy, language proficiency, and problem-solving capabilities (Landorf, 2006; Moeller et al., 2013).

The NeuroARTifact Project

The NeuroARTifact project began with a seemingly simple question: What happens when we observe an artifact? The project aims to define the act of examining an aesthetic procedure, recognizing that observation is a complex process involving multiple senses and motor functions as well as cognitive processes.

The question of what occurs in the brain during a neuroaesthetic experience is highly intricate and can only be partially addressed through a single project. In this case, the main research question is focused on the evaluation of this experience during the observation of an artifact in the empirical space of a museum and in virtual reality. The key study is the Sarcophagus of the Spouses, at the Etruscan National Museum of Villa Giulia in Rome.

A key aspect of the virtual experiment was the 1:1 scale reproduction of the artifact throughout the digital simulation (Figure 6.2). This means that the virtual

Figure 6.2 3D Virtual Model of the Sarcophagus.

object was created to match the exact size and proportions of the original artifact, providing a realistic and spatially accurate representation. Through the use of a virtual reality helmet, the virtual object acquires its own embodied simulation and digital ontology, resulting in a kinesthetic impact on the observer. In other words, the virtual object is not merely a visual representation but a subject that can be explored and investigated, with its own set of advantages and disadvantages compared to the physical artifact.

To fully understand the comparison between an immersive replica of a physical object and its cybernetic (informational) and aesthetic counterpart, both qualitative and quantitative analyses of the observer's mental state and subconscious reactions are necessary. This involves examining the cognitive, emotional, and physiological responses elicited by the virtual experience and comparing them to those elicited by the physical artifact.

Participating in the data acquisition phases between November 2021 and May 2022 were fifty-seven individuals between the ages of seventeen and sixty-three who were affiliated with different institutions and with a background in medicine, cultural heritage, archaeology, economics, engineering, psychology, and statistics, as well as work related to project-related disciplines.

The Sarcophagus of the Spouses

The Sarcophagus of the Spouses, which was reconstructed from approximately 400 fragments, is an urn designed to contain the physical remains of the deceased. The artwork depicts a couple in the traditional banquet position, with their busts raised in front of them while reclining on a bed (kline). The man envelops the woman's shoulders with his right arm, bringing their faces in close proximity while they maintain their characteristic "archaic smile." The configuration of the woman's fingers and hands implies the potential existence of now-lost objects, such as a miniature vase utilized to pour precious perfume or a cup for sipping wine.

The Sarcophagus is an artifact that gives rise to various sociocultural, anthropological, and archaeological issues that are partially relevant to the present project study. The complexity of its "affordances," as well as its connections to its original context, space-time, and the communication and media language of its material form, should not be obscured by its spatial isolation in a museum. The sarcophagus defies straightforward classification, and, on closer inspection, one feels observed. As an essential element of the initial communicative principle, the gaze of the statues intersects with the symbolic-funeral function of the artistic endeavor. The Sarcophagus is a "medium" whose malleability with respect to semantics must be investigated. The present case illustrates how the overarching theme of neuroarchaeological inquiry is expressed through two distinct lines of inquiry: the aesthetic outcome or consumption of the artifact from the perspective of the observer, and its performative role as a spatial object, specifically its degree of embodied simulation (embodiment; see Kiverstein and Miller, 2015).

These are two subjects that appear to be linked exclusively with the modern era, given that similar inquiries were addressed in Etruscan and archaeological investigations concerning the object's material and symbolic worth. What was the impact in its original context? In its imagined (celebration of the live coupling) and actual (funeral, post-death) spatial contexts of reference, what function did it serve? Evidently, this form of representation amalgamates fantastical situations with funerary purposes, with the tomb presumably being reopened to commemorate symbolic anniversaries or memory-related rituals. In each of the aforementioned scenarios, the sarcophagus and the spouses are not immobile entities; instead, they are differentiated by their actions during and after their lives, and additionally by aesthetic conventions that were fully understood by the target audience, the society to which they belonged.

EEG and Eye Tracking: NeuroARTifact

Experiments conducted at the National Etruscan Museum, visual observations, and statistical data analysis of the gathered data are essential for resolving the research questions that have been posed thus far. In particular, by employing multivariate analysis methods, the data obtained from the eye-tracker (Figures 6.3 and 6.4) and

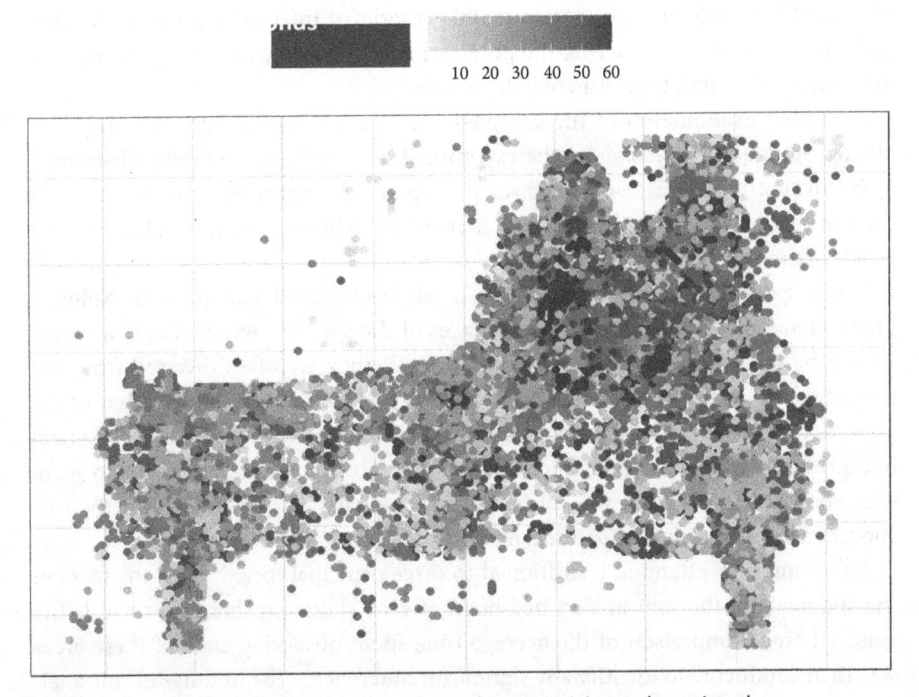

Figure 6.3 Cumulative heat maps by eye tracking: 42 visitors observing the sarcophagus for 60 seconds.

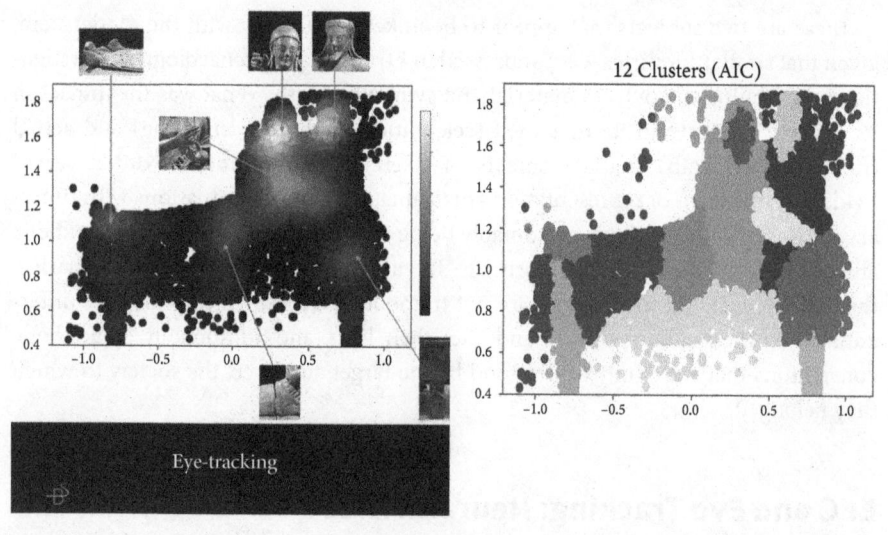

Figure 6.4 Cumulative heat maps and visual analyses. On the left the most relevant regions of interest, on the right the subdivision in clusters of the main visual features.

the EEG (Figure 6.5) can be linked to determine (i) the areas of greatest interest (ROIs), (ii) the duration of time devoted to each ROI, (iii) the prioritization of ROI attention, (iv) potential disparities in the aesthetic experience based on gender or educational attainment, and (v) discernible emotional intensities when confronted with specific ROIs. Considering the potential research avenues and the uniqueness of the available dataset, the list could be infinite.

An initial examination of the complete set of eye tracking data indicates that, during the initial 15 seconds of the experiment, observations are evenly distributed across the entire artwork, with no discernible patterns (Figure 6.2). Nevertheless, as the experiment progresses, there is an increasing inclination to concentrate on the hands of the couple.

When examining gender disparities, it has been noted that women exhibit a greater tendency to concentrate on the faces of the spouses, whereas men are captivated by the left hand of the woman. However, they are often diverted from the subject by the joint that separates the two halves of the sarcophagus situated in the artwork's center. While the sample does not contain any men with art-historical backgrounds, women without such backgrounds exhibit similar behavior to men. Consequently, the women who place greater emphasis on the features of the two spouses are those with art-historical backgrounds.

Following that, attention transitioned to three principal focal points: the faces of the spouses and the central clenched hand of each statue on their right hand. The gender-based comparison of the average time spent observing each of these areas was then conducted to identify any significant differences. The findings of this analysis were as follows: (i) the duration of attention devoted to the man's face did not differ significantly between men and women, (ii) women devoted a greater amount

Figure 6.5 Example of eye-tracking and EEG session of one visitor. The graph, on the right, shows the workload, the attention and the emotional index. In this case the metrics indicates that this visual experience is not consistent in the three indexes because of the complexity of the observation.

of time to scrutinizing the intricacies of the woman's face in comparison to men and the man's hands, and (iii) men devoted an approximately equivalent amount of time to observing both the man's hands and the woman's face.

In conclusion, the 1-minute experience of each participant was partitioned into four distinct ordered windows of observation, each lasting 15 seconds: [0s, 15s], [15s, 30s], [30s, 45s], [45s, 60s]. The eye tracking data were subsequently correlated with the emotional index (EI) value derived from the EEG to ascertain whether the participant was emotionally arousable at each time point relative to their baseline state, which was measured prior to the commencement of the investigation. It is feasible to ascertain an individual's visual orientation during an exhilarated or unexcited state as well as to discern diverse patterns within the experience (e.g., Do we experience excitement exclusively at the outset or toward its culmination?) using this methodology.

Do we find pleasure solely in facial features? The figure illustrates the experience of a randomly selected individual and reveals that the EI was lower than the initial value for the initial 30 seconds. However, it subsequently rose over the subsequent 30 seconds, with a higher concentration of observations occurring later over the bodies of the spouses (Figure 6.4).

Experimental EEGs were performed at the National Etruscan Museum and in virtual reality. By examining emerging neurophysiological parameters during cognitive and emotional processing, the neurocognitive approach enables researchers to discern those factors that elicit excitement in the general populace as well as to distinguish the perceptions of visitors based on a variety of criteria (e.g., age, gender, educational attainment, and so forth). By adopting this contemporary perspective on artistic perception, the visitor can contribute to the enhancement of the artistic heritage, thereby becoming an essential component of the artistic experience.

The visitor, who is generally the ultimate recipient of art dissemination, is actively engaged in the development of the dissemination experience throughout this procedure. Specifically, by conducting an examination of the neurophysiological and declarative reactions generated by an artistic piece in a prospective viewer, it becomes feasible to optimize both the process of disclosure and the audience's impromptu engagement.

This project, as opposed to conventional research on cognition and art that focuses on identifying the specific brain regions involved in artistic processing, seeks to comprehend the conscious and unconscious perception of the observer by examining the cognitive and emotional dynamics occurring in his or her mind, irrespective of the activation of brain regions. The utilization of portable and wireless devices is crucial for assessing visitors' perception in a highly realistic environment because they enable (i) noninvasive monitoring of nervous system activity and (ii) direct measurement of such activity within the museum, which is the customary setting for art perception.

The portable Revive EEG device, which was designed and developed by BrainSigns, a startup originating from the Industrial Neuroscience Lab at La Sapienza University, was employed in conjunction with the portable Shimmer device, which is capable of quantifying heart rate and perspiration (a participant donning the sensors while viewing the museum is depicted Figure 6.4, which features a three-dimensional reproduction of the virtual environment).

Using EEG, pulse rate, and perspiration, it is possible to determine the mental state of the observer. We specifically focused on the amount of cognitive exertion required to successfully accomplish a given task: allocating mental resources to analyze a stimulus or perform a task constitutes attention. An emotional response can be defined as a composite of two qualities: intensity and valence (positive or negative or feeble or intense). The participants were provided with instructions to investigate the actual sarcophagus and a high-quality replica using a virtual reality viewer. The cognitive and affective parameters mentioned above were obtained throughout the two experiences with the purpose of conducting a comparative analysis. It was discovered that the degree of attention was similar in both conditions; however, museum observation demanded a higher level of cognitive engagement, or mental burden, than virtual reality observation. Regarding the context in which an artwork is appreciated, this result validates previous research: "cognitive fluency," or the effort needed to complete the task, is enhanced when the artwork is observed or evaluated in a context that is considered appropriate and suitable. The regulations of the museum and the social impact of the environment in which the artwork is viewed influence this phenomenon. It has been shown that the museum not only engages visitors more but also demonstrates a greater capacity to stimulate them. The EI value exhibited a significantly greater magnitude during museum observation in comparison to virtual reality observation. The actual work elicited a more intense and positive emotional reaction from observers. The data that have been gathered suggest that the affective and cognitive engagement with an aesthetic object is greater in person than when experienced in its digital reproduction. Although the participants maintained an equivalent level of attentiveness throughout both experiences, they demonstrated greater affective engagement and expended more energy while viewing the actual artwork. These findings not only reaffirm the distinctiveness of the authentic aesthetic experience—which is likely more intricate—but also illustrate the effective application of cognitive neuroscience within the artistic sphere and how the audience can actively engage in the popularization process without assuming the role of a "passive" observer.

In 2019, researchers published an exhaustive review of more than 3,000 scientific studies on the relationship between the arts, well-being, and health in an effort to combat disease and enhance clinical outcomes. This review categorized an extensive body of research into two main groups: those focused on prevention and treatment and those in which the subjects merely engaged in artistic appreciation (e.g., viewing artworks, listening to music, etc.) versus those in which the subjects actively participated in the creative process (e.g., drawing, playing an instrument, discussing it). Numerous studies have demonstrated that the impacts of high-resolution digital reproductions are analogous to those of the originals. Nevertheless, it has been noted that an excursion to a museum encompasses not only cognitive and perceptual aspects, but also a motor experience characterized by exploration.

An additional research activity of NeuroARTifact was focused specifically on individuals requiring neurorehabilitation. For this scope, eleven stroke patients who had been committed to the Scientific Institute for Research, Hospitalization and Healthcare (IRCCS) Fondazione Santa Lucia in Rome were involved in this study. Three hours of motor and cognitive neurorehabilitation per day are beneficial for these patients; however, during the remaining inpatient hours, they require a stimulating environment if they are to remain active and motivated. Bernhardt et al. (2004) emphasize the critical nature of this matter in their article "Inactive and alone: Physical activity within the first 14 days of acute stroke unit." By developing virtual reality helmets that could be used to explore and view digital replicas of Etruscan artifacts, the NeuroARTifact project successfully led hospitalized individuals through a virtual tour comprising three randomized digital scenarios derived from the most significant digital artifacts on display at the National Etruscan Museum of Villa Giulia in Rome. After donning the virtual reality helmets, the patients were granted access to a virtual environment that isolated them from the hospital environment. Within this environment, they were able to observe three-dimensional digital reconstructions of the Sarcophagus of the Spouses as well as two distinct spatial perspectives of the pediment of the Temple of Pyrgi—one from below, as in a museum, and the other just in front of the subject. The patients expressed in their comments their satisfaction with the opportunity to virtually spend their hospital day at the museum. Additionally, the patients' eye movements were documented utilizing the eye monitoring system integrated into the virtual reality headgear. These data were subsequently compared to those of healthy subjects who were exposed to identical tasks in the same virtual environment. This research is focused on promoting so-called *cultural welfare*, or welfare promoted through culture, which in a country with a rich cultural heritage and an elderly population, like Italy, can be a crucial strategy.

Preliminary Conclusions

First and foremost, the NeuroARTifact Project is a work in progress. Even though a substantial research team has been engaged for a number of months, data processing and interpretation still require considerable effort. Certain eye tracking and EEG responses are intuitive, whereas others are not; the outcomes of these experiments are complex and multivariate, not binary.

Significantly, neurorehabilitation specialists, art historians, psychologists, statisticians, neuroscientists, and cognitive scientists comprised our team. The migration of data from multiple platforms utilizing complex exchange formats constitutes a protracted procedure. One must not overestimate the significance of these methodologies, notwithstanding their groundbreaking and innovative nature. Our understanding of the human mind remains limited, and the portable instruments currently available are often insufficient, much like the research inquiries we pursue. Despite this, the initial results are without a doubt highly intriguing and present uncharted territories for further academic inquiry and advancement. In particular, a new working protocol is established through the utilization of eye tracking and EEG during both empirical observation experiences and virtual simulation phases.

The case study of the Sarcophagus of the Spouses is highly relevant and brings to mind a contemporary concern: the interplay between museums, their visitors, and renowned artworks. Historically, numerous archaeological museums have succumbed to fossilization in their intermittent endeavors to secure visitors' opinions. To ascertain the popularity or disfavor of their collections—or the museum in its entirety—these institutions have employed questionnaires and statistics. The NeuroARTifact initiative, on the other hand, investigates the conscious and subliminal associations individuals have with artifacts alongside their kinesthetic learning and aesthetic appreciation. Because the investigation centers on the artifact, the museum functions merely as a setting.

Initial results suggest that these interdisciplinary studies have implications for numerous fields, commencing with an examination of historical phenomena, progressing to an evaluation of public perception of cultural heritage, culminating in the development of innovative approaches to promoting cultural heritage that cater to the cognitive and emotional requirements of visitors, and incorporating insights into the responses of both young and old visitors into the learning sector, all while implementing inventive paths and activities associated with the museum experience, including educational environments. Application in the realm of wellness promotion is of the utmost importance, integrating technologies and methodologies utilized in neurological and motor rehabilitation to transport museum artifacts to care facilities while also providing stress-reducing access to cultural heritage.

Acknowledgments

The authors thank Vittoria Lecce and Valentino Nizzo for their collaboration during the experiments and for promoting the project within the activities of the Villa Giulia Museum.

Bibliography

Bernhardt, J., Dewey, H., Thrift, A., & Donnan, G. Inactive and alone: physical activity within the first 14 days of acute stroke unit care. Stroke, (2004), 35(4), 1005–1009.

Forte, M. Perceiving Etruscan Art: AI and Visual Perception. Humans 2024, 4, 409–429. https://doi.org/10.3390/humans4040027

Freedberg, D., and V. Gallese. "Motion, emotion and empathy in aesthetic experience." *Trends in Cognitive Sciences* 11.5 (2007), 197–203.

Hailey, D., A. Miller, P., and Yenawine. "Understanding visual literacy: The visual thinking strategies approach." In *Essentials of Teaching and Integrating Visual and Media Literacy*, edited by D. M. Baylen and A. D'Alba, 49–73. New York: Springer, 2015.

Housen, A., & Yenawine, P. Visual Thinking Strategies Basic Manual Grades (2000), 3–5. New York: Visual Understanding in Education.

Housen, A. "Aesthetic thought, critical thinking and transfer." *Arts and Learning Research Journal* 18.1 (2002), 99–132.

Kiverstein, J., M., and M. Miller. "The embodied brain: Towards a radical embodied cognitive neuroscience." *Frontiers in Human Neuroscience* 9 (2015), 237.

Landorf, H. "What's going on in this picture? Visual thinking strategies and adult learning." *New Horizons in Adult Education and Human Resource Development* 20.4 (2006), 28–32.

Malafouris, L. *How Things Shape the Mind: A Theory of Material Engagement*. Cambridge, MA: MIT Press, 2013.

Moeller, M., K. Cutler, D. Fiedler, and L. Weier. "Visual thinking strategies = creative and critical thinking." *Phi Delta Kappan* 95.3 (2013), 56–60.

Renfrew, C. "Neuroarchaeology: Exploring the links between neural and cultural processes." *Science* 362.6417 (2008), 619–624.

Shifrin, S. "Visual literacy in North American secondary schools: Arts-centered learning, student creativity, and the fulfillment of state standards." *International Journal of Education through Art* 4.1 (2008), 85–100.

Yenawine, P. *Visual Thinking Strategies: Using Art to Deepen Learning Across School Disciplines*. Cambridge, MA: Harvard Education Press, 2013.

Maurizio Forte, Vincenza Ferrara, Marco Mingione, Pierfrancesco Alaimo Di Loro, Andrea Giorgi, Stefano Menicocci, Fabio Babiloni, and Marco Iosa, *The NeuroARTifact Project: Seeing with the Mind* In: *A New Etruscan Archaeology: Twenty-First Century Techniques and Methods*. Edited by: Maurizio Forte, Oxford University Press.
© Oxford University Press 2025. DOI: 10.1093/9780197582053.003.0007

7

Conservation Practice

The Tomb of the Sphinx in Vulci

Teresa Carta

Introduction

A cursory review of the tumultuous history of archaeological structure conservation in Italy is sufficient to provide an overview of the current state of affairs. The nineteenth-century rationalization efforts for monument conservation resulted in the complete abandonment of ancient ruins to their fate. Archaeological areas were falling apart until the 1990s. The common practice of "archaeological digs," which frequently left sites in a state that was "incomprehensible" to both the public and archaeologists, and the lack of recognition of restoration as a means of resurrecting a material record replete with useful information, contributed to this decline. The conflict between archaeologists and architects from different disciplines, which remains unresolved today, has significantly contributed to this phenomenon, as has the oversimplified application of Cesare Brandi's principles from his "Carta del Restauro" (1972). Indeed, in the 1950s, Brandi's philosophy often distorted the principle that "everything is material in an artwork," distinguishing between material as a support and as a means of revealing the image, leading archaeologists to view monuments as untouchable due to their fear of falsification.

Later, with the technological revolution, the idea took root that ancient buildings had a structural and static behavior that was similar to modern constructions of reinforced concrete, thereby leading to the use of the same technologies in this sector, too. Moreover, the construction industry used industrial materials like Portland cement, believing them superior to ancient cement, without properly verifying their compatibility with original materials. These methods, primarily used in the 1960s and 1970s, quickly proved harmful, as evidenced by the Arch of Constantine, the Column of Antoninus Pius in Rome, and the Arch of Trajan in Benevento. The painted tombs at Tarquinia are an example of this practice in Etruscan archaeology. Due to their precarious condition at the time of discovery, workers often removed the wall paintings or, alternatively, consolidated the plaster with metal clamps and cement-based mortars. With increasingly more resources available, invasive interventions were seen in the case of many kinds of ancient monuments. In Italy, these interventions borrowed from civil construction, a trend that was also often adopted abroadin large-scale anastylosis reconstructions, such as the Acropolis in Athens.

It wasn't until the 1990s that enlightened interventions became benchmarks and reference points in terms of the methods used, such as the restoration work at the Roman Forum, the intervention program at Paestum, and the work carried out at Cornus in Sardinia. An archaeological conference in November 1991 also established initial principles for conservation. These principles mandated the evaluation of methods and materials from other sectors for their appropriateness and compatibility before use, established a minimal intervention criterion that effectively eliminated the need for durable materials and "definitive" interventions, and emphasized the importance of architectural safeguards.

In the archaeological field today, the relationship between the discoveries made during an excavation and the original territory and environment is becoming increasingly important. The contextualization of objects mandates conserving the relations of time, space, and cultural relations that left their mark on these artifacts, and thus in situ conservation is of great importance today. In an effort to restore the painted tombs of Tarquinia, there has been a long-standing tendency to preserve the painted components on the original wall to the greatest extent possible, rather than removing them. This approach is based on a thorough examination of the surrounding environment and structure, as well as the substitution of outdated cement-based mortars with materials that possess chemical and physical properties comparable to the original materials. The harsh underground environments that make the materials prone to condensation prompted this action.

Conserving an archaeological area is certainly not an easy task because often we find ourselves dealing with a heterogeneous system with different degrees of material robustness. The first challenge arises when the chemical and physical status of the finds changes during the excavation phase. The most common questions facing specialists today are how to make the unearthing of "fragile" objects (structures made from tuff, masonry, floors, mosaics, plaster, etc.) less traumatic, how to best conserve these structures, and how to present and make them accessible to visitors.

Preventive and Active Conservation at Archaeological Sites

Italian research institutes have recognized the importance of in situ conservation and developed methods to implement during the excavation phase. "Active conservation" refers to these methods, which encompass immediate action, restoration, and maintenance. "Preventive conservation," which works with active conservation to slow the damage to exposed features (mostly through protective roofing and backfill) focuses on the environment around the exposed features.

When weather conditions easily damage archaeological remains, contact-based protection systems, typically geotextiles, can be used in conjunction with infill and/ or inert composites such as sand, pozzolana, expanded clay aggregate, large gravel, and so on. For example, in excavation areas with low architectural remains, the backfill can be prepared by affixing strata of a permeable substance, such as expanded clay, sand, or another inert material, within small-mesh plastic netting that has been custom-formed to conform to the contours of the feature to be protected.

Regardless, each situation must be assessed according to the nature of the element to be preserved, the backfill's lifespan, and the presence of supplementary protection systems, such as temporary roofing. Protective roofing construction, whether temporary during the excavation and restoration phases or permanent, is critical for allowing visitors to access the site during conservation efforts. Temporary roofing not only reduces the size of the imbalance of conditions between underground and the open air during uncovering and excavation but also slows the chemical exchange between the find's surface and the environment. It also protects against the destructive action of atmospheric agents, reducing the scale of subsequent restoration work and limiting or wholly preventing the loss of information useful for context study.

In addition, the Istituto Superiore per la Conservazione e il Resauro (ISCR), in collaboration with other research institutes like the Ente Nazionale per le Energie Alternative (ENEA), has conducted specialist studies and experiments on the physical interaction between roofing and the archaeological features it safeguards. Thanks to this work, there are now guidelines for the construction of free-standing roofs. It is necessary to ensure that the archaeological remains are not disturbed excessively, that they are shielded from the effects of weather and climate, that natural or artificial lighting is utilized in a manner that does not cause undue harm to plants or animals, that the work can be undone, that runoff water is effectively removed, and that it creates no condensation or greenhouse effect.

These recommendations are very important in the design of these protective structures because, even today, there is a tendency to attach more importance to the formal and aesthetic aspects of architectural features than to the actual conservation of remains. As previously stated, the design and implementation of the most suitable intervention methods, based on what is imagined right from the excavation phase, are of great help in conservation.

Using some kind of overhead cover can make the change from subsoil levels to the outside world more gradual. Covers can also be used to create localized protection over items that require slow drying out or over horizontal elements (e.g., floors, mosaics, etc.) to ensure their safety during the gradual excavation process, from both foot traffic and potential accidents caused by site workers.

There are specific tools used for both active conservation as well as quick intervention operations that mostly involve stabilizing artifacts against static and mechanical collapse, which causes cracks, fissures, and the loss of material, with pieces coming loose and falling off. These methods consist of creating physical supports that must meet the essential requirements of reversibility and lack of interaction with the original material. A highly effective method for supporting portions of rock, masonry structures, or even plasterwork on walls is "shoring up," which entails the installation of panels supported by metal shafts or timbers.

This system demonstrates utility not solely in excavation processes, but also in procedures involving plaster and wall coverings, wherein portions that have become severed from their supports are anchored via the injection of a consolidant. Materials that could crumble or shatter during excavation are subjected to quick mechanical intervention procedures. These techniques include temporary fixing with synthetic resins or injections of desalinated mortar, as well as temporary stuccowork and sealants using "lean lime" cements. These materials have fewer bonding agents, making them easier to undo during the final intervention. However, each case must be examined individually, considering the type of feature and the duration between excavation and restoration.

Tuff Features: Conservation Experience at Vulci

The techniques described thus far serve as a preparatory step for conservation intervention, particularly when dealing with extremely fragile materials like archaeological features made of tuff. The conservation issues with this material are usually very complicated because tuff contains reactive minerals like zeolites, is very porous, and doesn't have a lot of mechanical or abrasion resistance. The oldest settlement phases in Vulci frequently used this type of stone. Large rectangular blocks of "red tuff with black scoria" serve as the sole construction material in Vulci's monumental and defensive complexes, including the Great Temple and the City Walls. Red tuff (identifiable as type C ignimbrite from Vico) and blocks of sandstone and siltstone from the local substrate form the perimeter wall of the Domus del Criptoportico. Researchers dug large tombs in the Osteria Necropolis area, including the Tomb of the Carved Ceilings (also known as the EPT Tomb), the Silver Hands Tomb, and the Tomb of the Sphinx (both discovered in 2012/2013), directly into the tuff-pyroclastic terrain of a geomorphological plain that surrounds the archaeological area of the ancient Etruscan city.

By establishing its initial module at the end of the 1990s, the Vulci Archaeological Park aimed to facilitate certain restoration and conservation initiatives as well as provide the public with access to new visitor routes within the archaeological area. Outside specialists and the park's laboratory conducted a series of investigations for analysis and diagnostics.

We designed tests on samples to study and identify materials that would consolidate the red tuff with black scoria. The results of these studies revealed the presence of a consolidant, ethyl silicate, and a protective material, Akeogard CO, a fluoroelastomer. We selected the latter option because it exhibited "inert" behavior toward the material, was reversible, and had greater permeability to water vapor. This is a crucial attribute considering the high porosity of tuff.

However, tests in the field with these products did not yield good results because the tuff rock in the archaeological features does not stick together well and presents problems when reattaching flakes or granules. No product that combines rocks can fix this problem without completely changing the rock's chemical and physical properties.

Starting with the restoration and reconstruction intervention of the Tempio Grande, researchers investigated a physical protection method known as "surface sacrifice." Researchers designed this system to safeguard masonry structures made from squared blocks of red tuff that emerged during the excavation campaigns of 2000 and 2001. Canopy roofs could not protect these structures due to their size and placement. Inherently designed for reconstruction work, the chosen method involved laying blocks of tuff, similar in size to the original blocks, to cap the dry-stone walls. The blocks were of a different color, adhering to the original pattern, and protruded by approximately 6 centimeters to emphasize their protective function. The intervention, still visible today on portions of Vulci's outer city walls, is reversible; we laid the restoration blocks using the dry-stone technique and secured them to each other with metal clamps, ensuring no keying to the original parts. In instances where this approach was not feasible for tuff structures, the surface fissures were sealed with a mortar composed of sand, pulverized tuff, and lime mortar, followed by the application of colored lime grouts for surface reinforcement. Before proceeding, we disinfected and cleansed the surfaces to remove any potential microbes.

This latter method produced good results from an aesthetic point of view, but, without the protection of roofing against meteorological and climatic agents, the tuff stones that received this treatment needed continual maintenance. Today, after more than twenty years, "surface sacrifice" affords a fair degree of conservation of the tuff-built masonry structures, even though maintenance continues to play a vital role in the good conservation of features.

The conservation of features found in the Osteria Necropolis is more problematic. Tuffite bedrock, a sedimentary rock of mixed origin that consists of pyroclastic and detrital elements held together by a calcareous or clay-based matrix, forms the tombs. Due to its unique geomorphological features, this rock maintains a delicate environmental balance, with almost stable dampness conditions determining its survival. Post-excavation decay is rapid and manifests as flaking, fracturing, fissures, and material loss. The particular conformation of these underground monuments makes conservation of these places a highly complex intervention owing to the high degree of humidity in the air and the dampness of the structures themselves, on top of which there are often precarious static conditions.

The Archaeological Superintendency for Southern Etruria discovered the tomb in 1967, during a rescue excavation at the request of the Finance Police, and immediately backfilled it again. The Archaeological Superintendency for Southern Etruria undertook its restoration and erected a protective roof over it using metal sheeting and scaffolding tubes. During this initial intervention, we filled large gaps in the walls of the dromos with cement-based mortar and capped the upper part of the dromos, which was approximately 4 meters deep, to prevent rainwater from seeping inside the tomb. Additionally, we installed metal reinforcements along the dromos to stabilize large damaged parts in the silty bedrock.

Prior to the intervention that took place in 2002, we carried out particular experiments and monitored the fundamental microclimate to gain a more in-depth understanding of the chemistry, mineralogy, and other properties of the building materials.

The state of conservation of the underground tomb was very poor: in some chambers, parts of the carved ceilings were detached due to the infiltration of water, and, in addition, an evident microbiological attack affected several parts of the dromos due to the malfunctioning of the protective roofing. The stone's surface also showed signs of gradual deterioration, including flaking, fractures, and cracks. The first intervention involved altering the protective roof by relocating runoff to the west side of the tomb, away from the chambers, and rearranging the entrance to create a more accessible way in.

Following the standard procedures of capturing survey drawings and photos to demonstrate the tomb's preservation, the team cleaned and disinfected it to eradicate any potential microbes. Simultaneously, an initial investigation was conducted outside the dromos, excavating a strip of earth 3 meters wide and as deep as the surface of the rock into which the tomb was dug. The aim was to identify any cracks perpendicular to the silt bedrock, which could be responsible for the very high humidity present within some chambers. Subsequently, the excavation was expanded to cover the entire site, uncovering a surface area of approximately 200 square meters. This revealed several deep cracks that aligned with the chamber positions, indicating a clear rock break-up phenomenon.

When the old restoration grouting was mechanically removed along the upper edge of the dromos, it became clear that more flaking had occurred. This led to a decision to only remove the oxidized metal rods from the old intervention and replace them with rods of the same size that adhere better and are galvanized to protect them from iron corrosion. To fix the large flaking areas, a desalinated mortar was used, and, for the grouting, a mortar with siltstone-like properties was prepared. This was achieved by drawing comparisons with the restoration of other "subterranean buildings" whose material composition most closely resembled the case at hand.

Several trials were carried out, and the final choice rested on two mortars: the first, used on the part of the bedrock nearer the surface,[1] was made up of natural hydraulic lime and powdered red tuff and pumice; the second, used on the walls, was composed of hydraulic lime and two different kinds of powdered tuff, with the addition of a small amount of yellow natural earth to match the original color.

---

[1] In the overall stratigraphical scheme, we see three strata, starting with the surface and excluding farm soil(20–30 cm): (a) meso-macrogranular layer of pumice interspersed with fine deposits of clayey soil, being of average compactness (40–60 cm thick), and horizontal; (b) a microgranular layer or bedrock of tuffite, originating from ash deposits, with a total thickness of 2.0–2.5 meters, orientation subhorizontal; and (c) a layer of lamina tuffite bedrock continually interspersed with meso-macrogranular material; the orientation is variable from subhorizontal to variously inclined, with a thickness between 1.3 and 1.6–1.7 meters.

After sealing the dromos walls, the stability of the old cement-based mortar additions was checked and a color revision of the surface was conducted. The very high level of dampness in the 2002 intervention prevented the restoration of the carved ceilings in two chambers because the material had become impregnated with water. Therefore, an attempt was made to examine the bedrock after removing the soil. All the cracks were filled with a pozzolana-based cement, and the surface was "waterproofed" by placing a thick polythene sheet between two layers of beaten earth, following the slope outward to prevent water from collecting and forming pockets. Meanwhile, a temporary forced ventilation system was implemented, using ventilators inside the chambers to gradually lower the humidity level. Supports were constructed to secure those parts of the ceiling that were at risk of collapse. All this work will remain in place for as long as necessary, until it might be possible to take steps to consolidate the damage under more suitable conditions.

After the intervention, monitoring did not show any significant improvements in the situation. The level of humidity in the two underground rooms is still very high, and the dromos also poses conservation problems. As a result, a new intervention has already been scheduled that will also encompass other underground structures near the tomb. This intervention will include a specific study to construct adequate roofing for the entire area as well as conservation work using more innovative materials, such as nanosilica, which we have already used in the Tomb of the Sphinx.

The Intervention on the Tomb of the Sphinx

Preliminary Considerations

In 2011, the Osteria Necropolis underwent archaeological research as part of a project to enhance the Vulci Archeological and Nature Park.[2] The goal was to gather additional information about the historical and topographical layout of the necropolis, which resulted in the discovery of several highly significant structures. Prominent among these is Tomb 14 in Sector B of the area. Due to the discovery of a very fine nenfro sculpture inside it, which depicts a fantastic animal with a woman's face, the tomb is known as the Tomb of the Sphinx.[3]

The plan reveals a fairly complex layout for the tomb, which dates to the years after the mid-seventh century BCE and belonged to high-status individuals. It has long dromos, which lead to an extended antechamber. Three doors give way to this antechamber, leading to the burial chambers: one on the left; two on the right, aligned with each other; and, at the back, three chambers arranged in a cross-shaped pattern around a central atrium (Figure 7.1).

[2] Regione Lazio. Programma Operativo Regionale—F.E.S.R. 2007–2013 Lazio. Asse II Attività 5-Valorizzazione e promozione del patrimonio culturale e paesistico nelle aree di particolare pregioProgetto di Valorizzazione del Sistema Territoriale Etruschi del Lazio-Parco Archeologico di Vulci.

[3] In reality, the artifact was discovered in a secondary location within the antechamber, in the infill of a vast covert excavation, and therefore did not belong to the tomb.

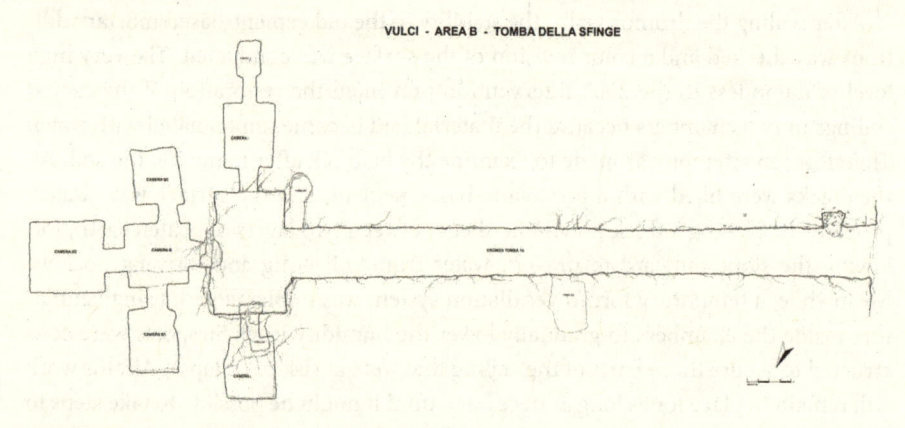

Figure 7.1 Plan of the Sphynx Tomb.

The underground structure is well-made, with architectural details originally high-lighted in color, as seen in Chamber Gamma, where faint remnants of a decoration consisting of thin red bands follow the contours of the *columen*.[4]

During restoration work, we later found traces of yellow, black, and red pigment on the walls of the antechamber and on the door closing the right-hand side chamber (Gamma), which consists of a large squared block of tuffite split into two parts.

Description and State of Preservation

Figure 7.2 depicts the dromos of this monumental tomb, a corridor open to the sky that is 26.5 meters long and 2.2 meters wide, carved into the silt bedrock.

The degradation takes the form of cracks, flaking, and material loss, especially in the upper parts, where the moisture release was most sudden. Indeed, during the excavation process, it was necessary to shore up the upper section of the central dromos's walls. Another at-risk zone exists on the southern side, where excavation temporarily filled in a large gap in the wall (approximately 2×2.5 meters) with small blocks of tuff. On the southern side, near the antechamber, the upper part of the dromos appears to have lost a section, owing to the presence of a niche that was dug into the rock to contain the remains of a cremation. Two other tombs are located along the dromos: an inhumation burial on the northern side, roughly halfway along the dromos, and another one on the southern side, near the entrance. On both sides of the dromos, there are small clay-filled gaps in the bedrock. These somewhat inhomogeneous interventions are probably ancient attempts to restore silt bedrock.

Three doors connect the antechamber (5.40×3.5 meters). Cracks, small fractures, and flaking are present on the walls, and a microbiological attack has damaged some

[4] Moretti A. M., L. Ricciardi, and E. Eutizi. "Vulci, necropoli dell'Osteria, campagna di scavo 2011–2012: dati preliminari," in Mercuri L. and Zaccagnini R. (eds), *Etruria in Progress*: la ricerca archeologica in Etruria meridionale, 106–111, Roma: Cangemi editore, 2014.

Figure 7.2 Tomb of the Sphinx prior to intervention.

areas in the lower section. A square-block siltstone door on the western wall leads to Chamber Beta. In the upper part of the bedrock, near this door, there are large missing portions due to the holes made in modern times for installing electricity poles. Like the dromos, small gaps in the walls were visible, filled in with clay. However, the repeated flooding of the underground structure has left no trace of the internal clay-based infill. Indeed, catastrophic events like the floods of 2012 and 2014 have further altered the tomb since its discovery, causing serious damage, such as the collapse of part of the southern wall of the dromos, as depicted in the Figure 7.3.

The Analysis and Restoration Intervention

Completed in January 2015,[5] the complex preservation intervention involved the first instance of roofing construction. By protecting the rock against atmospheric agents, this was designed to create the most favorable environmental conditions for the conservation of the underground structure[6] and the use, in the restoration phase, of products and materials compatible with the nature of the rock into which the tomb had been dug. To address this latest aspect, we conducted prior consolidation

---

[5] In this project restoration work was only carried out on surfaces, and only on the dromos and the tomb's antechamber. Restoration of the chambers is part of a new project that should commence shortly.

[6] Temporary roofing was erected, with sheeting supported by scaffolding tubes. Meanwhile the definitive roofing was designed by the architects Carla Pasqualini and Arnaldo Vicari, who also followed and directed structural consolidation work on the tomb, and the design of the new area of the Osteria Necropolis at Vulci.

Figure 7.3 Collapse of southern wall of dromos following torrential rain on 2 October 2014.

tests on rock samples to determine the most suitable product for restoring surface cohesion.[7] Indeed, the samples demonstrated problems with breakup and surface crumbling. Four products were tested: (1) ethyl silicate (70% solution), (2) water-based acrylic microemulsion, (3) liquid potassium silicate, and (4) nanosilica.

The tests used the total immersion technique, which relies on capillary action, a phenomenon in which a liquid spontaneously penetrates a porous solid. Although we cannot apply this method for consolidating the artifact in question, we used it to compare the effectiveness of the four products based on the percentage absorbed and their aesthetic compatibility (chromatic value).

The tests revealed that two products were most easily absorbed by the material, with a value of around 10 percent and a greater consolidating effect: nanosilica and ethyl silicate. Specifically, nanosilica displayed the largest total imbition coefficient ($\Delta P\%$). Furthermore, experts recommended nanosilica over the other two products due to its innovative nature in restoring and conserving stone materials.

Nanotechnology is a field of study that has led to the creation of new products for heritage restoration in recent years, including nanosilica.[8] This is an inorganic

[7] The study was carried out by Anna Stefani, from Calchèra San Giorgio, a research centre that formulates materials for specialists in architectural restoration - Grigno (TN).

[8] A silanized nanodispersion of colloidal silica in a water-based solution. By penetrating the pores of the stone, this product manages to form a gel, partially filling the voids in the structure. After application, only the water begins to evaporate off, and the particles begin to draw closer together, until they form a three-dimensional structure (xerogel) that acts as a consolidant.

consolidant that has a low environmental impact because it is a water-based dispersion of nanometric silica that poses no safety risks for conservation workers or the environment. Furthermore, it is totally "artifact-compatible," from the chemical and physical point of view, with the substrate of the works when compared to organic consolidants.

The decision was made to try nanosilica[9] as a bonding agent in this intervention to create an inorganic mortar with good adhesive properties and excellent permeability to water vapor. The selected inert materials consisted of finely crushed siltstone, powdered tuff, and silica sand. Subsequently, this paste mixture was employed to micro-repair and fill in lacking components, as illustrated in Figures 7.4 and 7.5. In the interim, broken components were repaired and fissures were filled with a fluid mortar that comprised nanosilica and aerated pozzolana (see Figures 7.4 and 7.5).

Surface preparation was accomplished by employing mechanical implements such as whisk fibers, animal hairbrushes, and small metal and wooden spatulas to eliminate bonded and loose soil and earth deposits. Thorough and arduous labor was required to mechanically remove the soil deposits, specifically from within the profound fissures of the rock, after which they were consolidated. The microbiological assaults were remedied by employing a quaternary ammonium salt solution (NEW DES 50) in 5 percent water, which was applied with a brush. The fractured regions and ancient clay restorations in the solid rock were remedied through the dilution of nanosilica in demineralized water. Following this, a fluid cement comprising aerated pozzolana and nanosilica was introduced to reattach the fragments. Concurrently,

Figure 7.4 Detail of degradation of rock.

[9] Nano Estel, a product made by C.T.S. s.r.l., was used.

Figure 7.5 Detail of rock after sealing.

separate granite segments were reattached utilizing a system of rods, which were occasionally constructed from fiberglass or steel. The task of repositioning the four sizable rock fragments that had become dislodged from the southern wall of the dromos was notably intricate. In consideration of the material's susceptibility, we initially thinned the detached rock sections on the reverse side subsequent to the structural consolidation of the wall and subsequently fortified them with a "dressing."

By employing photographic documentation and post-collapse drawings, we successfully identified the precise locations of the fragments, affixed them to the wall using low-pressure infusions of hyperfluid grout, and secured them in place using stainless steel clamps and rods.

Hydraulic lime cement with siltstone, tuff, sand, and natural earths completed the final infill of the missing part on the southern wall and the gaps in the antechamber. Cleaning, gluing fragments in place with epoxy resin, and filling in missing portions were all part of the conservation intervention on the door leading to Chamber Gamma, which allowed for the door's museumification near the chamber's entrance and its placement on a zinc-plated iron and steel support (Figures 7.6 and 7.7).

Conclusion

The market for restoration products is somewhat heterogeneous due to the wide variety of substances it includes: chemical formulations developed by companies for sectors other than restoration but also used in conservation; natural chemical substances; products and mixtures prepared by individual conservators; and, more

Figure 7.6 The tomb's dromos.

Figure 7.7 After the intervention.

recently, chemical formulations and products specifically designed by industry for heritage conservation. In the past, the absence of controls and the heterogeneity of formulations resulted in the dispersion and loss of accumulated experience, which was often characterized by direct and unwise experiments on works of art. The tragic floods that struck Florence and Venice in 1966 gave rise to the modern science of conservation, necessitating the search for new methods to restore and conserve an immense cultural heritage. Thus, in the past thirty years, we have seen significant developments in conservation science: the development of colloids and interfaces, together with materials science, has provided the skills and tools for advancing the study of the degradation processes affecting works of art. Similarly, these fields have developed innovative and secure methods for safeguarding artifacts, including dispersions of nanoparticles, microemulsions, gels, nanocomposites, and nanosensors, the latter of which can monitor conservation artifacts. The use of nanoparticles of different chemical elements has led to the formulation of nanoparticle products for use as biocides and for the consolidation and cleaning of various different materials: silicate rocks, carbonate rocks, marble, cement, paintings on canvas, wall paintings, wood, and paper. The list also includes deacidification treatments and products for cleaning papers, such as painted paper and ancient parchment.

As previously mentioned, these conservation systems significantly surpass traditional methods due to their advanced features, such as their high physical and chemical compatibility with artwork parts and their significantly lower toxicity compared to traditional restoration materials. In contrast to conventional cleaning techniques, they afford greater autonomy in managing restoration interventions. For instance, chemical hydrogels and microemulsions can be utilized to achieve extremely precise cleansing. The innovative methods put forward are feasible, safe, and, in many cases, simpler and faster than traditional methods. Prior to the COVID-19 pandemic, the market for conservation of the historical and cultural heritage in Europe was a very lively sector, estimated to be worth around €5 billion per year. It might have increased in the following years, thanks to the wider use of nanomaterials, but the after-effects of the pandemic had a negative effect on restoration work. Going forward, the most effective path to this industry's recovery is for research objectives to include improved damage assessment, the development of new conservation strategies, and the implementation of more advanced technology to better maintain and appreciate the creative and historical substrate.

In relation to our case study, preliminary assessments of the condition of the Tomb of the Sphinx, specifically the antechamber and dromos, have thus far validated the efficacy of the intervention.

The normally fast breakdown of tuffite seems to have slowed; the structures still look good, and the areas sealed with cement made from nanosilicas seem more stable and the nanosilica better suited to the rock than lime mortar. However, the rock's geomorphological properties, which limit its survival in the unstable temperatures and moisture levels of open-air settings, are primarily responsible for the emergence of new, thin cracks. Even though the roofing is efficient in its function of protecting against the direct action of rainwater and meteorological and climate agents, regular checks on and maintenance of these tombs, which are so fragile, are very important.

Recently, researchers discovered a microbiological attack within the central chamber near the entrance door; this occurred due to its exposure to sunlight during a specific time of the year. Periodic checks on the monument were able to identify this problem, which was difficult to anticipate during the roof design. Maintaining the roof, checking its functionality, and implementing small-scale actions such as, in our case, sealing new cracks, treating surface plants and microbiological attacks, and removing abundant animal dung and cobwebs may ensure proper, long-lasting conservation of the monument. An upcoming project will enable the completion of conservation work in the underground chambers, including the resolution of identified issues. The project will also enable the restoration of other significant monuments in the Osteria Necropolis, including the Tomba a Dado and the Tomb of the Carved Ceilings, utilizing advanced techniques and materials to safeguard the tuffite.

Bibliography

Brandi, C. *Teoria del restauro*. Milano: Piccola Biblioteca Einaudi, 2000.

Charola, E. *Lavas and Volcanic Tuffs: Proceedings of the International Meeting, EasterIsland, Chile*. Rome: Senior Editor, 1990.

Lazzarini, L., and M. Laurenzi Tabasso, *Il restauro della pietra*. Padua: CEDAM, 1986.

Masetti Bitelli, L., ed. *La conservazione e il restauro oggi 3, Archeologia recupero e conservazione*. Florence: Nardini editore, 1993.

Ministero degli Affari Esteri, *Il restauro in Italia: Arte e tecnologia nell'attività dell'Istituto Superiore per la Conservazione ed il Restauro*, Rome: Cangemi editore S.p.A., 2013.

Morbidelli, L. *Le rocce e i loro costituenti*, Rome: Bardi, 2010.

Nardi, L. *La conservazione sullo scavo archeologico*. Rome: ICCROM e CCA, Centro di conservazione archeologica, 1986.

NORMAL, 1/88. *Alterazioni macroscopiche dei materiali lapidei: Lessico*. Rome: CNR-ICR, 1990.

NORMAL, 3/80. *Materiali lapidei: Campionamento*. Rome: CNR-ICR, 1980.

Naso, A. *La pittura etrusca*. Rome: L'Ermadi Bretschneider, 2005.

Pedelì, C., and Pulga, S. *Pratiche conservative sullo scavo archeologico: Principi e metodi*, prima edizione, Florence: All'insegna del Giglio, 2002.

Webliography

www.ipac.regione.fvg.it

L. R. 26/2005 ART. 21 - Progetto NANOCOAT 4 L'impiego di nanotecnologie e nanomateriali per il recupero e la conservazione dei beni culturali Consorzio Innova FVG.

Teresa Carta, *Conservation Practice: The Tomb of the Sphinx in Vulci* In: *A New Etruscan Archaeology: Twenty-First Century Techniques and Methods*. Edited by: Maurizio Forte, Oxford University Press.
© Oxford University Press 2025. DOI: 10.1093/9780197582053.003.0008

8

Etruscan Painting

Interdisciplinary Approaches to Protection and Conservation

Daniele Federico Maras, Adele Cecchini, and Antonio Giglio

Introduction

Early Painting in the Classical World

Although painting was considered one of the major forms of art in the Classical world, alongside sculpture, very little remains of ancient painted monuments. Large polychrome megalographies applied on plaster decorated the most important Greek temples in the mid-seventh century BCE, such as the temple of Apollo at Abai (Kalapodi) and that of Poseidon at Isthmia, as the scattered remains found in modern excavations show.

Pliny the Elder narrates that the Lydian King Kandaules purchased a large wooden panel with a painting by Boularchos, which depicted a battle of the Magnesians. This passage provides the earliest literary evidence for the existence of painting on wood, possibly in a nonsacred context, even though we should probably postpone the episode from the late eighth century (when Kandaules reigned) to the mid-seventh century BCE (Hurwit, 2012).

Early architecture in Greece and elsewhere in the Mediterranean featured cheap and poor building materials, including wooden structures and raw bricks. And this tradition continued even later where the quality of stones and economic resources did not allow for better building techniques, as in many parts of Sicily and Italy (Marconi, 2007, 3–15 and 36–60). Terracotta roofs with broadly overhanging slopes provided the necessary protection from weathering for perishable structures over time (Winter, 2009). In addition, the walls were protected from time to time with either plaster or wooden panels, both of which certainly provided a favored space for painted decorations (D. F. Maras, in Agnoli et al., 2019, 59–61).

Unfortunately, only sparse fragments have been found of Archaic Greek painted plaster, and virtually nothing remains of Greek panel painting on wood, which included some of the most important works of famous Greek artists celebrated by the ancient authors.

We are luckier, however, with some durable substitutes for wood, which were used from time to time in monumental buildings. For instance, an unusual painted plaque from the mid-seventh century from the agora of Athens depicts a deity in frontal view, painted in red between snakes and with a high relief head.

Around 625 BCE, a famous group of painted terracotta plaques, currently on display at the National Archaeological Museum of Athens, decorated the temple of Apollo at Thermon in Aetolia. The scenes depict myths and bear labels; they likely originated as wall frescoes rather than roof decorations. Another example are the terracotta plaques with geometrical patterns associated with the earliest Marasà temple at Locri in southern Italy (Cosentino and Maras, 2019–2020, 103–105).

Literary sources do not explicitly mention free painting on terracotta, with the possible exception of some works by Zeuxis at Ambracia (*figlina opera*), which are, however, several centuries later than the archaeological examples.

Painting in Etruria

Our understanding of Archaic painting would be rather poor and partial if we had no Etruscan evidence. The use of wall painting in chamber tombs, especially but not only at Tarquinia, has preserved the largest and most precious collection of free painting in the ancient Mediterranean before the Roman period. In addition, the Etruscans (who did not have good-quality stone supplies) continued the tradition of terracotta revetments for buildings until the late Hellenistic period, including a large number of terracotta painted plaques used for wall decoration in the sixth and fifth centuries BCE.

Several hut-shaped impasto urns, as well as some splendid Orientalizing white-on-red house-shaped urns from the Villanovan period in Etruria, attest to the figural or geometrical decoration of private building walls. On these premises, we can argue that the painted walls of the Orientalizing tombs—for instance, at Veii and Caere—imitated the actual decoration of residential buildings, even though the subjects were probably different, as suitable for funerary contexts.

The earliest examples of funerary painting occur at Veii, where the Tomba dei Leoni Ruggenti dates from around 690 BCE and the Tomba delle Anatre from 680–670 BCE. The surfaces were smoothed and covered with a preparatory layer (possibly diatomite in the former and clay in the latter) before application of a limited palette of pigments (red, yellow, and black) (Boitani, 2019a, 2019b).

Geometric painted decorations are attested in several tombs of this period in Etruria; however, the use of painted friezes is attested in other seventh-century tombs at Veii (Tomba Campana), Caere (tombs della Nave and dei Leoni Dipinti), Magliano (Tomba Dipinta), and finally Tarquinia (Tomba delle Pantere; Figure 8.1) (Colonna, 1989).

This last inaugurates the outstanding series of painted tombs at Tarquinia, whose tradition continued steadily from the end of the seventh to the third century BCE, with a progressive development of techniques, material, and artistic features, as described below.

Figure 8.1 Tarquinia, *Tomba delle Pantere*: painted decoration of the back wall. End of the seventh century BCE.

Funerary paintings in elite tombs from the fourth and third centuries BCE appeared in other Etruscan metropolises, too, such as Volsinii, Vulci, and Chiusi. However, the necropolis of Tarquinia holds first place as the largest gallery of paintings in the ancient Mediterranean before the Roman period, with more than 130 painted tombs whose decorations have been sufficiently preserved (out of the 500 with painted remains) (Adinolfi et al., 2019a; Steingräber, 1984, 2006).

Unfortunately, these paintings belong exclusively to funerary contexts, with a selection of subjects depending on beliefs and symbolic references. Putting together this evidence and that deriving from painted pottery, one can glean only limited information on the use of painting in Etruscan daily life, in habitations as well as in public and sacred contexts.

In fact, wall painting was probably widespread in the ancient world, as was painting on revetments and mobile supports. Therefore, since there is no evidence for painted plaster in Etruscan habitation contexts, it is likely that the favored supports for these decorations were wood panels. However, some south Etruscan contexts began using painted terracotta plaques for wall decoration in the sixth century BCE.

The protruding "wings" on the back side of the earliest examples of these plaques—used for wall hanging—led to their misinterpretation as roof tiles in the past. These include white-on-red productions, such as a series dating from 575–550 BCE found in the residential context of Acquarossa and decorated with horses, birds, and snakes. A fragmentary example of uncertain origin, dating from 540–530 BCE, preserves the central part of a standing figure depicted over three plaques. Finally, a third tile-shaped example comes from the temple of Hera at Manganello in Caere, dating back to 510–500 BCE (Cosentino and Maras, 2019–2020, 105–106).

Apart from this early type, the most widespread model for painted plaques at Caere in the late sixth and early fifth centuries BCE was 120–130 centimeters tall and 50–60 centimeters wide. These were plain rectangular plaques with holes in the upper part used to attach them to the wall. These plaques were most likely supported by the wooden revetments covering the lower portion of the walls.

Fortunately, researchers have found the remains of several examples from a single series, but, regrettably, most of these discoveries have occurred during illegal excavations or on the international antiques market.

This is the case, for instance, for a series depicting Herakles's labors, which originally included more than thirty plaques, as proved by the numeral marks painted on the upper rim of some examples (Figure 8.2). Further series depicted dance and sports scenes as well as mythological narratives.

Although it is not clear where these plaques came to light, it is most likely that some of the earliest series originally decorated elite residences, and, in some cases, a selected number of plaques followed their owners into their tombs. According to Greek tradition, most series ended up in sacred buildings.

Figure 8.2 Caere, three terracotta plaques of the series with Herakles' labors on display at Centrale Montemartini in Rome. End of the sixth century BCE.

Caere's most recent production dates to the first half of the fifth century BCE. During this period, sanctuaries in Veii, at the temple of Portonaccio, and in Orvieto, at Campo della Fiera, attested different plaque models, shorter in height and featuring a different hanging system.

After this period, the fashion of decorating walls with painted plaques came abruptly to an end, presumably in correspondence with a different building technique for the walls of public buildings, thus condemning the archaic use of terracotta painting to oblivion, possibly because it was too reminiscent of an old-fashioned aristocratic lifestyle.

Interdisciplinary Approaches

Recent experiences in the study and conservation of painted surfaces, including wall paintings and terracotta plaques, have highlighted the importance of incorporating methods, analyses, and approaches from diverse disciplines into comprehensive conservation projects.

To achieve this, a network of public and private institutions, including universities and international research institutes and recognized associations of specialists, along with the expertise of independent professionals, surrounds the offices of the Italian Ministry of Culture responsible for the protection and conservation of archaeological sites and materials.

For instance, at the sites of the painted tombs at Veii and Tarquinia, a vast operation of geological monitoring of the bedrock in which the tombs are carved is carried out by a research group led by Daniele Spizzichino at the Italian Institute for Environmental Protection and Research (ISPRA) (Spizzichino et al., 2019).

An in-depth analysis of the microbiological population of the bedrock within the funerary chambers of the necropolis of Monterozzi at Tarquinia is part of a research project by Teresa Rinaldi at the Sapienza University of Rome (Rinaldi et al., 2018; Tomassetti et al., 2017).

A group of Italian and Korean researchers led by Giulia Caneva (University of Roma Tre) and Yong Jae Chung (Korea National University of Cultural Heritage) is studying the biological risk to painted hypogea to determine ways to stabilize the microclimate and use biocides that are safe for the environment (Caneva et al., 2021; Isola et al., 2021).

The placement and shaping of the mounds on the surface above the tombs of Tarquinia is the subject of experimental research by Matilde Marzullo and Andrea Garzulino, through the application of digital technologies, at the University of Milan (Marzullo, 2016, 2017).

Germana Barone and Paolo Mazzoleni lead a research group at the University of Catania that conducts an overall archaeometric analysis of pigments using mineralogical and chemical methods, in both the case of wall paintings and terracotta plaques (G. Barone et al., in Russo et al., 2018, 57–78; Barone et al., 2018, 2020).

Claudio Falcucci has systematically performed a complete set of physical analyses, including thermoluminescence, stratigraphic examinations on thin sections with a scanning electron microscope, X-ray fluorescence, and infrared spectrophotometry, on a large number of fragments of terracotta painted plaques recently repatriated or discovered at new sites. The restorer Marina Angelini has also conducted technical analyses (C. Falcucci, in Russo et al., 2018, 47–56; M. Angelini, C. Falcucci, in Agnoli et al., 2019, 105–122; Angelini et al., 2019).

Last, but not least, a research group including Gloria Adinolfi, Rodolfo Carmagnola, Luciano Marras, and Vincenzo Palleschi have, in an innovative project, applied hyperspectral reflectometry and ultraviolet fluorescence to wall paintings in Etruscan tombs at Tarquinia, Veii, and Chiusi and recently to the painted terracotta plaques from Caere as well. Significantly, this new approach is providing outstanding results in detecting faded pigments and reconstructing apparently lost pictures, thus saving them definitively from oblivion (Adinolfi et al., 2005; Adinolfi et al., 2019b; Adinolfi et al., 2021).

Wall Painting at Tarquinia

A Unique Cultural Heritage

The UNESCO World Heritage List recognizes the Etruscan necropolises of Tarquinia as "masterpieces of creative genius." In particular, Tarquinia's large-scale wall paintings are considered "exceptional both for their formal qualities and for their content, which reveal aspects of life, death, and religious beliefs of the ancient Etruscans" (http://whc.unesco.org/en/list/1158/).

Following this prestigious international acknowledgment, Italian governmental authorities in charge of the protection of this site faced the enormous challenge of monitoring the conservation of the painted tombs, preserving them from degradation, and experimenting with new methods of protecting the archaeological compounds in their entirety to save them for posterity.

During the seasonal cycle, interdisciplinary methods and approaches are used to tackle the complexity of the environment in the painted tombs, ensuring and improving the knowledge, conservation, and protection of the site and its unique features. In addition to archaeology and conservation, the operations include aspects of geology, physics and optics, botany and biology, meteorology, and the archaeometric study of ancient painting techniques as well as special research on restoration methods and techniques.

In this regard, it is important to highlight that, in recent years, the protection and conservation of cultural heritage have been demonstrated to be as difficult as they are indispensable in diverse parts of the world, with special regard to archaeological sites. This has proved true not only where war, terrorism, and vandalism are involved, but also in cases of negligence and, sad to say, public indifference, as well as simply a lack of funding. In this framework, archaeologists, scholars, and curators of museums and sites have the moral duty to protect cultural heritage as a whole and hand it down to the next generation as a token of civilization and a flywheel of culture.

As a result, the task of protection and conservation necessitates the best efforts of all involved, gathered into a network that includes authorities, universities and research centers, professionals, associations, and foundations as well as the active participation of local citizens. This is the project that the Italian Ministry of Culture is carrying out through an institutional network coordinated by the Soprintendenza in the UNESCO heritage site at Tarquinia, with particular regard to the recent interdisciplinary collaboration involving public and private forces.

The specific challenge in the necropolis of Tarquinia is to coordinate the goal of enhancing the visibility of the tombs and their access to the general public with the necessity of protecting them and preserving their nature as works of art, as required by the Italian law for cultural heritage and landscapes (Legislative Decree nr. 42/2004, art. 3 and 6).

Since the discovery of the majority of the painted tombs at Tarquinia starting in the 1820s and running throughout the nineteenth and twentieth centuries, efforts to this end have been based on achieving a balance between opening tombs to visitors and protecting them from undue exploitation: this was accomplished by monitoring their state of conservation (often documenting it by means of watercolors, facsimiles, and photos; see, e.g., Cataldi, 2020; Cecchini, 2017), closing those hypogea at risk or at least limiting access to the public, and carrying out specific restorations when necessary and when funds were available.

The rapid increase in visitors over the past thirty years has further challenged this balance, necessitating improved monitoring practices and stricter procedures for decision-making and planning interventions. Fortunately, technologies and methods for protection and conservation have improved as well and allow us to have a better understanding of the actual conditions of each painted tomb. For instance, since 1989, the progressive installation of aluminum insulating doors with thermal breaks has achieved wonderful results in preserving the microclimate in tomb chambers (Bettini and Massa, 1994) while at the same time allowing visitors to see the paintings comfortably through the doors' transparent windows and self-defrosting electrical devices (Figure 8.3d).

Daniele Federico Maras

Ancient Painting Techniques

The chamber tombs were excavated in a calcareous rock, locally known as *macco*, which contains abundant fossil fragments that are visible without magnification. Some of the tombs were painted. First, the artists leveled the surface using cutting tools, then filled in gaps and lower areas where necessary and covered them with plaster (Cecchini, 2012).

Figure 8.3 Tarquinia, painted tombs. a. *Tomba dei Tori* (ca. 540 BCE), detail of the back wall: the clay 'wash' and the preparatory incisions are visible. b. *Tomba dei Demoni Azzurri* (late fifth century BCE), detail of the left wall: the scarce resistance of the "dry" paint is visible. c. *Tomba del Tifone* (mid-third century BCE), detail of the lower frieze with a dolphin outlined with the help of a template. d. The Tomba degli Scudi, a partially transparent insulating door with a thermal break, dates from the mid-fourth century BCE.

Generally, people applied plaster only to create a smooth surface for painting. The entire surface, if too irregular, could receive a complete coating. This was done only where necessary: in the Tomba della Caccia e della Pesca, the walls were completely plastered but not the ceiling; in the Tomba dei Tori, the walls were not plastered but the ceiling was, most likely to cover red veins in the rock. The plaster used was composed of the same macco stone, finely ground and mixed with lime.

Using a large, soft brush, the artists applied a preparatory layer to all the plastered areas destined for painting. In sixth-century BCE tombs, this layer was composed of limestone having the same technical and morphological characteristics as a white material widely known and appreciated in antiquity and described in some detail by Pliny (*Natural History*, 35.6): "Among the white pigments…paretonium is the oiliest and most resistant to plaster due to its smoothness." Writers of the day describe it as a lime-solidified foam that contains very fine shells. Vitruvius also reports that paretonium takes its name from "a locality in Egypt…200,000 steps distant from Alessandria."

The light-colored clay found in the ancient tombs of Tarquinia comes from a micro-fossiliferous limestone that is similar to paretonium in many ways. It seems to have been used for the same things, whether in plasters or as a base for the first layer that was applied with a brush. The macco bedrock itself, given its composition of fossils, limestone, and clay, apparently provided a similar service. This can be seen in the earliest tombs, where the painting is executed directly on the smoothed rock surface without any preparatory layer (examples include the tombs delle Pantere, dei Leoni Rossi, and dei Fiorellini, all dating to the sixth century BCE).

After smoothing the surfaces or applying plaster in six tombs of the Necropolis of Tarquinia from the sixth century BCE, the artists laid on a layer of gray clay of varying thickness to make the surface smoother and more homogeneous (Figure 8.3a), a technique similar to the earlier pictorial precedents of Mesopotamia and Anatolia as well as the painted tombs of nearby Veii and Tuscany. A chemical study of this substance was carried out by Barone and Mazzoleni, of the University of Catania, after a campaign of noninvasive in situ analyses on eight Tarquinian tombs by means of a portable X-ray fluorescence device (Barone et al., 2018, 2020). The results confirmed the use of a calcareous stone substrate known as macco, as well as a preparatory layer primarily composed of calcite. Furthermore, considering the remarkably similar ratios of calcium oxide to magnesium oxide and strontium oxide to calcium oxide, we can conclude that macco served as both a raw material and a support for the entire pictorial work in the preparatory layers. However, where limestone marl is present, it forms the gray layer.

The tombs of Tarquinia were painted using the same pigments as in the fresco technique, but, unlike the latter, the pigments were applied over a clay "wash" in tombs from the sixth century and first half of the fifth century BCE, and over a layer of lime in the tombs from the fourth and third centuries BCE (Figure 8.3c).

During the second half of the fifth century, the Etruscan painters of Tarquinia attempted to paint directly on wet plaster rather than on freshly spread "fresco" plaster. In Etruscan tradition, plaster was applied when the tomb was excavated in order to smooth the surfaces of the rocky walls. The painters of the later fifth century thus dampened the already dried plaster using sturdy brushes and then proceeded with the decorative and pictorial execution. The result was, in effect, a "dry" paint that was not very resistant (Figure 8.3b).

Researchers examined the pictorial layers of eight important tombs (Fior di Loto, Leonesse, Cacciatore, Barone, Bartoccini, Tori, Giocolieri, Caccia e Pesca) to get a new perspective on the use of color in Etruscan culture, especially in wall painting at Tarquinia. The results produced new ways to think about a topic that is still being debated, showing a complex framework of pigments employed that was closely related to the importance of each single painting. Significantly, precious pigments are present only in specific symbolic details within the paintings and in the most notable tombs. In some cases, we have observed the coexistence of uncommon Etruscan pigments on pictorial surfaces, such as Egyptian blue, malachite, lazurite, and possibly Tyrian purple, alongside more traditional pigments like ochre (Bicchieri et al., 2001). Barone et al. (2018, 2020) achieved interesting results regarding pictorial technology and hypothesized the origin of the pigments.

Methods of Conservation

An archaeological complex as important and unique as Tarquinia has serious conservation problems. The approximately 200 painted tombs present at the necropolis of Tarquinia are only a small part (about 3 percent) of the hypogea present in the area commonly known as "Monterozzi." This large number of tombs is, by its very nature, constantly subject to degradation and therefore requires equally constant and regular maintenance.

The sudden variations in temperature and humidity within the painted compartment upon opening are the primary cause of the paintings' deterioration. These variations, in turn, trigger a whole series of degenerative processes that are detrimental to the painted surfaces. However, periodic tomb inspections can easily temper these processes with immediate interventions. Hence, it is essential to constantly monitor the tombs and provide for the site's regular maintenance.

Various factors alter microclimatic systems, triggering different degradation processes that necessitate constant survey monitoring; these include: thermo-hygrometric variations, the overlying terrain's conformation (including the paths leading to the tombs), the penetration of roots, spores and biodegradogenic microorganisms, insects, and lighting systems. Damage can be of chemical-physical, biological, mechanical, and anthropic origin. In addition, the occasional revision of previous and unsuitable interventions is necessary.

Among the damages of chemical-physical origin, the most important is certainly the formation of white efflorescence on painted surfaces caused by the difference between the temperature of the air inside the tombs and the surface temperature of the walls. This process facilitates the migration of water from the rocky substrate to the surface, as well as the subsequent movement of soluble salts contained within the substrate.

The resulting evaporation forms a whitish patina that veils the original colors. If this veil remains unremoved, it may carbonate and harden, applying pressure to the painted surface and ultimately leading to the lifting and falling of the pictorial film.

An inadequate conformation of both the soil above the tombs and the mounds causes damage of mechanical origin. In certain weather situations, an accumulation of rainwater in the substrate penetrates into the burial chambers, causing losses in the painted layers of the tombs.

Farmers who plow too closely to the underlying hypogea cause further structural damage. And the penetration through the soil of the roots of surface vegetation causes the disintegration and fall of plaster and pictorial film due to their perforating action (Figure 8.4b, d). This damage is mechanical in nature and is often very serious (Caneva et al., 2021; Massa, 2017).

The tombs' internal microclimate is also altered and damaged by factors of biological origin, such as the roots of overlying plants, which, combined with the introduction of spores, cause the development of colonies that form a patina deriving from biodeteriogenic microorganisms such as streptomycetes, fungi, and bacteria. This patina generates chromatic changes on the surface. In other cases, salts, like the one we're highlighting here, produce a white, patina-like sedimentation. Likewise, lamps whose values do not fall within the prescribed parameters also cause biological damage, leading to the proliferation of algal colonies in the irradiation zone.

The presence of insects also causes damage of biological origin, as well as mechanical damage. Slugs produce organic mucus and excrement that often lead to disfiguring, biological damage (Figure 8.4a). Termites of the species *Reticulitermes lucifugus*

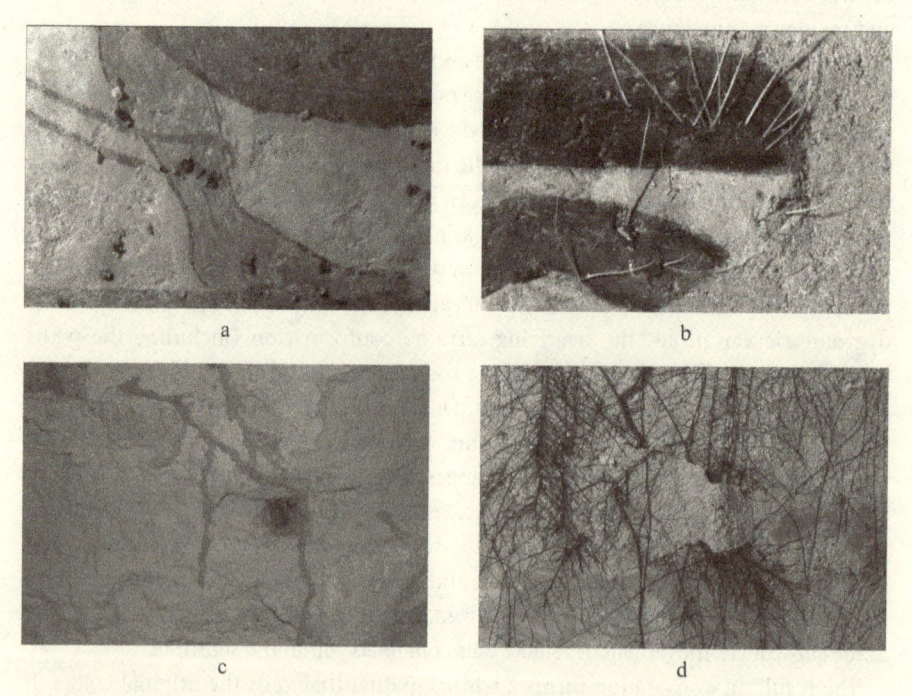

a   b

c   d

Figure 8.4 Tarquinia, painted tombs. a. *Tomba degli Auguri* (ca. 520–510 BCE): slug excrements on the painted wall. b. Tomba degli Auguri (ca. 520–510 BCE): mechanical damage resulting from the penetration of roots from the vegetation on the upper surface. c. *Tomba Francesca Giustiniani* (mid-fifth century BCE): tunnels excavated by termites (*Reticulitermes lucifugus*). d. *Tomba dei Vasi Dipinti* (end of the sixth century BCE): roots piercing the painted walls and lifting the pictorial coating.

build tunnels composed of a mixture of saliva, soil, and excrement in order to move through and across the painted surfaces (Figure 8.4c).

These are just a few examples of the degradation factors that constantly threaten the proper conservation of Tarquinia's painted tombs.

Maintenance of the hypogea and the area above them is an indispensable premise for accessing and conserving the painted tombs of the UNESCO Heritage Site of Tarquinia. Current methodologies demonstrate that an adequate and constant campaign of monitoring and rapid intervention is no longer a utopian vision; such campaigns successfully block the degradation of precious paintings and preserve them in situ.

To plan interventions and prevent damage from the factors that determine different types of degradation of the painted surfaces, monitoring the conservation status of the hypogea is the first essential step. Soprintendenza personnel, accompanied by a restorer who assesses the condition of the paintings and chambers, must carry out the initial and primary operation of inspecting the tombs twice a year, in autumn and spring. In the event of unusual weather events throughout the year, we organize further special inspections.

Adele Cecchini

Terracotta Painting at Caere

Recovering New Painted Plaques

As mentioned, the Etruscan terracotta painted plaques were presumably a durable substitute for the wooden tablets generally used to protect building walls and adapted as pictorial surfaces, often composing narrative friezes painted on a sequence of adjoining plaques.

In 1965, Francesco Roncalli conducted a seminal study on the terracotta painted plaques from Caere, studying and classifying fifty-three examples, including the renowned Campana Plaques at the Louvre and the Boccanera Plaques at the British Museum (Roncalli, 1965).

In 2016, the Carabinieri for the Protection of Cultural Heritage in Geneva seized a large number of new examples from the illicit antiquities market, with the help and support of the Swiss authorities (Russo, 2018–2019). The Italian Ministry and the Ny Carlsberg Glyptotek of Copenhagen, through an international deal of cooperation, repatriated a further group of plaques to Italy in the same year (J. Kindberg Jacobsen, G.P. Mittica, and J. Melender, in Russo et al., 2018, 25–32). Additionally, a few precious fragments of plaques were discovered in 2017–2018 during digs carried out by the Soprintendenza at the site of Manganello at Caere (Cosentino and Maras, 2019–2020).

The rescue and recovery of such a large number of examples (which raised to more than 400 the number of known Etruscan plaques) has provided an outstanding and unparalleled opportunity for appreciating and studying this form of art, but at the same time has challenged the skills of archaeologists, restorers, and scientists involved in their analysis and conservation.

In addition to two exhibitions at the Castle of Santa Severa in 2018 and the Centrale Montemartini in Rome in 2019–2020, the Soprintendenza presented the results of its research on the plaques at a congress in Santa Severa in 2018, whose proceedings are forthcoming (Agnoli et al., 2019; Russo et al., 2018).

Here, we present a resume of the current knowledge on the ancient production techniques and the modern restoration methods developed for the plaques (the latest discoveries in this field are presented in Bochicchio et al., 2024, and Maras and Zaccagnini, forthcoming).

Daniele Federico Maras

Ancient Production Techniques

The production of the terracotta plaques began by pressing clay into squared frames, as evidenced by marks on the back of some examples and the irregular rims of overflowing clay that frequently remain along the margins of the final products (Figure 8.5a).

Based on the available data, we reconstructed the height of the wooden frames used at approximately 30 millimeters. We measured the thickness of the resulting plaques within a range of 23 to 42 millimeters, taking into account the shrinkage that occurs during drying and firing, which frequently results in cracks on the back side.

The reddish color of the clay body, which is visible on the broken surfaces and behind the plaques, indicates that it is typically unrefined and contains iron oxides.

The shape of the plaques is generally rectangular, with a disproportion between the large dimension of the face to the relatively slim thickness. This often causes a deformation in the final product, producing a so-called sandwich effect that makes the plaque either concave or convex up to a maximum deviation of 20 millimeters at its far ends.

A slip of highly refined clay with a low content of iron oxides covered the surface of the pressed clay plaque after drying, giving it a light color after firing. The presence of vertical drops of liquid clay suggests that the finish was achieved by keeping the plaques in a vertical position, possibly to let excess clay trickle down (Figure 8.5c).

It is certain, however, that the subsequent phase of painting the polychrome decoration was executed vertically, as in easel painting, as evidenced by several droplets and streaks of colored pigment (Figure 8.5d). In this regard, it is important to highlight that terracotta painting, as opposed to any other type of painting, allows the painter only one coating, with no further possibility of making changes or retouching.

The palette used for polychrome decoration was limited to the possibilities of clays and metallic oxides—that is to say, red in its diverse hues, orange-yellow, black, and greenish gray.

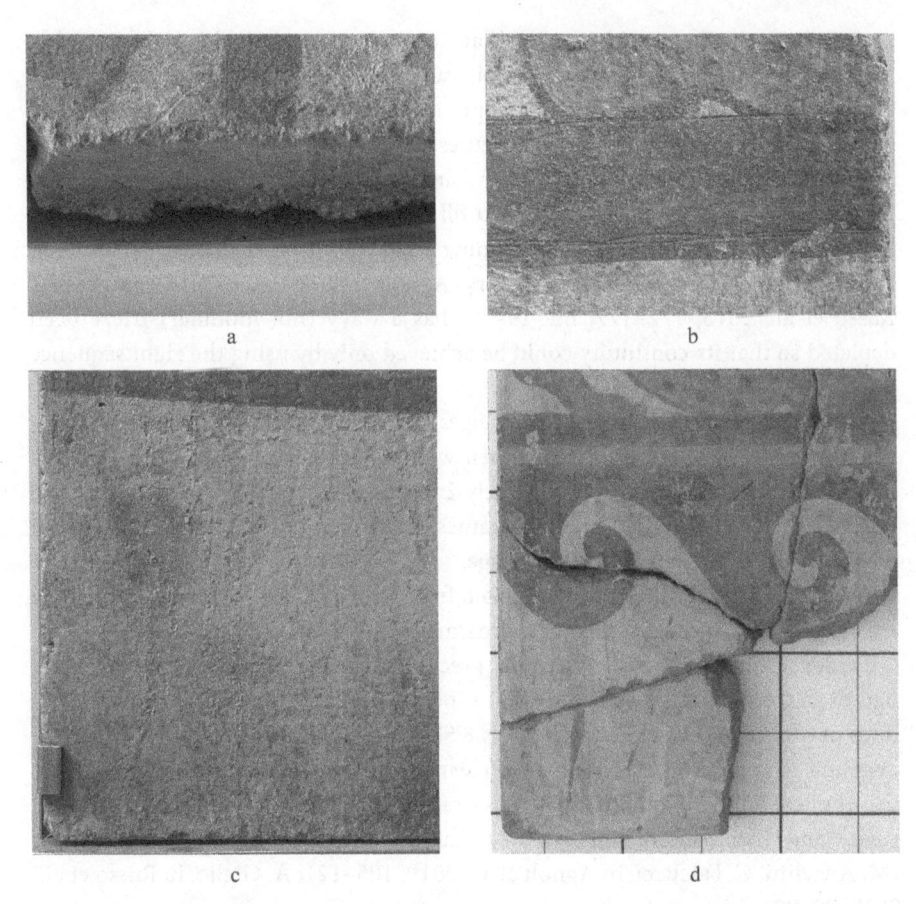

Figure 8.5 Shows Caere painting terracotta plaques. a. Margin of a plaque with an irregular rim of clay originally overflowing from the mold frame. b. A geometric partition. c. Remains of liquid clay trickled down from the background slip. d. Streaks of colored pigment dropped from the painting.

Diagnostic analyses executed on the pigments confirmed the use of manganese compounds for black color and of iron-oxides for red, yellow, and orange; the greenish gray was obtained by mixing dark manganese with the whitish clay of the background slip (Guidi et al., 2006; C. Falcucci, in Russo et al., 2018, 47–55; G. Barone et al., in Russo et al., 2018, 57–77; M. Angelini, C. Falcucci, in Agnoli et al., 2019, 105–121).

The upper part of the plaques' geometric decoration (including meanders and stripes) is typically red and black. As usual in Etruscan funerary wall painting, the color of the skin in human depictions differs: dark reddish brown for male figures and a light color for female figures. Females were depicted at times by either a sole outline, leaving the background color for their skin, or by adding a pinkish hue, or even, in a single case, by overlapping the whitish layer over a red one.

As previously mentioned, a series of adjacent plaques create pictorial friezes featuring mythological depictions of various subjects. The majority of known plaques present a tripartite scheme, with an upper frame and the lower band separated by stripes from the central scene, whose figures stand on the lower stripe.

The geometric modules of the upper frame usually have a regular rhythm, with a number of elements large enough to fill exactly the width of the plaque, thus making a continuous frieze with adjoining plaques, whatever their order. Only in the case of the series of Herakles's labors (Agnoli et al., 2019, 162–171, nn. 26–36; Russo et al., 2018, 172–177, nn. 19–38) has a wavy (not modular) frieze been depicted so that its continuity could be achieved only by using the right sequence of plaques.

The overall height of the plaques changes depending on the pictorial cycle, averaging around 100 centimeters, while their width seems to follow the rule of slightly more than 50 centimeters (approximately 2 foot in the italic measurement system). Possibly, the craftsmen had modular frames set up to produce plaques of standard measures, net drying and firing shrinkage.

On the grounds of measurements taken from whole plaques currently known, we estimate a width-to-height ratio of approximately 1:2.

Evidence for preparatory incisions preceding the subsequent painting of the figural decoration has been observed, especially in relation to the construction lines of geometric subdivision (Figures 8.5b and 8.6c). The guide lines for meanders and to separate stripes are often clearly visible. It is worth mentioning that the frames follow geometric patterns traced with the help of a tool (rod or ruler) and that usually brush strokes faithfully follow the preparatory track (M. Angelini, C. Falcucci, in Agnoli et al., 2019, 105–121; A. Giglio, in Russo et al., 2018, 79–92).

Methods of Conservation

All the known preserved plaques are fragmentary and usually incomplete: in some cases, the number of fragments is small; often each fragment is very small and there may be no more than fifty.

We lack data to determine the causes of plaque fragmentation as the vast majority have lost their original context. Most of the time, the rift lines align with compression events, likely caused by crashes or the collapse of architectural structures. However, in certain instances, we cannot rule out the possibility of voluntary blows to the surface, and we are uncertain if they occurred during the plaques' hanging on the walls or after their detachment.

The state of surface conservation often shows great differences in diverse areas of a single plaque. In all cases, reading the decoration of some areas is especially difficult because of the presence of either overlapping accretions, abrasions, loss of slip, or even damage to the clay body up to some millimeters in depth.

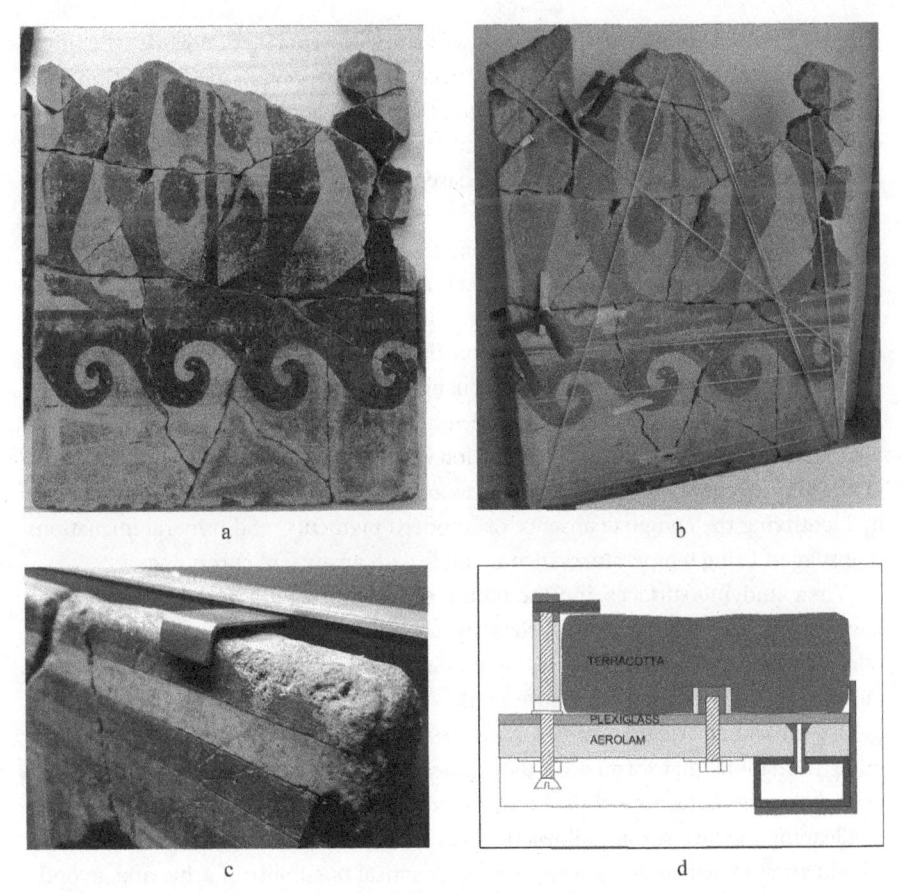

Figure 8.6 Shows Caere painting terracotta plaques. A fragmentary plaque from the series featuring Herakles' labors displays a dark patina of manganese compounds. b. Rubber bands and clamps secure the fragments of the same plaque while the adhesive dries. c. an L-shaped hook that attaches the upper side of a plaque to its support. d. A support scheme—a "tray" made of steel, aerolam, and plexiglass.

Some abrasions to the pictorial decoration could have been caused by a first cleaning performed by illicit diggers or by art dealers who put the plaques on the illegal market. Unfortunately, clumsy interventions executed with inadequate methods and tools can bring about the irreversible loss of entire parts of the decorations.

Besides the earth deposits concentrated on the back and on the broken margins, the presence of manganese deposits on the surfaces is often detected. Their formation is generally due to the alteration of organic substances during the long burial phase of the plaques: in this case, the peculiar conditions of the ground in which the plaques were laid gave these deposits extreme resistance and high-grade adhesion to the terracotta surfaces.

In this context, it is necessary to gather and document all available data on the state of the art before intervening directly with the fragments. After preparing detailed photo documentation in color, we compile a report that includes the initial preliminary observations. To separately record the treatments performed on each fragment, we number them on a photographic or graphic basis. We execute the first diagnostic campaign based on preliminary observations, initially through a series of nondestructive tests, and subsequently, based on their results, through the study of specifically focused samples.

The diagnostic study provides information on the nature of the material, the production techniques, and the state of conservation of the plaques. We get the samples we need for thermoluminescence dating (TLD) analysis by core drilling the broken edges and using only the middle section thickness of the plaque. We discard the outer layers of the core that might have changed because of exposure to the sunlight.

The study of pigments is also useful to either confirm or reject the compatibility of the manufacts with an Etruscan production (Brøns et al., 2018; C. Falcucci, in Russo et al., 2018, 47–55; G. Barone et al., in Russo et al., 2018, 57–77). We determine this by identifying the complete absence of "modern pigments" and mineral formations that suggest firing temperatures incompatible with an ancient chronology.

When studying surfaces and the nature of the overlying accretions, researchers have found that dark patinas, primarily composed of manganese minerals and referred to as metabolic processes by biodeteriogenic agents, indicate a very long burial period for the artifact (Figure 8.6a).

The subsequent cleaning phase aims to remove earth deposits, accretions, and other formations that formed on the surfaces of the fragments during their burial period. A perfect cleaning of the broken margins is required.

Cleaning the face surface allows the pictorial decoration to stand out clearly. We should always balance this goal against the practical possibility of achieving an optimal result without jeopardizing the original material or the remnants of ancient finishing operations. Therefore, we always recommend conducting a comprehensive diagnostic campaign to determine the nature of the existing deposits before initiating the cleaning phase.

To remove the majority of these deposits, we use a mixture of water and ethanol, small bristle brushes, cotton balls, and a scalpel. This first cleaning is critical for better understanding the original surfaces' state and identifying the presence of occasional insoluble or partially soluble deposits. In fact, these types of layers require a more complex cleaning intervention because they are often very firm and adhere to the fragile pictorial coatings.

A scalpel can mechanically reduce the thickness of calcareous deposits; for thin layers, one can use fiberglass brushes and ion-exchange resins, followed by rinsing the surface with deionized water. In exceptional cases, such as insoluble silica accretions adhering fast to fragile pictorial coatings, when any action is going to compromise the protection of the decoration, we consider preserving part of the deposit to avoid damaging the underlying pigments.

The manganese compounds that frequently make dark spots on the ceramic material found in excavations are usually obtrusive because they cover the underlying painted decorations. A chemical intervention on these compounds can be achieved by applying a cotton compress soaked in a solution prepared with specific hydrazine-sulfate products available on the market, possibly varying the concentration of the chemical compounds, their pH, and the time of contact (usually around 20 minutes).

The cleaning process becomes extremely complex when the manganese spots are widespread and mixed with other insoluble deposits to the point where remedial chemical action is ineffective; as a result, restorers alternate chemical interventions with the use of a scalpel and a magnifying glass. In any case, it is certainly helpful to have hyperspectral photos that allow the restorer to see more clearly what is difficult to detect with the naked eye.

The minimum intervention criteria is always the best course of action in archaeological restorations. Therefore, since the artifact is going to be preserved, presumably in controlled and protected environments that can counter possible degradation effects, each treatment should be justified by specific necessities after accurately evaluating its benefit-cost ratio. Any routine application of products or methods might be excessive intervention, producing secondary effects that are difficult to evaluate in advance when compared to the current problem.

With this in mind, it is necessary to determine the necessity and extent of the consolidation of the pictorial coating and engobe, taking into account the state of conservation of each manufact. The large dimensions and weight of the plaques necessitate adequate adherence between the fragments to withstand the strain on glued parts and, above all, sufficient mechanical resistance of the terracotta to prevent the creation of new cracks and breakage. Consolidation, achieved by applying products in depth to reach the undamaged layers of the material, can reduce the occasional phenomenon of de-cohesion when necessary.

Adherence needs to be reversible and adequate to the strain: therefore, such operations could require the application of two different products. A layer of acrylic resin in a high-concentration solution applied to the broken surface—taking care that it does not reach the face of the plaque—creates a thin protective layer that allows for reversibility of the adherence. After the complete evaporation of the solvent (24–48 hours) the use of a medium-viscosity epoxy resin (one neither so thin it is absorbed nor so thick that it forms a layer) creates adequate adhesiveness.

During the gluing process, it is advisable to use rubber bands and wooden sticks held by clamps to keep the fragments together; we avoid applying paper adhesive tapes that could risk damaging the painted surface (Figure 8.6b).

The time factor is one more element to consider when putting the fragments together. Despite large dimensions and a high number of fragments, it is advisable to perform the operation in a single day using a slow-setting adhesive to allow for minor corrections. Additionally, during this phase, we maintain the plaque in a vertical position to allow the fragments' weight to contribute to the strength of the rubber bands, resulting in the fragments returning to their original position.

Recent conservation interventions have opted not to integrate the relatively large lacunae and missing fragments, taking into account the plaques' illicit provenience and the potential for future rescue of missing fragments. Consequently, special "trays" designed for transport and exhibition of the manufacts provide support (Figure 8.2).

The supports recently designed for this purpose are composed of a stainless-steel frame, resistant to bending and twisting, which holds an aerolam panel covered by a satin-finish Plexiglass sheet (Figure 8.6d). When vertical, the plaques are held in place by a steel plate soldered to the lower base of the frame and by L-shaped hooks that fix them to the support on all sides (Figure 8.6c). An aluminum frame encloses the entire structure, and a horizontal rod at the back secures it to the wall.

To enhance the viewer's appreciation of the decorations, the final phase of conservation involves integrating the pigments with water-based paint. This is possible only where the engobe is preserved. We apply a semi-transparent colored dimming to the scraped surface in order to reduce its contrast with the preserved pigments. Although watercolors are completely reversible, it is appropriate to apply a protective layer in advance to avoid direct contact with the original surface. In a recent intervention, a polyvinyl butyral (PVB)-based vinylic resin (Mowital B 60HH) in a 1 percent ethanol solution was used (Angelini et al., 2019; M. Angelini, A. Giglio, in Russo et al., 2018, 33–45).

Antonio Giglio

Bibliography

Adinolfi, G., R. Carmagnola, and M. Cataldi. "La tomba dei Demoni Azzurri: le pitture." In *Pittura parietale, pittura vascolare. Ricerche in corso tra Etruria e Campania*, Atti della Giornata di studio (Santa Maria Capua Vetere, 28 maggio 2003), Rome: Scienze e Lettere, 2005.

Adinolfi, G., R. Carmagnola, and M. Cataldi. "*Istantanee*" dal passato. Pittura etrusca a Tarquinia / Vision of the Past. Etruscan Tomb Painting at Tarquinia*, Tarquinia: Associazione Amici delle Tombe Dipinte, 2019a.

Adinolfi, G., R. Carmagnola, M. Cataldi, L. Marras, and V. Palleschi. "Recovery of a lost wall painting at the Etruscan tomb of Blue Demons in Tarquinia (Viterbo, Italy) by multispectral reflectometry and UV fluorescence imaging." *Archaeometry* 61, 2 (2019b), 450–458.

Adinolfi, G., R, Carmagnola, L. Marras, and V. Palleschi. "Oltre il visibile: indagini iperspettrali nella tomba di Thesanthei di Tarquinia." *Studi Etruschi*, 83 (2021), 131–161.

Agnoli, N., L. Bochicchio, D.F. Maras, and R. Zaccagnini, eds. *Colori degli Etruschi. Tesori di terracotta alla Centrale Montemartini*, Catalog of the exhibition (Rome, Centrale Montemartini, 11 July 2019–2 February 2020), Rome: Gangemi, 2019.

Angelini, M., C. Falcucci, and A. Giglio. "Le lastre dipinte da Cerveteri: un intervento di restauro in equilibrio tra terracotta e pittura." In *Il restauro della ceramica. Studio dei materiali e delle forme di degrado, progettazione di interventi di restauro e conservazione*, edited by C. Casali and V. Mazzotti V., Atti della giornata di studio, Faenza, 29 November 2019, *FAENZA, Bollettino del Museo Internazionale delle Ceramiche in Faenza*, 105, 1–2 (2019), 40–49.

Barone, G., P. Mazzoleni, A. Cecchini, and A. Russo. "In situ Raman e pXRF spectroscopic study on the wall paintings of Etruscan Tarquinia tombs." *Dyes and Pigments*, 150 (2018), 390–403.

Barone, G., P. Mazzoleni, A. Cecchini, A. Russo, and M. Fugazzotto. "I pigmenti delle tombe etrusche di Tarquinia: un esempio di archeometria sul territorio." *Geologia tecnica e ambientale* 1/20 (2020). Rivista quadrimestrale dell'ordine dei geologi.

Bettini, C., and S. Massa. "Sistemi di protezione ambientale: tombe dipinte di Tarquinia." In *Atti del 49° congresso nazionale ATI*, Perugia, 26–30 September 1994, IV, Padova: SGEditoriali, 1994, 77–92.

Bicchieri, M., M. Nardone, P.A. Russo, A., Sodo, M. Corsi, G. Cristoforetti, V. Palleschi, A Salvetti, and E. Tognoni. "Characterization of azurite and lazurite based pigments by laser induced breakdown spectroscopy and micro-Raman spectroscopy." *Spectrochimica Acta Part B Atomic Spectroscopy*, 56 (2001), 915–922.

Bochicchio, L., A. Giglio, D.F. Maras, R. Zaccagnini, "Quattro nuove lastre etrusche di terracotta dipinta da Cerveteri in un recupero della Guardia di Finanza." *Rendiconti della Pontificia Accademia Romana di Archeologia* 95 (2023), 455–500.

Boitani, F. "Gli esordi della grande pittura nell'ideologia funeraria veiente." In *Società e pratiche funerarie a Veio. Dalle origini alla conquista romana*, edited by M. Arizza, Rome: Sapienza University Press, 2019a, 141–158.

Boitani, F. "Wall painting." In *Veii*, edited by J. Tabolli, Austin: Texas University Press, 2019b, 187–191.

Brøns, C., S. Buccarella Hedegaard, S., and K. Lund Rasmussen. "The real thing? Polychromy research employed in authenticity studies of Etruscan pinakes in the Ny Carlsberg Glyptotek." *Studi Etruschi* 79, 2018, 195–223.

Caneva, G., S. Langone, F. Bartoli, A. Cecchini, and C. Meneghini. "Vegetation Cover and Tumuli's Shape as Affecting Factors of Microclimate and Biodeterioration Risk for the Conservation of Etruscan Tombs (Tarquinia, Italy)". *Sustainability*, 13.6 (2021), 3393.

Cataldi, M. "La tomba del Tifone restaurata." In *Aeimnestos. Miscellanea di studi per Mauro Cristofani*, edited by B. Adembri, II, Rome: Centro Di, 2005, 668–675.

Cataldi, M. *Documentare l'arte con l'arte. Le pitture delle tombe etrusche di Tarquinia nell'opera di Adolfo Ajelli*, Tarquinia: Associazione Amici delle Tombe Dipinte, 2020.

Cecchini, A., and F. Adamo. "La tomba Bruschi Falgari di Tarquinia." *Kermes, la rivista del restauro*, 57 (2005), 65–74.

Cecchini, A. *Le tombe dipinte di Tarquinia: vicenda conservativa, restauri, tecnica di esecuzione*, Florence 2012.

Cecchini, A. "Le tombe tarquiniesi riprodotte nelle copie della Collezione Morani: conservazione e restauri." In *L'Etruria di Alessandro Morani Riproduzioni di pitture etrusche dalle collezioni dell'Istituto Svedese di Studi Classici a Roma*, edited by A. Capoferro and S. Renzetti, Rome: Polistampa, 2017, 179–195.

Colonna, G. "Gli Etruschi e l'invenzione della pittura." In *Pittura etrusca al Museo di Villa Giulia*, edited by M.A. Rizzo, Cat. of the exhibition, Rome, 7 giugno - 31 dicembre 1989, Rome: De Luca Edizioni d'Arte, 1989, 19–25.

Cosentino, R., and D.F. Maras. "Scoperte inaspettate dal santuario del Manganello a Cerveteri: una nuova lastra dipinta e la «firma invisibile» di un artista etrusco." *Rendiconti della Pontificia Accademia Romana di Archeologia*, 92 (2019–2020), 75–146.

Guidi, F.F., V. Bellelli, and G. Trojsi, eds. *Il guerriero di Ceri: tecnologie per far rivivere e interpretare un capolavoro della pittura etrusca su terracotta*, Rome: Enea, 2006.

Hurwit, J.M. "The Chigi Painter, and the interdependence of free-painting and vase-painting in the Seventh Century." In *L'Olpe Chigi. Storia di un agalma*, edited by E. Mugione, Proceedings of the international congress (Salerno, 3–4 June 2010), *Ergasteria*, 2, Salerno: Pandemos, 2012, 103–110.

Isola, D., F. Bartoli, S. Langone, S. Ceschin, L. Zucconi, and G. Caneva. "Plant DNA Barcode as a Tool for Root Identification in Hypogea: The Case of the Etruscan Tombs of Tarquinia (Central Italy)." *Plants*, 10.6 (2021), 1138.

Maras, D.F., R. Zaccagnini, "Rientri d'eccezione: il materiale ceretano recuperato dalle forze dell'ordine e dalla diplomazia culturale." In *Cronache ceretane. Seminario sulla storia degli scavi e delle collezioni archeologiche disperse*, edited by A. Coen, A. Conti, L.M. Michetti, M. Micozzi, Proceedings of the seminar (Viterbo, 30 March; Cerveteri, 21 April; Rome, 27 May 2023), Rome: CNR, forthcoming.

Marconi, C., *Temple decoration and Cultural Identity in the Archaic Greek World. The Metopes of Selinus*, Cambridge University Press, 2007.

Marzullo, M. *Grotte Cornetane materiali e apparato critico per lo studio delle tombe dipinte di Tarquinia*, I–II, Milan: Ledizioni, 2016.

Marzullo, M. *Spazi sepolti e dimensioni dipinte nelle tombe etrusche di Tarquinia*, Milan: Ledizioni, 2017.

Massa, S. "Esigenze conservative di un ipogeo interessato da vegetazione sovrastante." In R. Mancini and I. Rossi Doria, *Ruderi & Vegetazione. Questioni di restauro*. Rome: Bentivoglio Ginevra Editoria, 2017, 265–289.

Rinaldi, T., A. Cirigliano, M.C. Tomassetti, M. Di Pietro, F. Mura, M.L. Maneschi, M.D. Gentili, B. Cardazzo, C. Arrighi, C. Mazzoni, and R. Negri. "Calcite Moonmilk of Microbial Origin in the Etruscan Tomba degli Scudi in Tarquinia." *Italy. Scientific Reports*, 8 (2018), 15839.

Roncalli, F. *Le lastre dipinte da Cerveteri*, Rome: Sansoni, 1965.

Russo, A. "Le lastre dipinte di Cerveteri: storia di un recupero." *Rendiconti della Pontificia Accademia Romana di Archeologia*, 91 (2018–2019), 3–20.

Russo, A., R. Cosentino, and R. Zaccagnini, eds. *Pittura di terracotta. Mito e immagine nelle lastre dipinte di Cerveteri*, Catalog of the exhibition (S. Marinella, Castello di S. Severa, 22 giugno - 22 dicembre 2018), Rome: Gangemi, 2018.

Spizzichino, D., G. Leoni, P.M. Guarino, D. Boldini, S. Mengoni, E. Marino, A. Cecchini, F. Trucco, and B. Casocavallo. "Influenza delle condizioni climatiche sulla stabilità delle tombe etrusche della necropoli di Monterozzi a Tarquinia." In *Monitoraggio e Manutenzione delle aree archeologiche. Cambiamenti climatici, dissesto idrogeologico, degrado chimico ambientale*, edited by A. Russo and I. Della Giovampaola, Proceedings of the international congress (Rome, Parco Archeologico del Colosseo, Curia Iulia, 20–21 March 2019), Rome: L'Erma di Bretschneider, 2020, 227–230.

Steingräber, S. *Catalogo ragionato della pittura etrusca*, Milan: Jaca Book, 1984.

Steingräber S. *Abundance of Life. Etruscan Wall Painting*, Los Angeles: The J. Paul Getty Museum, 2006.

Tomassetti, M.C., A. Cirigliano, C. Arrighi, R. Negri, F. Mura, M.L. Maneschi, M.D. Gentili, M. Stirpe, C. Mazzoni, and T. Rinaldi. "A Role for Microbial Selection in Frescoes' Deterioration in Tomba degli Scudi in Tarquinia." *Ituly. Scientific Reports*, 7 (2017), 6027.

Winter, N. *Symbols of Wealth and Power: Architectural Terracotta Decorationin Etruria and Central Italy, 40–510 B.C.* (*MemAmAc*, Suppl., 9), Ann Arbor: University of Michigan Press, 2009.

Daniele Federico Maras, Adele Cecchini, and Antonio Giglio, *Etruscan Painting: Interdisciplinary Approaches to Protection and Conservation* In: *A New Etruscan Archaeology: Twenty-First Century Techniques and Methods*. Edited by: Maurizio Forte, Oxford University Press. © Oxford University Press 2025. DOI:10.1093/9780197582053.003.0009

9

Environmental Approaches to Etruscan Studies

Revisiting Negri 1927 Almost One Hundred Years Later

Meryl Shriver-Rice, Anna Maria Mercuri, Angela Trentacoste, Assunta Florenzano, and Simon Stoddart

Introduction

As Nigel Spivey acknowledged in 1991, "Etruscan archaeology is always slow to adapt to new fashions." Palaeoenvironmental reconstructions supported by extensive and diverse bioarchaeological and geoarchaeological sampling (soil cores, plant macroremains, microremains including pollen and phytoliths, animal microfossils, key vertebrate species) have long been common practice for pre-Roman and Roman Central European sites, but little attention has been paid to environmental sampling in Italy (Mercuri et al., 2010; Lodwick and Rowan 2022; Shriver-Rice and Schmidt 2022; Spivey, 1986; Spivey and Stoddart, 1990, 65–67; Stoddart, 2020a). As evidence of this fact, the first attempts to synthesize macro archaeobotanical data across Etruscan and Roman sites in Italy were done fairly recently (Bosi et al., 2015, 2017; Motta and Beydler, 2020; Trentacoste and Lodwick 2023; Sadori et al., 2015). The promise is nevertheless considerable. When combined with geoarchaeological methods, bioarchaeological sampling can provide significant new insights into human ecology, the intertwining of past natural and cultural landscapes (e.g., Mercuri, 2014). How Etruscan settlements interacted with, cultivated, and transformed their surrounding environments both affected and reflected ways in which the people of Etruria actively ordered their social relations.

Landscapes in ancient Etruria would have been deliberately and less consciously (Brown and Ellis, 1995; Hunt and Gilbertson, 1995) altered by inhabitants based on generationally shared received knowledge that may have differed by region (Bender, 2002; Stoddart, 2020b). This physical engagement with the environment would have been negotiated through accepted social boundaries developed by centuries of religious and political beliefs that governed accepted land management practices and localized traditions of access and constraint (Edlund-Berry, 2006, 2013; Hastorf, 2017). The forests of Etruria looked nothing like the managed lands of Tuscany today (Sadori 2018; see also Di Pasquale's forest reconstruction of Chiusi in 2003, Stoddart et al., 2019), although through further pollen analyses the processes of deforestation or forest sustainability during the first millennium BCE can be better understood. Little is known from the standpoint of environmental archaeology of Etruscan agricultural practices, field locations, climate adaptations, strategies of wild resource procurement, and control of arable lands (Motta and Beydler, 2020; Stoddart, 2020b, 73–79; Shriver-Rice and Schmidt 2022; Trentacoste and Lodwick, 2023). Grain production as a form of power and social debt is documented by the Romans as early as the fifth century BCE, when Etruria provided grain to Rome during several famines (Pieraccini, 2013: Dio. Hal. *Ant.* VII, 1, 2–5; Livy II, 34–3, IV, 52; XXII, 3, 1–7). Beyond questions of crop production (and the current narrow focus on the "Mediterranean triad"), climatic variation between regions and climate change through time inevitably conditioned the availability of resources and strategies of sustainability concerning wild resources. Through palynological research, a handful of rich environmental datasets exist to reconstruct climate and ecoregions at some Italian sites, providing detailed taxa lists alongside the existence of microregional land-use variabilities (Drescher-Schneider et al., 2007; Mercuri et al., 2010, 2019; Sadori, 2018; Sadori and Giardini, 2007; Sadori et al., 2010; Stoddart et al., 2019). But there is much we still do not know about the rich embedded cultural ecology of Etruscan settlements, and it is these details that have the greatest potential to shed new light on issues at the core of Etruscan archaeology: territorial control, technological innovation, resource mobilization for trade, and cultural adoptions of food practices and cuisines. New research seeks to understand more nuanced relationships between people and their environment, possible adaptations to climate oscillations, and the complex social implications of these decisions. In our chapter, we begin by surveying the history of palaeoenvironmental studies in Etruscan archaeology, starting with Negri's 1927 *Studi Etruschi* article. We then discuss the innovative range of interdisciplinary environmental methods, from geoarchaeology and palaeobotany to zooarchaeology, that might illuminate the complex set of relations between environment, biological need, and society in Etruria. Though the contributors of this chapter divided authorship according to disciplinary expertise, the endeavor of palaeoenvironmental studies in Etruscan archaeology—in life as in this chapter—is a collaborative one, which has been championed for decades by the influential work of Mercuri's archaeobotanical lab and the geomorphological research and prehistoric lens employed by Stoddart.

Giovanni Negri's 1927 prescient article "Come si possa ricostruire la fisonomia della vegetazione della Toscana durante il periodo etrusco" opens by asserting that experts are needed for interdisciplinary research in Etruscan studies, in particular botanists and geomorphologists. Nearly a century before environmental studies would find its footing in Etruscan archaeology, Negri investigated the possible ecological changes that might have occurred in ancient Etruria, tracing potentially introduced plants, changes in tree distribution, and theorizing on how and why the landscape was altered through millennia. Beyond lists of plant species that held economic value, Negri proposed the importance of complex palaeoenvironmental reconstruction for understanding the emergence of Etruscan social and state organization, reminding the reader that vegetation represents such a major factor within the human world of possibilities that it must always be evaluated to fully understand interpretations of human events in any time and specific region. He also pointed to the critical need to understand how other animals (both wild and domesticated) are embedded within Etruscan landscapes.

There are many facts that Negri got right. For example, he writes that, in general, cereals, flax, vines, and fruit trees were all likely to have been cultivated in Etruria. But there are a few assertions that we now know, reflecting back nearly one hundred years later, miss the mark, such as the idea that the Villanovans were much more "primitive" in their agriculture and pastoralism than the later Etruscans. As this chapter demonstrates, from the few sites that have been environmentally sampled, it is scale rather than agricultural regimes that change from the Late Bronze Age onward. Negri also mused that the mention by ancient authors of spelt (*Triticum spelta*) grown in Etruria was likely to have been emmer instead (*Triticum dioccum*), and we now know that both grains were cultivated in ancient Etruria. While he was correct that mostly wild species of olive would have been known in northern Etruria, he was incorrect to claim that domesticated forms were only introduced to the Italian peninsula by Greek settlers. His major point—that the poetic Mediterranean landscape of modern Tuscany, massively deforested and dotted with familiar cypress trees, would have been foreign to ancient Etruscans—still stands. His observation that much is still be to be known about the movement of ancient soils and hydrological systems also still stands and is investigated in the next section.

Geomorphology and Landscape

In common with other sectors of scientific research, the study of the geomorphology of the Etruscans has suffered from a lack of attention to the specific period of the Etruscans. The central question, in common with other contributions to this chapter, is the degree of human impact on the landscape, measured by stability and erosion. Since study areas of geomorphology have not focused on the first millennium BCE, the general measure of Etruscan impact has been considered modest, particularly compared with the full Roman period (Stoddart et al., 2019).

Current State of the Art

The current state of the art (Stoddart and Malone, 2022) can be categorized as follows: the implications of structural geology on settlements, the impact of erosion and alluviation on landscape, comparative sea level studies, and the interpretation of modern soil distributions in the relationship between the structural geology and settlement organization. Walter Alvarez, the famous American geologist who identified the K/T horizon event in the Gubbio Valley, was earlier in his career involved in important studies of Southeast Etruria during the directorship of John Ward-Perkins at the British School at Rome. His study of the evolution of the lower Tiber (Alvarez, 1975, 1976) developed into an analysis of the consequences for settlement opportunity in the volcanic province north of Rome for great Etruscan cities such as Veii; Faliscan cities such as Falerii Veteres, Narce, and Nepi (Alvarez, 1972); and, by implication, other Etruscan cities such as Cerveteri, Orvieto, and Vulci. He noted that volcanic eruptions disrupted the natural course of the Tiber, and the subsequent recapture of base level by the Treia and other rivers created the characteristic tuff outcrops of different sizes, separated by canyons that gave access to diverse resources that ranged from water to clay. The range of size of volcanic outcrops gave opportunity to different political systems; small outcrops during the Final Bronze Age and the Archaic; larger outcrops during the Villanovan and the developing powerful places that followed. The effect was not precisely the same for Cerveteri and Vulci, but the plateau system was similarly created by fluvial action (Figure 9.1). The location of Orvieto was formed out of harder volcanic material standing prominently above its landscape. Sadly, this achievement has been apparently forgotten in scholarship since the same points have been recently made by Force (2015) with no reference to his distinguished predecessor.

An independent Italian tradition of *geologia applicata* has investigated many of the eminences that provide the foundation of Etruscan cities since a substantial number have continued as prominent features of the urban landscape. Orvieto itself has been the focus of a number of projects by the local *comune* to protect the stability of the medieval and modern city. In the case of Orvieto, the historic monuments were placed on the relatively solid *Apparato Vulsino* (c. 315,000 years ago), which in turn rested on much more fragile Middle Pliocene clay (Cencetti et al., 2005). Over the course of time, this has led to considerable instability of the upper layers that required remedial action based on detailed geological investigation. These investigations have led to the discovery of ancient water systems and cavities within the substrata. Similar recuperative investigations have taken place in a number of Etruscan cities, but most notably Perugia, which was located on a very different relict

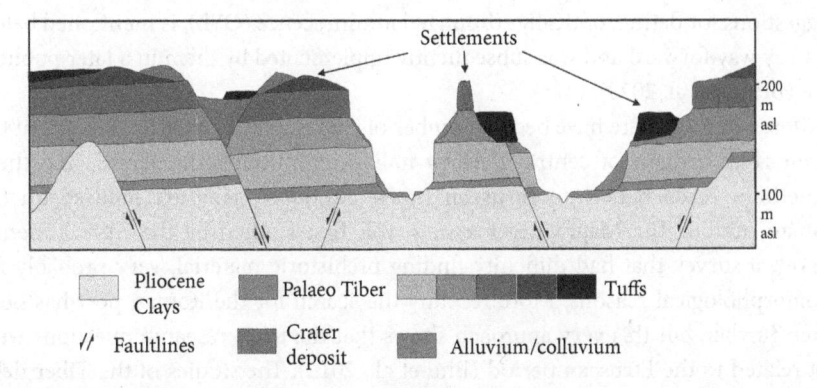

Figure 9.1 Settlements and structural geology. After Alvarez 1972.

palaeo-delta of the Upper Tiber. In this case, the exploration of the underlying hydrology has been important in understanding the development of the city from its first Final Bronze Age phases (Bertacchini, 2014, 49–50).

The politically powerful places of the Etruscans most probably had a similarly powerful but localized environmental effect (in comparison with the Romans) on their local colluvial and alluvial environment. Another American scholar, Sheldon Judson, once again working alongside Ward-Perkins, was the first to attempt to measure this effect by examining visible sections of alluvial bottoms in the volcanic landscape to measure erosion rates (Judson, 1963). Douglas Cherkauer (1976) undertook a seminal study of the fluvial regime of Narce alongside the excavation of Tim Potter, recording in detail the river regime in relationship to the occupation of the settlement. As a professor in Wisconsin, he went on to develop an understanding of the relationship between urbanism and geomorphological regimes (Cherkauer, 1978), but the implications of his important work were not continued in Italy. Tim Potter (1976) generally interpreted this work as representing climatic rather than anthropic effect, but more recent work has shown the enormous regional variation of erosion and alluviation that is more likely to be a response to the level of urban activity and mitigation (as explored by Judson himself; Judson and Kahane, 1963) by urban societies.

Vita-Finzi's parallel work (1970) has been more developed in the erosional regimes of North Africa, Greece, and Turkey, but Brown and Ellis (1995) did commence a regional exploration of the measurement of erosion and consequent alluvial accumulation in South Etruria (Figure 9.2). They came up against a severe problem of dating the onset, weight, and frequency of the alluvial processes. Judson, Cherkauer, Vita Finzi, and others had used material culture and soil color as a guide to dating the major phases of the Older and Younger fills of the Mediterranean. At a gross level, very early events in the Older Fill can be dated by distinctive struck chert and later events by Classical pottery, but a subtler dating of very substantial deposits eluded even the more recent work of Brown and Ellis. They systematically searched for sections broadly in South Etruria and attempted to supplement cultural evidence with palaeomagnetic dating. The broad results of their work suggested a very dramatic Roman alluviation but no clear evidence for the Etruscan phase. One of their suggestions for dating, optically stimulated luminescence (OSL), is mentioned below as a key way forward and was subsequently implemented by them in a later publication (Brown et al. 2023).

More recently, there have been a number of studies of the estuaries of some of the major river systems of central Italy by Italian interdisciplinary teams, and these sometimes reach back into Etruscan times, although many are focused on the Roman period. The Magra River system was first studied by the Ager Lunensis survey, a survey that had difficulty finding prehistoric material, very probably for geomorphological reasons. More recently the search for the Roman port has been taken further, but this very approach shows that the main research questions were not related to the Etruscan period (Bini et al., 2012). The studies of the Tiber delta are also substantially related to the port facilities of the Imperial Roman period (Bellotti et al., 2011; Milli et al., 2013, 2016). The landscape regime in the Etruscan

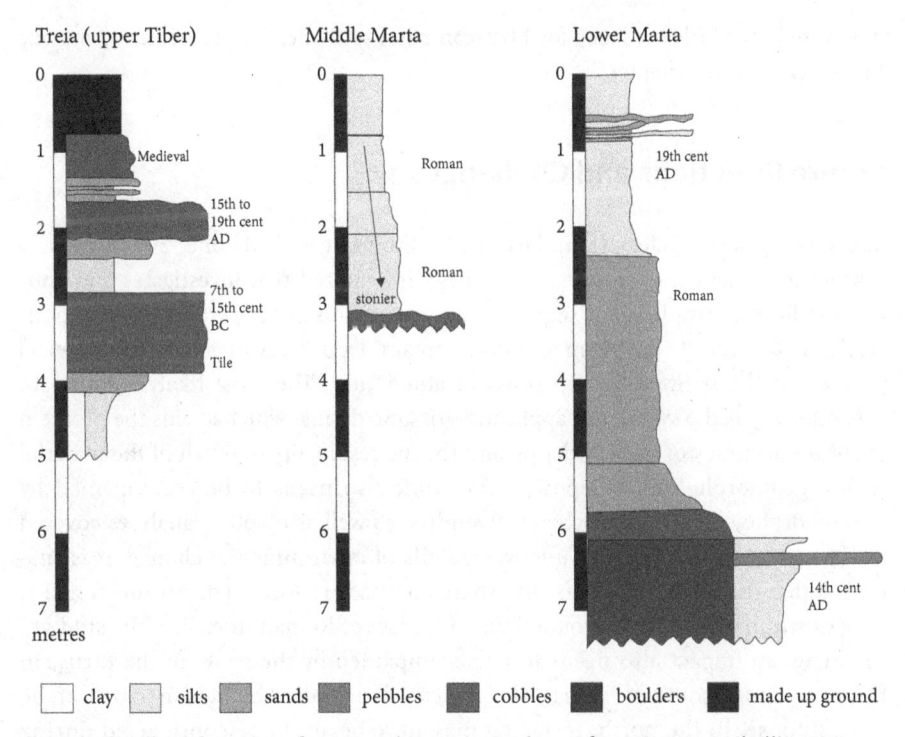

Figure 9.2 Alluvial sections from South Etruria. Redrawn from Brown and Ellis 1995.

phase seems to have been substantially oak woodland surrounding marshland. The study of the Arno delta has, however, demonstrated the importance of the Etruscan phase. This has shown that the geomorphological regime became more suitable for human settlement during the first millennium BCE (Amorosi et al., 2013; Sarti et al., 2015), even if the full-scale effects were not felt until later. A related long-standing theme has been the attempt to use material remains to understand the sea level of the Etrurian coast. This enterprise is more complicated than it might seem because of the neotectonic nature of central Italy. This means that the effects of sea level change can be very localized, relating to local fluvial regimes, coastal erosion, and uplift/fall from tectonic action. Bronze Age sites at the mouth of the Albegna Valley have been very effective at dating and assessing the stability of sandbars on the coast. Major stone structures such as the sanctuaries of Gravisca and Pyrgi can give major stratigraphic information of the position of the coast in various periods. However, the majority of key datable markers are provided by Roman period activity (Auriemma and Solinas, 2009). A complementary powerful methodology led by Dutch scholars has been inference from modern soil distributions, often employing the concept of land utilization type (LUT) (Vaccaro et al., 2013). Much of this work has been done in the part of Lazio south of Rome, but more recently the Roman Peasant Project has applied the same methodology to the Ombrone catchment of Northern Etruria (Bowes et al., 2015). This latter project focused on the Roman period and therefore uncovered very little evidence for Etruscan rural settlement so its results lie outside the purview of this chapter.

Future Directions and Challenges

The way forward is clear (Stoddart 2020b; Stoddart and Malone, 2022), namely that an integrated city–countryside strategy is required that investigates and connects well-dated stratigraphic sequences and palaeosols in city/settlement and countryside and connects upstream and downstream deposits. A major methodological problem is the dating of the process of alluviation. The most likely solution to this difficulty is the systematic application of OSL dating, which avoids the problem (a) of the accuracy of pottery dating and (b) the residuality of much of the material within geomorphological deposits. The work also needs to be accompanied by micromorphological and geochemical studies, as well as by other analyses covered in the rest of this chapter, to uncover details of environmental change. It is suspected that the impact of Etruscan urbanism was very localized, but this remains a supposition of an effect shrouded in the impact of Roman intensity. The study of the Etruscan impact also needs to be accompanied by the study of the Etruscan response. In the south of Etruria, the *cuniculi* first studied by Judson appear to be one response. In the north, terracing may have begun to be constructed during the Etruscan period. At present, we do not have modern studies of either of these issues from a geoarchaeological perspective that could provide time capsules of human activity.

Palynology and Cultural Ecology

Palynology is one of the strongest tools in the palaeoenvironmental research toolbox, providing direct evidence of environmental transformations and human influence over the past millennia. This is especially intriguing when dealing with historical periods for which iconography and archaeological evidence have been largely or uniquely used to reconstruct environmental contexts until recent times. On one hand, plant finds are real bioindicators of the flora, plant cover, habitat features, and hydrological/climatic variations of a certain region and a certain period. On another hand, the study of pollen, nonpollen palynomorphs, phytoliths, and microcharcoals, integrated with plant macroremains, is an "old but new" approach because, despite the fact that all these records have been analyzed for at least one century (Edwards et al., 2017), the way they are interpreted is constantly updated in the framework of interdisciplinary analyses. For example, when samples are available, pollen shows the local environmental transformations that occurred at the onset of new villages or the cultural choices and social needs influencing plant selection for food, fuel, or other purposes.

Current State of the Art

It is well known that an enormous quantity of microscopic plant records has been accumulated in sediments of lakes and terrestrial deposits (off-site) and of archaeological contexts (on-site) over the millennia. Therefore, biostratigraphies are fundamental archives to investigate the relationships between humans and plants and the transformations of ecosystems depending on natural and anthropogenic pressure in a certain region. Vertical sampling along trenches is useful to give diachronic reconstructions of environmental transformations; horizontal sampling is especially useful to discover different destination uses of the different sectors of an archaeological site. Contexts are not all the same, and data from palynology cannot be interpreted as simple "lists of taxa" because they depend on each (on/off) context, on the agent of transport of the plants, and on the taphonomy of the deposits. In this sense, data from archaeological sites are more useful to reconstruct human actions and economy, with local details, rather than the regional landscape. To simplify interpretation and data elaboration, including comparisons between sites of different regions or chronology, phytoecological sums of microremains are considered and their main significance is reported in Table 9.1.

The Etruscan landscape and economy are still underexplored from a palynological point of view. In the area between southern Tuscany, Umbria, and Latium, the region in which Etruscan culture developed, the thin woodlands drawn by pollen appear to have been richer of species during the Etruscan period than today. The archaeobotanical study of four archaeological sites, dated to the Iron Age, showed how Etruscans modified the forest vegetation of the area around the Gulf of Follonica, in front of the Elba Island. Pollen samples were taken from two farms at Val Petraia and Pian d'Alma, from many furnaces for iron ore reduction at Rondelli, and from a necropolis at Populonia (Mariotti Lippi et al., 2000; Sadori et al., 2010). Together with charcoal and seeds/fruits (Buonincontri et al., 2013; Di Pasquale, 2003), data showed that, during the Etruscan period, the landscape was generally characterized by an open vegetation close to the archaeological sites. Large farms or necropolis have features that make low forest cover expected in the place where houses, fields, or burials are located. Nevertheless, the forest cover continued to be similar (with low values in pollen spectra) in several small rural sites mainly dated to Roman contexts, between the 1st century BCE to the 1st century CE, in southern Tuscany. This suggested that an extensive clearance of lowland forested areas, causing soil erosion on hills and slopes, had already begun for agricultural purposes in the Etruscan period but was locally concentrated around sites rather than more generalized over the wider landscape, as in the Roman phases (Bowes et al., 2015; Rattighieri et al., 2013).

We can therefore ask what made the lush green environment of this specific region so favorable to the development of Etruscan and later Roman economy? The pollen trapped in the ship site of Pisa allowed scholars to recognize traits of the vegetation before and from the Etruscan to Roman period (Mariotti Lippi and Secci, 2007). During the first phase (not unequivocally dated), woods included

Table 9.1 Plant microremains as bioindicators of past environments in response to research questions about environmental transformations.

Research question	Sum	Information	Records
Human indicators: Deforestation?	AP = Arboreal Plants	Wood exploitation	Decrease or oscillation of pollen of woody plants (trees, shrubs, lianas)
Climate indicators: Temperature or dryness/humidity?	AP = Arboreal Plants	Wood cover	Decrease or oscillation of pollen of woody plants (trees, shrubs, lianas)
Climate indicators: dryness/humidity?	Hygro-hydrophilous Plants	Humid phases	Increase in wetland plant; presence of non-pollen palynomorphs like algae
	Dry phase or human action (e.g., reclamation)	Aridification	Increase in open vegetation: steppic indicators and decrease in wetland plants
	Natural vs. anthropogenic fires	Fire history	Microcharcoals; some fungi
Anthropization process: Arboriculture development	OJC = olive, chestnut and walnut trees (Mercuri et al., 2013a, 2021)	Care/cultivation of trees	Pollen of *Olea, Castanea, Juglans*
Anthropization process: Care/cultivation of woody plants	Other cultivated trees and woody plants collected in the wild	Human action	Pollen of *Corylus, Cornus, Morus, Pistacia, Prunus, Ribes, Rubus, Vitis*
Anthropization process: Crop fields	Cultivated/Cultivable herbs	Agriculture	Pollen of cereals (*Avena/Triticum* group, *Hordeum* group, *Secale cereale*), *Cannabis, Linum usitatissimum, Lathyrus, Medicago, Mentha, Salvia, Vicia*
Anthropization process: Farming contexts and open disturbed ground	Weeds and ruderals	Human action/presence	Pollen of *Artemisia, Campanula, Centaurea, Cerastium*-type, *Convolvulus, Cuscuta europaea*-type, *Galium*-type, *Mercurialis, Papaver, Plantago, Polygonum, Rumex, Silene dioica*-type, *Urtica dioica*-type, *Urtica*
Anthropization process: Human occupation and activities	Anthropogenic Pollen Indicators (API) (Behre, 1986; Mercuri et al., 2013b)	Human action/presence	Pollen of *Alchemilla/Aphanes*-type, *Anagallis, Artemisia, Centaurea*, cereals, Cichorieae, *Cirsium, Convolvulus, Galium*-type, *Mercurialis, Papaver rhoeas*-type, *Plantago, Polygonum, Rumex, Urtica*

Continued

Table 9.1 *Continued*

Research question	Sum	Information	Records
Anthropization process: Local pastoral activities (breeding/pasture)	Local Pastoral Pollen Indicators (LPPI) (Mazier, 2007; Mazier et al., 2009)	Human action	Pollen of Asteroideae, Cichorieae, *Cirsium*, *Galium*-type, *Potentilla*-type, Ranunculaceae, *Stellaria*-type
Anthropization process: Human activities at the regional spatial scale	Regional Human Activities Pollen Indicators (RHAPI) (Mazier, 2007; Mazier et al., 2009)	Human action	Pollen of *Artemisia*, cereals, Chenopodiaceae, *Plantago*, *Rumex*, *Urtica*
Anthropization process: Pastoral activities	Pollen Disturbance Index (PDI) (Kouli, 2015)	Human action	Pollen of *Centaurea*, Cichorieae, *Plantago*, *Polygonum aviculare*-type, *Pteridium*, *Ranunculus acris*-type, *Sarcopoterium*, *Urtica dioica*-type
Biodiversity	Upland forest vegetation	Wood composition	Pollen of *Abies*, *Betula*, *Fagus*, *Picea*, *Pinus*
Biodiversity	Mixed deciduous forest	Wood composition	Pollen of *Acer campestre*-type, *Carpinus*, *Corylus*, *Fraxinus*, *Ostrya carpinifolia/ Carpinus orientalis*, broadleaved *Quercus*, *Tilia*, *Ulmus*
Biodiversity	Mediterranean trees/shrubs	Wood composition under human influence	Pollen of *Erica*, *Fraxinus ornus*, *Juniperus*-type, *Ligustrum*, *Myrtus*, *Phillyrea*, *Pistacia*, *Quercus ilex*-type
Biodiversity	Riverine vegetation (trees)	Wood composition	Pollen of *Alnus*, *Populus*, *Salix*, *Tamarix*
Biodiversity	Wetland herbs	Aquatic flora	Pollen of *Alisma*-type, *Butomus*, *Callitriche*, *Ceratophyllum*, Cyperaceae, *Hydrocharis*, *Lemna*, *Lythrum*, *Myriophyllum*, *Nuphar*, *Nymphaea alba*-type, *Phragmites*, *Potamogeton*, *Ranunculus aquatilis* group, *Sagittaria*, *Typha/Sparganium*, *Typha latifolia*-type
Biodiversity	Open land vegetation	Steppe vegetation	Pollen of *Artemisia*, Chenopodiaceae, Poaceae wild grass group

This table is based on the overview of the pollen evidence from the Central Mediterranean (Kouli et al., 2018), modified according to the plant landscape in ancient Etruria (Bowes et al., 2015). Note that *Vitis* cannot be included in the OJC group (cared/cultivated trees; Mercuri et al., 2013a) since the wild and domesticated subspecies have different pollen morphology and pollen dispersal (Mercuri et al., 2021).

species belonging to the mountain belt, particularly *Fagus* spreading in the lowlands. The presence of beech at low altitude might have been related to flooding hazards that were also responsible for repeated catastrophic destruction of the Pisa ship site; this occurred during a wet and cool climate oscillation, probably at the first millennium BCE (the so-called sub-Atlantic cold phase; Lamb, 1995). In almost the same period, peaks or increasing values of *Fagus* pollen were recorded at Lago di Vico in central Italy (Magri and Sadori, 1999) and in southern France (Delhon and Thiébault, 2005).

Therefore, just before and at the beginning of the Etruscan period, the tree cover was characterized by taxa suggesting a cool, moist climate. Later, the vegetation became characterized by deciduous and evergreen oaks and heather in the region, suggesting a trend toward a warmer climate. At this later date, people shaped the environment by actively maintaining the vegetation as a macchia shrubland dominated by *Erica arborea* and probably enhanced the xeric features of the regional vegetation. However, the Mediterranean vegetation did not yet include significant specimens of wild olive trees (Mercuri et al., 2019).

During the Etruscan period, Mediterranean evergreen vegetation was characterized by *Quercus ilex* and *Erica arborea* with remnants of the mesophilous deciduous oak woods. The holm oak trees and the heather shrubs were part of the natural mature woods. Pollen suggests that these woodlands, originally dominated by oaks, gave good resources to Etruscans who exploited trees by practicing a short-turn coppicing to sustain their economy and to obtain fuel for iron metallurgy. The deciduous oaks (mainly *Quercus pubescens*, less frequently *Q. cerris*) were used for structural parts of the buildings while *Erica arborea* was the most important wood for metal reduction (Mariotti Lippi et al., 2000, 2002). The cutting activities were also evident in the pollen diagram of Lago dell'Accesa, itself next to a small settlement (Camporeale, 1997), showing that, during the Etruscan period, there was a clear decrease of evergreen oaks in the local area. In addition to the deciduous oaks, there was the floristic composition of coppiced wood that included species of secondary forest canopy like *Erica, Arbutus, Pinus* (*P. sylvestris* type), *Pistacia, Myrtus,* and the significant presence of *Corylus, Betula, Pistacia, Juniperus,* and *Pteridium aquilinum* at around 2800 cal BP, resulting in a prominent clearing at around 2600–2500 cal BP (Drescher-Schneider et al., 2007). The pollen diagram is characterized by a continuous presence of *Castanea, Juglans,* and *Olea* (Drescher-Schneider et al., 2007). Considering the data from Lago di Mezzano (Sadori, 2018) and Lago di Nemi (Mercuri et al., 2002), there is evidence that Etruscans encouraged the spread of chestnut trees and possibly walnut trees. The cultivated *Olea europaea* became a feature of the landscape only later, during post-Roman times in Tuscany (Mercuri et al., 2019). The impact of these two lakeside Etruscan settlements is shown also in the increasing pollen values of arable crops, including *Linum usitatissimum* and *Secale,* and the anthropogenic indicators (evidence of human-induced environment) including Chenopodieae, *Plantago lanceolata,* and *Rumex* (Mercuri et al., 2013b).

Future Directions and Challenges

Pollen studies have revealed that environment and vegetation in the Etruscan period were quite different from those of the present day because of the richer flora and the scant presence of olive trees. Moreover, the draining of coastal areas in the first half of the twentieth century has dried up coastal lagoons and marsh land and enabled the cultivation of areas that were previously exploited only for pasture (Perkins, 2017). Outside the core Etruscan region, Etruscan culture was also investigated in the settlement of Pianella di Monte Savino-Monte Bibele, near Bologna, giving information on diet and landscape of the Celtic-Etruscan village (Bosi et al., 2005; Lopane et al., 1998). At Verucchio, a vessel from a tomb in the Necropoli Lippi contained traces of cereals, fruit trees, and grapevine (Marchesini and Marvelli, 2010). In general, pollen diagrams of the Etruscan period are characterized by anthropogenic pollen indicators that demonstrate their skilled ability to manage their local landscapes. As already inferred by Negri (1927), the wild status of wooded areas and open lands have been heavily altered by people throughout millennia. In future research, it is important to be careful with how pollen sampling (the number of samples and which contexts are selected) is employed as it is crucial to the interpretation of reliable palaeoenvironmental reconstructions; one must remember that the set of microscopic evidence is quite complex and must be considered carefully in relation to the many variables of each environmental and cultural context. Increasingly more samples from on- and off-site records and integrated micro- and macrobotanical analyses, combined with geological sampling strategies and interpretation, means that the power of pollen analyses is increasing the information that can be obtained at a resolution useful for archaeology.

Cultural Ecology and Agriculture

Despite advances in multidisciplinary scientific investigations of human–environment interactions by members of the Botanical Records of Archaeobotany Italian Network (BRAIN) (Mariotti et al., 2018; Mercuri et al., 2015) and recent strides by a few key scholars, the first millennium BCE in central Italy is still greatly understudied in comparison to earlier prehistoric sites in Italy (Alonso et al., 2007; Mariotti Lippi et al., 2002; Mercuri et al., 2019). This is surprising, given that one of the main arguments (alongside advances in metallurgy) for the shift toward urbanism from the Late Bronze Age through the Iron Age into Archaic Etruscan urban centers relies on changes in agricultural strategies more geared toward surplus production. The presence of visible elites in the eighth century BCE is theorized to have been made possible by such agricultural surplus, yet the archaeobotanical evidence for how this was achieved is scarce (Motta and Beydler 2020; Shriver-Rice and Schmidt 2022; Stoddart, 2020b; Trentacoste and Lodwick, 2023). Heavy clay-laden sediments are partly to blame for the challenges of systematic environmental sampling (Malone et al., 2014; Perkins and Attoloni 1992; Shriver-Rice 2017; Shriver-Rice and Schmidt 2022); however, the widespread deficiency of environmental sampling at Etruscan-era sites also has been attributed to an academic emphasis on cultural and artistic aspects, as well as information from written sources (Malone et al., 2014; Stoddart, 2020a).

Very few excavations to date of Etruscan sites have benefited from systematic environmental sampling and reporting. Without systematic sampling of macrobotanical material and zooarchaeological microremains through soil flotation, excavation methods bias what types of zooarchaeological and archaeobotanical remains are recovered so that larger, highly visible bones, fruits, nuts, and recognizable grains and grape pips are hand-picked from the soil. Italian archaeobotanists have noted the "scarce attention paid by classical archaeologists to organic remains" beyond ideas of the much-discussed Mediterranean triad of grain, grapes, and olives, particularly in Roman and Etruscan archaeology (Mercuri et al., 2010, 862), but the situation is changing rapidly, with systematic flotation now more common on Etruscan excavations, with recent examples offered by Orvieto (George et al., 2017), Cetamura del Chianti (Mariotti Lippi et al., 2020), Tarquinia (Stoddart 2024) and Col di Marzo (Malone et al., 2014) (Figure 9.3).[1]

From the few Etruscan-era sites where macro archaeobotanical remains have been recovered, what can be surmised about the agricultural field systems is a diverse cereal and pulse crop repertoire that is similar to the sites from the mid- to late Bronze Age in central Italy in terms of species present (Bellini et al., 2008; Motta and Beydler, 2020; Trentacoste and Lodwick, 2023). Further evidence of indigenous development of subsistence strategies in Etruria has been established through faunal remains (Trentacoste, 2016). While it is known that cereal crops included free-threshing wheat, hulled wheats (emmer, spelt, einkorn), barley, millet, and rye (pulses included chickpeas, garden peas, lentils, and fava beans), little is known about the specific strategies employed at Etruscan farms and rural settlements (Motta and Beydler, 2020; Shriver-Rice and Schmidt 2022; Trentacoste and Lodwick 2023). For example, does the less frequent occurrence of free-threshing wheat (a much less labor-intensive crop to process) on sites in central Italy reflect specifically Etrurian practices, or does it merely reflect prior excavation methods? Recent recovery of free-threshing wheat from Poggio Civitate points to the latter (Shriver-Rice and Schmidt 2022). Comparative presence or absence studies of crop species is just the start of our making sense of agricultural strategies in Italy. Plant and animal agricultural regimes in ancient Etruria would have been actively adaptive and seasonally and regionally attuned—not a monolithic, timeless activity, but an actively changing medium of production.

---

[1] Also, the ongoing work of Angela Trentacoste and Erica Rowan at Orvieto, Frijda Schmidt's work on Tarquinia, Lisa Lodwick and Angela Trentacoste's work at Poggio Colla, Frijda Schmidt and Meryl Shriver-Rice's work at Poggio Civitate, and Laura Motta's work on archaic Rome (2002, see also Constantini and Giorgi, 2001).

Figure 9.3 Flotation machine used at Poggio Civitate. Photograph by Meryl Shriver-Rice.

Range of Research Questions

Our understanding of human–landscape interaction requires further integrated investigation to search for clear anthropogenic indicators of the human exploitation of Italian landscapes such as the presence of cereals; tree crops such as walnut, chestnut, and olive (Mercuri et al., 2013a); and weed seeds associated with agriculture and deforestation (i.e., slash-and-burn land management). Within central Italy's unique convergence of environmental conditions between two phytogeographical areas of high biodiversity, there is dramatic variation in seasonal precipitation and diverse soil types and elevational regimes because of a complex geological history (Atauri and De Lucio, 2001; Tomei and Bertacchi, 2006). Control of the most fertile and nearest-located rainfed arable land (Stoddart and Zeviani, 2021, 64) may have been held by specific families and kin groups so that the landscape surrounding settlements would have acted as a vast tapestry reflecting groups' symbolic demonstrations of power.

Many details are still unknown on how and why varieties of livestock and plant cultivars were exploited and how different populations might have been preferred and artificially selected for certain traits within a single species. Such unanswered questions include determining which grape varieties were related to wine production (raised as a future direction by Motta and Beydler (2020), how sheep flocks with different fleece qualities were managed (overlapping with textile evidence for fibers) (Trentacoste, 2020), and which crops were grown specifically for taste and preference of regional dishes rather than for highest yield? As prehistoric research sheds new light on the early exploitation for grapes and olives, there is much to be understood beyond the simplistic narrative that Greeks introduced new agricultural technologies to southern Italy (Caracuta, 2020; Lentjes and Saltini Semerari, 2016). We are now met with the challenge to untangle more precisely how, when, and why management strategies changed. Outside the agricultural contexts of crop sowing, harvesting, processing, animal foddering, manure production, and livestock management, evidence for the ritual use of plants and animals has implications for reconstructing ritual activity and related sociocultural acts such as gifting, destruction or erasure of power, and establishment of new physical boundaries (Shriver-Rice and Schmidt 2022). Costly display and the redistribution of subsistence resources often carry broader social and economic implications (Trentacoste, 2020), and ritual/religious motivations were woven throughout decision-making, not limited to a particular sphere.

Current State of the Art

Zooarchaeological analyses and syntheses published in the past decade are increasingly the result of integrated research agendas (Briccola et al., 2013; Colivicchi et al., 2016; Corbino and Fonzo, 2017; Cucinotta et al., 2010; Curci, 2010; Curci and Sertori, 2019; De Grossi Mazzorin, 2016; De Grossi Mazzorin and Minniti, 2015; Kansa and MacKinnon, 2014; Malone et al., 2014; Moses and Fusco, 2018; Rask, 2014; Rinaldi et al., 2016; Trentacoste, 2013, 2016). Syntheses of zooarchaeological data across sites have emphasized a rise in pork consumption over the first millennium BCE, especially in Rome and Etruria *padana* (De Grossi Mazzorin and Minniti, 2017; Trentacoste, 2016). New material studies and meta-data analyses are adding nuance to these broad trends, fleshing out the different modes and rhythms of animal exploitation across multiple scales, both in Etruria and neighboring Latium (Moses, 2020; Moses and Alhaique, 2022; Prato, 2023; Trentacoste and Lodwick, 2023). Domestic

Figure 9.4 Zooarchaeological remains being sorted at Orvieto. Photograph by Angela Trentacoste.

livestock increased in size over the Etruscan period, as part of a trend potentially beginning as early as the Bronze–Iron Age transition (De Grossi Mazzorin and Minniti, 2017, 2019; Trentacoste et al., 2018). This increase occured throughout Italy, though it appears particularly pronounced in some Etruscan territories.

Until recently, the only synthesis of archaeobotanical remains for central Italy was done in 2008, by Bellini et al., from the Mesolithic until 1000 BCE. More recent works investigating agricultural evidence for have updated the picture for plant and animal remains fromMore recent works investigating agricultural evidence for have updated the picture for plant and animal remains from Iron Age and Archaic Italy (Bosi et al., 2023; Caracuta, 2020; Motta and Beydler, 2020; Stoddart, 2020b). At the site level, archaeobotanical investigation has not received the same attention as faunal remains, as demonstrated by the low number of recent publications (Costantini et al., 2012; Gran Aymerich and Domínguez-Arranz, 2011; Malone et al., 2014; Marchesini et al., 2010; Mariotti Lippi et al., 2020). Low output is clearly not a reflection of the number of Etruscan excavations but of continued lack of the prioritization of archaeobotany as a research agenda. The recent expansion of systematic environmental research, including flotation programs at Tarquinia, Poggio Civitate, and Orvieto, promises hope for future research developments (Figure 9.4).

Future Directions and Challenges

The future of Etruscan plant and animal studies is very bright, and new approaches like geometric morphometrics (GMM), genetics, and stable isotope analyses are now revealing details on Etruscan management practices. GMM analysis is a nondestructive technique that has the potential to provide significant insight into ancient plant and animal populations, for example separating grape varieties (Bouby et al., 2021) and assessing shape change in animal populations relating to management regimes (Colominas et al., 2019; Haruda et al., 2019). At Cetamura, GMM analysis of grape pips has shown that completely domestic grape forms were exploited alongside wild fruits, providing valuable new data on vine cultivation (De Grummond, 2017, 2018; Mariotti Lippi et al., 2020). Stable isotope analysis has the potential to reveal high-resolution insights on how ancient crops and animals were managed (Lee-Thorp, 2008; Makarewicz and Sealy, 2015), and these approaches are becoming more common in pre-Roman contexts (Trentacoste et al., 2020; Gavériaux et al., 2022). However, plenty of promising research questions outside the realm of archaeological science remain, particularly in terms of cuisine and consumption. Detailed studies like Maini and Curci's (2013) investigation of food offerings in graves at Monte Bibele have the potential to add further depth to our understanding of ancient food culture and regional taste (Hastorf, 2017). There is also huge potential to better understand human–environment interaction and its socioeconomic implications through the investigation of, for example, agro-ecology and seasonality (Bogaard et al., 2016), crop processing (as implied for Rome by Motta, 2011), and microfaunal remains as palaeoenvironmental indicators (Mainland, 2008). Agriculture was the most essential form of production in ancient Etruria; therefore, further studies of plant and animal resources should view agricultural practices and products as active components in a constantly renegotiated world (Fairbairn et al., 2005), exploited and valued in their own terms within the specific traditions and social systems of the Etruscan people who grew and used them.

Destructive and inadequate sampling are two of the greatest challenges to the collection and analysis of environmental datasets. Recovery of macrobotanical and microfaunal environmental material at Etruscan sites has occurred on an ad hoc basis, often with samples that are not systematically collected or at sizes that are far too small to be considered (Lennstrom and Hastorf, 1995). Flotation machines capable of processing large samples (at least 40 liters of soil per context) are required for sufficient blanket sampling. While such machines are relatively easy to construct, an environmental team must be supported by the site director in terms of human labor. A number of people are needed to run the flotation machine, sort through the heavy residue, and hang and dry the light residue in preparation for processing in a laboratory setting.

As isotopic and genetic analysis are increasingly applied to biological remains, care should be taken to balance analytical results with the destruction of cultural heritage. It has already been pointed out that plant and animal remains are not "a limitless resource," and sampling strategies should therefore address the ethical implications of destructive procedures (Pálsdóttir et al., 2019). For excavators who have recovered assemblages of tens of thousands of bioarchaeological fragments, these considerations might appear overly cautious; however, sample sizes quickly reduce when the specimens targeted by genetic and isotopic analyses are considered. Even in an assemblage of thousands of specimens, only a handful of the preferred target sample might be present within a species once unsuitable materials are excluded (e.g., unstratified, broken, etc.). Destructive sampling not only removes material from a sample: it can also preclude the application of nondestructive techniques like GMM. Considering that the biggest research questions for Etruscan cultural ecology are less about defining the types of materials employed and are more focused on understanding the nuances of how their exploitation developed in different environmental and social contexts, the high-resolution data provided by GMM, isotopic chemistry, and genetic analysis are essential. However, we must be careful that short-term gains do not outweigh longer-term planning—a decision best made within an integrated and collaborative research program.

Environmental and bioarchaeological studies have established the main crop and animal species exploited by Etruscan farmers, but this is only the start of our understanding of the Etruscans' embeddedness in their landscape. Key research questions now require finer-resolution variation in how and why plants and animals were managed, what local ecological diversity meant for local inhabitants, and the socioeconomic implications of management strategies such as risk aversion, building social capital, symbolic use, and paying off or creating social debt. These analyses need to be evaluated within their sedimentary setting through techniques such as geochemistry, micromorphology, and precise dating (e.g., AMS and OSL). A sound environmental sampling strategy is critical at all sites, and we hope this chapter has provided greater motivation for the time and expense needed for the initial stages of data creation. Isotopic, genetic, and morphometric research will play an increasing role in this agenda and open new avenues into Etruscan cultural ecology.

Conclusion

The future of Etruscan archaeology is collaborative, and the more widespread adoption of interdisciplinary archaeological science allows for new publishing trajectories and "high-impact" articles in top journals. Considering the importance of the Etruscan period to the urbanization, mobility, and historical development of Italy, the Mediterranean, and Europe, it is natural that Etruscan environmental data have a seat at the wider prehistoric and classical archaeology table and participate in top-level scientific discussions. In this process, archaeologists and local stakeholders should demand significant input into sampling strategy and dissemination, not only to avoid erroneous conclusions (e.g., de Grummond, 2018), but also to achieve a greater understanding of those human activities that underpinned broader trends, like pollen evidence for deforestation and rural settlement infill. Palynology recently turned one hundred years old, but its applications and potential have continuously changed as interdisciplinary research has developed in the field of archaeology. Nearly a century after his seminal work, we can say that Negri was correct in the claim that the Etruscans cleared and actively managed local landscapes around settlements for agricultural purposes. However, we require more environmental sampling to determine whether such clearances were widespread or if large-scale deforestation only occurred after the post-Roman period, as is currently indicated by palynological evidence. We should also heed his call to be cautious in our reconstruction of the Etruscan landscape and bear in mind that modern-day Tuscany is much changed from its ancient landscape. The forests were richer with wild species and the tree cover was greater, yet much is still unknown about the cultural ecology and landscape of ancient Etruria.

Bibliography

Alonso, N., R. Buxó, and N. Rovira. "Recherches sur l'alimentation vegetale et l'agriculture du site de Port Ariane: Étude des semences et fruits." *Lattara* 20 (2007), 219–249.

Alvarez, W. "The Treia valley north of Rome: Volcanic stratigraphy, topographic evolution and geographical influence on human settlement." *Geologia Romana* 11 (1972), 153–176.

Alvarez, W. "The Pleistocene volcanoes north of Rome." In *Geology of Italy*, edited by C. Squyres, 355–377. Tripoli: Earth Science Society, 1975.

Alvarez, W. "The tectonic significance of Mediterranean volcanoes." *Geologia Romana* 15 (1976), 311–313.

Amorosi, A., M. Bini, S. Giacomelli, M. Pappalardo, C. Ribecai, V. Rossi, I. Sammartino, and G. Sarti. "Middle to late Holocene environmental evolution of the Pisa coastal plain (Tuscany, Italy) and early human settlements." *Quaternary International* 303 (2013), 93–106.

Atauri, J. A., and J. V. De Lucio. "The role of landscape structure in species richness distribution of birds, amphibians, reptiles and lepidopterans in Mediterranean landscapes." *Landscape Ecology* 16 (2001), 147–159.

Auriemma, R., and E. Solinas. "Archaeological remains as sea level change markers: A review." *Quaternary International* 206.1 (2009), 134–146.

Behre, K. E. *Anthropogenic Indicators in Pollen Diagrams*. Rotterdam: Balkema, 1986.

Bellini, C., M. Mariotti Lippi, M. M. Secci, B. Aranguren, and P. Perazzi "Plant gathering and cultivation in prehistoric Tuscany (Italy)." Proceedings of the Fourteenth Symposium of the International Work Group for Palaeoethnobotany (Krakow 2007). *Vegetation History and Archaeobotany* 17 Supplement (2008), S103–S112.

Bellotti, P., G. Calderoni, F. Di Rita, M. D'Orefice, C. D'Amico, D. Esu, D. Magri, M. P. Martinez, P. Tortora, and P. Valeri. "The Tiber river delta plain (central Italy), Coastal evolution and implications for the ancient Ostia Roman settlement." *Holocene* 21.7 (2011), 1105–1116.

Bender, B. "Time and landscape." *Current Anthropology* 43 (2002), S103–S112.

Bertacchini, M. "Il sottosuolo della cattedrale di Perugia. Una finestra sulla geologia del territorio Perugino." In *Perugia. La città antica sotto la Cattedrale di S. Lorenzo. I risultati degli scavi*, edited by L. Cenciaioli, 31–55. Napoli: Edizioni Scientifiche ed Artistiche, 2014.

Bini, M., H. Brückner, A. Chelli, M. Pappalardo, S. Da Prato, and L. Gervasini. "Palaeogeographies of the Magra Valley coastal plain to constrain the location of the Roman harbour of Luna (NW Italy)." *Palaeogeography, Palaeoclimatology, Palaeoecology* 337–338 (2012), 37–51.

Bogaard, A., J. Hodgson, E. Nitsch, G. Jones, A. Styring, C. Diffey, J. Pouncett, C. Christoph Herbig, M. Charles, F. Ertuğ, O. Tugay, D. Dragana Filipovic, and F. Fraser, "Combining Functional Weed Ecology and Crop Stable Isotope Ratios to Identify Cultivation Intensity: A Comparison of Cereal Production Regimes in Haute Provence, France and Asturias, Spain." *Vegetation History and Archaeobotany* 25 (2016), 57–73. doi:10.1007/s00334-015-0524-0

Bonghi Jovino, M., and F. Chiesa, eds. *Offerte dal regno vegetale e dal regno animale nelle manifestazione del sacro. Atti dell'incontro di studio Milano 26–27 giugno 2003*. Roma: L'Erma di Bretschneider, 2005.

Bosi, G., M. Mazzanti, M. C. Montecchi, P. Torri, and R. Rinaldi R. "The life of a Roman colony in Northern Italy: Ethnobotanical information from archaeobotanical analysis." *Quaternary International* 460 (2017), 135–156. doi:10.1016/j.quaint.2016.08.008

Bosi, G., C. A. Accorsi, M. Bandini Mazzanti, and L. Forlani. "The plant remains from the Etruscan-Celtic Village (IV–IIth cent. B.C.) of 'Pianella di Monte Savino' – Monte Bibele (Northern Italy)." In *Thirteenth Conference of the International Work Group for Palaeoethnobotany*, 103. Girona, Spain. Vegetation History and Archaeobotany 14, 4 (2005).

Bosi, G., A. M. Mercuri, M. Bandini Mazzanti, A. Florenzano, M. C. Montecchi, P. Torri, D. Labate, and R. Rinaldi. "The evolution of Roman urban environments through the archaeobotanical remains in Modena, Northern Italy." *Journal of Archaeological Science* 53 (2015), 19–31. doi:10.1016/j.jas.2014.09.020

Bosi, G., E. Castiglioni, M. Mazzanti, and M. Rottoli. "New crops in the 1st millennium CE in northern Italy. *Vegetation History and Archaeobotany* (2023). doi:10.1007/s00334-023-00955-9

Bouby, L., et al. "Tracking the history of grapevine cultivation in Georgia by combining geometric morphometrics and ancient DNA." *Vegetation History and Archaeobotany* 30 (2021), 63–76. doi:10.1007/s00334-020-00803-0

Bowes, K., A. M. Mercuri, E. Rattighieri, R. Rinaldi, A. Arnoldous-Huyzendveld, M. Ghisleni, C. Grey, M. Mackinnon, and E. Vaccaro. "Palaeoenvironment and land-use of Roman peasant farmhouses in southern Tuscany." *Plant Biosystems* 149 (2015), 174–184. doi:10.1080/11263504.2014.992997

Briccola, N., M. Bertolini, and U. Thun Hohenstein. "Gestione e sfruttamento delle risorse animali nell'abitato di Spina: Analisi archeozoologica dei reperti faunistici." In *Spina: Scavi nell'abitato della città etrusca, 2007–2009*, edited by C. C. Cassai, S. Giannini, and L. Malnati, 178–187. Firenze: Cooperativa Archeologica, 2013.

Brown, A. G., and C. Ellis. "People, climate and alluviation: Theory, research design and new sedimentological and stratigraphic data from Etruria." *Papers of British School at Rome* 64 (1995), 45–74.

Brown, A., Ellis, C. & Rhodes, E. The Natural Landscape and its Evolution. *In the Footsteps of the Etruscans: Changing Landscapes around Tuscania from Prehistory to Modernity* edited by G. Barker and T. Rasmussen, 61–84. Cambridge: Cambridge University Press, 2023.

Buonincontri, M., E. Allevato, and G. Di Pasquale. "The problem of the alternating dominance of deciduous and evergreen vegetation: Archaeo-anthracological data from Northern Maremma." *Annali di Botanica* 3 (2013), 165–171. doi:10.4462/annbotrm-10269

Camporeale, G. *L'abitato etrusco dell'Accesa: Il quartiere B*. (Archaeologica 122). Roma: G. Bretschneider, 1997.

Caracuta, V. "Olive growing in Puglia (southeastern Italy), A review of the evidence from the Mesolithic to the Middle Ages." *Vegetation History and Archaeobotany* 29 (2020), 595–620. doi:10.1007/s00334-019-00765-y

Cencetti, C., P. Conversini, and P. Tacconi. "The rock of Orvieto (Umbria, Central Italy)." *Giornale di Geologia Applicata* 1 (2005), 103–112.

Cherkauer, D. S. "Site K. The stratigraphy and chronology of the River Treia alluvial deposits." In *A Faliscan Town in South Etruria. Excavations at Narce 1966–71*, edited by T. W. Potter, 106–126. London: British School at Rome, 1976.

Cherkauer, D. S. "The effect of urbanization on kinetic energy distributions in small watersheds." *Journal of Geology* 86.4 (1978), 505–515.

Colivicchi, F., G. L. Gregori, M. Lanza, A. Lepone, M. Scalici, A. Trentacoste, and C. Zaccagnino. "New excavations in the urban area of Caere." *Mouseion* 13 (2016), 359–450.

Colominas, L., A. Evin, J. Burch, P. Campmajó, J. Casas, P. Castanyer, C. Carreras, J. Guardia, O. Olesti, E. Pons, J. Tremoleda, and J. M. Palet. "Behind the steps of ancient sheep mobility in Iberia: New insights from a geometric morphometric approach." *Archaeological and Anthropological Sciences* 11 (2019), 4971–4982. doi:10.1007/ s12520-019-00837-0

Corbino, C., and O. Fonzo. "The use of animals in Etruscan and Roman rituals at Cetamura del Chianti (SI)." In *Wells of Wonders: New Discoveries at Cetamura del Chianti*, edited by N. T. De Grummond, 323–335. Florence: Edifir, 2017.

Costantini, L., L. Costantini Biasini, F. Pica, and M. Stanzione. "Analisi archeobotaniche a Chiusi: Semi e carboni dello scavo del Petriolo." *Studi Etruschi* 75 (2012), 165–179.

Costantini, L., and J. Giorgi. "Charred plant remains of the Archaic period from the Forum and Palatine." *Journal of Roman Archaeology* 14 (2001), 239–248.

Cucinotta, C., J. de Grossi Mazzorin, and C. Minniti. "La città etrusca di Veio: Analisi archeozoologiche del pozzo US 469." In *Atti del 5° Convengo Nazionale di Archeozoologia.* edited by A. Tagliacozzo, I. Fiore, S. Marconi, and U. Tecchiati, 235–238. Rovereto, November 10–12, 2006. Rovereto: Edizioni Osiride, 2010.

Curci, A. "I dati archeozoologici." In *Marzabotto: La casa della regio IV – insula 2*. Vol. 2. I materiali, edited by E. Govi and G. Sassatelli, 397–420. Bologna: Ante Quem.

Curci, A., and S. Sertori. "Il cane in Etruria Padana: Usi domestici e valenze rituali." In *Atti 8° Convegno Nazionale di Archeozoologia* (Lecce, 2015), edited by J. De Grossi Mazzorin, I. Fiore, and C. Minniti, 297–306. Lecce: Università del Salento, 2019.

De Grossi Mazzorin, J. "Le offerte alimentari di origine animale del santuario di Monte Li Santi: Analisi archeozoologica." In *Il santuario di Monte Li Santi-Le Rote a Narce. Scavi 1985–1996, III*, edited by M. A. De Lucia Brolli, 9–56. Rome, 2016.

De Grossi Mazzorin, J., and C. Minniti. "Le hostiae animales dalla fossa rituale del saggio IV." In *Materiali per Populonia 11*, edited by V. Di Cola and F. Pitzalis, 139–158. Pisa: Edizioni ETS, 2015.

De Grossi Mazzorin, J., and C. Minniti. "Changes in lifestyle in ancient Rome (Italy) across the Iron Age/Roman transition: The evidence from animal remains." In *The Oxford Handbook of Zooarchaeology*, edited by U. Albarella, M. Rizzetto, H. Russ, K. Vickers, and S. Viner-Daniels, 127–146. Oxford: Oxford University Press, 2017.

De Grossi Mazzorin, J., and C. Minniti. "Variabilità dimensionale e sviluppo dei caprovini in Italia durante l'età del Ferro." In *Atti 8° Convegno Nazionale di Archeozoologia* (Lecce, 2015), edited by J. De Grossi Mazzorin, I. Fiore, and C. Minniti, 127–138. Lecce: Università del Salento, 2019.

De Grummond, N. T., ed. "Wells of wonders: New discoveries at Cetamura del Chianti." Catalog of the exhibition, June 9–September 30, 2017, Florence, National Archaeological Museum, MAF, Museo archeologico nazionale di Firenze. Florence: Edifir-Edizioni Firenze, 2017.

De Grummond, N. T. "Grape Pips from Etruscan and Roman Cetamura del Chianti: On Stratigraphy, Literary Sources and Pruning Hooks." *Etruscan Studies* 21 (2018) 1–31. doi:10.1515/etst-2018-0013

Delhon, C., and S. Thiébault. "The migration of beech (*Fagus sylvatica* L.) up the Rhone: The Mediterranean history of a 'mountain' species." *Vegetation History and Archaeobotany* 14.2 (2005), 119–132. doi:10.1007/s00334-005-0068-9

Di Pasquale, G. "I carboni di Chiusi: Una ipotesi di ricostruzione del paesaggio forestale." In *Manifattura ceramica etrusco-romana a Chiusi: Il complesso produttivo di Marcianella*, edited by G. Pucci and C. Mascione, 315–320. Bari: Bibar, Edipuglia srl, 2003.

Drescher-Schneider, R., J. De Beaulieu, M. Magny, A. Walter-Simonnet, G. Bossuet, L. Millet, E. Brugiapaglia, and A. Drescher. "Vegetation history, climate and human impact over the last 15,000 years at Lago dell'Accesa (Tuscany, Central Italy)." *Vegetation History Archaeobotany* 16 (2007), 279–299.

Edlund-Berry, I. E. M. "Ritual space and boundaries in Etruscan religion." In *The Religion of the Etruscans*, edited by N. T. De Grummond and E. Simon, 116–131. Austin: University of Texas Press, 2006.

Edlund-Berry, I. E. M. "Religion: The gods and the places." In *The Etruscan World*, edited by J. MacIntosh Turfa, 557–565. London: Routledge, 2013.

Edwards, K., R. Fyfe, and S. Jackson. "The first 100 years of pollen analysis." *Nature Plants* 3 (2017), 17001. doi:10.1038/nplants.2017.1

Evans, J. M., J. T. Troy Samuels, L. Motta, M. Naglak, and M. D'Acri. "An Iron Age settlement at Gabii: An interim report of the Gabii Project excavations in Area D, 2012–2015." *Etruscan Studies* 22.1–2 (2019), 6–38.

Fairbairn, A., E. Asouti, N. Russell, and J. G. Swogger. "Seasonality." In *Çatalhöyük Perspectives: Reports from the 1995–1999 Seasons*, edited by I. Hodder. BIAA Monograph No. 40. 2005.

Force, E. R. "Geologic aspects of ancient Villanovan settlement distributions in central Italy." *Catena* 125 (2015), 162–168.

George, D., C. Bizzarri, P. Bianco, A. Trentacoste, J. Whitlam, and J. Best. "Recent research in Cavità 254 (Orvieto, Italy)." *Etruscan Studies* 20.1 (2017), 58–76.

Gran Aymerich, J., and A. Domínguez-Arranz. *La Castellina a sud di Civitavecchia. Origini ed eredità: Origines protohistoriques et évolution d'un habitat étrusque* Rome: L'Erma di Bretschneider, 2011.

Grossi Mazzorin, J. "Il quadro attuale delle ricerche archeozoologiche in Etruria e nuove prospettive di ricerca." In *Animali tra uomini e dei. Archeozoologia del mondo preromano*, edited by A. Curci and D. Vitalli, 77–96. Bologna: Ante Quem.

Haruda, A. F., V. Varfolomeev, A. Goriachev, A. Yermolayeva, and A. K. Outram. "A new zooarchaeological application for geometric morphometric methods: Distinguishing *Ovis aries* morphotypes to address connectivity and mobility of prehistoric Central Asian pastoralists." *Journal of Archaeological Science* 107 (2019), 50–57. doi:10.1016/j.jas.2019.05.002

Hastorf, C. *The Social Archaeology of Food: Thinking about Eating from Prehistory to the Present*. Cambridge: Cambridge University Press, 2017.

Hunt, C. O., and D. D. Gilbertson. "Human activity, landscape change and valley alluviation in the Feccia Valley, Tuscany, Italy." In *Mediterranean Quaternary River*

Environments, edited by J. C. Woodward, M. G. Macklin, and J. Lewin, 167–176. Rotterdam: Balkema, 1995.

Judson, S. "Erosion and deposition of Italian stream valleys during historic time." *Science* 140 (1963), 898–899.

Kansa, S. W., and M. MacKinnon. "Etruscan economics: Forty-five years of faunal remains from Poggio Civitate." *Etruscan Studies* 17 (2014), 63–87.

Kouli, K. "Plant landscape and land use at the Neolithic lake settlement of Dispilió (Macedonia, northern Greece)." *Plant Biosystems* 149 (2015), 195–204.

Kouli K., A. Masi, A. M. Mercuri, A. Florenzano, and L. Sadori. "Regional vegetation histories: An overview of the pollen evidence from the central Mediterranean." In *Environment and Society in the Long Late Antiquity*, edited by A. Izbedski and M. Mulryan, 69–82. Leiden: Brill, 2018.

Lamb, H. H. "The rôle of ocean surface currents and water temperatures in the long-range weather forecasts problem: Early modern developments." *Wheather* 50.12 (1995), 407–412. doi:10.1002/j.1477-8696.1995.tb06066.x

Lee-Thorp, J. A. "On isotopes and old bones." *Archaeometry* 50 (2008), 925–950. doi:10.1111/j.1475-4754.2008.00441.x

Lennstrom, Heidi A., and Christine Hastorf. "Interpretation in context: Sampling and analysis in palaeoethnobotany." *American Antiquity* 60.4 (1995), 701–721.

Lentjes, D., and G. Saltini Semerari. "Big debates over small fruits: Wine and oil production in protohistoric Southern Italy (ca 1350–750 BC)." *BABESCH* 91 (2016), 1–16. doi:10.2143/BAB.91.0.3175640

Lodwick, L. and Rowan, E. "Archaeobotanical Research in Classical Archaeology." American Journal of Archaeology (2022) 126:4, 593–623.

Lopane, E., M. Bandini Mazzanti, and C. A. Accorsi. "Pollini e semi/frutti dell'abitato etrusco-celtico di Pianella di Monte Savino (Monte Bibele, Bologna – Nord Italia) Casa 24." In *Studi in ricordo di Daria Bertolani Marchetti*, edited by C. A. Accorsi, M. Bandini Mazzanti, D. Labate, and G. Trevisan Grandi, 359–365. Modena: Aedes Muratoriana, 1998.

Magri, D., and L. Sadori. "Late Pleistocene and Holocene pollenstratigraphy at Lago di Vico (central Italy)." *Vegetation History and Archaeobotany* 8 (1999), 247–260. doi:10.1007/BF01291777

Maini, E., and A. Curci. "The food of the dead: Alimentary offerings in the Etruscan-Celtic necropolis of Monterenzio Vecchio (Bologna, Italy)." *Anthropozoologica* 48 (2013), 341–354.

Mainland, I. L. "The uses of archaeological faunal remains in landscape archaeology." In *Handbook of Landscape Archaeology*, edited by B. David and J. Thomas, 544–551. London: Routledge, 2008.

Makarewicz, C. A., and J. Sealy. "Dietary reconstruction, mobility, and the analysis of ancient skeletal tissues: Expanding the prospects of stable isotope research in archaeology." *Journal of Archaeological Science* 56 (2015), 146–158. doi:10.1016/j.jas.2015.02.035

Malone, C., S. Stoddart, L. Ceccarelli, L. Cenciaioli, P. Duff, F. McCormick, J. Morales, S. Armstrong, J. Bates, J. Bennett, J. Cameron, G. Cifani, S. Cohen, T. Foley,

F. Fulminante, H. Hill, L. Mattacchoni, S. Neil, A. Rosatelli, D. Redhouse, and S. Volhard-Dearman. "Beyond feasting: Consumption and life style amongst the invisible Etruscans." In *Living in the Landscape: Essays in Honour of Graeme Barker*, edited by K. Boyle, R. J. Rabett, and C. O. Hunt, 257–266. Cambridge: McDonald Institute, 2014.

Marchesini, M., and S. Marvelli. "Analisi botaniche del contenuto del vaso biconico." In *Guerriero e Sacerdote: Autorità e comunità nell'età del ferro a Verucchio La Tomba del Trono*, edited by P. von Elòes, 299–307. Firenze: Quaderni di Archeologia dell'Emilia Romagna 6. All'Insegna del Giglio, 2010.

Marchesini, M., S. Marvelli, I. Gobbo, and E. Rizzoli. "Paesaggio, ambiente e attività antropica dalla Bologna villanoviana (VII-VI sec. a.C.) alla Bononia romana (I sec d.C.) attraverso le analisi archeobotaniche." In *Alla ricerca di Bologna antica e medieval: Da Felsina a Bononia negli scavi di via D'Azeglio*, edited by R. Curina, L. Malnati, C. Negrelli, and L. Pini, 145–162. Firenze: All'Insegna del Giglio, 2010.

Mariotti Lippi, M. "Ancient floras, vegetational reconstruction and man-plant relationships: Case studies from archaeological sites." *Bocconea* 24 (2012), 105–113.

Mariotti Lippi, M., P. L. Di Tommaso, G. Giachi, M. Mori Secci, and S. Paci. "Archaeobotanical investigations into an Etruscan farmhouse at Pian d'Alma (Grosseto, Italy)." *Atti Società Toscana Scienze Naturali* 109 (2002), 159–165.

Mariotti Lippi, M., A. Florenzano, R. Rinaldi, E. Allevato, D. Arobba, G. Bacchetta, M. C. Bal, M. Bandini Mazzanti, A. Benatti, J. Beneš, G. Bosi, M. Buonincontri, R. Caramiello, L. Castelletti, E. Castiglioni, A. Celant, E. Clò, L. Costantini, G. Di Pasquale, F. Di Rita, G. Fiorentino, G. Furlanetto, M. Giardini, O. Grillo, M. Guido, M. Herchenbach, D. Magri, M. Marchesini, M. Maritan, S. Marvelli, A. Masi, A. Miola, C. Montanari, M. C. Montecchi, S. Motella, R. Nisbet, M. Orrù, L. Peña-Chocarro, C. Pepe, R. Perego, E. Rattighieri, C. Ravazzi, M. Rottoli, E. Rowan, D. Sabato, L. Sadori, M. Sarigu, P. Torri, M. Ucchesu, and A. M. Mercuri. "The botanical record of archaeobotany Italian Network – BRAIN: A cooperative network, database and website." *Flora Mediterranea* 28 (2018), 365–376. doi:10.7320/FlMedit28.365

Mariotti Lippi, M., G. Giachi, S. Paci, and P. L. Di Tommaso. "Studi sulla vegetazione attuale e passata della Toscana meridionale (Follonica – Italia) e considerazioni sull'impatto ambientale dell'attività metallurgica etrusca nel VI-V secolo a.C." *Webbia* 55.2 (2000), 279–295.

Mariotti Lippi, M., and M. Mori Secci. "Richerche archeobotaniche nella Toscana preistorica." *Informatore Botanico Italiano* 39.2 (2007), 259–270.

Mariotti Lippi, M., M. Mori Secci, G. Giachi, L. Bouby, J.-F. Terral, E. Castiglioni, M. Cottini, M. Rottoli, and N. T. De Grummond. "Plant remains in an Etruscan-Roman well at Cetamura del Chianti, Italy." *Archaeological and Anthropological Sciences* 12 (2020), 35. doi:10.1007/s12520-019-00992-4

Mazier, F. *Modélisation de la relation entre pluie pollinique actuelle, végétation et pratiques pastorales en moyenne montagne (Pyrénées et Jura) application pour l'interprétation des données polliniques fossils.* PhD thesis, Universite de Franche Comté, 2007.

Mazier F., M. J. Gaillard, P. Kunes, S. Sugita, A.-K. Trondman, and A. Brostrom. "Testing the effect of site selection and parameter setting on REVEALS-model estimates of plant abundance using the Czech Quaternary Palynological database." *Review of Palaeobotany and Palynology* 187 (2012), 38–49.

Mercuri, A. M. "Genesis and evolution of the cultural landscape in central Mediterranean: The "where, when and how" through the palynological approach." *Landscape Ecology* 29 (2014), 1799–1810. doi:10.1007/s10980-014-0093-0

Mercuri, A. M., C. A. Accorsi, and M. Bandini Mazzanti. "The long history of *Cannabis* and its cultivation by the Romans in central Italy, shown by pollen records from Lago Albano and Lago di Nemi." *Vegetation History and Archaeobotany* 11 (2002), 263–276. doi:10.1007/s003340200039

Mercuri, A. M., E. Allevato, D. Arobba, M. Bandini, M. Mazzanti, G. Bosi, R. Caramiello, E. Castiglioni, M. L. Carra, A. Celant, L. Costantini, G. Di Pasquale, G. Fiorentino, A. Florenzano, M. Guido, M. Marchesini, M. Mariotti Lippi, S. Marvelli, A. Miola, C. Montanari, R. Nisbet, L. Peña-Chocarro, R. Perego, C. Ravazzi, M. Rottoli, L. Sadori, M. Ucchesu, and R. Rinaldi. "Pollen and macroremains from Holocene archaeological sites: A dataset for the understanding of the biocultural diversity of the Italian landscape." *Review of Palaeobotany and Palynology* 218 (2015), 250–266. doi:10.1016/j.revpalbo.2014.05.010

Mercuri, A. M., M. Bandini Mazzanti, A. Florenzano, M. C. Montecchi, and E. Rattighieri. "*Olea, Juglans* and *Castanea*: The OJC group as pollen evidence of the development of human-induced environments in the Italian peninsula." *Quaternary International* 303 (2013a), 24–42.

Mercuri, A. M., M. Bandini Mazzanti, A. Florenzano, M. C. Montecchi, E. Rattighieri, and P. Torri. "Anthropogenic Pollen Indicators (API) from archaeological sites as local evidence of human-induced environments in the Italian peninsula." *Annali di Botanica* 3 (2013b), 143–153. doi:10.4462/annbotrm-10316

Mercuri, A. M., A. Florenzano, F. Burjachs, M. Giardini, K. Kouli, A. Masi, L. Picornell-Gelabert, J. Revelles, L. Sadori, G. Servera-Vives, P. Torri, and R. Fyfe. "From influence to impact: The multifunctional land use in Mediterranean prehistory emerging from palynology of archaeological sites (8.0–2.8 ka BP)." *The Holocene* 29.5 (2019), 830–846. doi:10.1177/0959683619826631

Mercuri, A. M., L. Sadori, and C. Blasi. "Editorial: Archaeobotany for cultural landscape and human impact reconstructions." *Plant Biosystems* 144.4 (2010), 860–864. doi: 10.1080/11263504.2010.514137

Mercuri, A. M., P. Torri, A. Florenzano, E. Clò, M. Mariotti Lippi, E. Sgarbi, and C. Bignami. "Sharing the agrarian knowledge with archaeology: First evidence of the dimorphism of *Vitis* pollen from the Middle Bronze Age of North Italy (Terramara Santa Rosa di Poviglio)." *Sustainability* 13.4 (2021), 2287. doi:10.3390/su13042287

Milli, S., C. D'Ambrogi, P. Bellotti, G. Calderoni, M. G. Carboni, A. Celant, L. Di Bella, F. Di Rita, V. Frezza, D. Magri, R. M. Pichezzi, and V. Ricci. "The transition from wave-dominated estuary to wave-dominated delta: The Late Quaternary stratigraphic architecture of Tiber River deltaic succession (Italy)." *Sedimentary Geology* 284–285 (2013), 159–180.

Milli, S., M. Mancini, M. Moscatelli, F. Stigliano, M. Marini, and G. P. Cavinato. "From river to shelf, anatomy of a high-frequency depositional sequence: The Late Pleistocene to Holocene Tiber depositional sequence." *Sedimentology* 63.7 (2016), 1886–1928.

Moses, V. C. *The Zooarchaeology of Early Rome: Meat Production, Distribution, and Consumption in Public and Private Spaces 9th-5th Centuries BCE).* PhD. thesis,The University of Arizona, 2020.

Moses, V. C., and F. Alhaique. "Same place, changing patterns? Animal economy at Gabii (Latium, central Italy) from the Early Iron Age through the Imperial period." Journal of Archaeological Science: Reports 46 (2022): 103717.

Moses, V. C., and U. Fusco. "Urbanization, meat consumption, and ritual practices at Veii, 9th–4th centuries BCE: Zooarchaeological findings from Campetti, area Sud-Ovest excavations." *Journal of Archaeological Science: Reports* 20 (2018), 922–929. doi:10.1016/j.jasrep.2018.01.007

Motta, L. "Seeds and the city. Archaeobotany and state formation in early Rome." In *State Formation in Italy and Greece: Questioning the Neoevolutionist Paradigm*, edited by N. Terrenato and D. C. Haggis, 245–255. Oxford: Oxbow, 2011.

Motta, L., and K. Beydler. "Agriculture in Iron Age and Archaic Italy." In *A Companion to Ancient Agriculture*, edited by D. Hollander and T. Howe, 399–415. Hoboken, NJ: Wiley, 2020. doi:10.1002/9781118970959.ch19

Negri, G. "Come si possa ricostruire la fisonomia della vegetazione della Toscana durante il periodo etrusco." *Studi Etruschi* 1 (1927), 363–376.

Pálsdóttir, A. H., A. Bläuer, E. Rannamäe, S. Boessenkool, and J. H. Hallsson. "Not a limit-less resource: Ethics and guidelines for destructive sampling of archaeofaunal remains." *Royal Society Open Science* 6 (2019), 191059. doi:10.1098/rsos.191059

Perkins, P. "The landscape and environment of Etruria." In *Etruscology*, edited by A. Naso, 1239–1250. Berlin: De Gruyter, 2017.

Perkins, P., and I. Attolini. 1992. "An Etruscan Farm at Podere Tartuchino." *Papers of the British School at Rome* 60: 71–133.

Pieraccini, L. C. "Food and drink in the Etruscan world." In *The Etruscan World*, edited by J. MacIntosh Turfa, 812–819. London: Routledge, 2013.

Potter, T. W. "Valleys and settlement: Some new evidence." *World Archaeology* 8 (1976), 207–219.

Prato, O. *Intertwined Lives in the Mediterranean: Humans and Animals at Etruscan Tarquinia*. PhD thesis, University College London, 2023.

Rask, K. "Etruscan animal bones and their implications for sacrificial studies." *History of Religions* 53 (2014), 269–312.

Rattighieri, E., R. Rinaldi, K. Bowes, and A. M. Mercuri. "Land use from seasonal archae-ological sites: The archaeobotanical evidence of small Roman farmhouses in Cinigiano, South-Eastern Tuscany – Central Italy." *Annali Di Botanica* 3 (2013), 207–215. doi:10.4462/annbotrm-10267

Rinaldi, G., B. Abuhelaleh, and U. Thun Hohenstein. "Da Felsina a Bononia: studio archeozoologico e tafonomico dei resti faunistici provenienti dallo scavo urbano di Bologna in Via d'Azeglio." In *Atti del 7° Convegno Nazionale di Archeozoologia,* edited by U. Thun Hohenstein, M. Cangemi, I. Fiore, I. and J. De Grossi Mazzorin., 93–96. Ferrara: Annali dell'Università degli Studi di Ferrara, Museologia Scientifica e Naturalistica 11, 2016.

Sadori, L. "The Late glacial and Holocene vegetation and climate history of Lago di Mezzano (central Italy)." *Quaternary Science Reviews* 202 (2018), 30–44.

Sadori, L., E. Allevato, C. Bellini, A. Bertacchi, G. Boetto, G. Di Pasquale, G. Giachi, M. Giardini, A. Masi, C. Pepe, E. Russo Ermolli, and M. Mariotti Lippi. "Archaeobotany in Italian Ancient Roman harbours." *Review of Palaeobotany and Palynology* 218.1 (2015), 217–230.

Sadori, L., and M. Giardini. "Charcoal analysis, a method to study vegetation and climate of the Holocene: The case of Lago di Pergusa, Sicily (Italy)." *Geobiossystems* 40 (2007), 173–180.

Sadori, L., A. M. Mercuri, and M. Mariotti. "Reconstructing past cultural landscape and human impact using pollen and plant macroremains." *Plant Biosystems* 144 (2010), 940–951.

Sarti, G., V. Rossi, A. Amorosi, M. Bini, S. Giacomelli, M. Pappalardo, C. Ribecai, A. Ribolini, and I. Sammartino. "Climatic signature of two mid–late Holocene fluvial incisions formed under sea-level highstand conditions (Pisa coastal plain, NW Tuscany, Italy)." *Palaeogeography, Palaeoclimatology, Palaeoecology* 424 (2015), 183–195.

Shriver-Rice, M. "The challenges of environmental studies in pre-Roman first millennium BCE central Italy: A methodological case study." Conference presentation. Toronto Archaeological Institute of America, 2017.

Shriver-Rice, M., and F. Schmidt. "Environmental and Archaeobotanical Studies in Etruscan Archaeology: An Epistemological Overview and Future Considerations of Human–Plant Relationships. *Etruscan and Italic Studies* 25, no. 1-2, (2022), 113–147. doi:10.1515/etst-2022-0001

Shriver-Rice, M., Schneider, M. J., & Pardo, C. Charismatic megafauna, regional identity, and invasive species: what role does environmental archaeology play in contemporary conservation efforts? *World Archaeology,* 54(3) (2022), 429–446. doi:10.1080/0043824 3.2022.2118161

Spivey, N. S. "Review of Etruscan exhibition volumes." *Journal of Roman Studies* 75 (1986), 281–286.

Spivey, S. and Tomei, P., and A. Bertacchi. "The protection of biodiversity in Tuscany." *Nature Conservation Concepts and Practice,* edited by G. Gafta and J. Akeroyd, 87–89. Berlin: Springer 2006.

Stevens, C. "Plant remains." *Papers of the British School at Rome* 67 (2000), 330–333.

Stoddart, S. "An Etruscan urban agenda: The weaving together of traditions." *Journal of Urban Archaeology* 1 (2020a), 88–121.

Stoddart, S. *Power and Place in Etruria: The Spatial Dynamics of a Mediterranean Civilization, 1200–500 BC.* Cambridge: Cambridge University Press, 2020b.

Stoddart, S. 2024. Science@Tarquinia: Applying methods towards an understanding of site formation processes, mobility, diet, biology and human infrastructure in the early stages of Tarquinia. In *40 anni di scavi, ricerche e attività dell'Università degli Studi di Milano a Tarquinia*, Atti del convegno in omaggio a Maria Bonghi Jovino, Tarquinia 17–18 settembre 2022, edited by F. Bagnasco and A. P. Pernigotti, 33–44. Milano: Milano University Press.

Stoddart, S., and C. Malone. "A geoarchaeological agenda for Tyrrhenian central Italy." In *Inspired Geoarchaeology: Past Landscapes and Social Change. Essays in Honour of Professor Charly French*, edited by F. Sulas, H. Lewis, and M. Arroyo-Lewis. Cambridge: McDonald Institute. 157–165, 2022. doi:10.17863/CAM.91939

Stoddart, S., J. Woodbridge, A. Palmisano, A. M. Mercuri, S. Mensing, D. Colombaroli, L. Sadori, D. Magri, F. di Rita, M. Giardini, M. Mariotti Lippi, C. Montanari, C. Bellini, A. Florenzano, P. Torri, A. Bevan, S. Shennan, R. Fyfe, and N. Roberts. "Tyrrhenian central Italy: Holocene population and landscape dynamics." *The Holocene* 29(5) (2019), 761–775.

Stoddart, S. *Etruscan Italy*. London: B.T. Batsford (1990).

Trentacoste, A. "Faunal remains from the Etruscan sanctuary at Poggio Colla (Vicchio di Mugello)." *Etruscan Studies* 16 (2013), 75–105.

Trentacoste, A. "Etruscan foodways and demographic demands: Contextualizing proto-historic livestock husbandry in Northern Italy." *European Journal of Archaeology* 19 (2016), 279–315. doi:10.1179/1461957115Y.0000000015

Trentacoste, A. "Fodder for change: Animals, urbanisation, and socio-economic trans-formation in protohistoric Italy." *Theoretical Roman Archaeology Journal* 3 (2020). doi:10.16995/traj.414

Trentacoste, A., E. Lightfoot, P. Le Roux, M. Buckley, S. W. Kansa, C. Esposito, and M. Gleba. "Heading for the hills? A multi-isotope study of sheep management in first-millennium BC Italy." *Journal of Archaeological Science: Reports* 29 (2020), 102036. doi:10.1016/j.jasrep.2019.102036

Trentacoste, A., and L. Lodwick. "Agriculture and animal husbandry in first-millennium BC Italy: Towards an agroecology of the Roman expansion." In *The Roman Republic in the Long Fourth Century*, edited by S. Bernard, L. Mignone, and D. Padilla Peralta (2023).

Trentacoste, A., A. Nieto-Espinet, and S. Valenzuela-Lamas. "Pre-Roman improvements to agricultural production: Evidence from livestock husbandry in late prehistoric Italy." *PLOS One* 13 (2018), e0208109. doi:10.1371/journal.pone.0208109

Vaccaro, E., M. Ghisleni, A. Arnoldus-Huyzendveld, C. Grey, and K. Bowes. "Excavating the Roman peasant II: Excavations at Case Nuove, Cignano (GR)." *Papers of the British School at Rome* 81 (2013), 129–179.

Vita-Finzi, C. *The Mediterranean Valleys: Geological Changes in Historical Times*. London: Cambridge University Press, 1969.

Meryl Shriver-Rice, Anna Maria Mercuri, Angela Trentacoste, Assunta Florenzano, and Simon Stoddart, *Environmental Approaches to Etruscan Studies: Revisiting Negri 1927 Almost One Hundred Years Later* In: *A New Etruscan Archaeology: Twenty-First Century Techniques and Methods*. Edited by: Maurizio Forte, Oxford University Press. © Oxford University Press 2025. DOI: 10.1093/9780197582053.003.0010

10

Etruscan Textiles

Methods, Approaches, Results, and Future Perspectives

Margarita Gleba

Introduction

Until recently, the significant economic and social roles of textiles in Etruscan society stood in stark contrast with their limited consideration in scholarly debates. Over the past decades, however, new attention to the various sources of evidence and new analytical techniques and theoretical approaches have started to change this status quo. We are beginning to shift from qualitative to quantitative approaches in our treatment of the growing datasets that allow us to distil what is Etruscan and what is not.[1] These new data allow us to recontextualize the significance of textiles and textile production in Etruscan society and to interrogate the evidence with new questions in mind. In this chapter, I review the extant evidence, the latest methods, and the state of the art, as well as propose some future directions for the field of Etruscan textile research.[2]

Our evidence includes textiles themselves (Figure 10.1), tools used for their manufacture, zooarchaeological data consisting of sheep bones and muricid shells, archaeobotanical remains documenting flax and hemp cultivation and the presence of dye plants, iconographic depictions, and occasional written sources. Of these, archaeological evidence, in particular the textiles themselves and the textile tools, have seen the most significant methodological developments.

Ancient textiles in Etruria (and generally across Italy) only occasionally survive in the organic state, often due to waterlogging, the best examples being the wool fragments preserving color patterns recovered from the boat cenotaph at Sasso di Furbara near Cerveteri (Gleba et al., 2020) and the almost complete wool garments found in several burials at Verucchio.[3] Linen textiles are often preserved in their organic state when in close contact with bronze objects, as in the case of fragments from the Tomba del Guerriero in Tarquinia, currently conserved in Berlin (Stauffer, 2013); Tomba G at Casale Marittimo; (see Esposito, 1999, 71, fig. 67) or a fibula from Veii (Figure 10.1a). Occasionally, even wool textiles survive adhering to bronze and

[1] E.g., contrast Gleba (2013) and (Gleba 2017b).
[2] For the history of textile research in Italy, see Gleba (2008, 33–36).
[3] Stauffer (2012), with preceding bibliography.

preserve their original colors, for example the red and white checked textiles found in Tomb LXXII at the Cava della Pozzolana necropolis at Cerveteri and Tomb 72 at the Poggio Mengarelli cemetery of Vulci (Figure 10.1b) (Carosi and Regoli, 2021, 202 fig. 14.8). The vast majority of Etruscan textiles, however, survive in a mineralized state on iron or bronze objects included as grave goods (Figure 10.1c) (Gleba, 2017b). Sometimes referred to as *pseudomorphs*, mineralized textiles are created when a combination of chemical and physical conditions within a burial lead to the replacement of their organic components with inorganic ones, resulting in a positive or negative cast of the fabric and preserving its physical features, down to fiber morphology.[4] In a different type of mineralization, textiles can also be preserved in calcium-rich environments, as in the travertine burial urns of the Strozzacapponi necropolis at Perugia/Corciano, which, unlike the metal-replaced textiles, may retain their original color (Figure 10.1d) (Gleba et al., 2017a). Last but not least, while preservation through aridity is not typical for Etruria, one of the most famous Etruscan textile finds, the linen book of Zagreb, was preserved in the dry climate of Egypt (Figure 10.1e).[5]

In contrast to tools, which are ubiquitous in settlements as well as in burials and votive contexts (Gleba, 2008), textiles in Etruria survive almost exclusively in funerary contexts. This inevitably creates a bias toward high-status textiles and those likely used for garments or wrapping rather than other, utilitarian purposes, such as furnishings or sails. The geographical and chronological distribution of finds is also uneven, with certain areas (e.g., cemeteries of Vulci and Tarquinia) and certain chronological periods (e.g., Orientalizing period) better represented than others due to peculiarities of burial customs as well as excavation and conservation histories. Nevertheless, the wide spectrum of textiles recovered is to a significant degree representative of the Etruscan textile culture. In combination with other types of evidence, and thanks to the diverse methods of analysis now available, these textiles allow us to gain important new insights into Etruscan textile technologies.

Research Questions, Methods, and New Developments

Over the past twenty years the field of textile archaeology in Italy has seen significant developments thanks to the application of a growing suite of analytical approaches to the body of material that is itself growing thanks to improved excavation and conservation techniques as well as research interest. In the following overview, I outline these various approaches and discuss what types of archaeological questions they can help answer.

---

[4] Chen et al. (1998), with preceding bibliography.
[5] See van der Meer (2007), with preceding bibliography. The textiles are currently undergoing new analyses, including radiocarbon dating.

Figure 10.1 Different types of preservation of Etruscan textiles: (a) organic linen in contact with bronze, Veii; (b) organic wool in contact with bronze, Vulci; (c) mineralized wool on an iron fibula with textiles preserved in layers, Grotte di Castro; (d) calcified wool, Perugia; (e) organic linen preserved in arid climate, *Liber linteus zagrabiensis* (Images: Margarita Gleba).

Textile Structural Analysis

As a final product of a long and complex manufacturing process, any textile contains in it information about the various stages of its production, while its use context can tell about its intended function. Analysis of an archaeological textile find can thus provide data regarding the nature and quality of the raw materials and techniques used in its production, as well as its meaning for the past society that produced it. Examination of many textile specimens generates not only qualitative (based on presence and description) but also quantitative (i.e., quantifiable) data regarding the prevalence of specific textile cultures in specific areas and periods.

Much of the basic textile analytical work is done with a simple hand lens or a low-power microscope. Textiles have a precise structure that can be very accurately described, and, over the past half century, an internationally agreed terminology has been established (Barber, 1991; Emery, 1966; Grömer, 2016; Seiler-Baldinger, 1994). Structural analysis of a textile includes determination of thread parameters such as diameter of warp and weft (expressed in millimeters), thread twist direction in warp and weft, and tightness of twist angle (hard, medium, or loose) and of weave characteristics such as the type of textile weave or binding (plain weave/tabby, twill, etc.), thread count in warp and weft (expressed in number of threads per centimeter), presence of edges, weaving mistakes, and any other diagnostic features (Figure 10.2). These empirical features can inform our understanding of cultural aspects of textile production and use and, from the close study of many individual examples, much wider conclusions can be drawn about regional and chronological trends (Bender Jørgensen, 1986, 1992; Gleba, 2017a).

Although basic structural analysis constitutes the standard operating procedure in textile research, within recent decades textile investigation has been enriched by

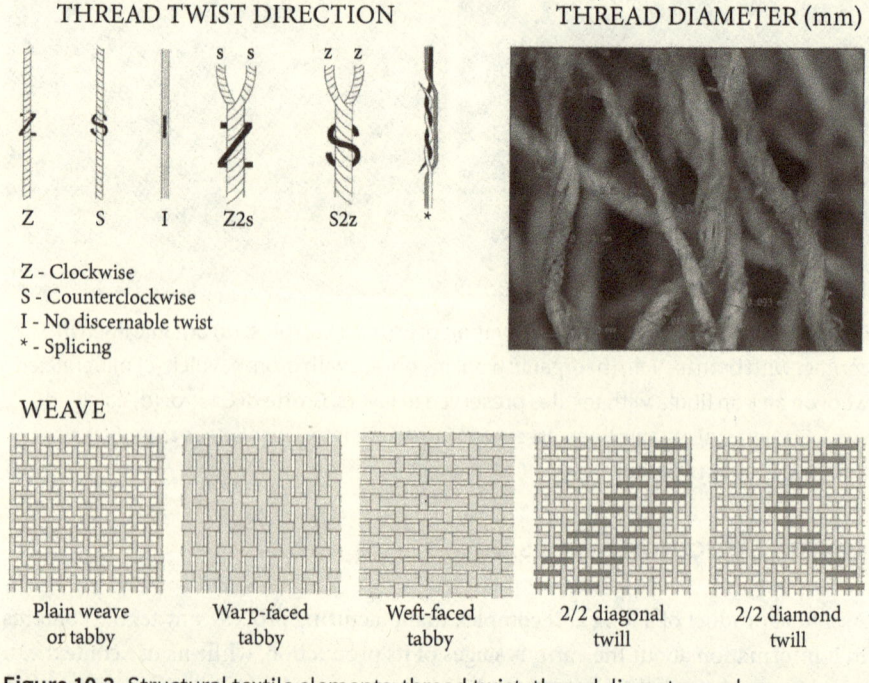

THREAD TWIST DIRECTION

Z   S   I   Z2s   S2z   *

Z - Clockwise
S - Counterclockwise
I - No discernable twist
* - Splicing

THREAD DIAMETER (mm)

WEAVE

Plain weave or tabby   Warp-faced tabby   Weft-faced tabby   2/2 diagonal twill   2/2 diamond twill

Figure 10.2 Structural textile elements: thread twist, thread diameter, and weave (Image: M. Gleba and V. Herring).

many new analytical methods stemming from the natural sciences that can be used to gain new kinds of information (Andersson et al., 2010; Good, 2001). Scientific analytical methods allow us to ask a variety of questions about many different aspects of textiles, in particular:

- *Characterization*: What materials were used to make the textile?
- *Technology*: How was the textile made?
- *Dating*: When was the textile made?
- *Provenance*: Where was the textile made?

Considering the perishable nature of textiles, their scientific analysis is also essential to understand the ways in which textiles deteriorate and to determine the best practice to preserve, conserve, handle, and protect these objects for the benefit of present and future generations.

Fiber Identification and Analysis

Textile quality and appearance depend on the materials of which the textile has been made—that is fiber and dye. Specific raw materials were used for different purposes. By studying fibers on a microscopic level we can come closer to understanding the types of raw materials used. Because they varied geographically and chronologically, such data may be indicative of textile origins.

Fibers in Etruria were primarily derived from plants (cellulose-based, such as flax and hemp) and animals (protein-based, such as sheep wool), with occasional use of minerals (asbestos) and gold thread. The fiber source may be identified by optical or digital microscopy on well-preserved textiles, using modern reference materials for comparison. Degraded fibers from archaeological textiles are often more difficult to identify and require more sophisticated methods. The best available method for fiber identification is currently scanning electron microscopy (Rast-Eicher, 2016), a technique particularly useful in the case of mineralized and charred specimens, which constitute the vast majority of the Etruscan finds. In the case of mineralized textiles, information about their raw material survives in the shape of negative or positive fiber casts, which often preserve detailed information about their original morphology (Figure 10.3).

The more advanced methods of fiber characterization include DNA and protein analyses, which are being developed in particular for protein-based fibers and hopefully will allow animal species identification and possibly even differentiation between breeds of the same species (Ørsted Brandt and Allentoft, 2020; Solazzo et al., 2014).

Fiber investigation, however, is more than just identification of material source. By studying fiber on a microscopic level we can come closer to understanding aspects of selective breeding (in sheep) and cultivation (in flax), processing of fibers

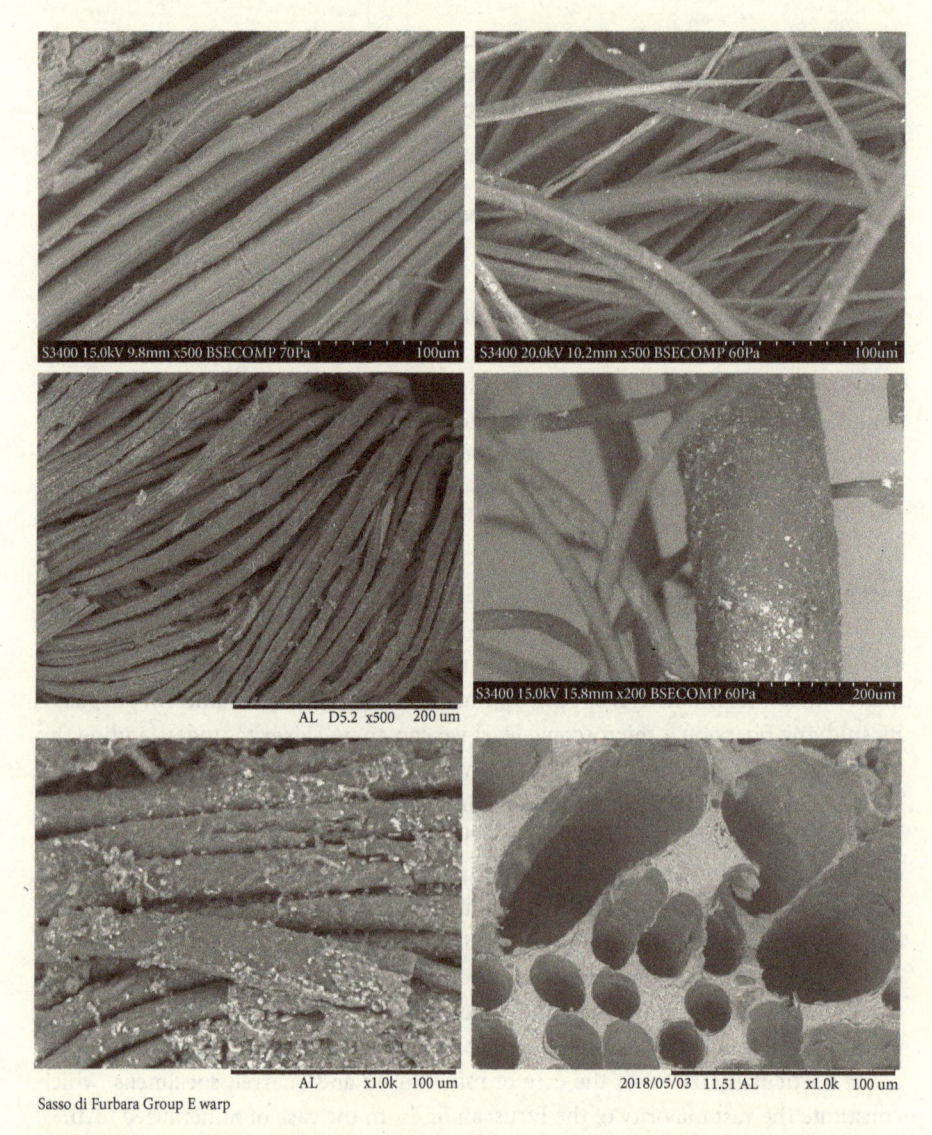

S3400 15.0kV 9.8mm x500 BSECOMP 70Pa   100um

S3400 20.0kV 10.2mm x500 BSECOMP 60Pa   100um

AL D5.2 x500   200 um

S3400 15.0kV 15.8mm x200 BSECOMP 60Pa   200um

AL   x1.0k 100 um

2018/05/03 11.51 AL   x1.0k 100 um

Sasso di Furbara Group E warp

Figure 10.3 Scanning Electron Micrographs of modern reference material (top), organic archaeological fibres (centre) and mineralized fibre casts (bottom) of flax (left) and wool (right) (Images: M. Gleba).

(e.g., wool sorting), and their wear, all of which are essential to the understanding of Etruscan agriculture, animal husbandry, domestication, processing technology, and textile use. Analyses of wool fiber fineness, for example, are used to determine the fleece type of prehistoric sheep. Assessment of fiber quality is based on the diameter measurement of 100 fibers per thread and statistical analyses resulting in a distribution diagram. Wool contains three parts, differing in structure and size: kemp, hair, and the wool itself. Michael Ryder established an evolutionary scheme for wool development based on fiber diameter measurements.[6] Ryder demonstrated that, over the course of time, selective breeding has produced increasingly finer and more uniform wool. Ryder's model has been adapted in recent investigations to account for the fact that the fiber in a textile is a product of numerous processes: breeding, selection, processing, and finishing (Skals et al., 2018). The method also allows distinguishing between sheep wool and goat fiber.

Dye Analysis

The addition of color has been an integral part of textile-making, contributing to pattern design (Cardon, 2007). Yet archaeological textiles in Etruria often survive as discolored rags or mineralized formations, making it difficult to visualize what color they originally had. This can in some cases be reconstructed through dye and mordant analysis Using high- or ultra-performance liquid chromatography (HPLC/UPLC), a technique in analytical chemistry used to separate, identify, and quantify each component in a mixture (Vanden Berghe et al., 2009). The method allows identification of chemical dye components and their combination, which can then be matched to a database of known plant and animal dye sources. This knowledge can help us to reconstruct Etruscan dyeing technology, as well as the aesthetics, value, and meaning of color for the Etruscan people. Dye identification can also be significant for tracing the origins of textiles, particularly in combination with fiber analysis, since certain dyes were extremely precious and traded over long distances.

Textile Dating

The most reliable way to accurately date fibers can be achieved by using accelerator mass spectrometry (AMS) radiocarbon analysis. Textiles made more than five hundred years ago are especially suitable for ^{14}C dating and may even give more precise dates than other material (Mannering et al., 2010). In the case of Etruscan textiles, however, this is not always possible, first because the majority of Etruscan textiles are mineralized and do not contain a sufficient quantity of organic material to be dated; and, second, due to the fact that several centuries of Etruscan culture fall within the so-called Hallstatt Plateau (van Geel et al., 1998). In most cases, we must rely on relative dating through association with other objects within the same burial context, although early and late Etruscan finds can be dated using the AMS.[7]

---

[6] Ryder (1983), with preceding bibliography.
[7] E.g., Gleba et al. (2020), on the dating of the Early Iron Age textiles from Sasso di Furbara.

Textile Provenance

An important aspect to understanding archaeological textiles is identifying where they were made and thus exploring the movements of raw materials and finished artifacts for what this can tell us about the social, economic, cultural, and technological links between sites and regions. Fiber type or quality, dye source, or weaving technique may occasionally help with identifying nonlocal textiles. Identifying the provenance of artifacts in absolute terms is, however, often difficult if not impossible. This is especially true of textiles, which, made with widespread and long-lasting techniques and materials, may defy typological classification, lack visible reference to their origin, and could be moved and traded over vast distances.

In archaeology, strontium (Sr) isotopes have been widely applied, mainly for the purpose of reconstructing human and animal migration routes in antiquity. Strontium isotopic signatures are conveyed from eroding geological materials through soils and the food chain into the human and animal skeleton, where Sr substitutes for calcium (Ca). Since the path of the strontium isotope ratio through the food chain is unfractionated, it is possible to apply the method also to animals and plants and hence to their products, in this case fiber and, consequently, textiles (Frei et al., 2009). This recently developed methodology using thermal ionization mass spectrometry can be used either independently or as a control for typological and/or technical analysis, although it should be applied with caution in some cases because recent studies indicate that 87Sr/86Sr ratios of archaeological wool textiles recovered from wet burial environments do not accurately reflect wool provenance even after cleaning (von Holstein et al., 2015), and the isoscapes may have been affected by recent anthropogenic factors (Thomsen and Andreasen, 2019). While it is not always possible to delineate precisely the exact geographical provenance, the technique provides a potential method for distinguishing between the local and nonlocal origin of textiles.

Combined carbon, nitrogen, and hydrogen isotopes are used in archaeology to establish geographic origin. Gradients in stable isotopes identified in modern studies of European sheep meat and wool have now been successfully applied to medieval archaeological wool samples from Iceland, the United Kingdom, Germany, and Sweden (von Holstein et al., 2016). Analysis has shown that the isotopic composition of wool and bone collagen samples are clustered strongly by settlement, demonstrating the feasibility of provenancing keratin preserved in anoxic waterlogged contexts. The same methodology could be extended to other animal and plant fibers in the future.

Textile Tool Analysis

The great number of implements associated with textile manufacture can be used to study the craft and its technological and economic aspects (Gleba, 2008). These include tools such as spindle whorls, distaffs, spools, loom weights, and needles.

These tools' ubiquitous presence, particularly in settlement sites (in contrast to textiles), makes them an excellent proxy for the investigation of textile production areas (via distribution mapping) and its intensity (quantitative analysis). The new method of functional tool analysis developed at the Centre for Textile Research in Copenhagen now also allows us to calculate the range of textile qualities obtainable using loom weights of specific weight and thickness[8]—an indispensable tool in the absence of actual textiles on many sites. When both textiles and tools are present, the technical information from the former allow us to check the validity of the functional analysis of the latter.

Furthermore, many textile tools have been found in votive and burial contexts, thus providing different interpretative frameworks. Analysis of tools found in votive contexts have been used to demonstrate that they were not only dedicated at sanctuaries but were also used there (Gleba, 2009; Meyers, 2013). In the meantime, textile tools found in Etruscan burials have provided strong evidence for women's involvement in textile production (Gleba, 2008; Lipkin, 2012).

Experimental Archaeology

Another important approach in textile studies is experimental archaeology, largely inspired by the long-standing tradition in northern Europe. For example, experiments carried out with replicas of Etruscan spindle whorls and spools (Ciccarelli and Perilli, 2017; Laurito, 2017), combined with traceological examination of both archaeological and experimental tools (Forte and Lemorini, 2017), allowed researchers to better understand their function and production processes (Figure 10.4a). Meanwhile, experimental tablet weaving has confirmed the techniques observed in poorly preserved archaeological material, in particular the fact that tablet-woven borders were integral to the ground twill-woven textiles and that the borders were woven simultaneously with the textile (Figure 10.4b) (Serges et al., 2018).

Zooarchaeology of Sheep Bones

Sheep bones are common on many Etruscan sites and can provide valuable data for our understanding of the Etruscan wool economy. The high percentage of sheep in comparison to other domesticates may be indicative of the site's specialization in wool production. The "age at slaughter" pattern or "harvest profile" of an assemblage is indicative of whether animals were kept for primary products such as meat, bone, and leather, or for their secondary products such as milk and wool. Predominance in the flock of adult animals, in particular castrated males, is generally considered to

---

[8] Andersson Strand and Nosch (2015); for an application of the method in Etruscan contexts, see Meyers (2013), Cutler et al. (2020).

Figure 10.4 Experimental archaeology: (a) skilled weaver Elena Ciccarelli spinning wool using a replica Etruscan spindle (Image: M. Gleba, reproduced with permission of E. Ciccarelli); (b) experimental weaving of a diamond twill with integral tablet-woven borders at the Experimental Laboratory of the University of Padua (Image: M.Gleba).

provide evidence of wool production. Change in animal size may indicate improvement (De Grossi Mazzorin and Minniti, 2018) or translocation of the domesticate species from one region to another (Gaastra, 2014). More recently, isotopic analyses of sheep bones have been used to investigate animal diet, seasonality, husbandry, and mobility, in particular short- and long-distance transhumance (Trentacoste et al., 2020).

Iconography

The large corpus of textile representations on Etruscan reliefs, paintings, statuary, and other artistic media has been used in studies of ancient dress for a long time since direct evidence of archaeological textiles is either too fragmentary to allow a meaningful reconstruction of garments or absent altogether. For example, Etruscan iconography helps us understand what a particular type of linen armor used by the Etruscans, a *linothorax*, looked like in the absence of direct evidence (Gleba, 2012). In other cases, archaeological finds corroborate the use of specific garments we observe in iconography, as in the case of semi-circular mantles, the early *tebennae*, found at Verucchio (Stauffer, 2012). Identifying clothing items, their combination into dress, and possible fashion influences has been a long-standing approach in iconographic studies of dress, and Etruscan iconography is no exception (Bonfante, 2003). Recently, a method has been developed for a more quantitative evaluation of textiles depicted in iconography, one that involves careful observation of textile layers and their number, length of garments on different figures, and consistency of specific elements like borders (Harris, 2022); ImageJ software is used to calculate the relative areas of different textiles (Gleba et al., forthcoming). These observations can be used to investigate the relationship between textiles and people of different gender, age, and class who wear them and textile consumption across space and time, leading to wider conclusions about textile economy and the social meaning of dress and its standardization. Other recent innovative approaches include using iconography of dancers' garments to interpret Etruscan performative dress, dance movements, and, through them, Etruscan music.[9]

Etruscan Textiles: State of the Art

The application of the methods and approaches reviewed above in recent years has generated data that allow us to have a broad yet sufficiently detailed view of the types of textiles Etruscans produced and consumed, how and with what materials these textiles were made, and how they compare to the fabrics produced by other civilizations of Central and Mediterranean Europe. We can also draw broader conclusions about Etruscan textile economy.

Etruscan Textile Culture

Structural and characterization analyses of hundreds of textile fragments provided for the first time a much more detailed picture of Etruscan textile culture. Tabbies or plain-weave textiles are generally common and constitute almost half of the textiles analyzed.

Where identified, they are mostly made in plant fiber, likely flax. The earliest linen textiles are warp-dominant tabbies, which have more warp than weft threads per unit of length (the thread counts range between 20 and 55 threads/cm in warp and 10–25 threads/cm in weft), are made of plant fiber and are woven with plied yarn that has been spliced rather than draft-spun (Figure 10.5a). Among the best examples of this type are fragments from the Tomba del Guerriero, in Tarquinia (Stauffer, 2013), and a fragment recently excavated in the Tomba dello Scarabeo Dorato, at Poggio Mengarelli, Vulci (Carosi and Regoli, 2021). Many of these

---

[9] Gouy (2023); Mauro Patricelli, a composer and ethnomusicologist, used Tarquinian banquet scenes of dancing and historical sources on the ancient Italian dance of *saltarello* for his documentary opera "Bella Ballerina": see https://www.youtube.com/watch?v=e9wulJr4alA

spliced textiles appear to have been used for wrapping of cremated remains as they are often found inside the ossuaries. From the sixth century BCE onward, there is a clear switch from splicing to draft spinning linen yarn (Figure 10.5b) (Gleba and Harris, 2019). Such textiles continued to be used as shrouds or as wrapping material for ossuaries or burial gifts (Gleba, 2014), but they were also used for inner garments, as in the case of the Orientalizing Tomb XIII at Veio Poggioverde (De Cristofaro and Piergrossi, 2017).

Another type of textiles are weft-faced tabbies, which have at least twice as many weft as warp threads per unit of length, and these are usually so tightly packed that the warp becomes invisible (Figure 10.5c). Where fiber identification was possible, all these textiles were determined to be made of wool. Another common characteristic of this group of textiles is that while the warp threads are hard z-twisted, the weft yarn has barely any twist. The thread counts range from 3 to 10 threads/cm in warp and 30 to 80 threads/cm in weft. The contexts and quality of these textiles suggest that they were likely used for garments. In the first half of the first millennium BCE, weft-faced tabbies appear only in unusual or exceptionally rich Etruscan burials. The earliest examples, dating to the early ninth century BCE, have been found at Sasso di Furbara and are likely imports (Gleba et al., 2020). Another find, also a likely import, comes from a sixth-century BCE burial at Grotte di Castro (Gleba and Laurito, 2015). Outside

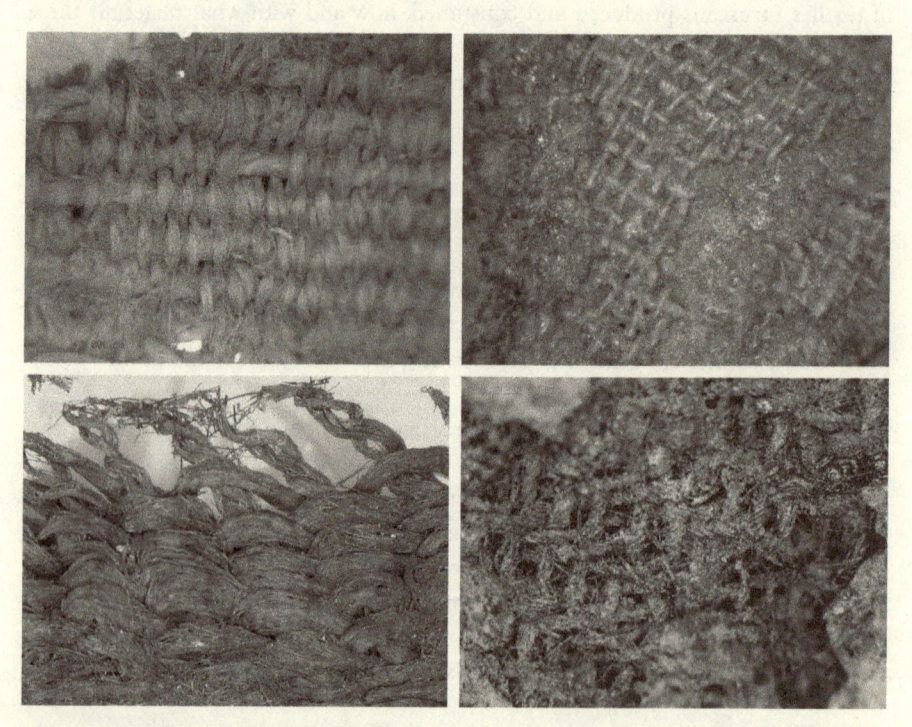

Figure 10.5 Different textile weave in Italy: (a) linen warp-dominant tabby in spliced yarn, Tarquinia, 8th century BCE; (b) linen balanced tabby in draft-spun yarn, Vulci, 6th century BCE; (c) wool weft-faced tabby, Sasso di Furbara, 9th cemtury BCE; (d) wool twill, Vulci, 7th c. BCE (Images: M. Gleba).

Etruria, weft-faced tabbies have been found in the Abruzzo region, an area that was culturally associated with the Adriatic basin during the Iron Age, and in the Greek settlements and coeval indigenous sites of south Italy. They are also typical in the eastern Mediterranean, including Greece and the Near East (Gleba, 2017a).

More than 40 percent of Etruscan textiles, however, fall into a different category: these are textiles woven in 2/2 twill weave (Figure 10.5d). All of the examples where raw material has been identified are made of wool. These twills are usually woven in z-twisted threads, but more than half are spin- or shadow-patterned (i.e., made using alternating groups of threads twisted in opposing directions in both warp and weft, which would have created a subtle striped or checked pattern when viewed with raking light). This can be seen particularly well in the garments of Verucchio (Stauffer, 2012). The thread counts range from 5 to 40 threads/cm, with the majority falling between 15 and 30 threads/cm. These twill textiles often have tablet-woven borders, also made of wool, where identified. Many of such tablet-woven borders are technically complex, extremely labor-intensive, and time-consuming (Ræder Knudsen, 2012). The twill textiles with tablet-woven borders were likely outer garments, such as the tunics and mantles recovered in the tombs of Verucchio (Stauffer, 2012).

While we cannot reconstruct the color of the mineralized textiles, dye analysis of some of the organically preserved finds indicates the use of sophisticated dyeing methods and a variety of plant- and animal-derived dyes by the Etruscans. The dye sources identified to date include woad (*Isatis tinctoria*) for blue, wild madder (*Rubia peregrina* or related species) for red, and unidentified yellow-producing plant species, as well as shellfish for purple (Gleba et al., 2017a; 2017b; Stauffer, 2012; Vanden Berghe and Gleba, forthcoming). The earliest dyed textiles in Italy come from Sasso di Furbara near Cerveteri and date to the early ninth century BCE (Gleba et al., 2020). These have patterns created in twill and tablet weaving using thread dyed with woad, madder, or a combination of two, while one of the presumably imported weft-faced tabbies has tested positive for traces of shellfish purple. One of the fabrics from Tomba dell'Aryballos sospeso at Tarquinia, dated to the late seventh–early sixth century BCE, had one of the systems dyed with shellfish purple, while another was originally dyed blue with woad (Gleba et al., 2017b). Shellfish purple was also identified in a textile from the second-century BCE burial at Strozzacapponi (Corciano/Perugia) (Gleba et al., 2017a). In the fine twills woven in white and red checks from the late Villanovan female Tomb LXXII of the Cava della Pozzolana necropolis at Cerveteri and Tomb 72 at Poggio Mengarelli Vulci (Figure 10.1b), the red threads were dyed with wild madder.

In addition, some Etruscan twills appear to have been decorated with various beads, buttons, and appliques in precious materials such as bronze, gold, amber, glass, and faïence, found in hundreds and even thousands in certain burials.[10] Small bronze domed buttons are particularly common over a very wide geographical area and occasionally preserve the remains of the spliced linen threads that were used to attach them to the fabric (Stauffer, 2013).

---

[10] E.g., at Verucchio; see von Eles (2007, 72).

Similar twills with color and weave patterns, decorated with tablet-woven borders and appliques are known in the Hallstatt cultural region (Germany, Austria, Slovenia, Croatia), but they stand in stark contrast to weft-faced tabbies in Greece and the Near East (Gleba, 2017a). Unlike twill, weft-faced tabby allows the creation of figural decoration. Indeed, iconography corroborates these differences, with geometric patterns prevalent in Etruscan textile representations and complex figural decorations observed on Greek and Near Eastern depictions of textiles. The different weaves—twills with tablet-woven borders in Etruria and weft-faced tabbies in Greece and the Near East—allowed for a different aesthetic expression of identity in dress in these geographical regions. This may explain the interest of Etruscans in new fashions, which arrived during the Orientalizing period and spread during the sixth century BCE. The colorful decorative border with lotus-palmette motif on the hem of the female Polledrara statue now in the British Museum may be an example of such new fashion (Verri et al., 2014).

When Greek settlements start appearing along the littoral of Southern Italy from the seventh century BCE onward, we see weft-faced tabbies appearing in several of the indigenous sites that had close connections with these colonies. In certain situations, contact with the weft-faced–tabby-based Greek textile culture gave way to the creation of new expressions, such as a weft-faced tabby cloth with a tablet-woven border at the indigenous south Italian site of Ripacandida—a hybrid of the Italian and Greek traditions and a result of the creation of a new transcultural identity (Gleba et al., 2018). Over time, however, the weft-faced tabby appears to have displaced twill as the dominant textile weave in Italy and in Etruria, with most of the fabrics dated to the Hellenistic period being of this new type (e.g., Gleba et al., 2017a), which became dominant during Roman times.

Etruscan Textile Production

While textile and iconographic evidence pertains primarily to the upper social classes, textile manufacture was practiced at all levels of society in Etruria and was arguably one of the most labor-intensive of all occupations. Etruscan textiles were produced using primarily locally available raw materials, which were transformed through multiple stages of the textile *chaîne opératoire*. The principal fibers used in Etruria were flax and sheep wool. Both materials required significant investment of time and resources and were clearly important elements of Etruscan agropastoral economy. While we have little archaeobotanical data on flax cultivation in Etruria to date, analyses of zooarchaeological remains indicate a relatively intensive sheep husbandry at many Etruscan settlement sites, with a prevalence of adult animals indicative of wool production.[11] A recent isotopic study of sheep bones from Poggio

---

[11] The most updated overview can be found in Trentacoste (2020).

Civitate di Murlo and Orvieto has furthermore demonstrated the complexity and diversity of husbandry regimes at these sites (Trentacoste et al., 2020).

The raw fibers had to undergo different processing to be usable. Selection and combing of wool before spinning is indicated by the microscopic observation of fibers with opposing scale patterns and the absence of thick or extremely thin fibers in many textiles. The processing of plant fibers undergoes a significant transformation in Etruria and broader across the Mediterranean region around 600 BCE. As noted above, the textile data show that until that point threads were produced by splicing, a technology in which strips of fibers are joined individually, often after having been stripped from the plant stalk directly and without or with only minimal retting (Gleba and Harris, 2019). In later linen textiles, the threads are made by draft spinning, whereby flax fibers that underwent retting, bracking, scutching, and heckling to separate, clean, and align them, are drawn out from a mass of fibers usually arranged on a distaff and twisted continuously using a rotating drop spindle. The draft spinning technology, used for millennia to spin wool fibers, appears have been transferred to flax around the middle of the first millennium BCE, at the time of significant growth in Etruscan long-distance trade, when the large numbers of sail-driven ships demanded the intensification of linen production (Gleba and Harris, 2019).

While we have no evidence regarding the tools used for splicing, spinning can be archaeologically traced using ceramic spindle whorls and distaffs in various materials (Gleba, 2008, 100–122). Functional analysis of spindle whorls found on Etruscan sites indicates that some sites, for example Poggio Civitate, specialized in the production of fine yarn, while others produced a broader range (Cutler et al., 2020). Depictions of spinners, found on objects such as the bronze *tintinnabulum* from Bologna, indicate that the type of spindle utilized in Etruria had the whorl attached to its lower end, in the low-whorl position.[12]

Weaving was accomplished on a vertical warp-weighted loom, which can be archaeologically traced through ceramic loom weights (Gleba, 2008, 122–138). Their functional analysis for some Etruscan sites, shows that they were particularly suitable for producing twills, but the range of textile qualities could vary more or less at different sites (Cutler et al., 2020). Ceramic spools, metal clasps, and bone spacers appear to document tablet weaving (Gleba, 2008). More than 800 spools excavated at Poggio Civitate di Murlo suggest that the site may have specialized in tablet weaving (Cutler et al., 2020).

The absolute prevalence of textile tools in both female burials and iconography indicate that textile production was by and large a female occupation. It is thus hardly surprising that tool evidence indicates that textiles were primarily produced at household level in Etruria, with only limited evidence for workshop production organization and that only from the Archaic period onward (Gleba, 2008).

---

[12] Cupitò and Vidale (2020), with preceding bibliography.

Etruscan Textile Consumption

Textiles were used for a wide variety of purposes in Etruria: clothing, furnishings, wrapping, sails, tents, linen armor, and many other utilitarian purposes. Only the first of these is archaeologically attested to any appreciable degree. We have seen that Etruscans used fine linen and wool textiles for their garments, often decorated using patterns, colors, and applied elements. Textiles were clearly among the most important and valuable prestige goods, and the emerging Etruscan elites used them to flaunt their high status, enabled through their likely control of not only local production but also long-distance connections allowing their acquisition from far-away sources (Harris, 2017). The importance of textiles is evident in the increasing detail with which they are depicted in Etruscan iconography from the Archaic period onward. The sheer volume and exuberance of cloth depicted in, for example, tomb paintings of Tarquinia trumps most other materials. As we have seen above, archaeological textiles provide a fairly good picture of what these luxury textiles were like. Yet we know next nothing about the sails, which were clearly produced and used on a vast scale if judging by the iconography of ships and the distribution of Etruscan exports all across the Mediterranean and Europe. This gap in our knowledge similarly applies to furnishings, tents, sacks, linen books, and other utilitarian textiles.

We also know little about the textiles consumed by the non-elite, although one example shows that the access to what we assume to be valuable textiles varied across time and space. Thus, shellfish or true purple, regarded as one of the most precious and prized dyes of antiquity, was identified in three textiles found in a quarry workers' cemetery at Strozzacapponi in Corciano/Perugia, dated second–first century BCE (Harris, 2017). The finest shellfish purple–dyed cloth was found in a humble coarse-ware ossuary. This suggests that Etruscan quarry workers had access to or could afford to use shellfish purple in their garments.

Conclusion

Textiles had great cultural and social importance and should be factored into any balanced assessment of the past. Over the past decade, textile studies have developed into an important new field of archaeological research in Italy. The accumulation of data and the constant development of analytical techniques are permitting a more synthetic approach to the history of textiles, demonstrating how much we can learn about the culture, society, technology, and economy of the past through textiles. Structural and raw material analyses permit us to define and trace past textile cultures chronologically and geographically, and this has important implications for reconstructing the various identities of people. Such analyses also highlight technological choices and innovations that had profound consequences for the ancient economies. Characterization and provenance studies of textiles are fundamental for our understanding of textile trade and exchange. Investigations of textile implements provide insights into the organization and scale of textile production. Paleoenvironmental data provide us information about textile resources and their exploitation. Last but not least, iconography illustrates the diverse uses of textiles even when textiles themselves no longer survive and, most importantly, shows us textile producers and consumers.

Etruscan textile studies have made a major qualitative and quantitative leap in the past decade thanks to the application of a variety of scientific methods. The field is nonetheless only at the beginning of its development. More analyses are needed to increase the statistical robustness of the data. Systematic census of specific sites for textiles preserved on metal objects may produce enough information to look at intra-site variation in the type and/or quality of textiles. Correlation of textiles with adornments is another underresearched area, one that may shed light on the complex expressions of identities through dress in Etruscan society (e.g., in specific cities, between different cities, in urban and rural contexts, etc.). Many of the methods described here may also be useful to investigate the range of sensory modality of Etruscan textiles (Harris, 2019). More and systematic archaeobotanical data are needed to understand flax cultivation, which must have occupied large expanses of land, if we think of sails production alone. Larger and systematic isotopic studies of sheep at both intra- and inter-site levels would allow the creation of much more sophisticated models of Etruscan sheep husbandry and mobility. Ancient DNA analysis has the potential to trace the development of various sheep breeds, particularly if combined with wool fiber quality analysis. There is still much to be discovered about the Etruscans and their textiles, and a plethora of methods at our disposition will allow us to do just that.

Bibliography

Andersson, E. B., K. M. Frei, M. Gleba, U. Mannering, M.-L. Nosch, and I. Skals. "Old textiles – new possibilities." *European Journal of Archaeology* 13(2), 149–73.

Andersson Strand, E., and M.-L. Nosch, eds. *Tools, Textiles and Contexts: Investigating Textile Production in the Aegean and Eastern Mediterranean Bronze Age*. Ancient Textiles Series 21. Oxford: Oxbow Books, 2015.

Barber, E. J. W. *Prehistoric Textiles: The Development of Cloth in the Neolithic and Bronze Ages*. Princeton, NJ: Princeton University Press, 1991.

Bender Jørgensen, L. *Forhistoriske textiler i Skandinavien. Prehistoric Scandinavian Textiles*. Nordiske Fortidsminder, ser. B, 9. Copenhagen, 1986.

Bender Jørgensen, L. *North European Textiles until AD 1000*. Aarhus: Aarhus University Press, 1992.

Bonfante, L. *Etruscan Dress*. 2nd ed. Baltimore: Johns Hopkins University Press, 2003.

Cardon, D. *Natural Dyes: Sources, Tradition, Technology and Science*. London: Archetype Publications, 2007.

Carosi, S., and C. Regoli. "Prolegomena to the material culture of Vulci during the Orientalizing period in the light of new discoveries." In *Making Cities: Economies of Production and Urbanisation in Mediterranean Europe 1000–500 BC*, edited by M. Gleba, B. Marín-Aguilera, and B. Dimova, 195–218. Cambridge: McDonald Institute Conversations Series, 2021. doi.org/10.17863/CAM.76133

Chen, H. L., K. A. Jakes, and D. W. Foreman. "Preservation of archaeological textiles through fibre mineralization." *Journal of Archaeological Science* 25 (1998), 1015–1021.

Ciccarelli, E., and A. Perilli. "Tracing the thread: Spinning experiments with Etruscan spindle whorl replicas." *Origini* 40.1 (2017), 155–164.

Cupitò, M., and M. Vidale. "Deep into the warp: Again on the tintinnabulum of Bologna: From technology, to society and ideology." *Eidola* 17 (2020), 39–64. doi:10.19272/2020 01101002.

Cutler J., B. Dimova, and M. Gleba. "Tools for textiles: Textile production at the Etruscan settlement of Poggio Civitate, Murlo, in the seventh and sixth centuries BC." *Papers of the British School at Rome* 2020, 1–30. doi:10.1017/S006824622000001X

De Cristofaro, A., and A. Piergrossi. "The clothes make the (wo)man: Historical and anthropological considerations on Etruscan female costumes between the 8th and 7th century BC." *Origini* 40 (2017), 65–82.

De Grossi Mazzorin, J., and C. Minniti. "Caprine varieties in Italy in the Iron Age: The evidence from archeozoological data." In *Purpureae Vestes VI: Textiles and Dyes in the Mediterranean Economy and Society. Proceedings of the International Symposium*, edited by M. S. Busana, M. Gleba, F. Meo, and A. R. Tricomi, 107–116. Padova-Este-Altino, 17–20 October 2016. Zaragoza: Libros Pòrtico, 2018.

Emery, I. *The Primary Structures of Fabrics: An Illustrated Classification*. Washington, DC: Textile Museum, 1966.

Esposito, A. M. *I principi guerrieri: La necropolis etrusca di Casale Marittimo*. Milan: Electa, 1999.

Forte, V., and C. Lemorini. "Traceological analyses applied to textile implements: An assessment of the method through the case study of the 1st millennium BCE ceramic tools in central Italy." *Origini* 40(2017), 165–182.

Frei, K. M., R. Frei, U. Mannering, M. Gleba, M.-L. Nosch, and H. Lyngstrøm. "Provenance of ancient textiles: A pilot study evaluating the sr isotope system in wool." *Archaeometry* 51.2 (2009), 252–276.

Gaastra, J. S. "Shipping sheep or creating cattle: Domesticate size changes with Greek colonisation in Magna Graecia." *Journal of Archaeological Science* 52 (2014), 483–496.

Gleba, M. *Textile Production in Pre-Roman Italy*. Ancient Textile Series 4. Oxford: Oxbow Books, 2008.

Gleba, M. "Textile tools in ancient Italian votive contexts: Evidence of dedication or production?" In *Votives, Places and Rituals in Etruscan Religion: Studies in Honour of Jean MacIntosh Turfa*, edited by M. Gleba and H. W. Becker, 69–84. Leiden: Brill, 2009.

Gleba, M. "Linen-clad Etruscan warriors." In *Wearing the Cloak: Dressing the Soldier in Roman Times*, Ancient Textiles Series 10, edited by M.-L. Nosch, 45–55. Oxford: Oxbow Books, 2012.

Gleba, M. "The World of Etruscan Textiles." In *The Etruscan World*, edited by J. Turfa, 798–811. London/New York: Routledge, 2013.

Gleba, M. "Wrapped up for safe keeping: 'Wrapping' customs in Early Iron Age Europe." In *Wrapping and Unwrapping Material Culture: Archaeological and Anthropological Perspectives*, edited by S. Harris and L. Douny, 135–146. Walnut Creek, CA: Left Coast Press, 2014.

Gleba, M. "Tracing textile cultures of Italy and Greece in the early first millennium BC." *Antiquity* 144 (2017a), 1205–22. doi:10.15184/aqy.2017.144

Gleba, M. "Textiles in pre-Roman Italy: From qualitative to quantitative approach." *Origini* 40 (2017b), 9–28.

Gleba M., and S. Harris. "The first plant fibre technology: Identifying splicing in archaeological textiles." *Archaeological and Anthropological Sciences* 11.5 (2019), 2326–2346. doi:10.1007/s12520-018-0677-8

Gleba M., S. Harris, J. Cutler, B. Marín-Aguilera, and B. Dimova. *Dressing Cities: Textile Economies in Mediterranean Europe 1000–500 BCE*. Cambridge: McDonald Institute Monographs, forthcoming.

Gleba, M., C. Heitz, H. Landenius Enegren, and F. Meo. "At the crossroads of textile cultures: Textile production and use at the south Italian archaic site of Ripacandida." *Journal of Mediterranean Archaeology* 31.1 (2018), 27–52. doi:10.1558/jma.36808

Gleba, M., and R. Laurito. "Appendice 1. Analisi delle tracce di tessuti rinvenuti a grotte di castro in località vigna la piazza." In E. Pellegrini, "Un aspetto delle necropoli etrusche di Grotte di Castro: Le tombe a fossa con circolo di Vigna La Piazza," 265–67. *Annali Faina* 20 (2015), 337–339, 346, figs. 1–4.

Gleba, M., A. Mandolesi, and M. R. Lucidi. "New textile finds from *Tomba Dell'aryballos Sospeso*, Tarquinia: Context, analysis and preliminary interpretation." *Origini* 40 (2017b), 29–44.

Gleba, M., E. Pizzuti, Vanden Berghe I., M. Boudin, A. Mostedoro, and A. Serges. "Iron Age textiles from Sasso di Furbara, Italy: Preliminary results of new scientific investigation." In *Purpureae Vestes VII: Redefining Textile Handcraft, Structures, Tools and Production Processes. Proceedings of the International Symposium*, edited by M. Bustamante Álvarez, E. H. Sánchez López and J. Jiménez Ávila, 201–210. Granada, October 2–4, 2019. Granada: University of Granada Press, 2020.

Gleba, M., Vanden Berghe I., and L. Cenciaioli. "Purple for the masses? Shellfish purple-dyed textiles from the quarry workers: Cemetery at Strozzacapponi (Perugia/Corciano), Italy." In *Treasures from the Sea: Sea Silk and Shellfish Purple Dye in Antiquity*, Ancient Textiles Series 30, edited by H. Landenius Enegren and F. Meo, 131–37. Oxford: Oxbow Books, 2017a.

Good, I. "Archaeological textiles: A review of current research." *Annual Review of Anthropology* 30 (2001), 209–226.

Gouy, A. "The performative clothing in pre-Roman Italy: Ritual function of Etruscan dress among Mediterranean interactions and cultural identity (6th–5th cent. BC)." In *Archaeology and Economy in the Ancient World. Proceedings of the 19. International Congress of Classical Archaeology*, edited by M. Bentz and M. Heinzelmann, 49–50. Cologne/Bonn, May 22–26, 2018. Heidelberg Heidelberg University Press, 2023.

Grömer, K. *The Art of Prehistoric Textile Making: The Development of Craft Traditions and Clothing in Central Europe*. Veröffentlichungen der Prähistorischen Abteilung 5. Vienna: Verlag des Naturhistorischen Museums Wien, 2016.

Harris, S. "From value to desirability: The allure of worldly things. *World Archaeology* 49.5 (2017), 681–699. doi:10.1080/00438243.2017.1413416

Harris, S. "The sensory archaeology of textiles." In *The Routledge Handbook of Sensory Archaeology*, edited by R. Skeates and J. Day, 210–232. Abingdon: Routledge, 2019.

Harris, S. "Abundance and splendour: Textiles of Archaic Greek statues of young women." In *Textiles in Ancient Mediterranean Iconography*, Ancient Textiles Series 38, edited by S. Harris, C. Brøns, and M. Żuchowska, 59–78. Oxford: Oxbow Books, 2022.

Laurito, R. "Testing ancient textile tools in southern Etruria (central Italy), experimental archaeology *versus* experiential archaeology." *Origini* 40 (2017), 141–154.

Lipkin, S. *Textile-Making in Central Tyrrhenian Italy from the Final Bronze Age to the Republican Period*. Oxford: BAR S2369, 2012.

Mannering, U., M. Gleba, I. Heinemeier, and G. Possnert. "Dating textiles and skins from bog finds by 14C-ams." *Journal of Archaeological Science* 37.2 (2010), 261–268.

Meyers, G. "Reconstructing ritual: The functional parameters of loom weights and spindle whorls as evidence for cult practice in ancient Etruria." In *NESAT XI: Proceedings of the Northern European Symposium on Archaeological Textiles*, edited by J. Banck-Burgess and C. Nübold, 251–256. Rahden/Westf.: Leidorf, 2013.

Ørsted Brandt, L., and M. Allentoft. "Archaeological wool textiles: A window into ancient sheep genetics?" In *The Textile Revolution in Bronze Age Europe*, edited by S. Sabatini and S. Bergerbrant, 274–303. Cambridge: Cambridge University Press, 2020.

Raeder Knudsen, L. "The tablet-woven borders of Verucchio." In *Textiles and Textile Production in Europe from Prehistory to AD 400*, Ancient Textiles Series 12, edited by M. Gleba and U. Mannering, 254–263. Oxford/Oakville: Oxbow Books, 2012.

Rast-Eicher, A. *Fibres: Microscopy of Archaeological Textiles and Furs*. Budapest: Archaeolingua, 2016.

Ryder, M. L. *Sheep and Man*. London: Duckworth, 1983.

Seiler-Baldinger, A. *Textiles: A Classification of Techniques*. Washington, DC: Smithsonian Institution Press, 1994.

Serges, A., E. Pizzuti, and M. Gleba. "Analisi preliminari e ipotesi ricostruttiva del bordo a tavolette rinvenuto al Sasso di Furbara: Nuove prospettive di studio." In *Trame di storia: Metodi e strumenti dell'archeologia sperimentale. Archeofest 2017*, edited by M. Massussi, S. Tucci and R. Laurito, 157–172. Roma: Siaed SpA, 2018.

Skals, I., M. Gleba, M. Taube, and U. Mannering. "Wool textiles and archaeometry: Testing reliability of archaeological wool fibre diameter measurements." *Danish Journal of Archaeology* 7.2 (2018), 161–179. doi:10.1080/21662282.1495917

Stauffer, A. "Case study: The textiles from Verucchio, Italy." In *Textiles and Textile Production in Europe from Prehistory to AD 400*, Ancient Textiles Series 12, edited by M. Gleba and U. Mannering, 242–253. Oxford/Oakville: Oxbow Books, 2012.

Stauffer, A. "Textil." In *La Tomba del Guerriero di Tarquinia: Identità elitaria, concentrazione del potere e networks dinamici nell'avanzato VIII sec. a. C.*, edited by A. Babbi and U. Peltz, 157–164. Mainz: Verlag des Römisch-Germanischen Zentralmuseums, 2013.

Solazzo, C., P. Walton-Rogers, L. Weber, H. F. Beaubien, J. Wilson, and M. J. Collins. "Species identification by peptide mass fingerprinting (PMF) in fibre products preserved by association with copper-alloy artefacts." *Journal of Archaeological Science* 49 (2014), 524–535.

Thomsen, E., and R. Andreasen. "Agricultural lime disturbs natural strontium isotope variations: Implications for provenance and migration studies." *Science Advances* 5.3 (2019). doi:10.1126/sciadv.aav8083

Trentacoste, A. "Fodder for change: Animals, urbanisation, and socio-economic transformation in protohistoric Italy." *Theoretical Roman Archaeology Journal* 3.1 (2020), 1. doi:10.16995/traj.414

Trentacoste, A., E. Lightfoot, P. Le Roux, M. Buckley, C. Esposito, and M. Gleba. "Heading for the hills? A multi-isotope study of sheep management in first millennium BC Italy. *Journal of Archaeological Science Reports* 29 (2020). doi:10.1016/j.jasrep.2019.102036

Vanden Berge I., and M. Gleba. Forthcoming. "Dyes of prehistoric Italy." *Journal of Archaeological Science Reports*, forthcoming.

Vanden Berghe, I., M. Gleba, and U. Mannering. "Towards the identification of dyestuffs in early Iron Age Scandinavian peat bog textiles." *Journal of Archaeological Science* 36.9 (2009), 1910–1921.

van der Meer, B. *The Liber linteus zagrabiensis [The Linen Book of Zagreb: A Comment on the Longest Etruscan Text]*. Monographs on Antiquity 4. Leuven: Peeters, 2007.

van Geel, B., O. M. Raspopov, J. van der Plicht, and H. Renssen. "Solar forcing of abrupt climate change around 850 calendar years BC." In *Natural Catastrophes during Bronze Age Civilisations*, edited by B. J. Peiser, T. Palmer, and M. E. Bailey, 162–168. Oxford: BAR International Series 728, 1998.

Verri G., M. Gleba, J. Swaddling, T. Long, J. Ambers, and T. Munden. "Etruscan women's clothing and its decoration: The polychrome gypsum statue from the 'Isis Tomb' at Vulci." *British Museum Technical Bulletin* 8 (2014), 59–71.

von Eles, P. "Famiglie gentilizie e donne a Verucchio: Linguaggi nascosti, rappresentazioni di ruoli e di rango." In *Le ore e i giorni delle donne: Dalla quotidianità alla sacralità tra VIII e VII secolo a. C.*, edited by P. von Eles, 71–85. Verucchio: Pazzini, 2007.

von Holstein, I. C. C., L. Font, E. E. Peacock, M. J. Collins, and G. R. Davies. "An assessment of procedures to remove exogenous Sr before 87Sr/86Sr analysis of wet archaeological wool textiles." *Journal of Archaeological Science*, 53 (2015), 84–93. https://doi.org/10.1016/j.jas.2014.10.006

von Holstein, I. C. C., P. Walton Rogers, O. E. Craig, K. E. H. Penkman, J. Newton, and M. J. Collins. "Provenancing archaeological wool textiles from medieval northern Europe by light stable isotope analysis (δ^{13}c, δ^{15}n, δ^{2}h)." *PLoS ONE* 11.10 (2016), e0162330. doi:10.1371/journal.pone.0162330

Margarita Gleba, *Etruscan Textiles: Methods, Approaches, Results, and Future Perspectives* In: *A New Etruscan Archaeology: Twenty-First Century Techniques and Methods*. Edited by: Maurizio Forte, Oxford University Press.
© Oxford University Press 2025. DOI: 10.1093/9780197582053.003.0011

11

Artificial Intelligence and Etruscan Archaeology

Maurizio Forte and Felipe Infante de Castro

Introduction

We are living through one of the most exciting and possibly even dangerous epochs of this evolving story: the emergence of artificial intelligence (AI) as an area of commercial development in the high-tech industry. Built on decades of academic research, AI as a field of investigation arguably started in 1943, when McCullogh and Pitts created the perceptron—the first model of an artificial neuron. Originally created for better understanding biological models, it was soon understood as a potentially useful model for electronic logical systems; however, its use was constrained by the technical difficulties of that era's rudimentary computing paradigms (Krizhevsky et al., 2017; Ramesh et al., 2021).

Starting in the 1980s, a renewed interest in AI brought about the introduction of fresh ideas and algorithms to the field, such as backpropagation (Rumelhart et al., 1986), convolutional neural networks (Le Cun, 1989), and long short-term memory (Hochreiter and Schmidhuber, 1997). These new techniques provided a glimpse of the capabilities that AI systems could achieve in handling complex tasks, but the world was still constrained by the lack of processing technology to scale the systems to a reliable and useful state.

The developments in the past few years in parallel processing technology—led by the makers of graphics processing unit (GPU) chips such as NVIDIA and AMD, and in AI algorithms, such as the advent of generative adversarial networks (Goodfellow et al., 2014) and especially the Transformers architecture (Vaswani et al., 2017)—changed this situation. For the first time, it was possible to adequate processing power to run and test the AI algorithms once theorized to work well and, perhaps more importantly, to rapidly iterate over them to test new paradigms and innovate on top of them.

Generative AI is the subset of those innovations that deal with AIs that are capable of creating original content. A realm of science fiction just a few years ago, generative AI has already become a reality in the day-to-day lives of millions of people, from students using it to write essays for school, to software developers applying it to create software using natural language as opposed to coding, to designers and artists leveraging it to create original drawings, images, and videos.

Definitions and Background

"Artificial intelligence" has historically been a loosely defined term, having been applied to systems as simple as formulaic responses to a hardcoded setup (as in a computer playing tic-tac-toe) and as complex as conversational chatbots such as Google Bard, ChatGPT, or Bing Chat, which passed the Turing test, as reported by several media. We subscribe to the definition that an AI is any artificial agent that receives percepts from the environment, maps percept sequences to actions, and performs them accordingly (Russel and Norvig, 2021). A subset of AI systems that gained prominence in the past few years are those that rely on machine learning (ML), defined as AI systems that exhibit the capacity to improve performance based on training and experience; the most well-known of those systems are *artificial neural networks*, algorithms that mimic the workings of biological neural networks by simulating each individual neuron and its interconnections with each other. Of special note are those AIs that are designed using multilayer neural networks, an approach called "deep learning" (Russel and Norvig, 2021).

The advent of deep learning AIs, coupled with the steady advance in graphics computing power and computer vision, have revolutionized the role that AI can play in art. The first AI capable of better-than-human performance in image categorization (identification of specific concepts within photos and images) was AlexNet, a deep learning AI that won the 2012 ImageNet Large Scale Image Recognition Challenge. AlexNet was a multilayer artificial neural network composed of 650,000 neurons and totaling 60 million parameters (Krizhevsky et al., 2017). Since then, there has been increasing interest in the use of deep learning AIs in the fields of image processing and handling, culminating in the advent of DALL-E in 2021 (Figure 11.1).

The Birth of Generative AI Art

In the context of art, OpenAI's DALL-E was the first public release of a *generative AI*—that is, an AI that can create original content, as opposed to just processing existing images. Launched in January 2021, DALL-E was a pioneering development over OpenAI's research on large language models (LLMs), which are AIs capable of reading texts and predicting future words in a sentence based on their relative frequency within a very large dataset of texts (and whose most well-known example currently is ChatGPT).

OpenAI's plan was to correlate a textual description with an image and then apply the probabilistic method used to forecast a word in a phrase to the problem of creating a new image. Instead of predicting a word in a text, however, DALL-E would start with a random noise image, and, through a number of iterations, slowly change the original image to create one that matched a textual prompt given by the user. To

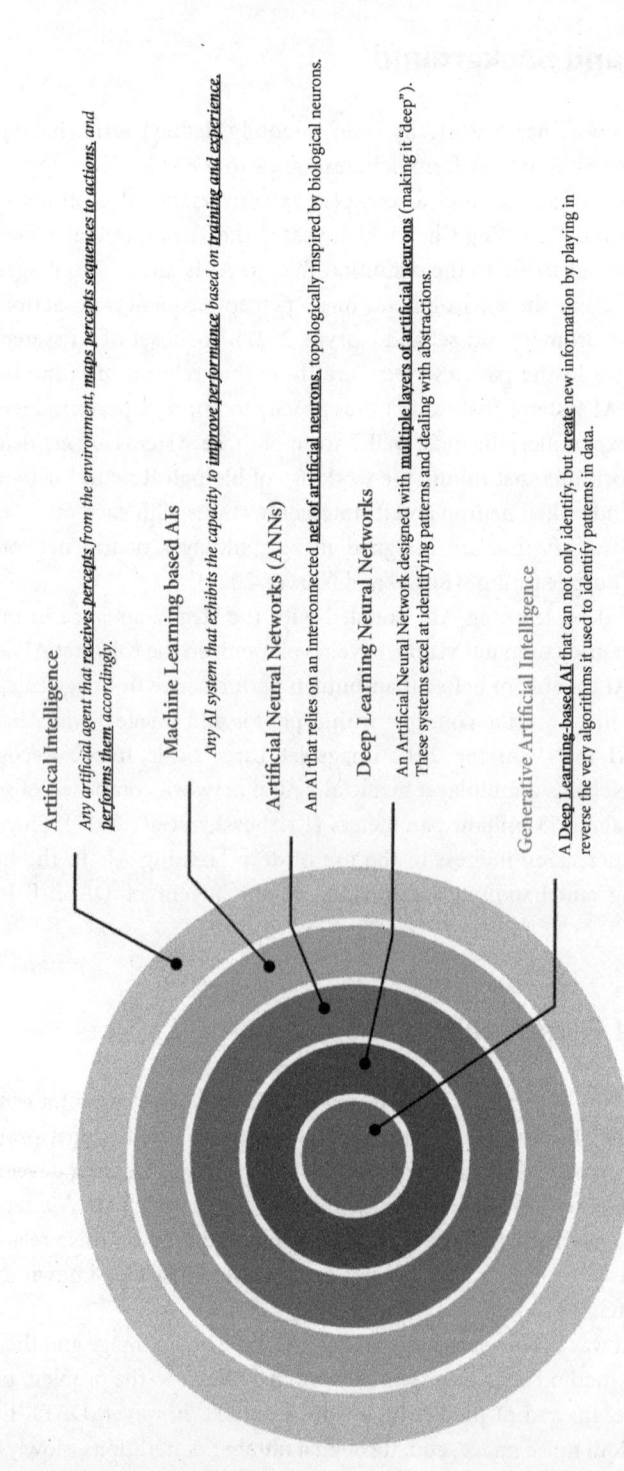

Artifical Intelligence
Any artificial agent that receives percepts from the environment, maps percepts sequences to actions, and performs them accordingly.

Machine Learning based AIs
Any AI system that exhibits the capacity to improve performance based on training and experience.

Artificial Neural Networks (ANNs)
An AI that relies on an interconnected net of artificial neurons, topologically inspired by biological neurons.

Deep Learning Neural Networks
An Artificial Neural Network designed with multiple layers of artificial neurons (making it "deep").
These systems excel at identifying patterns and dealing with abstractions.

Generative Artificial Intelligence
A Deep Learning-based AI that can not only identify, but create new information by playing in reverse the very algorithms it used to identify patterns in data.

Figure 11.1 A chart showing the evolution of generative AI.

learn how to do this, DALL-E had 12 billion parameters and was trained over a proprietary dataset of 250 million pairs of images with corresponding textual descriptions, which were scraped from the internet by OpenAI's team (Ramesh et al., 2021). Other generative AIs quickly came about, including Google's Imagen and Parti, Midjourney, and an improved version of DALL-E called DALL-E 2. By August 2022, a startup called Stability AI launched a new generative AI: Stable Diffusion.

Stable Diffusion is another revolutionary step in an already very active field. Thanks to a new paradigm in Deep Learning called Latent Diffusion Models (LDMs), Stability AI designed Stable Diffusion as a compact AI with only 900 million parameters, capable of being run locally in PCs equipped with consumer-grade GPUs. This is different from all other generative AIs made public until today, which are large models that can only be run in cloud-based servers and under the purview of their original developers (Rombach et al., 2022). In addition, Stability AI launched Stable Diffusion as a 100 percent open-source project: its source code, training datasets (LAION-5B, containing more than 5 billion image–text pairs), and trained model weights—whose creation requires significant computing power and time— are available for public use.

Launching Stable Diffusion as a compact and open-source AI resulted in an explosion of interest among developers, artists, and researchers, as indicated by engagement with the AI's primary code repository on GitHub. As of June 3, 2023, in less than a year since launch, the original Stable Diffusion[1] repository registered 55.3k stars (akin to GitHub "likes"), eclipsing other highly successful open-source projects such as WordPress[2] (leading CMS powering blogs and websites worldwide; 17.6k stars), WebTorrent[3] (peer-to-peer file transfer protocol; 27.9k stars), Ethereum[4] blockchain protocol (42.5k stars), and the Python[5] programming language (53.7k stars).

Accordingly, opening the technology to the crowd has brought about an avalanche of new tools and creative algorithms leveraging on the Stable Diffusion AI, ranging from algorithms to create animations using a sequence of AI-generated images (Deforum[6]), to complete web-based user interfaces (AUTOMATIC1111 Web UI[7]), to algorithms that give users the ability to control and constrain the image generation process (ControlNet[8]), or even to creating music snippets by way of generating audio spectrogram images and interpreting them as audio files (Riffusion[9]).

Particularly interesting are algorithms like Textual Inversion, DreamBooth, Low-Rank Adaptation (LoRA), and HyperNetworks that let users teach the AI. While

---

[1] Available at https://github.com/CompVis/stable-diffusion.
[2] Available at https://github.com/WordPress/WordPress.
[3] Available at https://github.com/webtorrent/webtorrent.
[4] Available at https://github.com/ethereum/go-ethereum.
[5] Available at https://github.com/python/cpython.
[6] Available https://github.com/deforum-art/deforum-for-automatic1111-webui.
[7] Available at https://github.com/AUTOMATIC1111/stable-diffusion-webui.
[8] Available at https://github.com/lllyasviel/ControlNet; see also Zhang et al. (2023).
[9] Available at https://github.com/riffusion/riffusion.

these algorithms work using distinct modeling paradigms, all of them ultimately relate to exposing the AI to a set of input images with their corresponding textual captions to fine tune its response to user input; in effect, what they all do is train the AI's "memory" to associate a specific instance whenever its corresponding name presents itself in a given prompt. These so-called fine-tuning algorithms allow the generative AI to produce results that are remarkably consistent across generative iterations, allowing for the recall of persistent entities upon user request.

Potential and Limitations of the Original AI Models

A very complex issue for archaeological taxonomy and datasets, in relation to AI, concerns the input (i.e., the selection process of the information we deliver to AI). This could be in the form of texts, images, videos, data sheets, or a combination of them. The uncertainty of the input selection and of the expected or unexpected result constitute both the potential and the limitation of AI models. In short, we don't know exactly how to formulate research questions—let's say a textual description—and how this can affect the visual output. A landscape or architectural classification, for example, can require very articulated analyses to have enough information; in other terms, narrative and visual reconstructions would require a certain level of consistency.

The aforementioned Ais possess significant computational prowess and have remarkable capabilities, although they are not exempt from certain inherent constraints. In the context of specialized applications such as archaeological interpretation, it is imperative to underscore the many inherent limits.

The issue of under- or overrepresentation arises when considering the presence of specific archaeological photos of certain examples and monuments in the collection. It is quite probable that these images have been underrepresented in comparison to more popular artifacts. In addition to the absence of a weighted training process that would account for the frequency of subjects, it is evident that the resulting AI possesses significant capabilities in generating highly realistic and versatile images of widely recognized entities. In archaeology, it would be important to have access to or filter specific databases to better connect input and output and make the training process more effective.

These limitations can be effectively mitigated through the fine-tuning procedure. To address the scarcity of domain-specific images, one can manually curate a collection of relevant images or capture new ones specifically for this purpose. Additionally, the problem of underrepresentation can be rectified by augmenting the fine-tuning process with an increased number of repetitions. Furthermore, the AI can be provided with manually generated text captions to facilitate its learning of precise and contextually appropriate terminology pertaining to the images.

Insufficient or inaccurate text captions can be observed in situations where the database utilized to train a first AI lacks comprehensive labeling or captioning, particularly in the context of archaeological terminology. The issue is exacerbated if the

photos sourced from the database underwent a filtering process through an additional AI model, which assessed caption accuracy but did not possess knowledge of
specialized archaeological terminology. There is a significant likelihood that a photograph depicting an Etruscan tumulus labeled solely as "Etruscan tumulus" would
be subject to filtration and exclusion. In instances where the filtering process fails to
remove some content, it is possible that the resulting output may have been assigned
a non–domain-specific label, such as a basic visual depiction of the image.
Consequently, the initial AI system has difficulties producing visual representations
when confronted with a domain-specific vocabulary.

Application Examples in Archeology

Generative AI applications in archaeology are very new (Resler *et al.* 2021) and at
the embryonic stage in Etruscan archaeology. Given the understanding of the limitations associated with AI models, it becomes apparent that a straightforward
approach to the application of AI in interpretative archaeology (IA) can be adopted.
First, it is advisable to select a compact yet powerful generative AI system that offers
flexibility and can be easily manipulated by an average user. Second, the AI system
should be trained to comprehend a specific concept by presenting instances of it
through a curated dataset consisting of photo–caption pairs. Last, the AI system
should be directed to generate original images depicting the precise concept it has
learned, thereby establishing a feedback loop that fosters an intuitive understanding
of how the concept may have manifested in the past.

Initial studies involved the utilization of AI techniques in many domains, namely
the examination of Etruscan tumuli, the creation of environmental reconstructions
pertaining to Etruscan and Roman environments, and, finally, the generation of AI
characters over the reconstruction of an Etruscan temple. This research provides a
limited insight into the potential of customized AI models, particularly if the community and users become more proficient in effectively utilizing AI's formida-
ble powers.

Etruscan tumuli, constructed during the seventh and sixth centuries BCE, serve
as aristocratic funerary structures. These monuments take the form of expansive
mounds that effectively communicate the symbolic authority held by these prominent families. Furthermore, the strategic placement of these burials within the urban
landscape and funerary settings enhances their visibility and significance. The
process of reconstruction and visualization using Stable Diffusion (as depicted
in Figure 11.2) and a particular animation developed in Deforum (an open-source
community of AI developers) exhibits a generative simulation of tumuli within
diverse geographic contexts and under varying environmental circumstances.

Due to the limitations of the initial Stable Diffusion AI in generating precise representations of Etruscan tumuli, a decision was made to enhance its understanding
of this subject matter. This was achieved through a process of fine-tuning, wherein

Figure 11.2 AI simulation of different models of Etruscan tumuli trained by real photos (bottom right). The simulation's goal is to study the shape and evolution of this funerary monument in relation to the ancient environment.

the AI was trained using a limited dataset comprising meticulously curated text and image pairs characterized by their high quality. Several crucial parameters employed for the process of fine-tuning include (a) the initial point of reference is the official Stable Diffusion 1.5, (b) the purpose of EveryDream 1.0 is to serve as a fine-tuning tool based on the DreamBooth platform, and (c) the training dataset consisted of 20–25 photographs of Etruscan tumuli sourced from the internet (Figure 11.2).

Each image was annotated with descriptive text, which included a distinct identifier "olis" that is recognized as a scarce token for the Stable Diffusion model. Following the completion of training, the AI will establish a correlation between the term "olis" and visual representations resembling Etruscan tumuli (Figures 11.3–11.4). Several experiments were conducted to develop a better understanding of the ideal number of training steps, which refers to the frequency at which each training image is shown to the model throughout the instructional phase. Additionally, the research aimed to determine the types and diversity of images that yield the highest quality outcome

The selection of the relatively optimal resulting artificial intelligences (AIs) was conducted through a process of trial and error, with the quality of the observed output serving as the criterion for evaluation.

It is crucial to emphasize the rapid pace at which this technology is advancing. Since the completion of the experiments, notable advancements and significant discoveries have been made in the field of Stable Diffusion models. These developments are expected to greatly enhance the capabilities of this AI, expanding the possibilities of its applications. One significant development in the field is the progress made in image-to-image creation techniques, particularly through the utilization

Figure 11.3 AI reconstruction of an Etruscan tumulus based on a machine-learning process and archaeological taxonomy.

of ControlNet. The notable feature of ControlNet is in its solution to the issue of spatial consistency. ControlNet addresses this issue by providing a technique that allows Stable Diffusion models to incorporate additional input conditions, thereby providing explicit instructions to guide the model's actions. In the past, there existed no effective method for providing explicit instructions to an AI model regarding the specific regions of an input image that should be preserved.

Artificial Intelligence and the Multiverse

The phenomenological study of generative AI is complex because it is at the intersection of technological revolutions and philosophical dilemmas. The hyperbole of

Figure 11.4 Aerial view of an Etruscan necropolis with scattered tumuli AI-generated. The simulation can help archaeologist to better understand the formation process of these aristocratic tombs.

AI is in the recreation of possible realities, new domains of real or digital modeling. All these ways to reproduce deep learning involve any kind of media: text, images, videos, models, scenarios. The combination of different media and digital sources opens endless research perspectives, often well beyond the multitasking capacity of the human brain to connect multifactorial information.

Virtual archaeology (1996–1997; see Forte and Siliotti, 1997), cyberarchaeology (2008; see Forte, 2015), and AI archaeology (2022; see Forte et al., 2023) mark significant junctures in the evolution of the digital representation of the past. If virtual archaeology was "model-oriented" (three-dimensional computer imagery), then cyberarchaeology aimed to simulate the past interactively, as a hyperreal world. This methodology is also applicable to the reconstruction of the past as an infinite process resulting from multiple simulations/representations. In this instance, the uncertainty of the interpretation is mitigated by diverse and multivocal perspectives, not by an idealized notion of fidelity, authenticity, or objectivity. In archaeology, material culture is the medium, and reconstructing its affordances and contexts requires a complex effort. This complex procedure generates data in various formats and according to specific ontologies in digital archaeology.

In each of these disciplines of study, the ability to simulate processes has played a vital role. In fact, AI archaeology offers up countless new perspectives in the process of interpretation and reconstruction. The application of AI in archaeology is not new and is a well-established research field, particularly in the automatic classification of objects and monumental structures, as well as in the remote sensing detection of sites. What is truly novel is the availability of extremely quick and open-access tools for infinite visualizations and graphical simulations, beginning with a simple textual syntax (text to image) or through image variants (image to image, image to videos, image/video to model). In other words, "deep learning."

We anticipate a near future in which AI will be able to generate visualizations, models, and complex simulations using only simple coding or textual instructions. Within an infinite framework of simulations, generative AI in virtual reality–real time settings could reevaluate digital consistency research problems. In accordance with this methodological approach, given the regime of ambiguity with which we contend and the subjectivity of our archaeological and historical interpretations, we "perform the past" as opposed to recreating it. In other words, the greater our capacity to reinterpret a place, monument, landscape, or relic, the greater the number of virtual/digital situations we produce.

The generative potential of AI visualizations multiplies and diversifies the content; in other words, the number of iterations and visualizations increases significantly. Given the uncertainty of reconstruction, AI archaeology research should concentrate on the connection between textual narrative (the "prompt"), image training, and visual simulations.

In response to a textual query, the AI software Stable Diffusion generates images by a database of more than 5 billion photos and their corresponding descriptions, allowing it to comprehend the concepts associated with the images themselves. Stable Diffusion is a completely open-source code, based on an open-source database (LAION-5B) and capable of operating locally on a consumer-grade computer.

AI archaeology will be viewed soon as a generative-autopoietic system that generates its own hypotheses, digital codes, models, and syntaxes using both human and artificial minds.

Artificial Intelligence and Mindscapes

The definition of "mindscape" refers to how individuals perceive, comprehend, and interpret their surroundings. The mindscape is a complex concept that encompasses physical reality, historical understanding, cultural convictions, and human imagination. It is an intellectual depiction or cognitive cartography of a setting, influenced by various factors such as individual encounters, societal heritage, and obtained information. If the original idea of mindscape was purely theoretical (Forte, 2003, 2005), then the potential of AI applications in the generation of landscapes/mindscapes makes this perspective realistic.

In fact, in a new experiment, "AI rethinks the past" (Figure 11.5; see https://rethinkingthepast.org/), Forte and de Castro applied generative AI to the reconstruction of Etruscan and Roman landscapes and environments, starting from paleoenvironmental data. By analyzing plant remains, paleobotanical analyses have

Figure 11.5 3D prints of ancient pollens from the Etruscan and Roman site of Vulci from the exhibition AI Rethinks the Past. The pollen allows reconstructing the paleoenvironment by AI neural networks.

proved to be especially useful in reconstructing the ancient environments and landscapes of archaeological sites. Pollen, charcoal, and diverse botanical remnants have been extracted from a wide range of archaeological sites, including the urban stratigraphic deposits of Roselle and a Roman cistern at Vulci. The samples comprise significant amounts of information regarding past flora and fauna, thus enabling researchers to carefully reconstruct ancient topographies. The pollen analysis conducted on the Roman cistern at Vulci provided evidence of this, showcasing a wide variety of plant species such as domesticated plants, cereals, legumes, and fruit trees. The pollen record indicates a notable abundance of cereals, which implies that the cistern was probably surrounded by agricultural fields. Additionally, the presence of untamed plants and fruit trees concurrently suggests that the vegetation cover on the cistern consisted of a combination of cultivated and wild plants (Figure 11.6).

Similarly, findings from charcoal analysis conducted in Roselle indicate the presence of a varied oakwood forest comprising holm oak, common oak, Mediterranean shrubs and vegetation, and hornbeam. Based on the data, the adjacent topography, comprising a varied composition of grassland, shrubland, and woodland habitats, exhibits signs of human intervention, including wood harvesting and land clearance.

By utilizing the complex taxonomy of the samples and training generative AI models with palaeobotanical data comprising extensive lists of scientific and botanical names, it has been possible to simulate and visualize ancient environments and landscapes (Figure 11.7) through text-to-image or text-to-videos processes. All the images and videos generated by this experiment reproduce very accurate models of Etruscan and Roman paleoenvironments just using soil and pollen analyses (Stable Diffusion and Runway tools). The main result of this AI project was the organization of the archaeological exhibition "AI Rethinks the Past", at Duke University in 2024.

Figure 11.6 AI reconstruction (Runway AI video generator) of wet environments around the Etruscan site of Vulci.

Figure 11.7 AI reconstruction of the landscape of Vulci in proximity to the Roman decumanus. The image has been obtained by training AI with the species of plants and vegetation in Roman times in combination with a contemporary view of the region of interest.

By bringing together specialists from natural sciences, computer science, archaeology, and history, the application of AI in landscape archaeology can facilitate new forms of interdisciplinary collaboration and expertise sharing. In summary, these experiments provide an intriguing insight into the revolutionary possibilities that generative AI technology may bring about regarding our comprehension and interaction with ancient environments and landscapes. By facilitating advanced and inventive ways of doing research, AI can challenge conventional notions of expertise and authority while aiding in the democratization and pluralization of historical and archaeological knowledge. AI-generated environmental reconstructions can increase the accessibility and applicability of archaeological knowledge to a broader audience.

Conclusion

Theoretically limitless, AI's visual generative power presents humanity with a new heuristic challenge: hyperrealism, which is more "real" than actual reality. What kind of knowledge can we transmit to a future where human and artificial intelligence will coexist? Can we conceptualize the past as we do in our modern societies? The hyperrealism generated by neural networks can generate visual simulations in a very brief amount of time and by searching online image and model archives containing billions of items. In relation to the generative power of AI, the concept of the past as a "multiverse" (Forte, 2025) is an intriguing and thought-provoking idea that calls into question our understanding of history, archaeology, and the very nature of reality.

In fact, cyberarchaeology's theoretical approach has introduced the concept of the "potential past" over the past decade, emphasizing the relativistic notion that the past is mutable and perceived differently by different societies across space and time.

The initial experiments in Stable Diffusion and Deforum demonstrate the success of an AI approach for simulating locations, artifacts, and ancient landscapes. At the intersection of space (such as a necropolis) and time (the development of a shape or morphology), all these variations are a part of a new interpretative process. Our modern view of the past as a multiverse is challenged by environmental settings and photorealism.

This research perspective replaces the traditional methodological perspective of the past's reconstruction with new forms that "blend" archaeological data through the generative and transformative power of neural networks as opposed to a single hypothesis derived from conventional scholarship. Things and objects are transitory and coevolve into something else: they are syntax, images, and models—this is the most accurate depiction of the past we might consider.

When contents are multiplied, new information is created and compels our minds to consider and evaluate a variety of alternatives, worlds, and contexts. Due to the simulation's metaphysical power, even a simple taxonomy can recreate a complex visual narrative from this perspective.

Deep learning AIs are an advanced form that has the potential to revolutionize the way we process and analyze large datasets, particularly in generative archaeology. These preliminary experiments reveal unexplored research avenues in the visualization and simulation of complex datasets and models and could mark the beginning of the systematic incorporation of deep learning AIs into the archaeological process.

Acknowledgments

This chapter is an elaborated and extended version of the article by Forte et al. (2023, 43–56).

Bibliography

Forte, M. "Mindscape: Ecological thinking, cyber-anthropology, and virtual archaeological landscapes." In *The Reconstruction of Archaeological Landscapes through Digital Technologies*, edited by M. Forte and P. R. Williams, 95–18. Proceedings of the First Italy–United States Workshop, Boston, Massachusetts, November 1–3, 2001. BAR International Series 1151. Oxford: Oxford University Press, 2003.

Forte M. "A digital "cyber" protocol for the reconstruction of the archaeological landscape: Virtual reality and mindscapes." In *Recording, Modeling and Visualization of Cultural Heritage*, edited by E. Baltsavias, A. Gruen, L. Van Gool, and M. Pateraki, 339–351. London: Taylor & Francis/Balkema, 2005.

Forte, M. Exploring Multiverses: Generative AI and Neuroaesthetic Perspectives. Heritage 2025, 8, 102. https://doi.org/10.3390/heritage8030102

Forte, M. "Cyberarchaelogy: A post-virtual perspective." In *Humanities and the Digital: A Visioning Statement*, edited by D. T. Golberg and P. Svensson, 295–309. Cambridge, MA: MIT Press, 2015.

Forte, M., and A. Siliotti, eds. *Virtual Archaeology* (foreword by C. Renfrew). London: Thames and Hudson Ltd., 1997.

Forte, M. F., I. De Castro, and I. Pkhovelishvili. "AI for IA: Artificial intelligence for inter-pretative archaeology." In *Proceedings of the International Workshop on AI and Cultural Heritage. Between Research and Creativity Workshop*, edited by A. Guidazzoli and M. C. Liguori, 43–56. CINECA Supercomputing Center, 2023. doi:10.1388/WORKSHOP-AICH-01

Goodfellow, I., J. Pouget-Abadie, M. Mirza, Bing Xu, D. Warde-Farley, S. Ozair, A. Courville, and Y. Bengio. "Generative adversarial nets." *Advances in Neural Information Processing Systems* 27 (2014) 2672–2680.

Hochreiter, S., and J. Schmidhuber. "Long short-term memory." *Neural Computation* 9.8 (1997), 1735–1780. doi:10.1162/neco.1997.9.8.1735

Krizhevsky, A., I. Sutskever, and G. E. Hinton. "ImageNet classification with deep convo-lutional neural networks." *Communications of the ACM* 60.6 (2017), 84–90. doi:10.1145/3065386. ISSN 0001-0782. S2CID 195908774.h

Le Cun, et al., Y. Le Cun, B. Boser, J. S. Denker, D. Henderson, R. E. Howard, W. Hubbard, and L. D. Jackel "Handwritten digit recognition with a back-propagation network." In *Advances in Neural Information Processing Systems 2*, 396–404. San Francisco: Morgan Kaufmann, 1989. doi:10.5555/109230.109279

Ramesh A., M. Pavlov, G. Goh, S. Gray, C. Voss, A. Radford, M. Chen, and I. Sutskever. "Zero-shot text-to-image generation." *arXiv* (2021), 12092v2.

Resler, A., Yeshurun, R., Natalio, F. et al. A deep-learning model for predictive archaeol-ogy and archaeological community detection. *Humanities and Social Sciences Communications* 8, 295 (2021). https://doi.org/10.1057/s41599-021-00970-z

Rombach R., A. Blattmann, D. Lorenz, P. Esser, and B. Ommer. "High-resolution image synthesis with latent diffusion models." *arXiv* (2022), 10752.

Rumelhart, D. E., G. E. Hinton, and R. J. Williams. "Learning representations by back-propagating errors." *Nature* 323.6088 (1986), 533–536. doi:10.1038/323533a0

Russell, S. J., & Norvig, P. (2021). Artificial Intelligence: A Modern Approach (4th ed.). Pearson. https://doi.org/10.1109/MSP.2017.2765202

Vaswani, A., N. Shazeer, N. Parmar, J. Uszkoreit, L. Jones, A. N. Gomez, Ł. Kaiser, and I. Polosukhin. "Attention is all you need." *Advances in Neural Information Processing Systems* 30 (2017), 1–15.

Zhang, L., A. Rao, and M. Agrawala. "Adding conditional control to text-to-image diffu-sion models." *arXiv* (2023), 05543. http://arxiv.org/abs/2302.05543, 1–12.

Maurizio Forte and Felipe Infante de Castro, *Artificial Intelligence and Etruscan Archaeology* In:
A New Etruscan Archaeology: Twenty-First Century Techniques and Methods. Edited by: Maurizio Forte,
Oxford University Press. © Oxford University Press 2025. DOI: 10.1093/9780197582053.003.0012

12
Conclusion and Future Perspectives

Maurizio Forte

The study of Etruscan archaeology has experienced remarkable transformations over the past decades. The incorporation of new methodologies and technologies has profoundly enhanced our understanding of Etruscan society, material culture, and the intricate environmental contexts in which the Etruscans thrived.

By embracing digital tools, remote sensing, and interdisciplinary approaches, the field has evolved beyond traditional boundaries, offering a more comprehensive and nuanced perspective on this society. Etruscan archaeology is more than just the study of artifacts and sites; it represents a complex interplay of social, cultural, and environmental factors that shaped the lives of the Etruscans and surrounding cultures. The integration of digital technologies, such as three-dimensional modeling, artificial intelligence (AI), remote sensing, and virtual reality, has revolutionized the field, allowing for detailed reconstructions of artifacts and sites. These tools facilitate improved preservation, study and public engagement, providing a dynamic and interactive platform for exploring the past. The advent of digital technologies has been a game-changer for Etruscan archaeology.

Technological Advancements in Etruscan Archaeology

Researchers can create accurate and detailed representations of artifacts and sites using three-dimensional modeling, which they can manipulate and study in a virtual environment. This technology has enabled archaeologists to examine construction techniques, analyze spatial relationships, and even simulate ancient environments. These models not only aid in research but also serve as valuable educational tools, making the past accessible to a wider audience. Geographic information systems (GISs) and drones equipped with remote sensing devices have transformed the way in which archaeologists study ancient landscapes. By integrating spatial data, researchers can analyze patterns of settlement, trade routes, and environmental changes over time. Spatial technology allows for the visualization of large datasets, providing insights into how the Etruscans interacted with their environment and organized their society. This technology has been instrumental in identifying previously unknown sites and understanding the broader landscape context of Etruscan settlements.

Virtual reality (VR) has opened new avenues for engaging with the past. By creating immersive experiences, VR allows users to explore reconstructed Etruscan sites on a very realistic scale. This technology not only enhances public engagement but also provides a powerful tool for researchers to test hypotheses about ancient spaces and interactions. For instance, by simulating the experience of walking through an Etruscan tomb, VR provides insights into the sensory and spatial dynamics of these sacred spaces. Virtual reality is also a very advanced simulation tool for archaeological excavations and landscape's analysis.

Remote sensing techniques, including ground penetrating radar (GPR) and magnetometry, have revolutionized archaeological surveys. These noninvasive methods allow archaeologists to detect and map subterranean structures without the need for intrusive excavation. By preserving the integrity of fragile sites, remote sensing techniques optimize resource use and provide a broader picture of the archaeological landscape. GPR, for instance, can reveal the layout of buried buildings, roads, and other features, helping researchers plan targeted excavations and conservation efforts.

Cognitive and Neuroscientific Approaches

The application of cognitive science and neuroscience to archaeological contexts has opened new avenues for understanding the experiential nature of Etruscan rituals and symbolic meanings. Studies on the aesthetic impact of Etruscan artifacts on the brain reveal how these objects influence emotional involvement and cognitive development, offering deeper insights into the cultural significance of material culture. The processual field of inquiry, cognitive archaeology, acknowledges that human cognition stems from perceptual and physical interaction with the material world. Researchers can better understand the cultural and symbolic meanings of Etruscan artifacts and monuments by examining how their original users experienced and interpreted these objects. For example, studies on the acoustic properties of Etruscan tombs have revealed how sound and music played a crucial role in funerary rituals, creating a sensory experience that reinforced the social and religious significance of the tomb space.

Researchers have also applied neuroscientific approaches to the study of Etruscan art. By using techniques such as electroencephalography (EEG) and eye tracking, researchers can measure the neural and emotional responses of viewers to Etruscan artifacts. These studies have shown that certain visual elements, such as color and symmetry, can evoke strong emotional reactions, suggesting that Etruscan artists deliberately used these techniques to engage and influence their audience. This research not only sheds light on the aesthetic preferences of the Etruscans but also highlights the universal principles of art and perception that continue to resonate with modern viewers.

Conservation Practices

Conservation practices have also seen significant progress, particularly using nanomaterials and noninvasive techniques. Projects like the preservation of the Tomb of the

Sphinx in Vulci highlight the importance of using compatible materials and minimally invasive methods to maintain the integrity of archaeological structures. Archaeological site conservation entails managing complex systems with varying degrees of material robustness. Traditional conservation methods often relied on invasive techniques that could cause further damage to fragile structures. Today, however, there is a growing emphasis on preventive conservation, which focuses on creating stable environmental conditions to slow the degradation of materials. This approach includes measures such as controlling temperature and humidity, protecting sites from water infiltration, and using noninvasive monitoring techniques to detect early signs of deterioration. Nanomaterials have emerged as a promising solution for the conservation of archaeological artifacts. We can engineer these materials at the molecular level to provide targeted and effective treatments, for instance, using nanosilica dispersions to consolidate porous stone, enhancing its mechanical strength without changing its appearance. Similarly, the use of nanocalcium hydroxide particles can be used to stabilize fragile frescoes and wall paintings, thereby preserving their original colors and textures.

The use of noninvasive techniques in conservation has also gained traction in recent years. Methods such as laser cleaning and infrared thermography allow conservators to remove dirt and contaminants from artifacts without physical contact. These techniques are particularly useful for delicate materials that cannot withstand traditional cleaning methods. Infrared thermography, for instance, can reveal hidden layers of paint and detect areas of structural weakness, thus guiding conservators in their efforts to preserve these valuable cultural treasures.

Environmental Research and Textiles

Environmental and landscape studies have provided valuable insights into the relationship between the Etruscans and their environment. Paleoenvironmental research, which combines methods such as geomorphology, palynology, and zooarchaeology, has revealed how environmental factors influenced settlement patterns, agricultural practices, and social structures. Researchers have reconstructed Etruria's ancient vegetation by examining pollen records and have reconstructed the ancient vegetation of Etruria, revealing a landscape rich in diverse flora. These studies have shown that the Etruscans practiced sophisticated land and water management techniques, such as coppicing and crop rotation, to sustain their economy and obtain fuel for metallurgy. Paleoenvironmental research has also highlighted the role of climate in shaping the formation and transformation of Etruscan cities, providing valuable lessons for understanding contemporary environmental challenges.

The study of Etruscan textiles, using both traditional and scientific methods, has shed light on production techniques, raw materials, and the social significance of textiles in Etruscan society. Textile analysis combines archaeological, iconographic, and scientific data to reconstruct the history and technological advancements of Etruscan textile production. By examining textile tools, zooarchaeological data, and mineralized textile remains, researchers can gain insights into the types of fibers used, weaving techniques, and the cultural context of textile production. Recent studies have revealed that Etruscan textiles were characterized by plain-weave linen fabrics and wool twills with tablet-woven borders. The use of sophisticated dyeing methods and the production of luxury textiles played a significant role in elite status displays. These findings highlight the importance of textiles in Etruscan society, not only as everyday items but also as symbols of wealth and power.

The Role of Artificial Intelligence and Big Data in Etruscan Archaeology

Looking to the future, the integration of generative AI in archaeology holds vast potential, with applications ranging from environmental reconstructions to artifact generation. AI can process and analyze large datasets, providing new interpretations and simulations of ancient contexts. Continued development and integration of AI technologies will further revolutionize the field. Generative AI, which uses algorithms to create original content, has the potential to transform archaeological research. For instance, researchers can visualize and study ancient artifacts in their entirety by using AI to generate three-dimensional models based on partial or fragmented remains. Researchers can also use AI to simulate ancient environments, reconstructing landscapes and architectural features using historical data and environmental evidence. The use of AI in archaeological interpretation is still in its early stages, but initial results are very promising. AI algorithms can identify patterns and relationships in large datasets that may not be immediately apparent to human researchers. By analyzing spatial data, artifact distributions, and environmental factors, AI can generate new multifactorial hypotheses and insights about ancient societies. These tools can also aid in the identification and classification of artifacts, streamlining the analysis process and improving accuracy. The integration of AI with big data analytics allows archaeologists to handle the vast amounts of information generated by modern research methods. From high-resolution scans of artifacts to extensive environmental datasets, the ability to process and analyze large volumes of data is essential for advancing our understanding of the past. AI-powered tools can help researchers uncover hidden patterns, correlations, and trends, providing a more comprehensive view of ancient societies.

Interdisciplinary Research

The field must continue to embrace interdisciplinary research, integrating insights from archaeology, anthropology, cognitive science, environmental studies, and the digital humanities. Such a holistic approach will deepen our understanding of the Etruscan world and its contributions to Mediterranean culture. Interdisciplinary collaboration is essential for addressing the complex questions and challenges of Etruscan archaeology. By combining the expertise and methodologies of different fields, researchers can gain a more comprehensive understanding of ancient societies. For example, the integration of cognitive science and neuroscience with archaeology provides new insights into the sensory and experiential aspects of Etruscan rituals, while environmental studies offer a broader context for understanding the relationship between the Etruscans and their landscape. The study of Etruscan material culture benefits greatly from the integration of scientific techniques such as radiocarbon dating, DNA analysis, and stable isotope analysis. These methods provide precise chronological frameworks and reveal information about the diet, health, and mobility of ancient populations. By combining scientific data with traditional archaeological methods, researchers can build a more detailed and accurate picture of Etruscan life.

Final Remarks

The advancements in Etruscan archaeology over the past decades have significantly expanded our knowledge and understanding of this ancient civilization. The field will remain at the forefront of archaeological research and social sciences by continuing to integrate new technologies, interdisciplinary approaches, and sustainable practices, thus ensuring the preservation and appreciation of Etruscology for future generations.

Etruscan archaeology represents a dynamic and evolving field, one driven by technological innovations and interdisciplinary collaboration. The integration of digital tools, remote sensing, and cognitive science has transformed our understanding of Etruscan society, providing new insights into their material culture, social structures, and environmental interactions (Figure 12.1).

Looking to the future, the continued development and application of generative AI and big data analytics hold immense potential for furthering our understanding of the Etruscan world. By harnessing the power of these technologies, researchers can uncover new patterns, generate innovative hypotheses, and create detailed reconstructions of ancient contexts. Public engagement and education initiatives will play a crucial role in promoting Etruscan archaeology, making it accessible to a wider audience and fostering a greater appreciation for cultural heritage (Figure 12.2). Ultimately, the collaborative efforts of researchers, scholars, and the public will drive the field of Etruscan archaeology to continue its multidisciplinary trajectory of growth and innovation.

Maurizio Forte, *Conclusion and Future Perspectives* In: *A New Etruscan Archaeology: Twenty-First Century Techniques and Methods*. Edited by: Maurizio Forte, Oxford University Press. © Oxford University Press 2025.
DOI: 10.1093/9780197582053.003.0013

Figure 12.1 Heat map/cumulative eye-tracking of a group of observers engaged with the site without a background in archeology. The core visual region of interest is very small and central. The dark dot in the middle shows the core region of interest.

Figure 12.2 Heat map/cumulative eye-tracking of a group of observers engaged with the site, with an archeological background). There are two large regions of interest and they involve almost all the excavation area. See the darker cloud over most past of the excavations.

Index

Since the index has been created to work across multiple formats, indexed terms for which a page range is given (e.g., 52–53, 66–70, etc.) may occasionally appear only on some, but not all of the pages within the range.